THE VIEW FROM DAMASCUS

The View from Damascus:

State, Political Community and Foreign Relations in Twentieth-Century Syria

ITAMAR RABINOVICH

VALLENTINE MITCHELL
LONDON • PORTLAND, OR

First published in 2008 by *Vallentine Mitchell*

Suite 314, Premier House,
112–114 Station Road,
Edgware, Middlesex HA8 7BJ, UK

920 NE 58th Avenue, Suite 300
Portland, Oregon,
97213-3786, USA

www.vmbooks.com

British Library Cataloguing in Publication Data:

Rabinovich, Itamar, 1942-
The view from Damascus : state, political community and
foreign relations in 20th century Syria
1. Syria - Politics and government - 20th century 2. Syria
- Foreign relations - 20th century 3. Syria - Foreign
relations - Israel 4. Israel - Foreign relations - Syria
I. Title
320.9¤'5691'0904

ISBN 978 0 85303 800 9 (cloth)

Library of Congress Cataloging-in-Publication Data:
A catalog record has been applied for

Printed by Biddles Ltd, King's Lynn, Norfolk

To Efrat

Contents

PART III
THE BA'TH REGIME

PART IV
SYRIA AND ISRAEL

Introduction

'The View from Damascus' is the title of an essay written in 2000 by the Syrian public intellectual Sadiq al-'Azm, quoted extensively in Chapter 19 of the present volume. 'Azm's essay deals with the Syrian state's and the Syrian public's attitude towards peace with Israel in the spring of 2000. It occurred to me, as I put together the essays and chapters included in this volume, that this could also be an excellent title for a book dealing with several major themes in Syria's modern and contemporary history.

The idea of putting this volume together came from the late Frank Cass who, as publisher of books and journals, had an important impact on Middle Eastern studies. His untimely death was a great loss for the field. Of the papers I have written on modern Syria, eighteen seemed to me worthy of reprinting, supplemented by chapters and segments from three of my books.

These essays and chapters revolve, as suggested by the subtitle, around three principal themes: (1) The evolution of the notion of a modern Syrian state and the successive efforts to convert these notions into an actual political entity; (2) The contending concepts of the political community that should inhabit and dominate that entity; (3) Syria's relations with external powers and neighbouring states and entities.

The term Syria referred in the late nineteenth and early twentieth century to a geographic entity, known at various times as 'Greater Syria', 'Geographic Syria' or 'Natural Syria', comprising the territory occupied today by Syria, Lebanon, Israel, Jordan and The Palestinian Authority. Chapters 1, 3, 6 and 12 describe the process which led to the crystallization of the Syrian state in its present boundaries, initially frail and eventually, under Hafiz al-Asad, quite powerful in part of 'Geographic Syria'.

The notion of a Syrian entity was propagated prior to the First World War mostly by French advocates of France's 'special position' in the Levant and by Lebanese and Syrian Christians. It was soon overshadowed by the sway of Arab nationalism. When France finally obtained a League of Nations mandate for Syria and Lebanon the architects of its policies in the

Levant realized that a Syrian state with Damascus as its capital would in fact be an Arab Syria, hostile to France's 'mission'. They chose to create a 'Greater Lebanon' as the anvil of their dominion and to break the remaining territory into a series of statelets as well as to cultivate minority separatism as a bulwark against Arab nationalism, which they viewed as an anti-French British creation.

It took more than two decades for the Arab nationalist leaders in Syria to create and gain independence for a unified Syrian state. But the independent Syrian state of 1945 was weak and beleaguered. The traditional nationalist leadership was beset by weakness and illegitimacy. The prevailing sense was that a Syrian state within these particular boundaries was artificial. The Syrian nationalist leaders had irredentist claims in Turkey, Lebanon and Palestine. More significantly, Syria was the object of other, more powerful, actors' ambitions. The impact of these ambitions and the schemes they bred was magnified by the fact that many in Syria were genuinely committed to the ideology of pan-Arab nationalism, which cast a long shadow over the legitimacy of the Syrian state. Why not erase the boundaries set by the colonial powers and merge Syria in a larger Arab entity as the first step towards the implementation of the vision and dream of Arab unity?

It was against this backdrop that Syria glided into an unsuccessful union with Egypt (February 1958–September 1961). In the event, the trauma of a failed union with a large, assertive Arab state served to reinforce the sense of Syrian identity and, after a transitional period, enabled Hafiz al-Asad to consolidate Syria's separate existence and to build it into a powerful state. On that basis Asad began to conduct an ambitious regional and foreign policy, seeking to impose Syria's hegemony over its weaker Arab neighbours. For a brief period Asad's regime invoked the notion of a 'Greater Syria' in order to rationalize and legitimize its ambitions.

In earlier decades the notion of 'Greater Syria' was anathema to Arab nationalists. It was associated with the legacy of French ambitions and with the teachings of Antun Sa'adeh, the Lebanese Christian founder of The Syrian Social Nationalist Party (SSNP), who formulated a doctrine of secular pan-Syrian nationalism, that was and is seen as inimical anti-Arab nationalist (see Chapters 6 and 10).

The rise and development of political ideologies in twentieth-century Syria can only be studied in the context of the ethnic, religious and communal make up of the country's population. It is, of course, one variable in a complex equation, but a very important one. The 60 per cent or so Sunni Arabs have tended as a rule to be affiliated with main stream Arab nationalism or with the Muslim Brotherhood. Members of the minorities (Christian and heterodox Muslims) tended to join radical parties seeking or offering to transform the political community and landscape through secular Arab nationalism (the Ba'th), secular pan-Syranism (the SSNP) or Marxism (the Communist Party, whose leader for many years was a Syrian Kurd, Khaled Bakdash). Young 'Alawi officers of Hafiz al-Asad's age group tended to be either Ba'this or Syrian Nationalists (see Chapters 9 and 10).

The Ba'th Party's appeal to members of minority communities (including the 'Alawis) and the lingering effect of France's policy of recruiting members of the same communities to the 'native' army under the Mandate produced a disproportionate number of minoritarian and Ba'thi officers in the ranks of independent Syria's army. Through a complex process (described in Chapter 9) a large number of non 'Alawi and non Ba'thi officers were removed from the Syrian army in the late 1950s and early 1960s and left 'Alawi–Ba'thi officers in control of the army and subsequently of the regime. What began to unfold without plan or premeditation became in the late 1960s a calculated strategy for preserving the regime and the 'Alawi community's privileged position.

The emergence in the 1970s of a relatively stable and robust regime in Syria transformed the country's foreign relations. During the first half of the twentieth century Syria was mostly a passive object, buffeted by colonial powers and more powerful neighbours. Under Hafiz al-Asad Syria became an influential regional power (Chapters 12, 15 and 16) and used its new position to replace a simple patron-client relationship with the Soviet Union with a far more complex relationship with both superpowers.

Syria has had adversarial relations with all its neighbours – Turkey, Iraq, Jordan, Lebanon, Israel and the Palestinians. Of these relationships the last three are of particular interest and importance. Syria has refused to recognize the legitimacy of the Lebanese state, which it has viewed implicitly and explicitly as part of Syria. In 1976 Syria intervened militarily in the Lebanese civil war. For thirty years the presence of Syria's army was the mainstay of its hegemony in Lebanon. In 2005 it was forced to withdraw but its influence is perpetuated through other means and resources. The Lebanese patrimony is a hub of numerous interests of the Ba'th regime and it has demonstrated several times that it was willing to go to great lengths in order to protect it.

Syria' s view of, and policy toward, the Palestinian issue is different from that of other influential Arab states – Egypt, Iraq or Saudi Arabia – that have sought during different periods to shape Palestinian politics and affect the direction of Palestinian nationalism. The notion of 'Palestine as

Southern Syria' is ever present, even when not articulated. At some points in time Syria's leaders have challenged the Palestinian nationalist leadership by asserting that Damascus was the real custodian of the Palestinian cause. At other times Damascus was willing to settle on a more modest role of just seeking to influence the course of Palestinian nationalism. Presently by hosting Hamas and Islamic Jihad in Damascus and in league with Iran and Hizballah Syria is trying to undermine the PLO's and al-Fath's leadership of Palestinian nationalism.

A significant portion of this volume deals with Syria's relationship with Israel – conflict, wars and, so far, an unsuccessful peace process. With the exception of the intriguing episode described in Chapter 14, Syria's conflict with Israel was, until 1991, particularly bitter. As the Arab nationalist state par excellence with a claim to a special relationship with Palestine and the Palestinians and as the seat of regimes dominated by military officers and ideological politicians, Syria had traditionally been at the head of Arab opposition to, and struggle against, Israel. This made the volte-face of 1991, coming to the Madrid Peace conference, all the more dramatic. There ensued a decade of negotiations that brought Israel and Syria to 'the brink of peace' (see Chapter 18) but did not cross it. The broad lines of an Israeli–Syrian peace agreement were drawn in the course of these negotiations. The failure to transform them into an actual agreement is the subject matter of a controversy shared by policy makers and academic observers (see Chapter 20).

The Israeli–Syrian peace process collapsed in 2000 and all efforts to revive it have so far failed. In fact, the two countries are facing the danger of sliding back into violent conflict. The effort to check this spiral and to restore a Syrian Israeli dialogue is a crucial issue on the Middle Eastern and international policy agenda.

Several developments which occurred in 2000–01 have pushed the Israeli–Syrian track of the peace process to the sidelines: Hafez Al-Asad's death, Ariel Sharon's opposition to withdrawal from the Golan, Syria's greater dependence on Iran and, most important, the Bush administration's hostility to Bashar Al-Asad and his regime. These issues are dealt with in some detail in the final chapter of the present volume.

I
HISTORICAL BACKGROUND AND THE PERIOD OF THE FRENCH MANDATE

1

Syria and the Syrian Land:
The Nineteenth-century Roots of
Twentieth-century Developments[1]

For the student of twentieth-century Syrian history the topic of this volume raises questions of both terminology and periodization. For the past several decades the term Syria has denoted the state which won its independence in the aftermath of the Second World War. Syrian statehood and independence within these particular boundaries were the product of a long drawn conflict over the identity and size of the Syrian state and its relationship to the other parts of the larger Geographic Syria (Suriyya al-Jughrafiyya). The roots of this conflict date back to the nineteenth century. The present chapter seeks to trace the divergence and respective evolutions of the contending notions of Syria and the Syrian Land and follow them through the first half of the twentieth century. It will become readily apparent – and hardly surprising – that from this vantage point, too, the year 1900 was rather meaningless in that the significant transition was not from the nineteenth to the twentieth century but from the Ottoman to the post-Ottoman period.

It was during the latter part of the nineteenth century that the traditional terms Bilad al-Sham, Barr al-Sham, and 'Arabistan, designating the territory of Geographic Syria were replaced by the revived term Suriyya and that the new term acquired a hitherto unfamiliar political significance. Bilad al-Sham had referred to a geographic entity whose existence was vaguely sensed despite its immersion in the larger Ottoman Empire and its division into several administrative units. The term Suriyya reappeared during the first half of the nineteenth century and later in the century it gradually replaced Bilad al-Sham and 'Arabistan as denoting the area of Geographic Syria.[2] Syria became also the focus of novel sentiments and ideas of patriotism and nationalism and became the object of new internal and external political ambitions.

Several developments and forces at work converged to produce these

changes. One was the administrative decision taken first by Ibrahim Pasha
and then, well after his eviction from Syria, by the Ottoman government,
to group together some of their Syrian provinces in order to create a
province (*vilayet*) of Syria. The Ottoman government's experiment with the
Province of Syria (1865–88) was particularly significant in this context. As
a rule after recapturing Syria from Ibrahim Pasha the Ottomans reversed
his policies. Among other things they abolished the Egyptian Province of
Syria and reinstated Syria's administrative division into smaller *vilayets*.
Their decision twenty-five years later to recreate a larger Syrian province
thus clearly went beyond considerations of administrative efficiency and
convenience. The notion that the new province represented more than an
administrative entity and that its creation was to tie its inhabitants through
a novel bond to the Empire was reflected in an article published in the first
issue of the new province's newspaper, *Suriyya*. The article offered an outline of Syria's history from ancient times to Napoleon's invasion. Like subsequent similar surveys it carried a message – this time implicit – that Syria
was a distinct territorial and historical entity.[3]

When the new Province of Syria was created a Lebanese Protestant,
Butrus al-Bustani, had already begun the publication of his *Nafir Suriyya*
(Syria's Clarion). Bustani, like other members of his circle and generation
like Nasif al-Yaziji and Khalil al-Khuri advocated a Syrian patriotism imbued
with an equally strong Arab sentiment. Their Syria was an Arab Syria and
their writings and activities were landmarks as important in the evolution
of Arab nationalism as in the formulation of the notion of a Syrian entity. It
is equally important to point to the specific sources of inspiration affecting
the thinking of Bustani and his circle: the arrival of the new notions of
nationalism and patriotism, in reaction to the massacres of 1860, ideas
propagated by American missionaries in Lebanon, and the quest for a secular basis for a newly defined political community. For Greek Orthodox and
Protestant Christians a secular Arabism and a territorially based Syria seemed
to offer a haven from both Muslim and Maronite-Catholic domination.[4]

By the 1860s, then, the notion of a Syrian entity, both as an ideological
construct and as an administrative and proto-political reality, had been
introduced into the course of the region's history. It remained a marginal
theme of that history during the last decades of the nineteenth century.
Thus, in the late 1880s when Midhat Pasha served as governor of Syria he
was suspected and accused by sundry detractors of seeking to follow the
example of Muhammad Ali and his successors and to make himself the
Khedive of an autonomous Syria. Contemporary consular reports tied
Midhat to the anti-Ottoman placards posted in Beirut whose authorship
has been ascribed at different times to a secret Christian society and to the

Muslim Sunni Society of Benevolent Intentions. But recent scholarship has clearly shown that Midhat did not plan a secession from the Ottoman Empire, that there was no segment of Syrian society that would have served as the local basis for such action and that neither the small Christian group nor the Sunni notables affiliated with the Society of Benevolent Intentions were the forerunners of Arab or Syrian-Arab nationalism.[5]

It was only on the eve of the First World War that the idea of a Syrian entity acquired an altogether different importance. This was to some extent a reflection of the dominant trends of the period – the preparations made by the European powers in anticipation of the Ottoman Empire's collapse and partition, the exacerbation of Arab-Turkish tensions and the spread of nationalism at the expense of primordial solidarities and the traditional allegiance to the Ottoman state.

In more specific terms Syria was defined, alongside Lebanon, as the focus of French interests and ambitions in the Levant. In 1912, Raymond Poincaré as prime minister and foreign minister, obtained from the British government a statement of disinterest in Syria and publicly declared France's determination to ensure 'respect for her traditional interests' in Syria and Lebanon.[6] In the minds of the advocates of French control of or influence in the Levant the term 'Syria' referred sometimes to the whole of Geographic Syria and on other occasions to those parts of Syria other than Lebanon and Palestine. Thus, a typical pronouncement by a member of the French colonial lobby in 1911 argued that: 'the axis of French policy is in the Mediterranean. One of its poles is to the West through Algeria, Tunisia and Morocco. The other pole must be to the east: Syria, Lebanon and Palestine.'[7]

At the same time other proponents of French preponderance in Syria were seeking to prove that there was a Syrian entity that was neither Arab nor Muslim, the existence of which could be gleaned from a proper study of the region's history. George Samné and Henri Lammens published books arguing this thesis in 1920 and 1921 but had been advocating their views, in different fashions, before the war. Lammens was a Belgian Jesuit, a student of Islam and the region's history who settled in Beirut where he taught and preached his views. Samné, a Greek Catholic doctor from Damascus, had emigrated to Paris and had been one of several Levantine Christians who wrote and worked to promote French influence in Syria. One of Samné's colleagues, the Lebanese Maronite, Khayrallah Khayrallah, published his ideas on the nature of the Syrian entity before the war. Given the fact that Syria was a diverse country that had never had a national government, Khayrallah maintained that a unified secular Syria could not be established all at once. As a transitional phase Syria should first be constituted as

a loose federation of largely self-governing districts, each with a stable ethnic or religious basis and so delimited that each important community had
a region in which it was in the majority.[8]

This concept of Syria was characteristic of a period in which the lines
between Syrian, Lebanese and Arab orientations did not have to be drawn
very sharply. A colleague of Samné and Khayrallah, Shukri Ghanim was the
author of a poetic drama, '*Antar* that in 1910 was a box office success in
Paris and popularized a 'romantic vision of the rise of the Arab people'.[9]
Another Lebanese, with no connection to the group mentioned earlier,
Bulus Nujayyim published in 1908 under the pseudonym M. Jouplain a
book in French on the Lebanese question. It is curious that one modern
historian chose to characterize the book as laying the ground for the subsequent demand to create a Greater Lebanon,[10] while another historian
chose to place the author among those who saw Lebanon as playing a special role in a Syrian entity that should be created at a later stage.[11]

In 1913 the British Admiralty published *A Handbook of Syria (including
Palestine)*. The authors defined Syria in the broadest sense of the term, as the
country lying between the Eastern Mediterranean and the Arabian deserts.
It also referred to the narrower sense of the term – that part of Syria that
was not including Palestine. This, stated the handbook, was the standard
French use of the term. But it is difficult to believe that the French would
have agreed to the authors' demarcation of the border between Palestine
and Syria as a line following the Litani and reaching just south of
Damascus. They even went so far as to suggest that the area could possibly
be so divided as to include Damascus in Palestine.[12]

It is curious that while the French and their supporters were preoccupied with the nature of the relationship between Syria and Lebanon the
British were interested in the demarcation line separating Syria from
Palestine. It was a reflection of ambitions and designs as well as of percep-
tions. For Europeans interested in the Levant on the eve of the First World
War Syria was an entity but Palestine and Lebanon, while pertaining to the
larger Syrian entity had their own identities.

Palestine was defined first and foremost by its history but by 1913 two
modern forces had been at work whose subsequent cooperation was to
shape Palestinian's separate history: the Zionist movement and British policy. In the early years of the twentieth century, British interest in Palestine
and in Southern Syria was determined by two geopolitical considerations:
defence of the Suez Canal and the plan to create in the event of the
Ottoman Empire's partition a landbridge under British control from the
Persian Gulf to a port on the Eastern Mediterranean. Broader foreign policy considerations induced the British to recognize France's pre-eminence

in Syria but they had a clear interest in limiting the scope of France's prospective sphere of influence in that ill-defined entity. Britain's own territorial ambitions in the southern part of Geographic Syria were fully articulated by the De Bunsen committee in 1915 whose task was to define Britain's war aims in the region.[13]

Lebanon had since 1861 been recognized as an administrative entity – the autonomous *mutasarrifiyya*, but it was ill at ease with its environment. The Maronites, the mainstay of the Lebanese entity, possessed several of the attributes of a nation except sufficient size and a distinctive language and their nationalism was formulated in Lebanese rather than Maronite terms. Lebanese nationalism laid a claim to territories lying outside the boundaries of the *mutasarrifiyya*, inhabited by Muslim or non-Catholic Christians and considered part of Syria. The three major demands or expectations of the Maronite nationalists were separation (or independence) from the rest of Syria, territorial expansion and French protection. These expectations were not shared by some Maronites, and by most non-Catholic residents of the *mutasarrifiyya* and by those residing in the outlying areas that had belonged to the Lebanese emirate during the periods of great success and expansion in the past. Beirut in this respect was not a Lebanese but a Syrian city whose society and politics produced a group like the 'Beirut Reform Society'. The Society was affiliated to the Ottoman Party of Administrative Decentralization and its activities were conducted in an Ottoman, Arab and Syrian rather than in a Lebanese context.[14]

It was significant that Lesser, Smaller or Inland Syria was defined during that period in negative terms, as composed of those parts of Geographic Syria that did not form part of either Lebanon or Palestine. Unlike these two regions, Inland Syria was not, indeed, defined by either the ambitions of a foreign power or by a local movement or political force. On the eve of the First World War, Arabism had developed into a significant political force in Syria's cities but it had yet to produce an actual political movement. The origins and early development of Arabism have attracted much scholarly attention even though most Syrians remained loyal Ottomanists until the Empire's final collapse at the war's end.[15]

Most pre-war Syrian Arabists thought in terms of Arab rights and autonomy, not ideas of 'some loose form of Syrian territorial unity'. Notions of British tutelage and secession from the Ottoman Empire did appear. In contradistinction to the early Christian advocates of Syrian and Arab patriotism, most Syrian Arabists of the pre-war years were Sunni Muslims, some of them hailing from the most prominent Muslim families of the Syrian provinces and some affiliated to or influenced by the Islamic reform movement.[16]

It was during the formative period of 1914–21 that Arabism was transformed into a dominant idea and political force under the combined impact of the Ottoman Empire's collapse and the alliance between British policy and embryonic Arab nationalism of the time. But this did not serve to fashion an Arab state in Greater Syria. Other forces at work, French policy, Maronite-Lebanese nationalism, the parallel British-Zionist alliance and Britain's ambitions resulted in the partition of Geographic Syria into several political entities.

An attempt to create a Syrian state which claimed jurisdiction over the entire territory of Bilad al-Sham was made by Faysal's Arab government – October 1918 to July 1920. It was installed in Damascus by General Allenby and his political advisors with a view to forming an Arab state under Faysal in Inland Syria.[17] Faysal himself tended as a rule to settle on that slice of the pie realizing that he could not hope to dislodge the British, the French and their allies from Palestine, Lebanon and perhaps from other parts as well. But his more radical supporters wanted an Arab Syria in the entire territory of Bilad al-Sham. Their demands and perspective were expressed primarily through the work of the Syrian Congress. The willingness of the Palestinian Arab nationalists to submerge themselves in a greater Syrian Arab entity under the term Southern Syria belongs to the same phase. It was only occasionally that Faysal was tempted, or lost control, and tried to extend his sway into the area of direct French control.[18] In March 1920 Faysal was swept by the radicals and agreed to be crowned as King of Syria. But his state – and coronation – were not recognized by the international order and his short lived kingdom whose partial sway remained in fact limited to Inland Syria, did not constitute an actual state.

One particularly interesting aspect of this period was the evolution of French attitudes toward the notion of a Syrian entity. As we saw, the idea of a secular non-Arab Syrian entity was closely linked on the eve of the First World War to the idea of French control of such an entity. France's takeover of Syria proved to be more difficult than expected and France ended up with a smaller part of Syria that she had hoped to have. But in July 1920 France was in control of most of Syria, Damascus included, and could in theory realize the historical vision and establish a Syrian state. But two considerations militated against such a policy.

One was the adoption of a two-tier Lebanese policy – the establishment of a separate Lebanese state and the expansion of its territory at Syria's expense. The creation of a French dominated Syria would have required Lebanon's inclusion in its territory. The Maronites and France's other Catholic friends would in that case have become the mainstay of French rule in a larger Syria. The idea, as we saw, had surfaced before the war and was advocated by one of the contending schools of thought regarding Lebanon's character and future. But by 1920 a powerful Maronite lobby was at work determined to have a separate – and larger – Lebanon. Recent research has shown that it was this lobby which played the major role in the process which led to the establishment of Greater Lebanon in September 1920.[19]

The work of the Greater Lebanon lobby was facilitated by the fact that the leaders of the small but extremely effective 'Syrian lobby' which had operated within the French government was taking a more complex and cool-headed view of its own success. Men like Robert de Caix who had endeavoured prior to and during the First World War to bring Syria under French control realized in 1920 that France's interests in Syria did not warrant the investment that French control of Syria in the teeth of Arab-Muslim opposition would require. They could – and did – lay the blame on Britain for Arab nationalism's anti-French orientation. But they could not ignore the fact that France came to Inland Syria after destroying Faysal's Arab government and that Arab nationalism was the dominant political force in Inland Syria. The French had made two attempts to explore the possibility of coming to terms with Faysal. These attempts were led by Clemenceau who was not particularly interested in Syria and was fully aware of the discrepancy between France's interests in Syria and the cost involved in any attempt to take and maintain control over it.

But the efforts proved futile. After destroying Faysal's government and having decided to create a Greater Lebanon they had to decide how they wished to organize the rest of the territory under their control.

Well before July 1920 Robert de Caix, the chief architect of French policy in the Levant, had argued against the creation of a unified Syrian state in the territory left after the creation of a separate Lebanese state. He argued that it would have Arab and Muslim orientation, would be hostile to France and would project a dangerous influence into French North Africa. As against this Syrian state he advocated the creation of 'une syrie federale cantonale'. Syria would be divided into a number of small states thus reflecting the country's regional and ethnic diversity. There would be no Syrian state as such. De Caix's program, it should be noted, clearly resembles the plan set in Khayrallah's 1912 article. Given de Caix's role in France's pre-war colonial lobby and the connections between Khayrallah and his circle and the Quai d'Orsay and the colonial lobby, it can be assumed quite safely that their pre-war ideas thus had an important influence on French policy in the Levant in 1920.

De Caix's policy was implemented in this respect by the High Commissioner, General Gouraud. A Syrian state was not created in

September 1920. It was only in January 1925 that de Caix's policy was abandoned and a state of Syria was established by the unification of the states of Damascus and Aleppo. The outlying areas, organized into a series of autonomous states and governments, went through several changes of status before being finally included in the independent Syrian state which emerged from the Second World War.

GREATER SYRIA, 1921–45

Geographic Syria's partition during the 1914–21 period had a contradictory effect on the region's subsequent history. The four principal units into which the territory was divided proved (unlike the French-made statelets in Inland Syria) rather durable and in time developed ruling establishments with a vested interest in the status quo and at least a measure of legitimacy. Nowhere were the effects of this process more striking than among Lebanon's Sunni Muslims where several prominent Arab and Syrian nationalists gradually came to accept the Lebanese polity and to play leading roles in its affairs.[20] In a less dramatic fashion a similar process of political habituation occurred in Inland Syria and in the Jordanian Emirate. Both entities, the one truncated and the other created *ex nihilo*, developed ruling establishments interested in consolidating their existence.

At the same time, the area's partition and the difficulties it presented to several groups and communities produced, particularly in the war's immediate aftermath a yearning for a larger Syria. Among Arab nationalists Faysal's short lived reign in Damascus appeared through a nostalgic myth as an all too brief golden age, though Faysal's own efforts to return to Damascus in the late 1920s and early 1930s were rebuffed by his own former supporters.

Beyond such vague sentiments three bids or programmes emerged during this period for the unification of *Biald al-Sham* into one state.[21]

One was manifested in the refusal of Arab nationalists in the truncated Syrian state to accept the region's partition and their insistence that not just French dominated Syria but all of Geographic Syria should be united into one Arab state with Damascus as capital. Thus, when the Syrian state's constituent assembly met for the first time in 1927 it endorsed a draft constitution whose first article stated that Syria including Transjordan, Palestine and the Lebanon was 'one and indivisible' and repudiated its partition by the victorious allies.[22]

The Syrian Arab nationalists rejected France's demand to rescind this article and the constituent assembly was prorogued *sine die*.

But the significance of this Syrian Arab nationalist claim to the whole of

Syria was rather limited. For one thing the truncated Syrian state was and remained weak until well into the latter half of the twentieth century. It could not quite translate the irridentist claim into an effective policy. Even more important was the Syrian Arab nationalists' de facto abandonment of the claim and their willingness, as early as 1936 to settle on independence within the area of French dominated Syria.

Among the Syrian Arab nationalists who provided the backbone of the national movement in Mandatory Syria, an outlook developed that advocated an Arab nationalism in which Syria, while still viewed as part of the larger Arab homeland was to hold a special position and play a special role.[23] The lack of sharp distinction between Syrianism and Arabism that had first become apparent in the nineteenth century was thus perpetuated in a different form.

A second bid was the Amir 'Abdallah's call for the establishment of a Greater Syrian Kingdom with Damascus as capital and himself as king. 'Abdallah's plan reflected the frustration of a man who saw himself (with considerable justification) as Sharif Husayn's most capable son who was twice denied his fair share of the spoils. Dissatisfied with the small, isolated and hardly significant principality allotted him he had invested efforts since the early 1920s in both Syria and Palestine. But it was only during the Second World War that he developed and propagated his Greater Syrian scheme.[24]

What is particularly interesting from our perspective was the ideological argumentation developed by 'Abdallah. 'Abdallah placed his drive for the establishment of a Greater Syrian state within an Arab nationalist framework. The Arab nation, according to 'Abdallah, was formed by history and territory. That territory encompassed the Arabian Peninsula and the Fertile Crescent (to the exclusion of Egypt). Within this territory Syria and Damascus occupied a central position. Their centrality was further magnified by the Arab Revolt – a crucial event in the Hashemite view of modern Arab history.

Syria for 'Abdallah was under several names Greater Syria, Bilad al-Sham, Suriyya al-Kubra, Suriyya al-Tabi'iyya, and Suriyya al-Jughrafiyya. The truncated Syrian state created by the French was merely – 'northern Syria'. The resurrection of Greater Syria would not only implement one of the central goals of the Arab Revolt and undo a grave injustice, but would be a crucial step toward solving the fundamental problems of the whole Arab nation.[25]

The most comprehensive and ambitious programme for the creation of a Greater Syrian state was formulated during the inter-war period by the Lebanese Antun Sa'adeh. Sa'adeh developed an elaborate ideology of pan-Syrian nationalism buttressed by a theory of nationalism and an interpretation of Syria's history since antiquity. Sa'adeh argued that nations were formed by territorial entities; and given the fact that a Syrian entity had existed since ancient times an unfulfilled Syrian nation existed as well. Syria's reunification would enable this nation to realize itself.

Like 'Abdallah, but from an entirely different perspective, Sa'adeh saw the period of the First World War as the crucial phase during which the Syrian entity was partitioned. As he put it, 'Syria at that time had yet to undergo a national and social revival that would consolidate its personality and rights' and was therefore not in a position to oppose 'the foreign deals'. The mission of Sa'adeh's party was to generate the national consciousness that would enable Syria to overcome religious and other divisions and to assert and implement its unity.[26]

Sa'adeh's platform pitted him at one and the same time against Arab nationalists and supporters of the status quo. His party attracted several thousand members, some of them well known intellectuals, in Lebanon, Syria and among the Palestinians, but failed to shake either the sway held by Arab nationalism or the territorial status quo.

Some of the party's attraction had little to do with its ideology. Many were attracted to it by Sa'adeh's personal magnetism and by his proto-fascist platform and style. But others were attracted by the doctrine – Greek Orthodox Lebanese, unhappy with French-Maronite domination of Lebanon or Syrian 'Alawis seeking a secular territorial definition of the political community.

To some extent at least Sa'adeh's doctrine seems to have reflected pre-First World War experiences. Sa'adeh was born in Lebanon to Khalil Sa'adeh, a Greek Orthodox physician who spent many years in Egypt and Brazil. Khalil Sa'adeh was a writer and a political activist, who propagated ideas of Syrian nationalism and secularism.

In the absence of an authoritative biography of Antun Sa'adeh much has to be surmised, particularly about the early and formative years of his life. More is known about the older Antun Sa'adeh whose activities were followed by security services and documented by his disciples, but precious little is known about Sa'adeh in the 1920s during which the doctrine was being formulated. Yet the context is quite clear: the direct influence of the father, the Greek Orthodox resistance and opposition to a Catholic Lebanon and the tendency of many Lebanese in the Diaspora, in Egypt as well as in Latin America, to view and present themselves as Syrian.

The role of the diaspora in the formulation of Syrian nationalism is particularly interesting. The phenomenon is well known from the history of other nationalist doctrines. As for the Egyptian part of the story it should be noted that the pattern was also to repeat itself. In the late 1950s a group of Syrian officers who were practically exiled by the UAR's authorities to Egypt formed the political group, the Military Committee, that in 1963 consolidated Syria's existence as a state. It was another case of a group of Syrians sensing their distinctiveness as against Egypt's mass and clear identity.

During the 1930s and early 1940s, Antun Sa'adeh, his party and his doctrine had a limited effect on the actual course of political events. For one thing, the area of Geographic Syria was dominated by France and Britain who were determined to maintain the territorial status quo and in a position to stifle any attempt to revise it. Local society and politics were controlled by traditional forces who sensed correctly that the new ideas and mood propagated and represented by the party constituted a grave challenge to their position. The attack on the Lebanese state and on Arab nationalism that attracted many of the party's early supporters in Lebanon and Syria antagonized a far larger number of Lebanese and Syrians in the mainstream of political opinion.

Like that of the other new ideological parties that appeared in the Arab world in the 1930s, the real impact of Sa'adeh and his movement was to be felt in the late 1940s and 1950s when the restraining influence of France and Britain had been removed. It was then that the generation that had had its political schooling in the 1930s came to play a real role in the politics of Syria and Lebanon. Men who as boys had been exposed to Sa'adeh's ideas and political techniques in Beirut, al-Hama and Latakia took part in the attack on the old order that was more effective in Syria than in Lebanon.

Yet it soon transpired that Sa'adeh's disciples were not to have a decisive influence on the actual course of political developments. But as the events of the past four decades have shown, the man's legacy and ideas proved durable. The quest for a secular definition of the political community and the sense and notion that there was a unity to Geographic Syria that transcended the territorial divisions of 1918–21 remained important elements in the politics of Syria, Lebanon and the Palestinian community. In this respect Sa'adeh's biography and ideas provide an intriguing line of continuity between the early modern notions of a Syrian entity in the nineteenth century and their more recent manifestations in the age of Syrian independence.

NOTES

1. This article was published in Thomas Philipp (ed.), *The Syrian Land in the 18th and 19th Century, Berliner Islamstudien*, Bd. 5 (Stuttgart: Frantz Steiner Verlag, 1992).

2. Butrus Abu Manneh, 'The Christians between Ottomanism and Syrian Nationalism: The Ideas of Butrus Bustani', *IJMES*, 11, 3 (1980), pp.287–304; Albert Hourani, *Arabic Thought in the Liberal Age* (London: Oxford University Press, 1962), pp.274ff. See also, C. Ernest Dawn, 'The Rise of Arabism in Syria', *Middle East Journal*, 16, 2 (1962), pp.145–68.

3. Abu Manneh, 'The Christians between Ottomanism and Syrian Nationalism'.

4. Hourani, *Arabic Thought in the Liberal Age*, and R.M. Haddad, *Syrian Christians in Muslim Society* (Princeton, NJ: Princeton University Press, 1970).

5. Shimon Shamir, 'Midhat Pasha and the Anti-Turkish Agitation in Syria', *MES*, 10 (1974), pp.115–41; and Fritz Steppat 'Eine Bewegung unter den Notabeln Syriens 1877–1878, Neues Licht auf die Enstehung des arabischen Nationalismus', *Deutscher Orientalistentag*, 17 (1968), Teil 2 ZDMG, Supplementia I (1969), pp.631–49.

6. C.M. Andrew and A.S. Kanya-Forstner, *France Overseas* (London: Thames and Hudson, 1981), pp.49–50.

7. Ibid.

8. Hourani, *Arabic Thought in the Liberal Age*, p.286.

9. Andrew and Kanya-Forstner, *France Overseas*, p.48.

10. M. Zamir, *The Formation of Modern Lebanon* (London: Croom Helm, 1985), pp.15–16.

11. Hourani, *Arabic Thought in the Liberal Age*, p.275.

12. Ibid., p.9.

13. A.S. Klieman, *Foundation of British Policy in the Middle East* (Baltimore, MD: John Hopkins Press, 1970), Chapter 1.

14. Elie Kedourie, 'Political Parties in the Arab World', in *Arabic Political Memoirs and Other Studies* (London: Frank Cass, 1974), pp.28–58.

15. Dawn, 'The Rise of Arabism in Syria', pp.145–68.

16. Philip Khoury, *Urban Notables and Arab Nationalism* (Cambridge: Cambridge University Press, 1983), Chapter 3 and David Commins, *Islamic Reform* (New York: Oxford University Press, 1990), Chapter 7.

17. For the history of that state see: Khayriyya al-Qasimiyya, *Al-Hukuma al-'arabiyya fi Dimashq 1918–1920* (Cairo: Dar al-ma'arif, 1971).

18. See Meir Zamir, *The Formation of Modern Lebanon* (London: Croom Helm, 1983).

19. See ibid., and Andrew and Kanya-Forstner, *France Overseas*, passim.

20. Raghid al-Solh, 'The Attitude of the Arab Nationalists towards Greater Lebanon during the 1930s', in Nadim Shehadi and Dana Haffar Mills (eds), *Lebanon, A History of Conflict and Consensus* (London: Center for Lebanese Studies with I.B. Tauris, 1988), pp.149–65.

21. See Daniel Pipes, *Greater Syria: The History of an Ambition* (New York, NY: Oxford University Press, 1990).

22. S.H. Longrigg, *Syria and Lebanon Under French Mandate* (London: Oxford University Press, 1958), p. 184.

23. A. Hourani, *Syria and Lebanon* (London: Oxford University Press, 1946), pp.119–20. Hourani correctly points to the fact that between this outlook and the rival doctrine of Syrian territorial nationalism (see below) there is a certain overlapping. See also Khoury, *Urban Notables and Arab Nationalism*.

24. Mary Wilson, *King 'Abdallah, Britain and the Making of Jordan* (Cambridge: Cambridge University Press, 1987).

25. This summary of 'Abdallah's writings and statements on the subject is based on I. Gershoni, 'The Arab Nation, The House of Hashem and Greater Syria in 'Abdallah's Writings', in *Hamizrah Hehadash*, 25 (1975), pp.165–70 [in Hebrew].

26. Sa'adeh's letter to the Social Nationalists and the Syrian Nation on the thirtieth anniversary of the Balfour Declaration (2 November 1947), reproduced in a party publication: *The Leader Through the Phases of the Palestine Question (Al-Zaim fi mar?hil al-masala al-filastiniyya)* (Beirut, 1949).

2

France and the Levant[1]

The title 'France and the Levant' evokes a powerful imagery and a long history. Since the crusades there existed both a special bond between France and the Levant and a consciousness of this bond that was often more important than the bond itself. The relationship had been full of ambiguities the first of which concerns the very term Levant. In the broadest sense the term denotes the coast of the Eastern Mediterranean, from Greece to Alexandria, but it could, in other contexts, have a narrower scope and refer specifically to the coastal region of Geographic Syria. Likewise France's relationship with the region and its inhabitants can be seen as a spectrum extending from a vague protective commitment to the Christian particularly Catholic communities of the whole region, to a much firmer nexus with the Maronites of Lebanon.

The ambiguity was given practical significance by the new political conditions, which emerged in the nineteenth century. France was one of the European powers whose ambitions and activities contributed to the Ottoman Empire's weakening and decline. It was known that in the event of the Empire's disintegration France had its eyes set, among other territories, on the Levant. The seriousness of France's claim was demonstrated in 1860 when it dispatched an expeditionary force to Lebanon to support the Maronites who had been badly defeated by their Druze rivals. And yet when the French government had to weigh its potential gains and losses if a partition of the Ottoman Empire were to take place a comprehensive view of France's interests and investments in the region led it to support the Empire's territorial integrity as the best option for French policy. The defeat of 1870 and the centrality of the quest to regain Alsace and Loraine in French nationalist thinking on foreign policy had a similar effect.[2] France's outlook on the Levant in the latter part of the nineteenth century and the Levantine Christian view of their French protectors were, thus, marked by a wide discrepancy between a mythical vision and a humbler reality.

Circumstances changed several times during the first two decades of the twentieth century but the ambiguity and ambivalence lasted until the summer of 1920. To the eve of the First World War French policy moved on the dual tracks of seeking to preserve the Ottoman Empire as the preferable option for maintaining France's interests and an effort to secure French control of 'La Syrie intégrale' in the event of the Empire's collapse. The war's outbreak put an end to this particular ambiguity. The allies decided to partition the Ottoman Empire and the questions now focused, from France's point of view, on its prospective share.[3]

But this well-defined focus did not remove all ambiguity and inconsistency from French policy in the Levant. During the period of the First World War and the ensuing peace settlement France's policies kept shifting – the area designated for French control or influence underwent several changes as did the French conception of the nature of this area and of the political entity or entities that should inhabit it. Was Syria one entity of which Christian Lebanon formed a part or should there be a separation between a Christian Lebanon and a different entity in the rest of Syria that would be Arab and Muslim? And if the latter option were to be adopted, what repercussions would the notion of a Syrian entity dominated by an Arab-Muslim national movement have on France's vital North African possessions?

France's vacillation between ambitious and more modest war aims in the Levant was governed by a variety of factors. The unusual influence wielded by a small but very effective colonial lobby within the French government and the pressures exerted by Levantine Christians tended to raise French sights. Counter pressures exerted by Britain and its Arab nationalist allies, the weakness of France's military presence in the region, post war weariness and the lack of genuinely important interests tilted French policy in the other direction. The contradictory effects of these sets of factors is best demonstrated by the sequence of events which led Clemenceau to first sign two abortive agreements with Prince Faysal in April 1919 and January 1920 and then to crush his Arab government in Damascus in July 1920.[4]

French doubts and uncertainties were matched by local responses. Arab nationalism became as a result of the First World War the dominant force among the Arab Muslim majority in 'La Syrie intégrale' and Arab nationalism viewed French ambitions in the Levant as a mortal danger. Arab nationalists were not impressed by the genuine French commitment to a mission civilizatrice in the Levant. To them it was a thinly veiled pretext for extending French control and influence as well as for promoting the interests of Christian minority groups over those of the Muslim majority. Among the Christians, the large and diffuse Greek Orthodox community resented France as the patron of its Catholic rivals. The latter, particularly the Maronites, were France's staunchest supporters. France's long awaited arrival was finally to provide them with effective support and security. But this element was horrified by Clemenceau's agreement with Faysal which envisaged a non-independent Lebanon forming part of a Syrian federation. Some French politicians may have seen the agreements as a matter of expediency and tactics. For many of their Christian Catholic supporters, nurtured by a long historical myth, it was seen as treason. It was difficult to restore the confidence thus shaken in the spring of 1919.

It is against this backdrop of a long history and complex ambiguities that the establishment of French rule in the Levant and its subsequent evolution should be seen. Things became defined. The Levant was now practically identified with the French mandated area, or part of it. In that area two states were established and the region's history and its relationship with France were conducted within this framework. French presence was no longer a prospect but became a reality and as such produced several disappointments. This was hardly surprising for Arab nationalists and Muslims who had opposed French control and influence, but for France and her traditional supporters the transformation of an erstwhile yearning into a relationship between the ruler and ruled was a painful process of disappointing discoveries.

The romantic and mysterious East was transformed into an actual arena of squalid local politics while, for the other side, France the savior came to be embodied by the usually unimpressive members of its colonial service. For France it was, on the whole, a disappointing experience. This was certainly the case in Syria. French rule, as originally established in 1920, was predicated on the concept of '*état cantonal*'. Its formulators, General Gouraud, the first High Commissioner and his influential aide, Robert de Caix, realized that the traditional French concept of a non-Arab Syrian entity was illusory. The territory of Geographic Syria was predominantly Arab and among the Arabs pan-Arab nationalism held sway. They therefore sought to take advantage of local and communal particularism in order to break Syria up and reshape it gradually to their liking.[5]

That original policy was abandoned in 1925 and an effort was made to open a dialogue with the Syrian Arab nationalists. The change in French policy was obscured by the outbreak in 1925 of a revolt in Syria that took two years to quash. In its aftermath a fresh and more determined effort was made to base French rule in Syria on cooperation with a local constitutional system. French policy now vacillated between attempts to cooperate with the Arab nationalists, the principal local political force, and equally frustrating efforts to govern through the so-called moderate local politicians. A treaty replacing the mandatory system was finally signed with the Syrian nationalists in 1936 but it was not ratified by the French government and ultimately was not implemented.[6]

The defeat of 1940 undermined among other things France's position in the Levant states. Free French forces participated in the British victory over Vichy forces in the Levant in 1941. They subsequently fought for over four years to preserve French hegemony against the Arab nationalists and their British (and this time American) supporters. As De Gaulle's memoirs clearly indicate, this particular arena of Anglo-French rivalry left a particularly bitter legacy in French consciousness. Indeed, French efforts to revive the treaty of 1936 were to no avail and France was evicted from the Levant in 1946 without any formal standing there.

The course of French policy in Lebanon in the 1920s and 1930s was smoother, but it led to an equally disappointing ending. The Lebanese state was created in its 1920 boundaries as a joint effort by the Maronite ultra-nationalists and the most radical members of the French colonial lobby. Robert de Caix, an important and sophisticated member of that lobby was opposed to the creation of the Grand Liban in its 1920 boundaries, arguing that such an expansion was bound to undermine the Maronites' position. He was, in this case, overruled by General Gouraud who acted under the pressure and spell of the Maronite ultra-nationalists. The creation of the Grand Liban implied a durable French protection.[7] How else could the Maronites hope to survive politically in a hostile environment when the demographic underpinning of a Christian Lebanon had been eroded? From this perspective the Fall of France in 1940 and its repercussions in the Levant were particularly significant in that France was no longer perceived by most Maronites and other Lebanese Catholics as an effective protector. The victory in 1943 of Bishara al-Khuri over Emile Eddé was, beyond its personal dimension, the victory of an orientation which sought to secure the Maronites' political future not through French support but by a partnership with the Sunni Muslim establishment in a pluralistic Lebanon. The National Pact, the compromise formula, which regulated Christian-Muslim relations in Lebanon provided also a modality for Lebanon's relationship with its Arab hinterland and enabled it to join the Arab League that was seen at the time as a British instrument.

In France this disappointing record had remarkably little influence. France's policies in the Levant never became an important domestic issue and were not the subject of a significant debate or editorial comment in the French press. Nor has it resulted in a sizeable body of academic writing. Memoirs aside, not a single major book was written in France on this national venture and general works dealing with French foreign and colonial policies in the inter-war period devote little space to the Levant.

The single most important factor accounting for this attitude seems to be the absence of genuine interest and interests. When the vague sense of

a long-standing historical connection had to be translated during this century's first two decades into an actual policy it transpired that the balance
between French interests in the Levant proper and the investment they
required was negative. France's decision to obtain the Levant despite this
negative balance was due to two factors: (1) the extraordinary effectiveness
of a small colonial lobby which operated inside and outside the governments of the day; (2) the fact that it was England which seemed to be on
the verge of taking over these traditional areas of French influence. This
turned the issue in 1919–20 to a nationalist *cause célèbre* and led a Prime
Minister like Clemenceau to commit his country to a policy course he may
not have otherwise have taken.

Indeed, it was the rivalry with Britain in the Levant, which continued
to have the greatest resonance in France. This was particularly true of the
Second World War period. Charles de Gaulle, as his memoirs clearly illustrate, saw British policy in the Levant as a lowly attempt to take advantage
of France's difficult hour in order to dispossess her from the Levant and
replace her as the paramount European power. The passion with which
these parts of the memoirs were written suggests that it had an impact on
this policy toward Britain in later decades.

The impact, immediate and lingering, of France's rule in the Levant on
the Syrian and Lebanese states it had created there, was far greater. In
Lebanon's case the lasting effects of France's action can be seen in the creation of Greater Lebanon and in the consolidation of the confessional political system. It is an interesting juxtaposition in that the confessional system
helped mitigate and postpone the disastrous effects of the creation of
Greater Lebanon.

Greater Lebanon was established on September 1 1920 when the
autonomous province of Mt Lebanon was expanded in all directions. The
gain in territory and economic viability was clearly outweighed by the loss
of a clear-cut Christian-Maronite majority, the disaffection of the Muslims
population and the Syrian irridenta. For years it had been assumed that the
creation of Greater Lebanon was a French act, designed to provide French
policy in the Levant with a large basis of support. Recent research conducted in the French archives has revealed that it was the Maronite community led by its patriarch that had played the principal role in bringing
that decision about. As has been suggested above, French policy makers
acted in response to Maronite initiative and were divided among themselves on this issue.

Several factors account for the fact that it took fifty-five years for that
prediction to come true, but chief among them is the confessional political system, which took its final shape under the French mandate. This form

of consociational democracy created a genuine partnership and a community of interests between the country's major communities or at least their political establishments and provided the country with a backbone that was not broken until 1975.

In Syria, a different French policy was pursued in an entirely different set of circumstances. In contradistinction to the partnership with the main political force in Lebanon French policy in Syria had been antagonistic to the Syrian Arab nationalists and to the idea of a large centralized Syria they sought to form. This goal was achieved in part in 1945, but unlike other parts of the Third World, the Syrian Arab nationalists did not emerge from the struggle with the prestige and coherence of a victorious national movement.

The weakness of the Sunni urban political establishment in independent Syria left the stage open to members of the 'Alawi community who twenty years after the independence, operating through the armed forces and the Ba'th Party seized power in Syria. This has for the past twenty years been a cardinal fact of Syrian political life and it can be related to an important dimension of French mandatory policy. France did not create the tension between Sunnis and 'Alawis but it certainly fostered it and cultivated 'Alawi separatism as a bulwark against the notion of a unified Arab Syria. More specifically it recruited many 'Alawis to the *troupes spéciales*, the local force which served as the basis of the future Syrian army. This is how the process which catapulted the 'Alawis at the top of the pyramid of power in Syria was launched.

Given the hostility between France and the nationalist movement in Syria and the circumstances in which France left the Levant it is curious to note how ephemeral the resentment of France's erstwhile opponents in the Levant turns out to have been. Some twenty-five years after its departure from the Levant, France, itself in an ambivalent relationship with its Western allies, no longer appeared to Arab nationalists and Muslim radicals in the Levant as a sinister Western power, but as different from, and sometimes an alternative to, what Charles de Gaulle used to call 'the Anglo-Saxon Powers'.

During the past few years two volumes have been added to the comparatively scant literature dealing with France and the Levant. A collection of documents from the French archives was edited and published: A. Hokayem, D. BouMalhab 'Atallah and J. Charif, *Documents Diplomatiques Francais Relatifs A L'Histoire Du Liban Et De La Syrie A L'Epoque Du Mandat: 1914–1946,* Tome 1; *Le Démantèlement de L'Empire Ottoman Et Les Preludes Du Mandat: 1914–1919,* Beyrouth et Paris, 2003. It is an invaluable source, shedding new light both on French policy and local politics.

In 2006 the British author David Pryce-Jones published Betrayal.[8] The main theme of the book, the anti-Semitic strand in the Quai d'Orsay and France's attitude toward and relationship with Zionism and the State of Israel, is not our concern in the present context, but Pryce-Jones conducted extensive research in the French archives and some of his finds are of great interest.

Pryce-Jones's work touches also on another theme worthy of a separate study: the quadruple relationship between Britain, France, Arab nationalism and Zionism. British policy was originally allied, often uncomfortably, with both Arab nationalism and Zionism. France, Britain rival's in the Levant, viewed both movements with suspicion as instruments of British policy. At various points in time, as British policy in Palestine tilted or seemed to tilt, toward the Arabs, the stage was set for French-Zionist cooperation. Several such episodes did occur, but at most times France continued to seek an accommodation with Arab nationalism while the Zionist movement and subsequently Israel saw a relationship with Britain and then with the United States as the mainstay of their foreign policy. Several years of close French-Israeli cooperation in the mid and late 1950s were significant but still an exception.

NOTES

1. Paper delivered in a conference held in Tel-Aviv University in 1982.
2. For books reflecting a French perspective on the notion of a Syrian entity and its history, see Henri Lammens, La Syrie: Précis Historique (Beyrouth: Imprimerie Catholique, 1921), pp.194–269; George Samné, La Syrie (Paris: Bossard, 1922); Tabitha Petran, Syria (London: Ernest Benn, 1978), pp.45–79. For a description of France's expansion into the Levant, see C.M. Andrew and A.S. Kanya-Forstner, France Overseas: The Great War and the Climax of French Imperial Expansion (London: Thames and Hudson, 1981). For a particularly intriguing case of the French relationship with an Arab Christian nationalist, see Martin Kramer, 'Azouri: A Further Episode', Middle Eastern Studies, 18, 4 (1982), pp.351–8.
3. On the period of the French Mandate and the links with the minorities, see Stephen Hemsley Longrigg, Syria and Lebanon Under French Mandate (London: Oxford University Press, 1958); Albert Hourani, Syria and Lebanon: A Political Essay (London: Oxford University Press, 1946).
4. For Clemenceau's policy and the events which led to the crushing of Faysal's regime, see Andrew and Kanya-Forstner, France Overseas, pp.137–82; 241–7.
5. For the French methods in Syria compared with those carried out in Morocco, and for French Policy, which reinforced divisions and cleavages among Syrian society, see Edmund Burke III, 'A Comparative View of French Native Policy in Morocco and Syria', Middle Eastern Studies, 9, 2 (1973), pp.175–86. See also in this volume: I. Rabinovich 'The Compact Minorities and the Syrian State, 1918–1945'.
6. Philip Khoury, 'Factionalism among Syrian Nationalists during the French Mandate', International Journal of Middle Eastern Studies, 13, 4 (1981), pp.441–69; Hemsley Longrigg, Syria and Lebanon Under French Mandate, pp.195–7.
7. For the emergence of a Lebanese entity and the establishment of Greater Lebanon, see Meir Zamir, The Formation of Modern Lebanon (London: Croom Helm, 1985), pp.1–96; Meir Zamir, Lebanon's Quest: The Road to Statehood, 1926–1939 (London: I.B.Tauris, 1997), pp.1–28.
8. David Pryce-Jones, Betrayal: France, The Arabs, and The Jews (New York, NY: Encounter Books, 2006).

3

Between Nationalists and 'Moderates':
France and Syria in the 1930s[1]

In November 1934 the new French High Commissioner, Comte de Martel, tried to have the draft French-Syrian treaty, prepared under his predecessor and signed by the Syrian Government, approved by the Syrian parliament. The treaty was to replace the League of Nations mandate as the basis of France's paramountcy in Syria, and to place French-Syrian relations on a footing similar to the apparently successful British-Iraqi relationship. The effort failed, and the Mandatory Authorities were forced to withdraw the proposed treaty and to suspend the uncooperative Chamber. The standard histories of the period ascribe the French failure to the effective opposition of the nationalists who, though a numerical minority in the Parliament, drew on their political skills, moral conviction, and popular support in order to defeat a text regarded as inadequate.[2]

A similar explanation was offered at the time by French diplomats and practitioners baffled by their inability to overcome the opposition of what they viewed as a manipulative urban minority:

> Elections thus regularly send to a Syrian parliament a majority of moderate rural notables, inclined to cooperate with the Mandatory Power, and an active minority of cultivated intellectuals who, in moments of political crisis, easily impose their manoeuvres on a so-called moderate majority, amorphous and lacking a political tradition. This is the underlying reason for the Mandatory Power's failure so far to resolve the Syrian question on a contractual basis.[3]

But in a note prepared by the Levant Department of the Quai d'Orsay in March 1934, in which President Doumergue and Foreign Minister Herriot were warned against Subhi Bey Barakat, the Speaker of the Syrian Parliament, a rather more complex explanation was offered for the debacle which had occurred some four months earlier. According to that version, the Speaker, who in 1932 had been elected to Parliament and to his position as a pro-French 'moderate', played an important role in aborting the High Commissioner's policy in November 1933. Subhi Bey was at the time a powerful and influential politician. He commanded a bloc of twenty-eight deputies in a Chamber of seventy, and was reelected in October for a second term by forty-six deputies. But the Speaker, for reasons that will be explained below, harboured a grudge against the High Commissioner, and took his revenge. He signed the nationalist manifesto that denounced the draft treaty and its Syrian signatories, and mobilized 'moderate' deputies to oppose it in Parliament. He further clashed with the Mandatory Authorities when the latter made a point of suspending the Chamber before it had the opportunity to reject the treaty formally. The speaker, the Quai d'Orsay charged subsequently, tried to 'falsify' the record of the meeting, so as to include in it the nationalist manifesto, and to create the impression that a majority of the delegates had adopted it and rejected the draft treaty.[4]

This fuller and, in all likelihood, correct[5] version of France's failure to obtain a satisfactory Syrian treaty in 1933 reveals a missing dimension in the traditional view of her policies toward mandatory Syria. That view has assigned much of the blame for the failure of these policies to France's inability to come to terms with Syrian Arab nationalism and its representatives, and to the inherent weakness of the more cooperative 'moderate' politicians through whom she chose or was forced to govern. It should be supplemented and nuanced by a recognition of the flaws and errors with which France's relationship with her Syrian supporters abounded. From this wider perspective, a less deterministic view of France's ultimate failure can be taken.[6]

FRANCE AND THE SYRIAN ARAB NATIONALISTS

During the first decade of her rule in Syria, France's attitude toward and relationship with the Syrian Arab nationalist politicians went through three phases.

The first began with the destruction of Faysal's Arab government in Damascus in July 1920, and lasted until 1925. It was shaped primarily by the mutual hostility between the French authorities and Syrian Arab nationalism whose roots can be traced to well before the First World War. A small but influential colonial lobby in France had been promoting a French claim to a sphere of influence in (an ill-defined) Syria.[7] To the nascent Arab nationalist movement the French claim, particularly its 'civilizing' dimension and the historic connection with the region's Christian communities, appeared threatening. The advocates of French hegemony in 'La Syrie intégrale', in turn, did not envisage an Arab-Muslim Syria, but a particular Syrian entity shaped by its distinctive history and cultural tradition.[8]

The antagonism was exacerbated by the circumstances of the First

World War and the ensuing peace settlement. France's claim to hegemony and influence in part of Geographic Syria was recognized and endorsed by her wartime allies. But an overlapping (not to say contradictory) commitment was given by the British to the Arab nationalist claim over Inland Syria, and an Arab nationalist government under the Hashimite prince Faysal was installed in Damascus with British support. To the Arab nationalists, the French now appeared as an enemy bent on destroying their achievements and dispossessing them. The French, in turn, viewed the Arab nationalists not only as obstacles to their influence, but also as the instrument of an inimical British policy. All efforts to effect an accommodation between France and Faysal having failed, the French dislodged him by force and established their rule on the ruins of his state.[9]

It was against this background that the French authorities organized their Mandatory Government in Syria. Syrian Arab nationalism was a hostile force to be combated and weakened. Robert de Caix, the chief architect of French policy in Syria and a leader of the colonial movement in France, was far from underestimating the challenge of Arab nationalism. To him it was a dangerous idea, whose influence could undermine France's position in her far more crucial North African possessions. But it could be checked through an alliance with the forces of particularism and traditionalism. A divided Syria controlled by the French through cooperative conservative local forces and leaders was the formula he advocated and subsequently applied together with General Gouraud, the first High Commissioner.[10]

This policy began to change, and then collapsed in 1925. The third High Commissioner, General Sarrail, in an effort to liberalize France's policy, allowed a nationalist opposition, the People's Party, to form and operate. But far more significant was his unwitting contribution to the outbreak of the Druze Revolt, which developed into a general rebellion that the French authorities were hard put to quell. Sarrail was recalled and his successor, Henri de Jouvenel, sought a political solution to the crisis. He dismissed the unpopular President Subhi Bey Barakat, and tried to replace him with Shaykh Taj al-Din al-Hasani, who was considered a moderate nationalist. However, the latter's conditions for taking office were unacceptable to the French and the choice finally fell on Damad Ahmad Nami Bey, whose Cabinet initially included nationalist ministers in its ranks. In 1926 de Jouvenel was replaced by a professional diplomat, Henri Ponsot, whose main task was to establish a constitutional and parliamentary framework in Syria, and to have a Syrian government, enjoying parliamentary support, sign a treaty with France. Ponsot's strategy was clearly inspired by Britain's apparent success in Iraq, where its control was exercised through a cooperative local elite with sound

Arab nationalist credentials. He was also operating under the other pressures that had constrained French policy in Syria from the outset: the asymmetry between her real interests and the investment required to sustain them, the need to meet France's obligations to the League of Nations, and the hostility of part of the French political spectrum to France's presence and policies in the Levant.

In any event, Ponsot's efforts to find a compromise solution failed. Elections were conducted by Taj al-Din al-Hasani, and they produced a constituent assembly with a large majority of 'moderate' rural notables. Still, the nationalist minority, now organized into a National Bloc, dominated the proceedings, and it introduced into the text of the proposed constitution several articles that the High Commissioner found absolutely unacceptable. The situation was deadlocked, the assembly was suspended, and Taj al-Din al-Hasani continued to govern Syria on behalf of the French, as an unsatisfactory but workable intermediate solution.

FRANCE AND THE 'MODERATE' POLITICIANS

Unwilling or unable to govern Syria through the nationalist politicians, the French Mandatory Authorities had to rely on a group of cooperative and pragmatic politicians who came to be known as moderates. Their function was defined succinctly by de Martel in 1935 in the following terms: 'A government sufficiently strong to undertake responsibility for the conduct of affairs to provide together with the French *délégués* and *conseillers* effective control that will be sufficiently discreet so that the men in power do not appear before public opinion as mere instruments in our hands.'[11]

Three of the politicians mentioned above (Subhi Bey Barakat, Damad Ahmad Nami Bey, and Shaykh Taj al-Din al-Hasani), together with Haqqi Bey al-'Azm, were the chief instruments of this policy. An attempt to identify the underlying differences between the group of Syrian politicians who chose to cooperate with the Mandatory Authorities and those who, as Syrian Arab nationalists, chose to oppose them, would fall outside the scope of this essay,[12] but an outline of the political careers of France's principal local allies should illuminate an important aspect of France's Syrian policy.

Haqqi Bey al-'Azm, a scion of one of Syria's most distinguished families, had been a member of the pre-First World War 'Ottoman Party for Decentralized Administration', a rather moderate group that advocated Arab autonomy within the Ottoman framework. In 1922 he was appointed governor of the State of Damascus, and in 1924 to the first cabinet of the newly created Syrian state. In 1929 he was one of the founders of the

Syrian Reform Party – a small group of traditional politicians without real membership or popular support.

In terms of both personality and career, Subhi Bey Barakat presents an interesting contrast with Haqqi Bey al-'Azm. A landed notable from the region of Antakya, he was ethnically more Turkish than Arab, and his command of Arabic was and remained imperfect. His leadership style was shaped by his powerful personality, but its effectiveness was compromised by the vindictive and violent streaks in his character. Nor was Subhi Bey very consistent: by the end of the 1920s he had gone through three changes of course and orientation. He began by fighting against the French in northern Syria, but subsequently made his peace with the new authorities and was willing to cooperate with them. In 1922, when the Mandatory Authorities decided to form a Syrian federation, they placed Subhi Bey at its head. His forceful personality, anti-French past, and north-Syrian orientation seemed to qualify him for the conduct of a policy seeking to demonstrate that a Syrian state was not necessarily identified with the Arab nationalism of the Damascene notables. When a Syrian state was established in January 1925, he was made its first head. Despite charges of nepotism and corruption, Subhi Bey was considered by the French a successful administrator. But the outbreak of the 1925 revolt marked the end of his success. His high-handed methods were in tune as long as the military effort to quash the rebellion continued, but once the new High Commissioner, de Jouvenel, decided to seek an accommodation with the nationalists, their Syrian foe had to be sacrificed.[13]

Subhi Bey did not go down gracefully. Before parting, he published a statement endorsing the nationalist platform. This was not forgotten by the High Commission's staff, and during the 1928 elections the French authorities and Shaykh Taj al-Din al-Hasani joined forces to keep him out of the constituent assembly.

Subhi Bey's successor as Syria's head of state in 1926 was Ahmad Nami Bey, who as a former son-in-law to a former Ottoman sultan was known as Damad. He was of Circassian extraction, grandson of the Ottoman governor of Tripoli whose family had settled in the Beirut area. He accepted the post only on the basis of a programme that the nationalists were also willing to endorse by joining his first cabinet.[14]

The Damad remained in office for twenty months. In early 1928 the High Commissioner, Ponsot, decided to hold elections for a constituent assembly and to appoint another head of government to conduct them. For one thing, the Damad had become too ambitious for the French – he actually exerted pressure on them to appoint him King of Syria. He seemed also to have completed a familiar cycle, and to have made too many enemies among both the nationalists and the other moderate politicians.[15]

The conduct of the 1928 elections was entrusted, instead, to Shaykh Taj al-Din al-Hasani, who had been the Mandatory Authorities' original choice in 1926. His platform and list of demands were too close to the nationalist position, and he was not willing then to accept the High Commission's terms. This added a mild nationalist aura to his other asset: he was the son of Shaykh Badr al-Din al-Hasani, a venerated and popular 'alim in Damascus. Once in office, he proved to be a very shrewd politician who managed very well with the local French authorities, and excelled in cultivating an effective lobby in metropolitan France.[16]

THE REASSESSMENT OF 1930

Effective as Shaykh Taj al-Din may have been as a political instrument, he and his government could not solve France's fundamental dilemma. The constituent assembly remained suspended, and a course of evolution leading through the passing of a constitution, parliamentary elections, the signing of a treaty with an elected government, and its approval by the Syrian parliament, did not seem feasible. The negotiations which preceded the Anglo-Iraqi treaty of 1930 and its eventual signing only served to underline the difference between Britain's apparent success and France's failure, and to aggravate the latter's predicament.

Against this background, Henri Ponsot and his High Commission's staff held in late 1929 and early 1930 a long series of meetings and consultations, with a view to devising a new political strategy. The process was completed in February 1930, and the conclusions drawn by the High Commission were summed up in an unusually revealing note penned by its staff.[17]

As the High Commission saw it, a fundamental choice had to be made in the first place between the nationalists and 'the so-called moderates'. The option of a deal with the nationalist mainstream, as represented by the National Bloc, was ruled out at the outset. The platform presented by the nationalist leader, Hashim al-Atasi, persuaded the High Commission that the gap between 'their interests and our prestige remained unbridgeable'.[18]

But an intermediate option could be considered. In their negotiations with the authorities, the nationalists had intimated that they were willing to settle on a practical compromise. Let the French force their hand by imposing the amended text of the constitution unilaterally, and proceed with the formation of a cabinet composed of 'second echelon' nationalists whose task it would be to negotiate a Franco-Syrian treaty. Despite its apparent attractiveness this option, too, was discarded by the High

Commission. Its memorandum cited two principal reasons which militated against such a compromise. It would, the High Commission argued, constitute too abrupt a change in a policy that should carefully prepare the transition from a *regime d'autorité* to a *regime de conseil*. A hasty transfer of power could produce a situation in which force would have to be employed. Nor was there, it continued, a sufficient measure of confidence or community of views that could enable France to overcome the residues of the past. Did this pessimistic view mean, as it seemed to imply, that France could never come to terms with the nationalists? Not necessarily, was the answer:

> We can hope that some day, when the normal working of the constitutional institutions brings the nationalists to power, it will also produce between us and them, between the positions we keep and the ones they acquire, a certain balance ... but we cannot rely on the nationalists to create this balance, or to help us in good faith to prepare the conditions for it. Handing power more or less directly into their hands, through the promulgation of the constitution, would be tantamount to deliberately providing them with all the opportunities, and to entering immediately into battle on a terrain which we will have no time to prepare.[19]

Having thus rejected the idea of a compromise with the nationalists, the High Commission was left to choose a 'moderate' politician to govern Syria on its behalf. It saw four possibilities:

a) A combination of the Hashimite Prince Haydar as King of Syria and Rashid Rida al-Rikabi as his prime minister. Both men were very attractive to the French, but their hour seemed to have passed. A Syrian monarchy was no longer feasible, and the authoritarian approach associated with Rikabi was out of tune with a French policy committed to a *programme sagement libéral*.[20]

b) Subhi Bey Barakat. The High Commission's rancour seemed to have dissipated when it described his qualifications: 'He enjoys the advantage ... of having provided proof of his governing ability, his loyalty and even disinterestedness. He rests in northern Syria on a clientele that is still vigorous and devoted.' But the countervailing considerations were more powerful. Subhi Bey was bound to unite against him both the 'nationalists' and all the other moderates. The Mandatory Authorities could in theory 'carry him on their arms' to electoral victory, but they felt that they did not 'presently possess the organization ... necessary for undertaking such an adventure ... it is too late or too early, the old structure of the authoritarian regime having been weakened morally and materially, and the future structure of a consultative regime being still too rudimentary.'[21]

c) The group of politicians and factions led by Haqqi Bey al-'Azm and the Damad Ahmad Nami Bey, and loosely federated under the title of 'The United Parties'. The High Commission had little esteem for either their effectiveness or their program. Al-'Azm was described rather uncharitably as 'of mediocre intelligence and weak character'. The Damad was described as 'a courteous and nonchalant gentleman, devoid of administrative experience and breadth of political views'. As a group, their governing capacity had been tested twice and found to be deficient. They were 'strong in speech and feeble in action, and history has taught us that they were the first sinkers of the destinies entrusted to them'.[22]

d) Having discarded these three alternatives, the High Commission was bound to settle on the fourth. The process of consultation and search departed from the assumption that the government of Shaykh Taj al-Din had to be replaced; it ended with the conclusion that under the circumstances the French would be best served by retaining it. The High Commission was far from starry-eyed about either the character or the political capacity of the incumbent, but it failed to discover a better choice. It tended to ascribe his bad reputation and lack of popularity to his competitors' jealousy rather than to a genuine popular sentiment. He had shown that he could run the country reasonably well without requiring a particular effort on the part of the Mandatory Authorities to sustain him. Given a facelift, his government should be able to proceed with the promulgation of the constitution and with the holding of elections.[23]

THE 1931–32 ELECTIONS

The High Commission's plan was indeed carried out in stages. Taj al-Din al-Hasani was retained and his government, following the promulgation of the amended constitution, supervised the parliamentary elections that were held in stages from November 1931 to January 1932. The new parliament was to meet in June 1932 to elect the president, the prime minister and its own speaker. The new administration's principal task would be the negotiation and signing of a Franco-Syrian treaty.

In retrospect, it becomes clear that in this sequence the elections of 1931–32, more specifically the elections in Aleppo, were of particular importance. Ironically, it transpired that the unexpected extent of the Mandatory Authorities' success in these elections was counterproductive to their own purposes.

As the 1928 elections to the Constituent Assembly had shown, it was difficult, despite the efforts of the French authorities and their Syrian partners, to reduce the nationalist representation beyond a certain point.

Leaders like Hashim al-Atasi in Hims, Sa'dallah al-Jabiri in Aleppo, and Jamil Mardam in Damascus commanded clienteles and networks that practically guaranteed electoral success. France's problem, as mentioned above, derived from the fact that the nationalist minority, once in Parliament, easily dominated the inchoate 'moderate' majority.

But in the 1931–32 elections the nationalists were totally defeated in Aleppo, and northern Syria dispatched to Parliament a solid bloc of twenty-eight deputies led by Subhi Bey Barakat. Some of the factors which explain this surprising outcome were inherent in the special circumstances in Aleppo: the large number of Christian and Jewish voters, particularly in the electoral college (224 Christians and Jews as against 280 Muslims), a primacy given to economic over political considerations, and a sense of local patriotism reinforced by a familiar resentment of Damascene hegemony. The availability of a powerful local leader and his (uncharacteristic) success in overcoming rivalries with other 'moderate' leaders and in reassuring the Christian communities of his own tolerance were crucial in channeling this political potential in one direction. Still more crucial were the efforts and pressures exerted by the French authorities. The *Délégué Adjoint* referred to these rather euphemistically when he subsequently congratulated himself and his colleagues: 'But it was necessary to allow that [silent] majority to liberate itself and become self-conscious, as well as to instill in it enough self-confidence in order to express itself.'[24]

Another report by the same *Délégué Adjoint* was more specific in describing his contribution to this outcome. In the first round of the elections on 20 December, he wrote: 'Twelve voting stations in the popular Muslim quarters were invaded by a throng of nationalist voters.' Determined to prevent 'a repetition of the situation which favored the nationalist party in 1928', and in view of the ineffectiveness of the Syrian police and gendarmerie, the *Délégué Adjoint* brought in Algerian and Senegalese units of the French army. Several nationalist candidates, among them the lawyer and writer Edmond Rabbath, were arrested. The others made the mistake of withdrawing their candidacies and resubmitting them on the next day, thus confounding their supporters. It was hardly surprising that when the votes were counted on 21 December, not a single nationalist candidate was chosen to the college of electors.[25]

This outcome led to protests and demonstrations both in Damascus and Aleppo. But the protest and violence were not purely the work of the nationalists. In Aleppo the French authorities traced them to the Syrian director of police and to the director of *Waqf*. Both were considered underlings of Shaykh Taj al-Din al-Hasani. The Shaykh, it was suggested, understood very well that the election results in Aleppo had turned Subhi Bey Barakat into a leading candidate for the presidency of the state, and was seeking to have the elections in Aleppo repeated. After all, commented the Délégué Adjoint in Aleppo: 'There have always existed among the moderates rivalries based on ambition, and no one can ignore the fact that during his incumbency Shaykh Taj al-Din invested a far greater effort against his moderate than against his nationalist rivals.'[26]

SUBHI BEY BARAKAT AND THE SYRIAN PRESIDENCY

We do not know how the High Commissioner and his staff reacted to their supporters' overwhelming success in Aleppo. Their representatives' satisfaction, however, clearly betrayed no sense of the disruptive effect it was to have on France's policy in Syria during the next few years.

In fact it did not require Taj al-Din's astuteness to understand that the election results were bound to inflate Subhi Bey's ambitions and to enhance his claim on the presidency of the state. He commanded an impressive bloc of twenty-eight in a chamber of seventy and, furthermore, interpreted the results as a moral victory and a vindication of his earlier policies. The High Commission, in turn, maintained the position it had taken in 1930: that the man was not suitable for leading Syria into a contractual relationship with France. On April 17, in the aftermath of an attempt on Subhi Bey's life, Henri Ponsot painted an uncharitable portrait of a politician who was 'yesterday the leader of a band and today the leader of a party. His manner is to force things, and his name remains closely associated in Damascus with the events of 1925. He embodies the North's animosity to the South, and conciliation is alien to his character'.[27]

The High Commissioner was clearly impressed by a memorandum submitted earlier that month by Haqqi Bey al-'Azm, who minced no words in denigrating Subhi Bey's character and record.[28] Subhi Bey himself had already discovered that the High Commission was determined to deny him the presidency, and came to argue his case. The record of his discussions with M. Chauvel and M. Reclus of the High Commission's staff is most interesting.

To M. Reclus he explained that he deserved the presidency in return for the many services he had rendered, particularly during the 1925 revolt. Furthermore, he had been invited by the Mandatory Authorities prior to the recent elections 'to rally the moderate elements of Northern Syria'. Having accomplished this task as well, he should be made president, and would not settle on the speakership of Parliament with which the French wanted to console him. If the French failed him, he threatened, he would resign together with his supporters, and confront them with a situation like that of 1928.

In M. Chauvel's ears, Subhi Bey developed other arguments, some of them rather ingenuous, in order to explain why he wanted to be president and did not want to be elected speaker. But more significant was his poignant allusion to the ambivalence which he had correctly detected in a French policy that could not come to terms with the nationalists, and yet would not commit itself fully to the 'moderate' collaborators with the Mandate. In his own words: 'He could not fail to notice among the mandatory officers two distinct tendencies; that a similar state of affairs had been the true and underlying cause of the events of 1925 and 1928, and that he must reach the conclusion that the same cause would lead once again to the same results.'[29]

In April, it thus became clear to the High Commission that the conflict with Subhi Bey Barakat could have serious repercussions on its policies. It was also causing tensions between M. Lavastre, the *délégué* in Aleppo, who took Subhi Bey's side, and his colleagues in Damascus and Beirut. In an effort to resolve these problems, the High Commissioner dispatched one of his aides, M. Solomiac, to Aleppo and the North, and then held, in the course of May 1932, three staff meetings in his office. The notes taken during these meetings on 14, 19, and 30 May provide a rare glimpse into the inner workings of the High Commission.[30]

Most of the first session was taken up by M. Solomiac's report on his northern tour. He heard from Subhi Bey Barakat yet another rendition of his familiar positions, and established in his conversations with other politicians that Subhi Bey indeed had the solid support of twenty-eight delegates. Subhi Bey outlined to M. Solomiac an interesting strategy for neutralizing the nationalists' opposition to his presidency. He was willing to let them head the cabinet, and even to have two of his supporters resign their seats, so that nationalist candidates could win them in by elections. With regard to the treaty he was willing to accommodate all of France's wishes.

The session held on 19 May consisted mostly of a debate between M. Lavastre and M. Solomiac, the first promoting Subhi Bey's candidacy for the presidency, and the latter opposing it. There was an obvious personal antagonism between the two administrators, but it is curious to observe to what an extent the traditional competition between Aleppo and Damascus was transformed into a French bureaucratic feud. M. Solomiac, in any event, reported that the nationalists in Damascus remained vehemently opposed to Subhi Bey Barakat. They were in a conciliatory mood, willing to accept moderate candidates for the three senior positions (president, prime minister and speaker) and to send their representatives to the new Cabinet, but all this on the condition that Subhi Bey did not become president. The disagreement was not resolved, and it was decided to hold another, final, session.

That session was held on 30 May. With the High Commissioner's support, M. Solomiac defeated M. Lavastre, and a decision was made to have Subhi Bey elected speaker. Two other candidates for the presidency, the nationalist Hashim al-Atasi and the moderate Muhammad 'Ali Bey al-'Abid were disqualified, and Haqqi Bey al-'Azm was chosen as the High Commissioner's candidate for the presidency. The assembled forum was aware of its candidate's 'weakness of character and lack of energy', but saw several advantages in him:

> Francophile since the first hour, who has never changed his attitude ... with regard to Syrian opinion he appears as a neutral personality. No serious hostility can be turned against him. He appeared together with nationalist candidates on the mixed list that had been formed in Damascus before the last elections. His election will be equally satisfying for the minorities, with regard to whom he had loyally followed our directions.[31]

But when the new parliament met on 6 June, Haqqi Bey was not elected president, and had to settle on the premiership. Subhi Bey was indeed elected speaker, and it was Muhammad 'Ali Bey al-'Abid who was elected president. 'Abid was the son of Ahmad 'Izzat Pasha al-'Abid, who had played a cardinal role in conducting Sultan 'Abd al-Hamid's Arab policy. His son (born in 1874) had not played an important role before his election to the presidency.[32] It is not known exactly what happened between 30 May and 6 June which led to Haqqi Bey's losing the presidency and Muhammad 'Ali Bey al-'Abid's winning it. The version offered by Khalid al-'Azm, that the latter succeeded in building a coalition of Damascene 'moderates' and nationalists to support him, may very well be true. It is also likely that the High Commission was anxious that Subhi Bey might seek the presidency after all, and might have tacitly supported 'Abid's deal with the nationalists.

FRANCE, SUBHI BEY, AND THE ABORTIVE TREATY

For nearly a year and a half the arrangements completed in June 1932 seemed to function well. Haqqi Bey al-'Azm was made prime minister, and as they had promised earlier, the nationalists endorsed his cabinet by taking two of the portfolios.

Subhi Bey also seemed to have made his peace with the Mandatory Authorities. In October 1932 he was reelected speaker by a sweeping majority of forty-six out of fifty (he was originally elected by thirty out of

sixty-eight in the second round of voting). In July 1933 the speaker
planned a trip to Paris, in the course of which he wanted to present his
own ideas on the question of the Franco-Syrian treaty to the Quai d'Orsay.
Some Syrian politicians excelled in manoeuvring between the politicians
and bureaucrats of Paris and the Beirut High Commission, but if Subhi Bey
tried to follow this strategy, he was not successful.

Thus on 25 July the Quai d'Orsay Levant Department, in coordination
with the High Commission in Beirut, submitted to the minister of foreign
affairs a background note on Subhi Bey, who had asked for an audience
with the minister. The note provided a lengthy account of the speaker's
political career that was somewhat critical, but on the whole fair-minded.
After reviewing the disagreement over the presidency in 1932, the note
stated that 'since his election he gave active support to the mandatory
power, but has not relinquished his ambition, namely to become – due to
a political crisis – president of the Syrian Republic'.[33] The Department and
the High Commissioner were in agreement on the political programme
that Subhi Bey wanted to present in Paris: 'On certain points the speaker
appears to be more demanding than the extremist circles. One cannot be
surprised by a spirit so devoid of any political finesse, and who certainly
lacks any sense of what can be nuanced political action.'

But since, in the Department's view, Subhi Bey had given France devoted service on several occasions, and since he did represent in Syria 'an
undeniable force', his request for an audience should be granted. The minister and his aides were warned, however, to treat their guest with caution,
and to avoid giving him the impression that his programme was acceptable to them. The cold shoulder given him in the Quai d'Orsay had no
soothing effect on Subhi Bey. After returning to Syria in autumn, he drew
closer to the nationalists, and it took the High Commissioner's intervention to foil his efforts to organize a joint delegation with the nationalists
that would go to Paris to present to the authorities there the wishes of the
Syrian population.[34]

His rapprochement with the nationalists culminated in the cooperation,
described above, which led on 19 November 1933 to the failure in
Parliament of the draft treaty signed by the government. From that point
on, it was open warfare between Subhi Bey and the French authorities, the
High Commission in Beirut and the Levant Department in Paris. One of his
attempts to get over their heads to the president of the Republic and to the
minister of foreign affairs, by sending them in March 1934 a telegram
complaining of the High Commissioner and the Syrian government, gave
the Levant Department another opportunity for reviewing the speaker's
career and his latest activities.[35]

The slight reserve and criticism of the July 1933 memorandum were replaced by acrimony. The speaker was now painted as an unusually ambitious and unprincipled authoritarian politician. It was now argued that he had been cooperating with the nationalists since June 1932, and his role in the debacle of November 1933 was described in great detail.

The telegram sent to Paris was seen by the Department as yet another piece of trouble-making. It strongly recommended that the president and the minister of foreign affairs not respond to it, and refrain even from acknowledging its receipt, because:

> the mere acknowledgment of the arrival of his telegram, banal as it is, addressed to the speaker is bound to be interpreted and presented by him as an encouragement to persevere in his nefarious ways .... In the present delicate circumstances of Syrian politics local opinion will be further confounded – which we have every interest to prevent.[36]

Compared to the damage he caused French policy in Syria in November 1933, these were irksome but minor incidents. The Mandatory Authorities had to contend for the duration of the Chamber's term with a hostile speaker, but in the larger scheme of things this was not one of their principal problems. In 1936 they finally decided to come to terms with the nationalists, and a new Chamber dominated by the National Bloc was elected. Subsequently, however, it transpired that ambivalence toward the Syrian Arab nationalists was inherent in French policy. France signed a treaty with the National Bloc, but did not ratify it. After some two years of government by the National Bloc, a 'moderate' team was called in 1939 to administer Syria on behalf of the French.[37]

CONCLUSION

The explanations generally offered for the failure of France's Mandate in Syria tend to emphasize French underestimation of Syrian Arab nationalism as the single most important flaw in France's Syrian policy. Closer examination of France's conduct in Syria in the 1930s, of the choices it could and did make, of its relations with rivals and supporters, and of the discourse used among the French officials and between them and their Syrian interlocutors, calls for a modification of that view.

The original concept of France's Mandatory Government in Syria had indeed been formulated by Robert de Caix with a view to combating Syrian Arab nationalism. But while he believed that it could be defeated, he was far from belittling it. De Caix's policy was relinquished in 1925, but the ambiguity toward Syrian Arab nationalism that was inherent in it lingered. By the end of the 1920s, France's policy makers had come to believe that Syrian Arab nationalism could not be defeated, and yet they could not devise a way of coming to terms with it. It is true, as Andre Raymond writes, that many of the French officials tended to see nationalism as an urban phenomenon whose hold was limited to Western-educated intellectuals, and which had no roots in the larger rural population.[38] That very language, as we saw, was still used with regard to Syria in 1935. But by then it was tempered by the realization that the small minority of nationalist intellectuals had the urban masses spellbound, and completely dominated the rural notables in any parliamentary setting.

If this was indeed the case, then it followed that the nationalist politicians represented the wave of the future, that they were bound to win, and that any policy not based on cooperation with them amounted to little more than playing for time. The *note confidentielle* of February 1930 came very close to saying as much. It also followed that there was something wrong and artificial about France's cooperation with the 'moderates'. The French knew that they could find a Syrian Isma'il Sidqi: Subhi Bey Barakat and Rida al-Rikabi could have played the role. But France did not possess the will, the resources, or even the true interests that such a policy required in the 1930s. The French preferred to rule through weaker politicians, some of whom they actually despised, and to pursue a policy clearly lacking in conviction. They were not the last European power to do so in the Middle East.

NOTES

1   This article was published in C.E. Bosworth, Charles Issawi *et al.* (eds), *The Islamic World: From Classical to Modern Times* (Princeton, NJ: Darwin Press, 1989), pp.801–19.
2.   A.H. Hourani, *Syria and Lebanon* (London: Oxford University Press, 1946), pp.194–6; and S.H. Longrigg, *Syria and Lebanon Under French Mandate* (London: Oxford University Press, 1958), pp.195–7.
3.   MAE (Ministère des Affaires Etrangères) Levant, 1918–1940, Syrie-Liban, vol. 490, pp.125–33, note written apparently at the Quai d'Orsay. Unless otherwise indicated, all documents from the French archives quoted below are from this series, and they will be identified by volume number alone.
4.   MAE, vol. 488, pp.101–6, note written on 9 March 1934 by the Levant Department with regard to Subhi Bey Barakat.
5.   The description in the Quai d'Orsay's note is matched by Khalid al-'Azm's version in his memoirs. Mudhakkirat Khalid al-'Azm, *Mudhakkirat* (The Memoirs) (Beirut: al-Dar al-Taqadumiyya lil-Nashr, 1973), vol. I, pp.173–5. Curiously, the incident was overlooked by the usually observant British Consul, who failed to devote much attention to the mandatory authorities' relationship with Subhi Bey.
6.   French policy in the Levant in the inter-war period has, until recently, been a neglected subject, certainly when compared to the study of British policy in the Middle East. Soon after the Second World War, Pierre Rondot published a perceptive study of France's failure in the Levant, 'L'Expérience du Mandate Français en Syrie et au Liban 1918–1945', *Revue Générale de Droit International Public*, 1948, pp.1–23. Albert Hourani's book is a study of Syria and Lebanon rather than of France's

policies, and Longrigg's book is very thorough but not the work of a historian. After a long hiatus, several studies have appeared which mark the beginning of a change in this picture: E. Burke III, 'A Comparative View of French Native Policy in Morocco and Syria', *Middle Eastern Studies*, 9, 2 (1973); C.M. Andrew and A.S. Kanya-Forstner, *France Overseas: The Great War and the Climax of French Imperial Expansion* (London: Themes and Hudson, 1981); A. Raymond, 'La Syrie Du Royaume Arabe a l'independance (1914–1946)', in A. Raymond (ed.), *La Syrie d'aujourd'hui* (Paris: Editions du Centre National de la Recherche Scientifique, 1980), and several recent essays by Philip S. Khoury.

7. For a rich and incisive study of the French colonial movement and its influence on French policy in the Levant up to 1920 see Andrew and Kanya-Forstner, *France Overseas*, passim.

8. See K. Salibi, 'Islam and Syria in the Writings of Henri Lammens', in B. Lewis and P.M. Holt (eds), *Historians of the Middle East* (London: Oxford University Press, 1962), pp.330–42.

9. Andrew and Kanya-Forstner, *France Overseas*, passim.

10. De Caix's views and plan were laid out in a seminal memorandum entitled 'Note sur la politique de l'accord avec Feysal' (26 January 1920). I am grateful to Prof. Elie Kedourie, who has made this document available to me. A comparison of de Caix's note with the policy implemented after July 1920 will immediately establish his profound influence on the actual course of events. See also Burke's article mentioned in note 6.

11. Note by de Martel, 12 March 1935, MAE, vol. 490, pp.102–8.

12. This subject is dealt with by Philip S. Khoury in his article 'Factionalism among Syrian Nationalists during the French Mandate', *International Journal of Middle Eastern Studies*, 13, 4 (1981), pp.441–69.

13. In retrospect the Quai d'Orsay came to believe, or at least argue, that Subhi Bey's conduct and mistakes contributed to the transformation of the Druze rebellion into a Syrian revolt. It thus argued that he had persecuted the leaders of the People's Party and pushed them into the arms of the Druze, that he had weakened the police and gendarmerie, etc. See the notes on Subhi Bey Barakat of July 1933 and March 1934, MAE, vol. 486, pp.1–4 and vol. 488, pp.101–6.

14. The composition and history of the Damad's cabinet are analyzed in an unusual document authored by Pierre 'Alyye, the *délégué* in Damascus, under the title 'Rapport sur le gouvernement national provisoire' (8 June 1926). The report is available in the Henri de Jouvenel Papers in the departmental archive of La Correze.

15. 'Note confidentielle sur la situation politique en Syrie', 20 February 1930, MAE, vol. 477, pp.232–59.

16. For a biographical note on Shaykh Taj al-Din see 'Note pour le service du protocole', 11 July 1935, MAE, vol. 491, pp.39–43.

17. See the 'Note confidentielle' cited in Note 15.

18. Ibid., pp.3–4, 11–15.

19. Ibid.

20. Ibid., pp.16–19.

21. Ibid., pp.19–21.

22. Ibid., pp.21–3.

23. Ibid., pp.23–6.

24. On the 1931–32 elections in Aleppo, see the *Délégué* Adjoint's two reports of 9 January, MAE, vol. 480, pp.245–56, and the account by M. Gennardi of the High Commission's 'Controle de Wakf', ibid.

25. Subhi Bey sorted out his differences with his local rival, Shakir al-Ni'mat, on the very eve of the elections, ibid.

26. The *Délégué* Adjoint's report of 13 February 1932, MAE, vol. 481, pp.27–30.

27. Henri Ponsot's telegram of 17 February 1932, MAE, vol. 481, pp.90–2.

28. 'Note confidentielle remise par Hakki Bey al-Azem au sujet de la Candidature de Soubhy Bey Barakat a la Preside nee de la République', MAE, vol. 481, pp.112–18.

29. 'Résumé d'un Entretien entre Soubhy Bey Barakat et M. Reclus', 14 April 1932; 'Resume des declarations faites par Soubhy Bey Barakat a M. Chauvel', 14 April 1932, MAE, vol. 491, pp.107–11.

30. 'Conférence Politique du 14 Mai 1932 Proces-Verbal sommaire', 'Entretien du 19 Mai 1932 sur la situation politique en Syrie et les prévisions concernant la réunion de la Chambre et les désignations aux differents postes à pouvoir'; 'memorandum d'un entretien au sujet de la Presidence de la Republique de Syrie', 30 May 1932, MAE, vol. 481, pp.119–27, 128–34, and 148–60.

31. Memorandum of 30 May 1932, cited in note 30.

32. See 'Notice biographique sur ... Muhammad 'Ali Bey Abed', MAE, vol. 481, pp.242–3.

33. Departmental note on Subhi Bey Barakat, 25 July 1933, MAE, vol. 486, pp.1–4.

34. Departmental note on Subhi Bey Barakat, March 1934.

35. Ibid.
36. Ibid.
37. Rondot, 'L'Expérience du Mandate Français en Syrie et au Liban 1918–1945', compares France's success in working through Charles Debbas in Lebanon to its failure to find an equally effective local prop in Syria.
38. A. Raymond, 'La Syrie Du Royaume Arabe a l'independance (1914–1946)', pp.67–8.

4

Oil and Local Politics: The French-Iraqi Negotiations of the Early 1930s[1]

To a European power looking at the Middle East through imperial and strategic lenses, the Levant coast has often been perceived as a vital link in its or its rivals' communication with the Persian Gulf and India. The importance of the overland route to India declined after the construction of the Suez Canal,[2] but acquired a renewed importance from a somewhat different perspective when oil was discovered in Iran and Iraq shortly before the First World War. Britain's preparations for and conduct of negotiation with allies and clients over the post-war disposition of the Arab provinces of the Ottoman Empire clearly reflected the desire to secure control over an area affording a territorial link between the Levant coast and the head of the Persian Gulf. This would enable Britain to lay pipelines as well as to construct a railway that could supplement, or substitute for, the canal.[3]

France, the other contender for the coast of the Levant, based its claims on rather different grounds that had more to do with the cultural and economic ties between the western and eastern Mediterranean than with the territories to the east.[4] French control of the Levant coast was not relished by British strategic planners, but while French claims for the Syrian interior could be challenged, Britain realized all along the intensity of the French attachment to the coastal area, Lebanon in particular, and hence the ultimate futility of a potential British effort to deny that area to France.

Consequently Britain's pied-à-terre on the Levant coast had to be established in Palestine, which had the additional advantage of reinforcing the defenses of Egypt and the Suez Canal. This was being prepared as of 1915 and was finalized in the course of the post-war Anglo-French negotiations, which revised their wartime agreements. While France conceded both Palestine and Mosul to Britain, the latter accepted French control of Syria and Lebanon and acquiesced in France's destruction of the Hashemite government in Damascus. France was also given a 23.75 per cent share in Iraq's oil, and undertook in turn to permit the construction of a pipeline and a related railway through its new possessions to the Mediterranean.[5] These could in fact be laid through territories purely under British control, but an alternative option must have seemed desirable in the early 1920s.

Britain's perspective regarding the pipelines carrying Iraq's oil to the Mediterranean and the related railway line changed a few years later when preparations for their construction were actually begun. These preparations entailed protracted and complex negotiations among several parties – the British, French, and Iraqi governments; the Iraq Petroleum company and its constituent elements; and British, French, American, and Dutch oil interests. A study of the negotiations that took place in the late 1920s and early 1930s on the basis of British and recently opened French archives offers fresh insights into various aspects of British and French policies in the Middle East in the inter-war period: the intensity but also the limits of the two-power rivalry; the intricacies of British oil policies and the interplay between national policy and oil interests; the mechanisms and styles adopted by London and Paris in the formulation and execution of their Middle Eastern policies; and the outlook of the two governments on the strategic significance of their respective possessions in the region. Of still greater interest was the convergence of the pipeline negotiations with Iraq's *Drang nach Westen* – the quest for hegemony in the Fertile Crescent and particularly for the reestablishment of Hashemite rule in Damascus, which began in earnest when independence was conceded in 1930. The fusion of the international negotiations on the Iraqi oil pipelines with the French-Iraqi negotiations on the future of Syria – an absorbing episode in its own right – also reflected the changes that had gradually occurred during the 1930s in the patterns of regional politics set by the post-war settlement.

BRITAIN, FRANCE AND IRAQI OIL

It is one of the ironies of the post-war settlement in the Middle East that Britain's control of Iraq afforded it only limited access to that country's most valuable national resource. Exploitation of Iraq's oil through the Turkish Petroleum Company, transformed in 1925 into the Iraq Petroleum Company, had to be shared with French, American, and Dutch interests. The IPC's convention of 1925 was drafted with a view to complying with – or evading – the new norms of international trade and politics, and was in many respects cumbersome and awkward. The IPC's character as an international company headed – sometimes manipulated, but certainly not dominated – by Sir John Cadman, the chairman of the Anglo-Persian Oil Company, gave rise to manifold conflicts of interest and fully illustrates the complexity of the relationship

between British government policy and private and semi-public oil interests. These issues were further compounded by the attempts of rival British
oil interests (the British Oil Development Syndicate) to acquire a share in
Iraq's oil and by the increasingly independent role of the Iraqi government.[6]

It was against this background that the British government sought in
the late 1920s to accomplish three goals: to replace the IPC convention
with a new, improved convention; to lay a pipeline carrying Iraq's oil to the
Mediterranean, with Haifa serving as its terminal point; and to construct
as inexpensively as possible a related railroad linking Baghdad to Palestine
– and thus also to Egypt.

Of the difficulties that confronted the implementation of these plans,
the most serious were posed by France's rival schemes. France wanted
Tripoli, in Lebanon, to serve as a terminal point for the Iraqi pipeline, and
planned its own railroad connecting Tripoli with Abu Kamal on the Syrian-
Iraqi border. Linked to the Iraqi railroad systems, it would make the projected Baghdad-Haifa line largely redundant and economically onerous.

France obviously had good reasons to insist on Tripoli as the terminal
for the pipeline: a part of France's oil supply would thus be guaranteed,
and economic advantages would accrue to continental France and to its
mandated territories in the Levant. But the British were right to suspect that
more was at stake, that France was trying to use its control of the Levant
coast in order to develop strategic and economic assets extending far
beyond the little 'balcony'[7] allocated to its share of the war spoils in the
East.

The Levant Africa Department of the Quai d'Orsay couched its view of
the matter in economic terms when it wrote a few years later that the
Levant states would be: 'le débouché sur la Méditerranée du traffic a desti-
nation ou en provenance de l'Irak et de la Perse'.[8]

Henri Ponsot, the French high commissioner in Syria, expounded his
vision of Tripoli as a crucial link between Iraq and Iran and the
Mediterranean to none other than the British high commissioner in Iraq
during the latter's visit to the Levant states in April 1931. In his account to
the colonial secretary, Humphrys described how his French counterpart
'gave me to understand that it was his ambition to link up Tripoli with
Mosul and Northern Persia by the Palmyra Deir ez-Zor route'. Tripoli in
turn, Henri Ponsot explained, would be connected to Marseilles through
an efficient service 'French Flying Boats'.[9]

It is easy to see why the British would be alarmed by a plan that in addition to jeopardizing their own projects threatened to provide a European
competitor with a commanding strategic asset in the Middle East. In the

Long-Berenger negotiations in 1919 the British had pressured the French to undertake to facilitate 'by every means at their command' the construction of two separate pipelines through the territory under their control. But ten years later the British could have the pipeline under their exclusive control and saw no reason to provide the French with a crucial advantage.

THE IRAQI PIPELINE NEGOTIATIONS

France's efforts to secure a northern alignment (a Tripoli terminal) for the Iraqi pipeline relied on one major advantage – this was the shortest and cheapest route. The British representatives on IPC's board estimated that if they insisted on a southern alignment, their French counterparts stood a very good chance of winning their case in the International Court of Justice.[10]

The British in turn could secure, in return for appropriate compensation elsewhere, the support of the American and Dutch partners in IPC and occasionally even that of a French representative ('a level-headed individual' was Sir John Cadman's definition of a cooperative Frenchman). They also exerted considerable influence on an Iraqi government hostile to France for its expulsion of King Faysal from Damascus less than a decade earlier. Thus in May 1930 the British high commissioner was able to produce ten reasons for the Iraqi government's strong preference for the southern alignment and opposition to the northern one. The high commissioner emphasized to his own government that he had 'scrupulously abstained from giving any advice to the Iraqi government upon this question' and had confined himself throughout 'to ascertaining their real views and putting them into plain language'.[11] It is a curious and significant fact that the ten reasons included no explicit reference to the hostility between France and the Iraqi Hashemite ruling house.

Still the British were unable to have Haifa designated as the sole terminal for Iraqi oil. The failure created tension between the British representatives on the IPC board and the British government. This tension was resolved when Sir John Cadman appeared in June 1930 before a special Iraqi Oil Committee of the British Labour cabinet under the chairmanship of Arthur Henderson, the secretary of state for foreign affairs. The minutes of the committee's deliberations and particularly of its exchange with Sir John Cadman shed an interesting light on the formulation and conduct of Britain's Middle Eastern oil policy. Sir John Cadman had no difficulty in persuading the cabinet members that their Conservative predecessors in the Baldwin government were to blame for their present difficulties. The

IPC board, he explained, was all ready for a tacit endorsement of the southern alignment when the previous government's insistence on the explicit mentioning of Haifa triggered French opposition.

A subsequent British attempt in 1930 to take advantage of Iraqi opposition to the Tripoli terminal failed as well, and the British accepted a compromise formula – a bifurcated pipeline leading to both Tripoli and Haifa. This created a new bone of contention: should the point of bifurcation be at Haditha, as the French wanted, or at Rutha, farther south, as the British and Iraqis wanted? Britain's final position was formulated by the cabinet's Iraq Oil Committee on 5 February 1931. The British government now agreed to bifurcation at Haditha provided that at least 50 per cent of the oil pumped by IPC be sent to Haifa and that the two pipelines be completed simultaneously (or virtually so) and at an early date (not later than the end of 1935). For what it viewed as a major concession on its part, the British government expected IPC to reciprocate by agreeing to delete from the company's new convention the clause empowering it to build railways outside its concession area. The Iraqi government and the company were to give the proposed Baghdad-Haifa Railway Board veto power over the construction of any railroad through Iraq to the Syrian border, preempting any future attempt by the French government to implement its designs for a strategic rail connection between the head of the Persian Gulf and the Levant coast.[12]

It should again be noted that when the secretary of state for foreign affairs briefed his colleagues about the various factors affecting British policy on Iraq's oil, he neglected to mention the French-Iraqi negotiations, which began in 1930 and were closely linked to the deliberations just described.

FRENCH-IRAQI RELATIONS

Iraq's outlook on France's desire to have its oil transported to the French-dominated port of Tripoli and its related, broader geopolitical schemes was naturally influenced by Iraq's own foreign policy ambitions as well as by the hostility between France and the Hashemite dynasty.

The foreign policy ambitions of the Iraqi state, boasting in 1930 of the fresh, though nominal, independence granted by the new Anglo-Iraqi treaty (and implemented in 1932), appeared as a mirror image of France's designs. While France wanted to use its control of the Levant coast to acquire influence over the remote hinterland, the Iraqi government sought to extend its influence from that hinterland westward. Particularly after 1930, these ambitions were translated into a championship of the pan-Arab nationalist cause and, on a different level, to an effort to secure the throne of Syria for King Faysal or another member of his family.[13]

A Hashemite return to Syria, now couched in broader nationalist terms, had been attempted by Faysal immediately after his ouster in July 1920 and throughout the 1920s. For this he had to negotiate with the French, whose position in Syria was recognized by the British and in the 1920s seemed unshakable. The French viewed Faysal and his family as instruments of British policy hostile to France and its position in the Middle East, but in 1925 and in 1928 they were willing to discuss with Faysal the possibility of a Hashemite return to Damascus in order to obtain tactical political gains.[14] The French negotiators had no intention of establishing a monarchy in Syria or of having a member of the Hashemite family as Syria's ruler. Their manipulation of Faysal's patent ambition added yet another dimension to the negative residue of French-Hashemite relations.

The balance in the French-Iraqi relationship changed somewhat in 1930. France wanted the pipeline to Tripoli, and the semi-independent Iraqi government – acting on its own initiative or, as the French suspected, under British guidance – had a role to play in making the decision for or against a northern alignment. The French government in Paris may not have been as enthusiastic as its emissaries in Beirut about the notion of a strategic nexus between the Levant and the Persian Gulf, but it was anxious to secure a steady supply of Iraqi oil for France. Pressure was brought to bear on the British government and, as in previous instances of Franco-British relations in the Middle East, the recognition that the fundamental alliance with France could not be jeopardized for relatively minor gains in the Middle East prompted London to make some concession to French demands. Now the goodwill of the Iraqi government had to be obtained and M. Lépissier, France's *chargé d'affaires* in Baghdad, was instructed to obtain it.

THE FRENCH-IRAQI NEGOTIATIONS

The French-Iraqi negotiations were conducted during much of 1931. The Quai d'Orsay's own account of the negotiations is complemented and modified at various points by British sources – who relied often on King Faysal's version – so as to clarify not only the course of events but also the interplay between the chief actors.[15]

The first phase of the negotiations began in January 1930 when Lépissier initiated a meeting with King Faysal. Lépissier had obviously assumed (or known for a fact) that Iraq's opposition to France's insistence on bifurcation at Haditha derived from political, not economic, considerations. A linkage between the oil pipeline and King Faysal's ambitions in Syria existed; Lépissier had only to turn it in the right direction. He did so by presenting the combined prospect of a potential promise-cum-threat – France was once again considering the possibility of a Syrian throne and the three candidates were Faysal's brother 'Ali or two archrivals: 'Sharif 'Ali Haydar [member of a rival branch of the Hashemite family] or one of the sons of Ibn Sa'ud.'[16]

A series of delicate manoeuvres followed as each party tried to have the other come out first with a concrete offer. Philippe Berthelot, the secretary-general of the Quai d'Orsay, who supervised the negotiations from Paris through Ponsot in Beirut and Lépissier in Baghdad, was not willing to go beyond a statement of willingness to discuss a *règlement d'ensemble* of the questions concerning Iraq's relations with Syria. Faysal tried in vain to seek clarifications, nor would he enumerate his own desires and expectations.

By 4 February the situation had changed. The king was now aware of the British cabinet's new line and sought to use it to his own advantage. He saw Lépissier again and after berating him about France's failure to clarify its position, expressed his willingness to promise bifurcation at Haditha and a flow of 50 per cent of Mosul's oil to the Tripoli terminal. But Faysal was still careful in outlining his demands for a quid pro quo. He first made a distinction between himself and his government, whose ambitions he shared 'fundamentally' but not necessarily in detail. He himself demanded from the French government 'a moral commitment to take into account, together with me, in its policy in the Levant the legitimate national aspirations common to Syria and Iraq'.[17]

The Quai d'Orsay's response, transmitted through Lépissier (with a commentary addressed to Ponsot), was drafted with studied caution:

> We are also inclined to establish between Iraq and the states of the Levant relations of friendship and interest. But as the Emir [sic] had already understood, the examinations and discussions that concern such complicated questions should be carried out thoroughly and in coordination with the High Commissioner. At this time except for the general promise that you had given him and which he must keep secret I ask that you emphasize in the King's ears how much a satisfactory settlement of the oil question (with regard to which our and Iraq's interests are compatible) will strengthen dispositions favourable to him in the League of Nations and in the Levant.[18]

In his telegram to Ponsot, Berthelot took pride in his cautious drafting. He had avoided repeating the term 'national aspirations' and by using 'the states of the Levant' rather than 'Syria', had preempted a potential Iraqi claim to have Syria separated from Lebanon within Iraq's 'orbit'. Berthelot then sought the high commissioner's advice on specific minor points that might come up later when the negotiations became more concrete. He was willing to please the Iraqis on various economic points, but a commitment to the Hashemites concerning the Syrian throne was simply not on the agenda. All that the Quai d'Orsay was willing to do on that issue was to remove the threat planted by Lépissier in January to install a rival family in Damascus.

Faysal was unable to extract a more concrete concession from France in return for his government's acceptance of the British position on 7 February. He tried his hand again during the second phase of the negotiations, triggered in early April by the need to have the new IPC convention approved by the Iraqi parliament. The king used the occasion to exert fresh pressure on the French government to come up with a firmer commitment on the issue uppermost in his mind.[19]

The French knew that with London on their side the ratification of the convention and the Haditha bifurcation was not in serious danger, but they were willing to invest some effort in order to facilitate the proceedings and retain Faysal's goodwill. Three issues were defined as outstanding between France and Iraq with regard to Syria. On two of them, the convening of an Iraqi-Syrian economic conference and the opening of an Iraqi consulate in Beirut, the Quai d'Orsay was willing to display magnanimity. Significantly, the high commissioner objected to an Iraqi consulate in Beirut, arguing that it would accentuate the uneven pace of political emancipation in Iraq and the Levant states, but he was overruled by the ministry. The Quai d'Orsay, though, was not willing to make more than cosmetic concessions on the one issue that was really important to Faysal. Its formal position was that Syria now had a republican constitution and France had no intention of 'provoking its modification'. What it could offer the Iraqis was the theoretical possibility of a subsequent constitutional change and a promise not to support the candidacy of Sharif 'Ali Haydar or one of Ibn Sa'ud's sons. That promise, furthermore, was to be made orally. There would be no written commitment.

Faysal was incensed. He easily saw the 'sens profond' of the French message and knew that he could not revoke the concessions already made to the French. All he could do was vent his frustration on the French *chargé*. France's attitude, he told him, was a step hostile to the legitimate ambitions of his family 'et surtout l'expression officelle du maintien en Syrie d'un régime base – prétend il – sur l'arbitrage qui éloigne définitivement les états du Levant de toutes les cooperations arabes'.[20]

Yet Faysal did not lose all hope. He took advantage of a trip to Europe in August 1931 to launch a third round of negotiations with the French government. Before meeting with Berthelot, he tried to prepare the ground through an old acquaintance, M. Georges Picot, telling him that he intended to discuss France's plans for Syria's future regime. Now that France had its oil pipeline to Tripoli, he was trying to entice it with the other strategic asset the French had originally desired. He alluded that personally he favoured 'l'établissement de communication de son pays avec le mer par le territoire syrien, la ligne de chemin de fer envisagée par Caiffa lui paraîssant trop longue et trop coûteuse'.[21]

But the French government knew better than to corrode the foundations of an agreement with Britain from which France had so clearly benefited. Only a brief French account of Faysal's meeting with Berthelot in August is available; it argues that from the official, courteous, and sympathetic reception given him by the French authorities, the Iraqi monarch erroneously deduced that his ambitions were in fact acceptable to them. In October the Quai d'Orsay was alarmed by reports from the region that on his way back from Europe, Faysal met with Syrian expatriates in Alexandria and led them to believe that he was about to mount the throne of Syria with France's blessing. His emissary Rustum Haydar brought a similar message to Beirut.

Interested or concerned Arab parties such as Ibn Sa'ud were not the only ones to take this rumour seriously. The British government, departing from its policy in previous instances of French-Iraqi negotiations, decided to take a serious look at the prospect of a Hashemite return to Damascus. The Standing Official Subcommittee on the Middle East met on 20 October 1931 to discuss the issue. Its recommendation was that the course most desirable to British interests would be for Syria to remain a republic with a Syrian as president. It was opposed to a joint Iraqi-Syrian monarchy or an attempt by King Faysal to transfer his throne to Damascus, yet saw no reason to oppose the candidacy of ex-king 'Ali should an offer be made to him by the French.[22]

The French, however, had no such intentions, as they had already explained to their own representatives in the area. They now had to abandon the ambiguity and subtleties that had served them so well in their earlier dealings with Faysal, and issue a flat denial. The king felt both cheated and humiliated and an atmosphere of 'acrimonious chill' descended on France's relations with the Iraqi Hashemites, which lasted well beyond Faysal's death in 1933.[23]

The ironies inherent in the encounter between the aristocratic professional diplomats of the Quai d'Orsay and their overly eager Iraqi counterparts are vividly illustrated by the French account of a subsequent discussion between

M. St Quentin, deputy director for Africa and the Levant, and the Iraqi political leader Nuri al-Sa'id. St Quentin tried to use Nuri's visit to Paris in October 1933 as an opportunity to argue for better cooperation and coordination between Baghdad and Beirut, so that unfortunate incidents, such as the one involving the Assyrian refugees, should not recur. Nuri responded with a litany of grievances, arguing in essence that France had been given its desiderata regarding the pipeline and that it was up to it to give Iraq its *contre-partie*. Having rendered Nuri's version of what had been given and promised in 1931, the French diplomat commented scornfully that it demonstrated the 'deformation caused by oriental imagination'.[24]

As a chapter in the diplomatic history of the inter-war Middle East, the French-Iraqi negotiations are therefore less significant for their actual impact on the course of events than for what they reveal about the forces and actors that shaped that course.[25] France's limited effort to amplify its strategic posture in the Middle East did not accomplish much, and Faysal's ambition to return to Damascus remained unrealistic in the face of France's unyielding opposition to him and to his family. Relations between the Iraqi government and France and its high commissioners were further embittered, but this was hardly a change in the pattern established during and immediately after the First World War. The negotiations did facilitate the Haditha bifurcation to Tripoli, but the fundamental decisions concerning the route of the Iraqi pipeline had been made earlier in London and Paris. The newly independent Iraqi state became an incipient actor in the regional politics of the Middle East, but in the early 1930s its role was still defined by Britain and France.

Subsequent developments have obviously altered the perspective from which the conflict over the route of the Iraqi oil pipeline to the Mediterranean has been seen. The Haifa extension was severed with the establishment of Israel, and the Tripoli extension became the exclusive outlet of Mosul's oil to the Mediterranean until the completion of the Kirkuk-Banyas pipeline in 1952. The radicalization of Syrian politics and the endemic tension in Syrian-Iraqi relations made this outlet tenuous and problematic. In 1965 the Syrian Ba'th regime shut off the Iraqi pipeline as part of a (successful) effort to increase Syria's own revenues from the pipeline. Still more ominous was Hafiz al-Asad's decision a decade later to shut off the pipeline as a means of exerting pressure on his Ba'thi rivals in Baghdad. The Iraqi government, in turn, sought to reduce its dependence on Syria by constructing an alternative pipeline through Turkish territory and by expanding the pipelines and terminals in the southern part of the country. But the renewal and exacerbation of the conflict with Iran has gravely threatened the transportation of Iraqi oil through the Persian Gulf.

Thus, fifty years after the French-Iraqi negotiations of 1931, the government of Iraq still has to contend with the problem of pumping its oil to the Levant coast across the territory of a Syrian state controlled by a hostile government, this time an Arab one.

NOTES

1. This article was published in Uriel Dann (ed.), *The Great Powers in the Middle East, 1919–1939* (New York: Holmes and Meier, 1988).
2. See A. Hoskins, *British Routes to India* (New York, NY: Longmans, Green and Company, 1928).
3. See E. Kedourie, *In the Anglo-Arab Labyrinth* (Cambridge: Cambridge University Press, 1976), particularly Part I.
4. See C.M. Andrew and A.S. Kanya-Forstner, *France Overseas* (London: Thames and Hudson, 1981).
5. Ibid.
6. On British oil policy in the Middle East during this period, see Y. Bilovich, 'The Quest for Oil in Bahrain 1923–1930: A Study in British and American Policy', in Uriel Dann (ed.), *The Great Powers in the Middle East 1919–1939* (New York: Holmes and Meier, 1988), pp.252–68. The specific background of Britain's oil policy in Iraq is illuminated by the minutes of the British cabinet's Iraq Oil Committee's deliberations in 1930 and 1931 available at the Public Record Office, CAB 27/436/27766.
7. I am obliged to Professor André Nouschi for this reference.
8. MAE (Ministère des Affaires Etrangères), Levant, Syrie-Liban 1918–1940, vol. 458, Note on 'The Iraqi Question' written on 1 March 1934.
9. Sir E. Humphrys to Lord Passfield, 1 May 1931, PRO, E2627/294/89.
10. Sir John Cadman before the Iraq Oil Committee, PRO, CAB 27/436/27766.
11. Paraphrase Telegram from the High Commissioner for Iraq to the Secretary of State for the Colonies, 16 June 1930, Appendix I to the Iraq Oil Committee's Deliberations, PRO, CAB 27/436/27766.
12. Report by the Iraq Oil Committee, 5 February 1931, ibid.
13. See K.S. Husry, 'King Faysal I and Arab Unity 1930–1933', *Journal of Contemporary History*, 10, 2 (1975), pp.323–40, and see in this volume, I. Rabinovich, 'Inter-Arab Relations Foreshadowed: The Question of the Syrian Throne in the 1920s and 1930s'.
14. Documented in 'The Question of the Syrian Throne', cited in note 13.
15. Of the various documents available in the Quai d'Orsay's archives on this subject, the most important is a long note prepared on 10 April 1934 under the title 'The Hashemite Candidature for the Syrian Throne', which describes the French version of the negotiations and the eventual deterioration with Iraq. Apologetic and occasionally less than candid, it is still a uniquely detailed and valuable source. MAE, Levant, Syrie-Liban 1918–1940, Vol. 459.
16. See the dispatches from Humphrys to Lord Passfield on 10 and 30 January 1931, PRO, FO 371/15364/7714.
17. MAE, 'The Hashemite Candidature'.
18. Ibid.
19. Ibid.
20. Ibid.
21. Memorandum on Georges-Picot's conversation with King Faysal, MAE, Levant, Syrie-Liban 1918–1940, Vol. 458, 24 August 1931.
22. PRO, FO 371/15366, 25 October 1931.
23. MAE, 'The Hashemite Candidature'.
24. Ibid.
25. See Chapter 21 of the present volume for more recent developments in this matter.

5

Inter-Arab Relations Foreshadowed:
The Question of the Syrian Throne
in the 1920s and 1930s[1]

A full-fledged system of inter-Arab relations developed in the Middle East in the aftermath of the Second World War, when the Arab League had been formed, several Arab states achieved their independence, and Britain and France lost much of their erstwhile influence over Arab politics. Within a few years a pattern of inter-Arab relations crystallized that was governed by a fundamental contradiction between a genuine quest for unity and union and the forces and processes which obstructed their implementation. Foremost among these were the vested interests which had developed within the existing Arab states and regimes, the rivalries among Arab dynasties and leaders, tension between an official-traditional brand of pan-Arab nationalism and a more radical, ideologically oriented one, and the interlacing of Arab regional politics with Great Power rivalries and domestic politics of the various Arab states. The two issues which first brought these dynamics into play were the Palestine problem and the future of Syria.

While this system became fully developed after 1945, its major attributes had been adumbrated during the preceding two decades. The prism through which this process can be most clearly examined is the issue of the Syrian throne – the successive efforts by and on behalf of a host of candidates throughout the 1920s and 1930s to acquire the prospective throne of Syria.

Most of these efforts were little more than brief and curious episodes, interesting not as exercises in *real politik* but as a testimony to the lingering effect of traditional political attitudes. One was the belief-current among British and French officials and some Arab politicians – that a monarchial regime was the natural political order in a Middle Eastern country and that it was likely to produce greater stability and effectiveness. Of still greater interest is the list of self-appointed and sponsored candidates, which included North African, Ottoman and Arabian princes and dignitaries and very few Syrians. Their candidacies reflected a residual belief in the primacy of common Islamic descent as a determinant of political allegiance and legitimacy.

Of an entirely different nature were the persistent efforts invested by various members of the Hashemite family throughout the inter-war period to establish a Syrian monarchy that would be added to the family's possessions. This was a serious and sustained effort predicated on claims to the leadership of Arab nationalism and to the implementation of its doctrine. Still, in the circumstances which prevailed in the region in the early 1920s, their initial efforts were not directed at their Arab constituency but rather at the British and French authorities.[2]

As mentioned above, French administrators in Syria in the early 1920s were not opposed to the notion of a Syrian monarchy as such. Like the British in Iraq, they believed that a monarchial form of government would contribute to the country's stability and facilitate the implementation of their policy with lesser effort and expense.[3] But the Hashemites appeared to represent almost everything that the French in Syria feared and detested. To establish their rule in the Syrian interior, the French found it necessary to destroy the Sharifian government which had been installed in Damascus with British help in October 1918. That government had been headed by the Hashemite Prince Faysal who in March 1920 was proclaimed (but not widely recognized) as king of (a Greater) Syria. The Hashemite family was then a mainstay of pan-Arab nationalism and closely allied with British policy in the Middle East, both of which were regarded by the French as inimical to their position in Syria.

In 1920 and 1921 that position appeared tenuous. The creation of a Greater Lebanon was carried out firmly and successfully, but the establishment of French control and an effective local government in the rest of the mandated territories encountered considerable difficulties. Inside Syria the French Administration had to contend with strong opposition in which members and supporters of the ousted Sharifian regime played a leading role. It also faced unfriendly neighbors on three borders: Kemalist Turkey in the north, Faysal, by then king of Iraq, in the east, and his brother 'Abdallah's embryonic Jordanian state in the south.

Against this background the French were advised at least twice, in the spring and early summer of 1921, that by placing a Hashemite, preferably the Amir 'Abdallah, on a Syrian throne in Damascus their rule would become acceptable to the Syrian populace and a potential threat to their position from the outside would be removed. This advice was given explicitly by General Haddad, King Faysal's aide, when he met Foreign Minister

Berthelot in Paris in April, and in a subtle and indirect fashion by Sir Herbert Samuel when he visited with General Gouraud, the French High Commissioner, in June.[4]

The French lost no time in rebuffing these initiatives. They regarded a Hashemite presence in Syria as incompatible with their own position there, especially when memories of their clashes with that family were so fresh. But the French went beyond rejecting British and Hashemite approaches. In a rather imaginative way they used the very notion of a Syrian monarchy in order to improve their own position and to embarrass the British whom they regarded in any case as the real power behind the Hashemites. During the spring and summer of 1921 the French appear to have encouraged the Ottoman Sultan's government in Istanbul, the former Khedive Abbas Hilmi and Prince Omar Tusun to believe that they seriously considered installing an Ottoman prince or one of the two Egyptian dignitaries as the head of a Syrian monarchy.[5] The thought of having any of the three in Damascus must have been most unsettling to the British and the Hashemites. The candidacy of an Ottoman prince could also serve as a bargaining chip in the French-Turkish negotiations, which ended in the Franklin-Bouillon agreement. It is doubtful whether the French government ever considered any of these three candidates seriously,[6] and the whole issue died down by 1922 with the consolidation of France's hold on Syria.

The Hashemites waited over two years before they tried their luck again with the French. In February 1924, on his way back to Baghdad from a visit to Amman, Nuri Sa'id, Faysal's aide, stopped in Beirut to discuss a series of issues with General Weygand, the French High Commissioner. The accounts given by both to the British were contradictory, but it seems that Nuri tried to sound Weygand out on the candidacy of ex-king 'Ali and possibly also of the Amir 'Abdallah and was given a clear negative answer.[7] The French were still unsuccessful in setting up a local government that would be effective, cooperative with them and acceptable to the local political classes. They were jealous of Britain's apparent success in so doing in Iraq, but were not ready to consider a Hashemite candidate for that purpose. The episode was also significant in demonstrating to the British that, where dynastic interests were concerned, they could not fully rely on the manner in which the Hashemites and the politicians who served them, consulted with and reported to the British authorities in Iraq.

France's attitude seemed to have undergone a complete change in November 1925, when King Faysal was in Paris and met with Foreign Minister Berthelot and French senior officials. The king was given a very friendly reception and had a long discussion with Berthelot. The latter sought Faysal's advice on how to deal with 'the Syrian question' and hinted that the French government would favourably consider one of Faysal's brothers as a candidate for a possible Syrian throne. He then asked him 'to do all he could by letters or otherwise to reassure his friends in Syria as to French intentions'.[8]

The change in France's position was not as far reaching as it seemed to King Faysal. October and November of 1925 were the most difficult months of the Syrian-Druze revolt of 1925–26, and the French could use help from any quarter in order to calm down the Syrian nationalists and to facilitate a political solution to the crisis. In order to encourage King Faysal's intervention with the nationalists, they did not shy from whetting his appetite and leading him to believe that one of his brothers would be acceptable to them as king of Syria, should it be decided to establish a Syrian monarchy. It is evident from his report to the British that Faysal failed to notice how careful Berthelot was not to commit himself in any way while attempting to solicit the king's services. Faysal was reported later, in the summer of 1926, to have attempted to mediate between the French and the Syrian nationalists and to have met for this purpose with Dr 'Abd al-Rahman Shahbandar and with Sultan al-Atrash, the leaders of the 1925–26 Syrian-Druze revolt.[9]

This short episode ended without immediate results. But by leading Faysal to believe that the Hashemites had become acceptable to them, the French helped to reveal new aspects of Faysal's dynastic and Arab policy. His earlier attempts to have one of his brothers installed in Syria had appeared as efforts to enhance the family's position and to solve a personal problem for one of his less successful brothers. However, in November 1925 Faysal seemed also moved by an ambition to restore, directly or indirectly, a position for himself in Syria. The future rivalry between the Iraqi and the Jordanian branches of the Hashemite family over Syria was also foreshadowed during these weeks. 'Abdallah regarded himself as the member of the family best entitled to rule Syria. He felt deprived by the settlement of 1921 and came out from his meetings with Churchill in that year with an impression, at least, that Britain would support his claim to Syria should the opportunity arise. But in 1925 Faysal, aside from his personal ambitions, clearly preferred to see Zayd, his younger brother, rather than 'Abdallah installed in Damascus.[10]

An important change in Syria's political complexion occurred in 1928 when the French Mandatory Administration launched an effort to come to terms with the Syrian nationalists, which culminated in the 1936 treaty. Hashemite and other contenders for Syria and the Syrian throne now had to address themselves in a much more serious fashion to the local politicians as well as to the French and British authorities.

In 1928 the course of Syrian domestic politics was governed by the elections for and the sessions of the short-lived Constituent Assembly. The formal position taken by the French High Commissioner, Ponsot, was that the choice of the form of government should be left to the Assembly. It was in order to influence the Assembly's deliberations that a monarchist party was organized in Damascus. Its activities at the time were described by the French authorities in the following terms: 'Au cours du mois [October 1928] le groupement monarchiste, dont la fondation remonte au mois de Juin, a intensifié sa propagande. Une mazbata [petition] d'un millier de signatures a du etre envoyée a Paris ... elle reclame l'etablissement du regime monarchique en Syrie'.[11]

But the monarchist party was a negligible factor in Syrian politics. The chief political force on the local scene was the National Bloc, the loose coalition into which the Syrian nationalists organized themselves. Some of the Bloc's leaders were real (Nasib al-Bakri) or declared (Fares al-Khuri) supporters of the Hashemites, but by the end of 1928 it clearly transpired that they were an ineffective minority. The delegates to the Constituent Assembly considered the principle of monarchy and a list of candidates, who among others included the Hashemites 'Ali and Zayd, the Saudi Prince (and later King) Faysal and Sharif 'Abd al-Majid, the son of Sharif 'Ali Haydar, a relative and rival of Husayn's branch of the Hashemite family. The great majority of the nationalist delegates favored a republican form of government and even among the advocates of monarchy support for the Hashemites was not certain. In fact, the Saudis were more popular with several leaders of the National Bloc, Shukri al-Quwatli in particular. This support stemmed from traditional family ties as well as a feeling that the Saudis were more genuine Arab nationalists and less dependent on the British than the Hashemites. Nuri Sa'id, Yasin Pasha and Rustum Haydar were dispatched from Baghdad on an extended mission to Syria to lobby on behalf of the Hashemites, but their efforts were to no avail.[12]

Beyond the immediate political issues that were at stake this episode is of interest because of the insight it offers into the conflict which developed first subtly and then overtly between the Hashemites and the leaders of the nationalist movement in Syria. In a broader sense this conflict represented the tension between the pan-Arab nationalist doctrine and movement and the local nationalist movements in the new states of the Fertile Crescent. The leaders of the nationalist movement in Syria subscribed to the doctrine of pan-Arab nationalism which regarded the state of Syria as it then exist-ed as an artificial creation which at some future date was to be submerged in a greater Arab entity. And yet in the later 1920s, after several years of struggle for the unification and independence of that state, an attachment

to it and to their own position of leadership had grown among the nationalist leaders. The Hashemites, furthermore, did not appear as selfless champions of Arab unity, nor was their close association with and dependence
on the British relished by many Syrian nationalists. Several of the latter had
cooperated with the Hashemites in the past, during the First World War and
Faysal's reign in Damascus. But when they were given a choice between
their own government in Syria or the acceptance of Hashemite suzerainty,
they opted for the former.

These, though, were not the conclusions drawn by King Faysal and his
aides after the failure of their efforts in 1928. Several factors account for
the king's failure to understand the mood and conduct of the Syrian
nationalists: his own obsession with the Syrian throne, the reluctance of
the Syrians to reject the Iraqi overtures in clear-cut terms, and the reluctance of his own aides to provide him with full and accurate accounts of
the Syrian response to his initiative. The report, which King Faysal's emissaries submitted upon their return to Baghdad in 1928, is most revealing
in this respect. Its authors had no illusions with regard to the French attitude and saw through the official position presented to them that Ponsot
was actually opposed to a Hashemite monarchy in Syria. But their account
of the Syrian attitude was tailored to suit the king's own wishes: 'If there
was no uncertainty as to the possible French opposition, there is no doubt
that the Syrian people would elect first King Faysal to be their king and. if
he refused, then the Amir Zayd. The French were not favorably disposed
toward the Amir Zayd, as he is believed to be pro-English. It would require
great effort to guarantee the election of ex-king 'Ali.'[13]

The Iraqi-Hashemite campaign in Syria was revived with greater intensity in the early 1930s as part of a more comprehensive new Arab policy.
The adoption of that policy derived from the 1930 Anglo-Iraqi treaty
which granted Iraq its formal independence. With that independence and
with the resources of the state available to them, the Iraqi leaders envisaged
for Iraq a role comparable to that played by Prussia and Piedmont in nineteenth-century Europe. At the same time pan-Arab nationalism seemed to
be on the rise again with the convening of the Islamic Congress in
Jerusalem in 1931, the formulation of an Arab Covenant and the revival of
the Istiqlal Party's activity. King Faysal sought to take charge of this recru-
descence and to make Baghdad the centre of pan-Arab nationalism. For this
purpose an Arab congress was convened in Baghdad and efforts were made
to secure the support of such figures as Shakib Arslan and 'Abd al-Rahman
Shahbandar.[14]

But in the early 1930s it was only in Syria that Faysal and his entourage
saw the prospect of concrete achievements. Accordingly, between 1930 and

1933 they worked in a variety of ways to secure the throne of Syria for King Faysal or for another member of his family who was acceptable to him. In addition to the efforts he directed at the British and the French, the king met in person with several Syrian politicians and solicited their support. His emissaries did the same in Cairo, Beirut and Damascus. A first-hand account by one such Syrian politician, Munir al-'Ajluni, sheds an interesting light on the king's *modus operandi*. Ajluni, we are told, met the king in Paris, at the end of August 1931. Ihsan al-Jabiri, the Aleppo nationalist who had arranged the meeting, had warned the king of 'Ajluni's republican sentiments. The king therefore opened the conversation by denying that he came to Paris to secure the throne of Syria for his brother 'Ali. He then proceeded to argue that an independent monarchy was preferable to a republic dominated by foreigners. 'Ajluni responded by stating that if a monarchy was to guarantee independence, he would be first among the royalists.[15]

However, as in 1928, Faysal's courting of the Syrian nationalists met with little success. The leaders of the Syrian-Palestinian Congress remained hostile or at best unreliable. Such Syrian nationalists as Ihsan al-Jabiri and Fares al-Khuri pledged their support when they met with him in Europe but became hesitant and ambivalent upon their return to Syria. The National Bloc as a party remained republican and anti-Hashemite. Its attitude was manifested in June 1933 when a delegation of Syrian politicians went to Amman to present King Faysal, stopping there on his way to Europe, with a petition to look after Syria's interests during his trip. The National Bloc first absented itself from the delegation and then decided on a modest representation so as not to offend the king.

This continued to be the National Bloc's attitude throughout most of the 1930s and even more so after the formation of its government in 1936. Some of the Bloc's leaders did support Iraqi bids for union and the Syrian throne due to personal and family ties or as a corollary of personal and regional rivalries, but they continued to represent a minority orientation. It was only on the eve of the Second World War, when France seemed determined to suppress the 1936 treaty, that several of the Bloc's major leaders were temporarily willing to support Hashemite unionist schemes as the only apparent means of achieving independence from French rule.[16]

The sustained Iraqi effort in Syria during the early 1930s also met with opposition from the Amir 'Abdallah, who was motivated by an equally potent ambition to extend his rule into Syria. 'It should be accepted as an always present factor' Sir Henry Cox, the British resident in Amman, wrote in 1939, 'that he will always take any opportunity he may see of bringing more Arabs and more Arab territory under his rule'.[17] It was probably

'Abdallah's pressure which brought King Faysal to publish, in March 1932, a statement in the Iraqi press in which he denied that there were disagreements between 'Abdallah and himself or that he wanted to interfere in the internal affairs of Syria.[18]

Eager as he was, 'Abdallah was more realistic than his brother and understood that in the early 1930s, with Syria squarely under French control he had no prospect of furthering his ambitions there. He began his campaign for a union of Syria and Transjordan under his rule in 1936 when the British and French hold over the area seemed to loosen. But his efforts at mobilizing the support of the mainstream nationalists in Syria were as unsuccessful as those of the Iraqi branch of his family. 'Abdallah sent messengers to the leaders of the National Bloc on the eve of the Syrian delegation's departure to Paris to negotiate the 1936 treaty. He proposed a union of Syria and Transjordan under his throne and suggested that the delegation stop in Amman on its way to Europe. The Bloc's leaders were more explicit with 'Abdallah than they had been with his brother. We are told that they responded to his offer by saying that 'they had their hands full with the task of extricating Syria from its present difficulties and could not consider complicating the issue between them and the French'.[19] 'Abdallah was able to win the support of a group of Syrian politicians, most notable among whom was Dr 'Abd al-Rahman Shahbandar, but the National Bloc continued to evade his overtures.

By 1936, though, the bids of both the Iraqi and Jordanian branches of the Hashemite family became closely intertwined with broader regional issues and designs. Thus, Nuri Sa'id and the Amir 'Abdallah were two of those who at that time advocated the idea of a Greater Syrian or Fertile Crescent federation. This idea had several aspects and versions. Its Hashemite promoters sought to respond to a clearly growing yearning for unity and to couch their ambitions in national rather than in personal or dynastic terms. In Britain the idea found support among those who hoped to mollify Arab nationalist opinion and particularly among those who saw it as the only solution to the Palestine problem. The latter saw no prospects for a solution whose scope was limited to Palestine proper and hoped to obtain Palestinian and other Arab acceptance of Jewish achievements in Palestine by linking them to comparable or even greater achievements for the cause of Arab unity.[20]

Nuri and 'Abdallah indeed indicated that in return for a British endorsement of their plans they would be willing to display flexibility in dealing with the Jewish population of Palestine and its political aspirations. While neither was at that stage willing to accept the notions of partition and Jewish sovereignty in part of Palestine, the new idea nourished a wave of diplomatic activity in which a variety of Arab, British and Zionist states-men, politicians and diplomats took part.[21]

In this context the aspirations of the chief Hashemite contenders for a Syrian throne appeared somewhat more realistic, but the major obstacles hindering their progress were not removed. Despite some British support, the French and the majority of the local Syrian politicians remained opposed to the Hashemites. Nor were the Hashemites capable of resolving their own differences as both branches sought to dominate the putative federation and to acquire the throne of Syria for themselves. The Iraqi posi-tion became further confounded in the late 1930s by the interest of 'Abd al-Illah, who became the regent after King Ghazi's death, in a Syrian throne for himself. In 1939 the Iraqis, worried by the impact of the conflict with 'Abdallah, took the initiative and suggested that the two branches coordi-nate their Arab policies. But the terms of the proposal implied the seniori-ty of Iraq and King Ghazi: coordination was to be achieved by a subordi-nation of 'Abdalah's policy to that of Iraq. 'Abdallah rejected the overture.[22]

Like the intra-Hashemite conflict and the response of the Syrian nation-alists, the reaction of Saudi Arabia and Egypt to the Hashemite designs on Syria adumbrated the pattern of the full-blown inter-Arab rivalries of the 1940s and 1950s.

The Saudis were initially drawn into the struggle over Syria's future in a passive fashion in 1928, when their clients and supporters raised the name of Faysal as a (counter) candidate for the Syrian throne. They repeat-ed their initiative in 1931 and 1935. Then in 1937 Ibn Sa'ud's unofficial adviser, St John Philby, was involved in abortive discussions with David Ben Gurion in which a role for Saudi Arabia in the Fertile Crescent was moot-ed.[23] But Ibn Sa'ud himself does not seem to have been carried away by any of these schemes, which as a realistic statesman he would regard as futile, farfetched and beyond Saudi Arabia's limited capabilities. His prime con-cern was not to extend his own influence to Syria but to prevent the aggrandizement of the rival dynasty. He explained his outlook to Sir Reader Bullard in October 1939 when the issue was raised for the last time before the war. 'I do not want Syria or anything else outside Saudi Arabia', he stat-ed, 'but fear lest addition of Syria to Transjordan or Iraq should facilitate designs on Hedjaz or the Nejd. Like His Majesty's government in Europe. I want balance of power in the Arab world. So long as no Hashemite becomes king of Syria let the Syrians choose for themselves [a] king from outside.'[24]

The Egyptian position was more complicated. Like Ibn Sa'ud, King Fu'ad was opposed to the prospect of a Hashemite monarchy in Syria, but he was still more alarmed by the candidacy of the ex-Khedive 'Abbas

Hilmi, which was revived in 1931. 'Abbas Hilmi, in turn, was supported by Turkey as a measure designed both to prevent the union of Syria and Iraq and to install a Turkish client should the French proceed seriously with the establishment of a Syrian monarchy. Tension thus developed between Turkey and Egypt which led to an angry exchange of letters in 1932.[25]

But the Egyptians went beyond passive resistance and they proposed alternative candidates from the house of Muhammad 'Ali. They did so in 1932 and again, more seriously, in March 1938, when King Faruq tried through Sir Miles Lampson to promote the candidacy of Prince 'Abd al-Mu'min. This was not an isolated episode but part of a new and more active Arab policy which the young king launched under the guidance of 'Ali Mahir and 'Abd al-Rahman 'Azzam. As a result of this policy Egypt became a full and active partner in the nascent system of inter-Arab relations and developed a greater interest in the course of Syrian politics.[26]

But in the 1930s the interest and meddling of the Egyptian, Hashemite and Saudi ruling houses in the affairs of Syria were of limited actual significance. Britain and France dominated the area, their position challenged but not shaken by Italy and Germany. The regional policies of Arab governments had to be conducted within the limits determined by Britain and France, their scope broadened occasionally by the rivalry between the latter two and inconsistencies within their policies.

In this respect the decisive fact was that towards the end of the 1930s the Quai d'Orsay did not seriously consider the establishment of a Syrian monarchy and it certainly did not change its mind with regard to the Hashemites. Yet the activity generated by the issue of the prospective Syrian throne was not always displeasing to the French and on several occasions, particularly in 1931, 1932 and 1934, appears even to have been encouraged by them.

This French attitude reflected a sense of comparative security and confidence in France's position in Syria that had been distinctly lacking in the early and mid-1920s. In the late 1920s and the 1930s the French authorities no longer felt as threatened by external intervention of the type that has been described above. They rather seem to have appreciated the advantages it offered from their vantage point.

For one thing, the debate over Syria's future form of government and the selection of candidates for a potential throne facilitated the task of French High Commissioners by dividing the ranks of the Syrian nationalists. More significantly, the fact that they could dispose of the prospective throne of Syria provided the French with an important asset for the implementation of their regional policies. The usefulness of this tool was illustrated by the development of their relations with the Iraqi Hashemites.

In 1921 the French were alarmed by Hashemite ambitions in Syria. In 1925 they used them in an effort to soothe the Syrian nationalists. In 1928 and in later years they used them in Iraq itself. Already in 1925 the French consul (and eventually the French *charge*) in Baghdad took advantage of the royal court's intense interest in Syria to break through the narrow confines designed by the British for the activity of foreign representatives in Iraq. He gained easy access to the palace and could conduct political and other business with the king and his entourage.[27] One such concern was the French attempt to attract Iraqi oil pipelines to a territory under France's control, and French encouragement of Hashemite hopes in Syria in 1931 was probably designed to help that attempt.[28]

These considerations were clear to the British and they explain in part their sceptical attitude to the notion of a Syrian monarchy in the late 1920s and throughout the 1930s. But there were additional, and more important, reasons. Despite France's growing confidence with regard to this issue, meddling in Syrian affairs by a British client could be embarrassing for Britain. It was also felt that even if the French were to accept an Iraqi Hashemite candidate in Damascus, the resulting intimate Iraqi involvement in Syria could reflect back on and endanger the stability of Iraqi politics.[29]

Later, Britain's position was further compounded by the rivalry within the Hashemite family and by the interest of the Saudi and Egyptian dynasties in the fortunes of the prospective Syrian throne.

The opinion of the Foreign Office was that it would be best not to have to choose between several rival claimants, all of whom were tied to Britain in one form or another. Prompted by King Faysal's bid for the Syrian throne in 1931, the Standing Official Subcommittee for Questions Concerning the Middle East met on October 20 1931. It formulated a position which was then submitted to a cabinet subcommittee. Its recommendations were that the outcome most desirable to British interests would be a republic with a Syrian as president. It was opposed to a joint Iraqi-Syrian monarchy or to an attempt by King Faysal to transfer his throne to Damascus. But it saw no reason to oppose the candidacy of ex-king 'Ali should an offer be made to him by the French.[30] In the next few years this position continued to guide British policy with regard to Hashemite ambitions in Syria.

The position formulated by the British government in 1938 in response to King Faruq's initiative was essentially the same and in fact mentioned specifically the conclusions reached in 1931. Lacy Baggallay, who transmitted the Foreign Office's reply to Sir Miles Lampson, added other considerations, two of which are particularly interesting. It was feared, he wrote, 'that such an extension of the family's influence might give its members exaggerated ideas of their importance'. And, he added, the elevation of an Egyptian prince, friendly to King Faruq, to the throne of Syria 'might provide King Faruq with powerful support for an Egyptian caliphate'.[31]

But alongside this official policy there existed another school of thought that was rather attracted by the potential advantages of a pro-British ruler in Damascus. This school continued to advocate the promotion of Arab union under Britain's auspices and aegis, much along the lines of the policy that was pursued during and immediately after the First World War.[32] Such a policy could not be adopted as long as France controlled Syria and her position there was accepted by Britain. But, as has been shown above, a change of outlook began to transpire in the late 1930s when British politicians and officials searched for novel ways to solve the problem of Palestine and mollify Arab opinion. This new attitude was formalized in a Foreign Office memorandum, which on the eve of the Second World War took stock of Britain's position with regard to Arab unity and unionist schemes. The memorandum still advocated the view that Britain should not actively foster such ideas and schemes but argued also that pan-Arabism was a phenomenon 'which has probably come to stay'. It would not be wise, the authors explained, to oppose this trend and 'His Majesty's Government had therefore taken the line that while they would be unwilling to take any initiative, which they believed should come from the Arabs themselves, they would endeavor to avoid displaying active opposition or open lack of sympathy'.[33]

This line was further developed during the course of the Second World War. France's hold over Syria and Lebanon was shaken and Britain acquired a predominant position in the Levant and while it did not formally adopt a policy which fostered Arab unity projects, it appeared to be sympathetic to them. Under these circumstances Hashemite efforts both from Iraq and Jordan to determine the future of Syria seemed for the first time to have real prospects of success. Their efforts were increased but so were those of their opponents. It was then, particularly in the later 1940s, that the validity of the caveats formulated by cautious British diplomats in 1931 and 1938 was to be painfully demonstrated.

NOTES

1. Research for this article has been supported by grants from the Ford Foundation received through the Israel Foundations' Trustees, and the French CNRS. The author also acknowledges the assistance of the Foreign Policy Research Institute. This article is an English version of an article published in *Zmanim, a Historical Quarterly* (in Hebrew), 1, 3 (1980), published by The Aranne School of History, Tel Aviv University, and Betan Zmora Publishing House.

2. The archives of the French Ministry of Foreign Affairs are open for part of the period under study. However, due to the fragmented state of the archives for Syria, French policy and the considerations which underlay it had to be reconstructed through their reflection in the British and American archives.

3. Jean Pichon, Le Partage du Proche Orient (Paris: J. Peyronnet, 1938), p.278.

4. General Haddad reported to the British on his conversation with Berthelot (note on conversation with General Haddad, FO371/6458, 19 April 1921). Samuel's detailed report to Churchill illuminates several aspects of Anglo-French relations in the area at that time (FO371/6455, 25 June 1921).

5. French intentions with regard to the Ottomans were reported to the British by a number of sources, one of which they regarded as particularly reliable. See FO371/6656, 10 September 1921. The candidacy of Egyptian princes was a matter of public knowledge and was reported by The Times (London) on 27 September 1921.

6. See FO371/6454, 3 December 1921 for Prime Minister Briand's categoric denial.

7. Nuri Pasha told the British High Commissioner of Iraq that the issue was raised by Weygand who 'hinted strongly' that he supported such an arrangement (FO371/10160, 29 February 1924). On 21 March the British Consul-General in Beirut, H.E. Satow, broached the subject to Weygand who rejected it offhand. On the basis of his understanding of French policy, Satow had no doubt that Weygand's version was correct.

8. Faysal reported on his meetings with Berthelot to Phipps in Paris (FO371/1085, 4 November 1921), and to George Lloyd in Cairo (FO391/10852, 10 November 1921).

9. Report by the American Vice Consul (in Damascus) Walter Rishter, for the period 8–21 August 1926, 890 D 00/636.

10. This came out in Faysal's conversation with George Lloyd and in a later conversation with the High Commissioner, Sir Henry Dobbs, in Baghdad. Dobbs was alarmed by the content of the discussion which he decided to communicate verbally. In view of what he heard, Dobbs doubted that Britain could in good faith encourage the French to invoke Faysal's help (FO371/10852, 18 November 1925).

11. Bulletin de Renseignements mensuel du service des Renseignements de l'Etat de Syrie et du Djebel Druze, Octobre 1928 in File 63 B3. Commandant Superieur Des Troupes Du Levant 1919–1939, in the French Military Archives, Chateau Vincennes, France.

12. Consul-General Satow described in a telegram to the High Commissioner of Iraq a meeting of nationalist leaders in Ba'al Bek in which support was raised for the candidacy of Faysal Ibn al-Sa'ud (FO371/13076, 8 June 1928). Several nationalist leaders did express support for a Hashemite candidate when speaking to Nuri Sa'id (report by British Consul in Damascus who repeatedly advised that the National Bloc was decidedly republican in sentiment: see, for instance, FO371/13076, 16 and 21 June).

13. FO371/13076, 28 July 1928.

14. See E. Kedourie, 'Pan-Arabism and British Policy' and 'The Kingdom of Iraq: a Retrospect', in his The Chatham House Version and Other Middle Eastern Studies (London: Weidenfeld and Nicolson, 1970), pp. 213–35; 236–82; A.M. Gomaa, The Foundation of the League of Arab States (London: Longman, 1977), pp.5–6; M.I. Darwaza, Al-Walula al 'Arabiyya (Cairo: al-Maktab al-Tijari lil-Tiba'ah wal-Tawzi'i wal-Nashr, 1957), pp.123–6; and C.E. Dawn, 'The Project of Greater Syria' (Unpublished PhD Dissertation, Princeton, 1968), pp.16–19. Some interesting aspects of King Faysal's efforts were recorded by the French Sûreté. These reports are kept in the French Military Archives, file 66 B3, section d'etude du Levant (1931–32).

15. French Military Archives, letter by Munir al-'Ajluni in Paris to his brother in Damascus (1 September 1931).

16. Report by E. Epstein (Eilat) to the Political Department of the Jewish Agency. Central Zionist Archives, Jerusalem, file S25-3500.

17. FO371/23276, 7 January 1939.

18. Letter from the Colonial Office to the Foreign Office, FO371/16086, 25 April 1932.

19. Report by H. Cox from Amman, FO371/20065, 26 March 1936.

20. See Dawn, 'The Project of Greater Syria', pp.27–30 and McMichael's letter to Shuckburgh, FO371/23280, 18 June 1939.

21. See Gomaa, The Foundation of the League of Arab States, pp.11–16.

22. Report from the British High Commissioner in Jerusalem, FO371/23276, 6 April 1939.

23. Gomaa, The Foundation of the League of Arab States.

24. FO371/23281, 16 October 1939.

25. FO371/15366, 29 November, 21 and 28 December 1931, and FO371/16086, 6 and 20 January 1932.
26. Gomaa, *The Foundation of the League of Arab States*, and Kedourie, 'Pan-Arabism and British Policy', pp.215–16.
27. Communication between the Colonial and Foreign Offices, FO371/10853, 29 December 1925.
28. Report by the High Commissioner to Lord Passfield, FO371/15366, 30 January 1931. See Chapter 4 of the present volume.
29. Ibid.
30. FO371/15366, 25 October 1931.
31. FO371/21913, 16 and 26 March 1938.
32. Dawn, 'The Project of Greater Syria', pp.31–3.
33. Gomaa, *The Foundation of the League of Arab States*, pp.27–8.

6

The Greater Syria Plan and Palestine Problem: Historical Roots, 1919–1939[1]

The emergence of a relatively stable and effective regime in Syria that is pursuing a dynamic foreign policy and acquiring influence over its neighbours – Jordan and Lebanon – as well as over the PLO has given rise in recent years to the assumption that President Hafiz al-Asad is seeking to set up a political entity in the territory of Greater Syria[2] to be dominated by the Syrian state which he heads.

This assumption is based on an analysis of the rationale which seems to underlie the regional policy of the Asad regime and on a number of statements made and actions taken by its leaders and spokesmen. The best known of these statements was made in March 1974 when Asad asserted, in response to an earlier statement made by the Israeli Prime Minister Golda Meir, that 'Palestine is none other than the principal part of Southern Syria'.[3] Since then, Syria's leaders have made but few explicit remarks on the subject and, when asked about this issue in the press, they have tended to avoid a direct response. They have, however, frequently alluded – particularly in 1976 and 1977 – that this was in fact their goal. Thus, Patrick Seale, a prominent British journalist and Asad's biographer, published in April 1977 an illuminating article based on an interview with Hafiz al-Asad. The article patently reflected the central motifs given prominence at the time. Seale noted:

> Asad has been a member in the Ba'th party dedicated to Arab unity, for 30 years. Moreover, the fact that he rules in Damascus, the heartland of Arabism, makes him heir to a remorseless drive to reach out beyond Syria's national boundaries. His current unionist campaign is two-pronged. First he sees Syria's two immediate neighbors, Lebanon and Jordan, as a natural extension of its territory, vital to its defense. This three-nation grouping is already a *fait accompli*, although in the

low profile Asad manner, without fanfare. Asad now rules by proxy in Lebanon, while the progressive integration with Jordan is well advanced. If the Palestinians ever recover a West Bank homeland, they will inevitably join his complex.[4]

Similar statements were published by the Syrian media. *Tishrin*, the mouth-piece of the Asad regime, published an article extolling its achievements in which is stated that 'political geography may have an important role in explaining the phenomenon of pan-Arab consciousness among the Syrian people, for the southern portion, that is Palestine, was severed from this steadfast country: it has lost Alexandretta, and Lebanon and Jordan and was hemmed in by the Sykes-Picot agreement'.[5]

It is also very significant that the Ba'th regime employs a Lebanese journalist named Shawqi Khayrallah, a veteran activist of the Syrian Social Nationalist Party, in its media network. The PPS (as the party was known according to the French acronym of its name) had advocated in the 1930s the creation of a Greater Syria based on a doctrine of secular territorial pan-Syrian nationalism. Khayrallah now expounds the implementation of a Greater Syria vision in a new guise. Thus, he published an article in the Syrian government newspaper *al-Thawra* on 29 August 1976, in anticipation of a visit by Lebanon's President, Elias Sarkis, to Damascus, in which he called for the setting up of a federation consisting of Syria, Lebanon, Jordan and Palestine.

The connection between this development, the Palestinian problem, and the Arab-Israel conflict is clear, but two aspects should be particularly stressed. First, the argument that the Syrian state has a special status regarding the Palestinian issue is derived from the claim that Palestine is part of an entity called Greater Syria. Consequently, Syria's position in the Arab-Israel conflict emanates not only out of pan-Arab solidarity, as in the case of Egypt or Iraq, but out of the direct relationship of one part of Greater Syria to another part of the same entity. Second, the plan to set up a state or federation in the region of Greater Syria would enable Asad's regime to offer its own solution to the Palestinian component of the Arab-Israel conflict; this would call for an autonomous Palestinian state to be set up on the West Bank and tied to both Jordan and Syria in a federal framework. The Palestinians would thus be given self-expression, while the link to Jordan and Syria would ensure the stability and legitimacy of this arrangement.[6]

The advantages accruing to Syria from the implementation of such a plan are obvious: Hafiz al-Asad's regime would be holding a unique key to resolving the Palestinian issue – a huge political and diplomatic asset. However, discussion of these advantages, as well as of the tensions inherent in the proposed plan and the extensive opposition it is bound to raise, is not our concern now.[7] In the following remarks, I wish to identify the Historical roots of the idea of a Greater Syria as they developed in the period between the two world wars, and the interplay between that plan and the Arab-Jewish conflict in Palestine as a recurrent theme in the political and diplomatic history of the region.

GREATER SYRIA AS AN ELEMENT IN THE STRUGGLE AGAINST ZIONISM

One of the more intriguing aspects of the historian's craft is the insight provided by looking at the present through an investigation of its historical roots and by looking at past events from the fresh perspective of the present. Thus one finds a striking similarity between some of the principal components of Asad regime's approach to the Palestinian issue, and the plan to set up an Arab federation in the region of Greater Syria with which the leadership of the Jewish community in Palestine was confronted in the 1930s and 1940s. The principal element in both cases is the assumption that the establishment of a single Arab entity in the territory of Greater Syria could serve as a basis for settling the Arab-Jewish conflict in Palestine or, alternatively lead to a more effective mobilization of resources for the Arab struggle against Zionism. This motif has remained a permanent element in the political and diplomatic history of the Levant, and its roots – like those of the Greater Syria plan – are to be found in the events of First World War and in the peace settlement that followed it.

On the eve of the First World War, the British Admiralty's handbook on Syria determined that Syria in its broadest sense is that land lying between the eastern shore of the Mediterranean and the Arabian Desert, and that in a more narrow sense the name refers to that part of Syria which is not included in Palestine.[8] This definition, like other uses and definitions of the term 'Syria' in the period prior to the First World War, reflected the lack of clear-cut distinction between Greater or Geographic, and Lesser Syria, the latter being the loosely defined political administrative unit located in the region between Damascus and Aleppo. In previous centuries, there was a vague notion of a geographical entity called Syria – today's Syria, Lebanon, Israel and Jordan. Establishing this entity as a political one was not a practical issue, given the historical and political circumstances of those centuries. Furthermore, broader loyalties (Islamic and Ottoman) and the existence of other entities in parts of Syria – such as Mount Lebanon, Palestine and inland-Syria – militated against any such notion.

With the political and ideological awakening of the last decades of the nineteenth and the beginning of the twentieth century, two contradictory views of Syria as a defined entity were put forward. According to one view, developed mainly by local Christians and French writers, Greater Syria (*la Syrie intégrale*) was defined as a geographic non-Arab entity that should be set up as a French protectorate. The other view claimed that Syria was an Arab entity and an integral part of the Arab world. An Arab state should be set up therein, to be integrated in the future within a framework that would realize the vision of Arab unity.[9]

The First World War brought in its wake the dismemberment of the Ottoman Empire, and created the possibility of setting up a new political entity in the region of Greater Syria. However, the complex reality emerging from the war thwarted this opportunity.

The secret agreement and promises of the war period gave rise to expectations and commitments to set up at least three political entities in Syrian territory: an Arab state, a Lebanese Christian state or a larger entity under French control and a Jewish National Home in Palestine. British wartime policy also provided a great impulse to pan-Arab nationalism and to the movement striving to achieve it. British policy focused the aspirations of the Arab nationalist movement on the region of Syria, by placing Amir Faysal at the head of an embryonic Syrian-Arab state having Damascus as its capital. It was the tension between these expectations that molded the dynamics of the Greater Syria issue in the period between the world wars. This phase can be divided into three sub-periods.

THE PEACE SETTLEMENT, OCTOBER 1918–JULY 1921

Clear patterns had not as yet emerged in this period, and the situation remained sufficiently fluid, so as to enable the main parties fighting for control in Syria, or parts of it, to try and steer the situation their way. These parties included France, Britain, Faysal and Arab nationalists in Damascus, the Zionist movement in Palestine, the Christian supporters of an independent Lebanon, the emerging Palestinian Arab nationalist movement, and 'Abdallah, Faysal's elder brother.

One cardinal aspect of this struggle revolved around the attempt to transform Faysal's administration in Damascus into the nucleus of a larger Syrian state with an Arab nationalist orientation. This effort manifested itself in the convening of the Syrian National Congress whose member delegates came also from Palestine, Lebanon, and Transjordan, in the recruitment of supporters in these areas and, finally, Faysal's coronation as king of Syria on 8 March 1920. But, despite brief hopeful spells, the idea came to naught. Faysal's government controlled a limited area and was dependent on Britain which, along with France, generally opposed the idea of a

Greater Syria and refused to recognize Faysal as its king. In Lebanon and Palestine there were strong centres of opposition to the idea, and apparently even Faysal himself did not have much faith in the prospect of his rule over these areas. The main supporters of the idea were the radical pan-Arab nationalists in Faysal's camp.[10]

Of special interest is the support for the idea of a Greater Syria among the leaders of the emerging nationalist movement of the Palestinian Arabs. This support led Yeoshua Porath to define those years as the 'southern Syria period' in the history of the Palestinian nationalist movement.[11] His analysis highlights three points:

1) There was no general support among the Arabs in Palestine for the idea that Palestine is southern Syria and part of a larger Syrian state.

2) Even at the peak of the Greater Syrian orientation, the Palestinian Arabs' attitude was ambivalent regarding Palestine's inclusion within its framework.

3) The attitude of the Palestinian Arab leaders was instrumental. They supported a Greater Syria entity in the hope and expectation that it would reinforce their opposition to Zionism. Indeed, when regime was toppled, this orientation almost completely disappeared from the spectrum of Palestinian political opinion, and a particularistic approach regained the ascendancy.

The period concluded with the formation of patterns that were to last throughout future decades. They were based on the division of Syrian territory into four units: a truncated state in inner-Syria (which would in fact only come into being in January 1925), Greater Lebanon, the Transjordanian Emirate, and Mandatory Palestine.

THE YEARS OF CONSOLIDATION, 1921–36

These years were marked by a process of consolidation which followed the rapid changes that occurred between 1914 and 1921. But the internal development within each of the four units varied according to its particular conditions.

In Lebanon, the Muslims, including the population in the regions detached from Syria in 1920, gradually adapted to the existence of the Lebanese state. The Maronites and Sunnites found a community of interests, resulting in the National Pact of 1943 and the establishment of the independent Lebanese Republic. Needless to say, however, the fundamental tensions within the Lebanese body politic were not resolved.

The negotiations which took place at the beginning of 1919 between the leaders of the Zionist movement (Weizmann and Frankfurter) and the Arab nationalist leaders demonstrated another aspect of the interplay between the Greater Syria notion and the emerging Jewish-Arab conflict. The Faysal-Weizmann agreement signed in February 1919 unsuccessfully attempted to strike a compromise between Zionism and the Arab nationalist movement. The assumption that guided the Zionist leadership is of great interest in that it presumed that if the Arabs were to achieve their ambitions in the territory surrounding Palestine, it would be easier for them to accept the existence of a Jewish-Zionist entity in Palestine itself. Faysal himself encouraged these hopes when he wrote to Frankfurter on 3 March 1919 that 'our movement is nationalistic and not imperialistic and there is room for both of us in Syria'.[12] This theme did not fade from Zionist political thought after the failure of the Faysal-Weizmann agreement.

In Lebanon the refusal of the Greek Orthodox (and to a lesser extent of other non-Catholic communities) to accept the Lebanese state as it was then defined was translated by Antun Sa'adeh into the doctrine of the Syrian Social Nationalist Party. According to this doctrine, Greater Syria was a natural geographic and political entity that had fashioned a Syrian nation. History decreed that this nation will express and fulfill itself through the formation of an independent Greater Syria state. The party's secular territorial nationalism was inimical both to Arab nationalism and to the smaller entities that had crystallized in the territory of Greater Syria.

The history of this intriguing party does not concern us here,[13] but a number of facts and characteristics should be mentioned. First, the party spread from Lebanon to all parts of Syria. Second, as a rule it attracted members of minority groups who were dissatisfied with the prevailing political order. Third, the party is still in existence today, after undergoing several metamorphoses in both form and orientation, and has contributed much to political thought and action in the region. It is particularly interesting to note that some of the Palestinian formulators of the idea of a 'secular democratic state' (the Sayigh brothers and Hisham Sharabi, for instance) are former members of this party.

Transjordan, created *ex nihilo* in 1921, was gradually taking shape as a state. Its ruler, Amir and later King 'Abdallah, was a revisionist and agitating element. In the politics of the region, 'Abdallah never reconciled himself to the idea that he emerged from the First World War and the peace settlement with a mere desert domain. Sir Henry Cox, the British Resident in Amman, observed in 1939 that 'it should be accepted as an always present factor, that he will always take any opportunity he may see of bringing more Arabs and more Arab territory under his rule'.[14] But 'Abdallah was a realist, and between 1921 and 1936 he did not venture beyond attempts to acquire supporters and influence in the Syrian state and in Western Palestine. Nor did 'Abdallah then nurture a vision of the unification of Syria under his rule; he was content with extending his rule either northward to include the Syrian state or part of it, westward to Palestine or its predominantly Arab part.

The truncated state set up in inner-Syria inherited the legacy of the Greater Syria which the Arab nationalists had tried to establish during the time of Faysal. When the constituent assembly of mandatory Syria met in 1928, the Drafting Committee determined that the Syrian territories severed from the empire were 'an indivisible political unit' and that the splitting up of this territory after the First World War was fundamentally invalid. This baggage, however, was too heavy for the political elite of the Syrian state. It is true that the ritual devotion to the vision of an Arab Greater Syria continued to exist, and the refusal to relinquish it was one of the factors that later led to the dispersal of the founding convention by the French Commissioner. But aside from the clear feeling that this dream was indeed hopeless, it was in fact neutralized by two other forces at work:

1) The powerful hold of pan-Arab nationalism. Ideological tension existed between this vision and that of a Greater Syria. It is true that the tension could have been mitigated by claiming that the establishment of Greater Syria would be a step on the road to Arab unity. But the idea of Greater Syria had a stigma of hostility to Arab nationalism attached to it. This originated in the French-Christian notion of Syrian statehood mentioned above and was reinforced during the 1930s by the appearance and activity of the Syrian Nationalist Party.
2) The truncated Syrian state acquired a degree of political vitality during the 1920s and early 1930s. The struggle of the nationalist movement against the French over the independence of this territory, and its struggle against the separatist movements in the peripheral regions, fostered new interest and loyalty within its ranks. Towards the middle of the 1930s most of the leaders of the nationalist movement in Syria were prepared to compromise regarding the independence of the Syrian state by relinquishing, at least formally and temporarily, not only the idea of a Greater Syria but also their claims to the regions annexed to Lebanon in 1920. This was one of the most important aspects of the treaty signed in 1936 between Syria and France for the purpose of granting Syria independence under French protection.[15]

HEYDAY OF AN IDEA, 1936–39

A more fluid situation prevailed during this period, for two main reasons:

1) Iraq, Syria and Lebanon gained nominal independence, with a degree of autonomy that enabled them to conduct a foreign policy and allowed greater intervention by the Arab states in each other's affairs.

2) The general international situation as well as the direct challenge by Germany and Italy weakened the grip of Britain and France over their protectorates.

This was the background for the competitive revival of the idea of a Greater Syria by the two Hashemite states. We have already mentioned 'Abdallah's ambitions to extend his kingdom toward Syria and Palestine in the peroid 1921–36, and his relatively low-key activities in this regard. The change in circumstances in 1936 led him to renew his activity with greater intensity. He set out to establish a monarchy in Syria and simultaneously to impose his rule on the Arabs of Palestine. On this basis he was able to propose to Britain that the consolidation of Syria, and the solution to the Jewish-Arab conflict in Palestine, were two good reasons for lifting British opposition to the plan.

The Iraqi interest in this plan was also familiar, although less well known. From the British archives opened up in recent years we learn that throughout the 1920s and 1930s the Iraqis were interested either in placing a Hashemite Iraqi prince on the throne in Syria, or in bringing about Iraqi-Syrian unity. This policy took on new dimensions in the 1930s, when Iraq, after achieving independence, became the center of the pan-Arab nationalist movement, and when a militant wave of nationalism swept through the middle of that decade. The Iraqi plan, conceived on the eve of the Second World War, to include Syria in an Arab federation, was a rival to the Jordanian plan. It sought to exploit the instability in Syria and Palestine and the aspirations for Arab unity, in order to establish Iraq's hegemony.

ATTITUDES OF THE SYRIAN NATIONALISTS

The leadership of the Syrian state, which gained nominal independence in 1936, was forced to react to external initiatives to set up an Arab federation in Greater Syria. On this issue, the heads of the Syrian nationalist bloc divided into two schools whose roots could be traced to previous years.[16] The dominant orientation was represented by Jamil Mardam, Prime

Minister of Syria during most of the period. This approach may be termed pragmatic. It primarily tried to implement the Syrian-French treaty and to ensure the independence and integrity of the territory under its nominal authority. The defensive approach of this leadership with its attachment to the territorial *status quo*, for fear that any change would endanger it, was described in the report sent from Damascus by Eliyahu Sasson to Moshe Sharett in the Political Department of the Jewish Agency on 20 March 1938 following a conversation with N.B. (= Nasib al-Bakri). Bakri claimed that 'Jamil Mardam feared a Turkish conquest of the northern part of Syria. The bloc leaders also decided to associate themselves more with England since they viewed her as a more influential power than France, and expressed the fear that she might reach agreement with Turkey and France over the division of Syria: the northern part of Turkey, the southern part of Transjordan, and Lebanon to France'.[17]

The second orientation within the nationalist bloc dew its inspiration from the pan-Arab ideology whose supporters were former members of the *Istiqlal* party headed by Shukri al-Quwatly and other leaders such as Nabih al-'Azmeh and Fakhri al-Barudi. They advocated acceptance of the pan-Arab policy even before Syria gained real independence. It was possible to implement such a policy by assisting the Arab revolt in Palestine, that was conducted from Damascus during a certain period. This assistance was given because of pan-Arab policy considerations and not necessarily because of an ambition to achieve control over the Palestinian nationalist movement. Assistance to Arab revolt in Palestine became a subject of contention in the internal policies of Syria during those years because it was, to a great extent, extended by radical elements on the fringes of the nationalist bloc or in the opposition, rather than by the Arab nationalist establishment.[18]

THE PRE-WAR CONSTELLATION

On the eve of First World War, support for the pan-Arab orientation gained strength among the ranks of the nationalist bloc. This was partly due to the weakness of Jamil Mardam, to the increasing intervention of other Arab states (Iraq, Saudi Arabia, and Transjordan), and to the suspicion that France did not intend to grant Syria independence. The Jewish Agency's Political Department was under the impression that the Quwatly group was 'pinning its hopes on the appearance of a pan-Arab trend in Britain's Near Eastern policy, believing that by applying pressure to France, Britain would be able to carry out her pan-Arab policies by integrating [inner] Syria into a federation'.[19]

This analysis can be interpreted as a reflection of the mood prevailing in Syria during the months and weeks before the war, rather than indicating the existence of political resources available to those wishing to set up a Greater Syria. Iraqi and Jordanian policy, as a concrete plan of action, earned very little support among the Arabs of Palestine. There it was supported by a number of nationalist activists such as Akram Zu'aytir, and in Syria by a pro-Hashemite monarchist party under the leadership of Dr 'Abd al-Rahman Shahbandar.[20] For the most part, however, the Hashemite plans met with a uniform opposition whose leaders – the Mufti in Palestine and some of the heads of the Syrian nationalist bloc – viewed them with suspicion and animosity. Other states in the region, Egypt, Saudi Arabia, and Turkey, also responded negatively. France viewed the plans as a British-Hashemite plot to remove her from Syria, and the British treated these plans, at least until First World War, with reservations. A completely new chapter opened with the outbreak of the war.[21]

THE JEWISH VIEW

These plans posed a dilemma for the leaders of the Jewish Community. On the one hand, Arab unity could build up strength which would change the balance of power between the Jewish community in Palestine and its Arab environment. On the other hand it might be assumed, just as in 1919, that such unity might satisfy Arab ambitions and that the latter would then ease their pressure with regard to the Palestine question. This second position was formulated by Eliyahu Eylath of the Jewish Agency's Political Department when he met the leaders of the Syrian nationalist bloc in Bludan on 1 August 1936: 'If the nationalist aspirations of the Arabs would eventually lead to the establishment of a federal [federative in Eylath's own language] political regime in our area, we would not object to it in principle, on condition that this federation is based on harmony and understanding among all the parties.'[22] The supporters of the idea of a federation, in Syria and elsewhere, resorted to familiar arguments when they tried to explain the latent advantages of their plan to the Zionist leaders. A prime example of this was the plea made in 1940 by one of the leaders of the Syrian nationalist bloc to a member of the Political Department of the Jewish Agency with whom he was on good terms. 'According to him,' reported the Agency's emissary, 'some of the Syrian leaders consider the federation as a solution to the Palestine problem. As long as that problem exists, and the Arabs of Palestine are battling the Jewish world, the greater is their fear of Jewish domination. If Palestine, Transjordan and Syria were to unite, this unity would safeguard the Arabs from the Jewish domination, and they would therefore be more amenable to making concessions.'[23]

A vast chasm existed in fact between the Jewish and Arab perspectives. But, since the plans to set up an Arab federation or to establish Greater Syria failed to reach the practical stage in the 1930s, the real contradiction between the Jewish and Arab assumptions did not become fully apparent. Yet it was there. The Zionist leaders endeavored to set up a Jewish state in Palestine. If an Arab federation was to be formed, Zionist diplomacy would attempt to exploit the situation so as to direct Arab nationalist ambitions away from Palestine. The Arab nationalists, however, viewed Palestine as an Arab entity and certainly as part of Greater Syria. Some of the Arab leaders saw no point in arousing Zionist opposition to the plans of Arab unity at an early stage, and some may have believed that it was possible to come to some sort of an arrangement by which the Zionist leaders would achieve some of their objectives. But even if there were Arab leaders who were interested in a settlement between the Arab federation of Greater Syria and the Jewish community in Palestine, they still had to overcome three important obstacles:

1) Potential supporters of a compromise were in a minority, compared to those who refused to concede the Arab nature of Palestine.

2) The question of the Arab federation and Greater Syria was part of the bitter conflict already unfolding within the emerging system of inter-Arab relations. Conflicts of this sort tend to reinforce radical trends and weaken tendencies toward compromise and agreement.

3) A settlement based on mutual recognition of the Arab federation and the rights of Jewish settlement in Palestine required a great degree of mutual trust, which did not exist.

There is no direct connection between these plans and the idea of Greater Syria which circulated in Damascus between 1974 and 1977. The political leadership in Damascus in the 1930s and 1940s was merely a passive participant in plans that were formulated outside of Syrian borders. Nor is there continuity between the two periods, since the idea of a Greater Syria remained dormant between the 1940s and the 1970s. A new Syrian leadership decided to revive the idea in the mid-1970s – either as a plan of action, or as an attempt to drum up ideological legitimacy for an expansionist foreign policy.

The waning and rebirth of historical ideas and concepts is a fascinating issue in its own right. It seems that the current geo-political situation, the weakness of several states in the region, and considerations of political benefit, all combined to revive the connection between the idea of Greater

Syria and the Palestine problem, as a new incarnation of a persistent theme in the history of the region during the past century.

NOTES

1. This article was published in *The Jerusalem Cathedra*, 2, 1982, pp.259–71. Translated by Aviva Damboritz. Research for this article was partly financed by the Israel Foundation Trustees, to whom I extend my thanks. I am also grateful to Mr Yoram Nimrod, who shared with me documents that he collected on the subject of the Central Zionist Archives, and the Ben Gurion Heritage Center for permission to quote from some of the documents in their collection.

2. For an illuminating study of the issue of Greater Syria, see: Daniel Pipes, *Greater Syria: The History of an Ambition* (New York: Oxford University Press, 1990).

3. Radio Damascus, 8 March 1974.

4. *The Observer* (London), 6 March 1977.

5. Tishrin, Damascus, 22 November 1976.

6. Similar ideas were put by the Syrian leaders to the Lebanese delegation in the summer of 1976. See *al-Sayyad* (Beirut), 9 September 1976. The idea was more generally developed by Albert Hourani in an article, 'Lebanon, Syria, Jordan and Iraq', in A.L. Udovitch (ed.), *The Middle East: Oil, Conflict and Hope* (Lexington, MA: D.C. Heath, 1976).

7. These elements are discussed in my essay 'Syria, Israel and the Palestine Question', in this volume.

8. British Admiralty, *A Handbook of Syria (including Palestine)* (London: HM Stationery Office, 1913), p.9.

9. A. Hourani, *Arabic Thought in the Liberal Age* (Cambridge: Cambridge University Press, 1962), pp.274–6; K.S. Salibi, 'Islam and Syria in the Writings of Henri Lammens', in B. Lewis and P.M. Holt (eds), *Historians of the Middle East* (London: Oxford University Press, 1962), pp.330–42.

10. The political history of the Faysal period in Syria not yet been sufficiently researched. A preliminary description of the various factions in Faysal's government can be found in Khayriyya al-Qasimiyya, *Al-hukuma al-'arabiyya fi Dimashq* (Cairo: Dar al Ma'arif, 1971).

11. Y. Porath, *The Growth of the Palestine Arab Nationalist Movement 1918–1929* (Hebrew), (Jerusalem: Hebrew University Press, 1971), pp.56–90.

12. See M. Verte, 'Arab-Zionist Negotiations in the Spring of 1919 and British Policy', *Zion*, 1–2 (5277/1967); M. Perlman, 'Arab-Jewish Diplomacy, 1918–1922', *Jewish Social Studies*, 6, 2, pp.123–54, Central Zionist Archives (CZA) S/25-3282.

13. E. Eylath, 'Antun Sa'adeh – Portrait of an Arab Revolutionary', in *Zionism and the Arabs* (Hebrew) (Tel Aviv: Devir, 1974), pp.368–72; also L.Z. Yamak, *The Syrian Social Nationalist Party: an Ideological Analysis* (Cambridge, MA: Harvard University Press, 1966), and see Chapter 10 of the present volume.

14. FO371/23276, a letter from the British Representative in Amman to the High Commissioner in Jerusalem, 7 January 1939.

15. In this connection, it is interesting to note President Asad's statements to the Kuwaiti newspaper *al-Ray al-'Aam* on 10 February 1977, in which he explained that Syria gave up her claim to areas annexed to Lebanon, in order to prevent the establishment of a small and ethnic Lebanon.

16. A description and analysis of these approaches is to be found in the memorandum written by Eliyahu Epstein (Eylath) (translated into English by A. Eban) at the end of 1939 on the political situation in Syria; CZA S/25-3500.

17. A letter from Sasson to Sharett on 20 March 1938 (013 6026), the Ben-Gurion heritage Center.

18. For further details on this topic see my article 'Germany and the Syrian political scene in the late 1930s', in Y. Wallach (ed.), *Germany and the Middle East 1835–1939* (Tel Aviv: Tel Aviv University, 1975), pp.191–8; also the report sent by Gilbert Mackereth, the British Consul in Damascus, to Sir Charles Tagert in Palestine, in which he described in great detail the activities of the participants and the supporters of the Palestinian rebellion in Syria. The report is found in the Tagert Papers in St Antony's College (Oxford), Box 3, File 5.

19. See above, n.16.

20. On Akram Zu'aytir and his activities, see Eylath, 'Antun Sa'adeh – Portrait of an Arab Revolutionary', pp.286, 241. Details on the supporters of the plan to set up a Hashemite monarchy in Greater Syria (or part of it) can be found in a memorandum written by a British officer, K.N. Donald Mills, in March 1946. The memorandums are found in the Spears Papers in St Antony's College, Oxford, Box 3, File 6.

21. This period is outside the scope of this article, but it is desirable to indicate the clear appearance

of the central motif mentioned here in the British plan of the solution of Palestine problem, where the establishment of a Jewish state in part of Palestine is connected with the establishment of an Arab federation. This subject is touched upon and analyzed in G. Cohen, *The British Cabinet and the Palestine Question* (Tel Aviv: Tel Aviv University, 1976).

22. Eylat, 'Antun Sa'adeh – Portrait of an Arab Revolutionary', pp.422–9.
23. CZA S/25-3500, report of 31 March 1940.

7

An Anthropologist as a Political Officer: Evans-Pritchard, the French and the 'Alawis (with Gitta Yaffe)[1]

In 1973 the great British anthropologist, Professor Sir Edward Evans-Pritchard, published a brief autobiographical note titled 'Genesis of a Social Anthropologist'. It was an engaging piece in which the section dealing with the Second World War period is of particular interest. When the war broke out Evans-Pritchard had already acquired a reputation as an anthropologist but not an established academic position. There was in him a restlessness and an adventurous streak which his activities during the war clearly reflected. He served in the Sudan Auxiliary Defence Force, was trained in the use of high-explosives in Palestine, was attached to the Spears Mission in Syria, returned to the Sudan Defence Force, served as the military governor of the Cyrene District in present-day Libya and then became a liaison officer with the Bedouin of that region. His stay in Cyrenaica resulted in an important work, The Sanusi of Cyrenaica. Soon after the war's end Evans-Pritchard was appointed Professor of Anthropology at Oxford.[2]

But while it was his Cyrenaican experience that produced his one important contribution to Middle Eastern studies, it is the section on Syria in Evans-Pritchard's 'autobiographical note' that raises curious questions. In it he wrote that:

> My friend John Hamilton got me attached to the Spears Mission in Syria, which was supposed to liaison with the Free French, though much of the time was spent in quarreling with them. Part of my time was spent in preparing clandestinely for what was rather vaguely called post-occupational sabotage, that is to say, if the Germans came through Turkey into Syria, at the time it was thought they might, I was to remain behind when our more or less token force withdrew and blow up roads, bridges and so forth and send out morse intelligence. I don't suppose that would have lasted long! However, our relations

with the French, in my case liaison with General Montclair [sic], a
brave man who liked having rows, being strained, I felt uncomfortable, especially as Montclair tried to have me court-martialed, and so
asked to be relieved of my duties.[3]

Written some thirty years after the event this brief account is as striking for
what it omits as it is for what it contains. Evans-Pritchard did not mention
that he was the Spears Mission's political officer in Latakia, provincial capital of Syria's 'Alawi region, whose main tasks were to report on the political scene in his area and to liaison with the local French authorities.
Working in close coordination with Sir Edward Spears, Captain Evans-
Pritchard exceeded his own mandate in trying to abort French policy
toward the 'Alawis. It was General Catroux, Free French Delegue General in
the Levant, rather than his own delegue adjoint in Latakia, General Monclar
(Evans-Pritchard curiously misspelled the name), who demanded that the
British authorities investigate Evans-Pritchard's conduct. A Court of Inquiry
set up by General Holmes, Commander of the Ninth Army, found on 16
September 1942, that Evans-Pritchard had 'acted outside the written
instructions for Officers of the Spears Mission'. Assuming, though, that
Evans-Pritchard had acted under verbal instructions from Spears himself,
the court took a light view of the matter. But General Holmes thought otherwise. In his opinion: 'Captain Evans-Pritchard has for some time desired
to be transferred; he is on bad terms with the local French officials, his
reports are coloured and his usefulness impaired. I recommend that he
should be found employment elsewhere. In the meantime he should be
granted leave outside the 'Alawite territory as soon as possible.'[4]

An examination of the specific incident which resulted in the British
Court of Inquiry will cast light on a host of significant issues: British and
French policies and rivalry in the Levant, the confused political circumstances obtaining in the Levant states following the allied invasion, and the
social and political evolution of the 'Alawi community. The role played in
this episode by Evans-Pritchard adds another dimension by touching on
the question of the relationship between the academic study of Middle
Eastern society and participation in its governance.

ANGLO-FRENCH RIVALRY IN THE LEVANT, 1942

Following the invasion of Syria and Lebanon by a predominantly British
force in June 1941 and the surrender of the pro-Vichy forces in July of that
year, a rather complicated arrangement was devised for the governance of
Syria and Lebanon.

On the eve of the allied invasion of Syria and Lebanon, the British persuaded the Free French to issue a declaration of independence for their mandated territories in the Levant. Their argument was that such a declaration would enhance the population's support for the allied cause. In the event General Catroux issued a declaration promising a termination of the mandate but failing to actually terminate it. The British had to settle for his formula and to recognize both the continuation of the mandate and France's nominal pre-eminence in Syria and Lebanon. But the reality was more complex. The De Gaulle-Lyttleton agreement of August 1941, the main document defining the British-French division of authority in the Levant, granted to the British military the supreme authority in matters of security. The distinction between matters of security and political affairs (given to French pre-eminence) in wartime was never fully clarified. In the particular conditions obtaining in the Levant, the resulting confusion was exacerbated by the paucity of French forces, the multiplicity of and lack of proper coordination between British agencies dealing with the Middle East and, above all, by the personality and policies of Sir Edward Spears.

Sir Edward Spears, an MP, a close personal friend of Churchill and a well-known Francophile was charged in 1940 with liaising with Charles de Gaulle and his Free French movement. In this capacity Spears and his staff – the Spears Mission – travelled with the Free French to the Levant. The Levant having become Free France's chief base, the Spears Mission soon settled there in classic bureaucratic fashion. Assuming additional tasks and responsibilities, it acquired a triple brief: British diplomatic representation in the Levant, liaison with the Free French and responsibility for domestic security. Spears himself became the British Minister in Beirut. His mission headquartered in that city, deployed its representatives as political officers in all parts of Syria and Lebanon. Their tasks were to report on local political and security conditions and to liaison with the French authorities. The Spears Mission thus became another British agency dealing with political affairs in the Levant alongside the Foreign Office, the Minister of State's Office in Cairo and the various military authorities.

Under the circumstances it did not take long for a difficult opinionated man with a direct line to the Prime Minister to become embroiled in bureaucratic quarrels with his British military and civilian superiors and colleagues. But this was not the main issue. Far more important for the history of British-French relations and the political evolution of Syria and Lebanon was the fact that Spears had a falling out with De Gaulle and that his criticism of the man and his policies extended also to Free France's policies in the Levant. Spears was converted to the Arab nationalist vision of Syria's and Lebanon's future; Syria as a unified state dominated by Arab nationalists and Lebanon as a state with a special (Christian) character but fully integrated in the Arab world. There was a school, in fact a dominant one, among British officials in the Middle East that saw the Arab national-ist movement as a natural ally of Britain and its victory as beneficial to British interests. From these premises there emanated a rejection of France's pre-eminence in the Levant and the set of French policies that were designed to preserve it.[5]

One of these French policies was the cultivation of 'Alawi separatism. This had been one of the tenets of France's original strategy in her man-dated territories from 1920 onwards. French policy makers regarded the Muslim heterodox and Christian minorities as allies against the Arab nationalism of the urban Sunni elite. In the case of the 'Alawis they were given autonomy within the 'Alawi territory. France's relationship with the 'Alawis was more comfortable than the one they had with the Druze. The 'Alawis' position, just north of Lebanon and along the full length of Syria's coast, placed them in a vital geopolitical position. Their territory could conceivably be used in order to create an area of French control along the whole Levant coast in contradistinction to the hostile hinterland. An important aspect of France's 'Alawi policy was the preservation of the tra-ditional social and political order within the community. The French, in the tradition of Marshal Hubert Lyautey's 'native policies', saw the communi-ty's traditional leaders as natural allies.[6]

In 1936 the French agreed to the incorporation of the 'Alawi territory (along with the autonomous Druze state) into the state of Syria. This was retracted in 1939 when the French-Syrian treaty of 1936 was suspended and the 'Alawi territory again became the *Terriroire Autonome Alaouite*. In January 1942 its status was changed yet again. As a concession to the Syrian government in Damascus, which had been granted nominal independence in September.1941, the 'Alawi territory was converted into an administra-tive province though one enjoying a semi-autonomous status under the title *Mohafazat du Djebel Alaouite* (a similar change was introduced in the Druze region). Regardless of the change in status, the French alliance with the separatist elements in the province was maintained. The Arab nationalists of the Syrian Interior and their local British supporters suspected that the Free French intended to use 'Alawi separatism as the principal instrument of a policy calculated to abort Syrian unity and independence.

Among France's 'Alawi collaborators, Sulayman al-Murshid occupied a particularly important and intriguing position. Murshid started life as a poor shepherd boy in the village of Jobeth Bourghal on the western slopes of the northern part of Jabal Ansariyya. As a teenager he acquired the rep-utation of having prophetic qualities and used this reputation to acquire

wealth and power. 'Alawi society was divided along both tribal and denominational lines. Murshid's ascension to a position of leadership resulted
accordingly in the creation of a new tribal confederation (the Ghassasneh)
which branched out of the Khayyatin (Murshid's own original confederation) and eventually a new denominational grouping (Murshidun). Thus
while other 'Alawi potentates were either religious or tribal leaders this
'new man' combined both capacities in his person.

Many of the methods employed by Murshid in the process of his
aggrandizement were coercive and deceptive. He used both force and ruse
to take over land in dozens of villages and turned the original small hold-
ers into virtual serfs and sharecroppers. By the end of the 1930s Murshid
controlled vast lands and dozens of villages in the northern mountain with
Jobeth Bourghal as his headquarters. He possessed a militia which consisted of a nucleus of several hundred regulars and additional thousands who
could be mobilized in times of need. The government apparatus in that part
of the Mountain, including the courts, was subservient to Murshid. His
position was further consolidated when he was elected to the Syrian parliament.[7]

The French Mandatory Authorities did not intervene in Murshid's activities and acquiesced in his rise to prominence and leadership. This suited a
general policy of refusal to interfere in the domestic affairs of a community whose traditional leadership tended to cooperate with the French
authorities. After 1936, when the issues of Syrian independence and unity
and French departure became pressing, those French who were opposed to
such changes viewed Murshid and other traditionalist 'Alawi leaders as
allies against Arab nationalism. It is against this background that the Bab
Jenneh incident of August 1942 should be seen.

THE BAB JENNEH INCIDENT, AUGUST 1942

On 14 August 1942 a group of Sulayman al-Murshid's retainers came to the
small village of Bab Jenneh, in the Haffe district, north-west of Jobeth
Bourghal. They set about to cut down trees in a piece of land which
Sulayman al-Murshid claimed to have bought. In fact this was the beginning
of a takeover of the village that Murshid had been planning for nearly a year.
Some of the villagers resisted and a fracas followed in which several men
were wounded. Murshid retaliated by expelling some of the villagers and
arresting others. Another group was conscripted to work on a new house
for Murshid.

This would probably have remained yet another incident in the long
series of misdeeds which built Murshid's growing patrimony. But in this

instance there was British intervention, On 16 August Captain Evans-Pritchard, the British political officer in Latakia, accompanied by three other British military, visited Bab Jenneh and Slenfe, where some of the villagers were kept under arrest and Murshid himself was staying in what was described as a rented summer house. Some of the facts remained disputed but it seems certain that Evans-Pritchard used strong language to warn Murshid and the qaimaqam that their conduct and the resulting state of affairs would not be tolerated. Evans-Pritchard then called on the French inspector of the Services Spéciaux and informed him that he was going to make a report to Generals Spears and Wilson on the state of insecurity in which the British troops found themselves as a consequence of the arming of Sulayman al Murshid's partisans.

On 19 August Spears sent a telegram to the Minister of State in Cairo and to the Foreign Office in which he tried to place the Bab Jenneh incident in a much larger context and recommended that the incident be used in order to bring about a showdown with De Gaulle. Spears used a variety of arguments to support his case. He began with a moral argument: Sulayman al-Murshid was exploiting and despoiling poor 'Alawi villagers and the area's Sunni Muslim population with French connivance. He then argued that given the danger of a German invasion (which then loomed as a possibility) it was vital to uphold British prestige among the 'Alawis and to guarantee the latter's goodwill, so as to ensure their cooperation if guerrilla activities had to be organized in the territory. He argued that Sulayman al-Murshid's activities were endangering these prospects and recommended that should General Catroux fail to take action, the British army be instructed to arrest Murshid.[8]

Spears was fully aware of the fact that De Gaulle was visiting the area. In fact it seems that De Gaulle's imminent visit to Latakia and his planned meeting with Murshid in a reception for 'Alawi dignitaries prompted Spears to act. He felt that should De Gaulle receive Murshid formally, the latter's position would be enhanced significantly. The Spears telegram of 19 August was reinforced by a brief memorandum written by Evans-Pritchard on the same day. In it he argued that the French supported Murshid 'for political reasons' and that 'British interests are compromised'. He warned that British prestige in the territory might he ruined and argued that 'As General Monclar lends him every support, it is necessary to remove the General.'[9]

Spears, however, failed to convince either the Foreign Office or the British military authorities in the Levant. On 24 August the Foreign Office replied to the Minister's telegram of the 19th. While it had no objection 'to the Army Commander taking this question up with the Fighting French on security grounds', the Foreign Office was not 'greatly impressed by the strength of our case for political intervention'. The Foreign Office detected in Spears' telegram the notion of seeking to set up the Sunni Muslims of the coastal plains against Murshid and the 'Alawis and rejected it. Its view was that the British should act against Murshid only if he interfered directly with British troops and convoys and it implicitly criticized Spears and his staff by asserting that the Political Officer should be instructed to avoid any interference with 'secular quarrels between Ansariyeh and Moslems and to concentrate on security of British troops and communications in the area'.[10] In a similar vein the Commander of the Ninth Army expressed the view that under the terms of the relevant Anglo-French agreements he had no authority to impose a state of siege as proposed by Spears.[11]

Furthermore, a reading of the minutes written in the Foreign Office prior to dispatching the reply to Spears, reveals the scepticism and reservations held there with regard to his policies. London found discrepancies between the alarming tone of the 19 August telegram and the routine weekly political summaries prepared by the Spears Mission. Gilbert MacKereth, Britain's former Consul in Damascus, a man with a profound knowledge of the Syrian political scene and an acerbic pen, shot large holes in the lines and arguments of both Spears and his political officer in Latakia: 'It is really nonsense to think that 'Amir Sulayman al-Murshid could be built up as a force of native resistance [in the eventuality of German occupation]' wrote MacKereth, 'if he leads 300 men he will certainly plunder everyone and anyone he can'. MacKereth in his familiar disillusioned fashion saw through France's 'cynical' use of Murshid's own harassment of the region's population and the Sunni element's effort to exploit Anglo-French rivalries. But he never lost sight of the larger political picture: 'Unless we are ready, and I gather that we are not, to administer Syria and the Lebanon directly ourselves, we should keep out of this business.'[12]

The Free French, for their part, responded to the Bab Jenneh incident in two ways. When De Gaulle visited Latakia he not only invited Sulayman al-Murshid to a luncheon but also granted him a private interview. Evans-Pritchard was not invited to the luncheon. Then, on 26 August General Catroux responded to a letter sent to him by General Holmes on the 19th. In that letter Holmes complained about the 'growing arrogance and local oppression exercised by Murshid' and argued that his activities endangered military security by undermining the effort to obtain the goodwill of the local population.

Catroux's letter highlights the difference between France's pragmatic (in MacKereth's language 'cynical') attitude to the 'Alawi question and the heavy moralism echoed in Spears' and Evans-Pritchard's pronouncements on the subject. He thus wrote that:

There was not, in the event, an act of terrorization by Sulayman al-Murshid and I should add that it would be exaggerated to use this characterization for this native leader's manner with the local population. It certainly happens that Sulayman al-Murshid commits abuses and from the point of view of our Western concepts of justice these abuses are to be condemned; indeed the administration, be it French or Syrian, acts to limit them. But these acts do not have the effect on the local population that one may have feared in other countries. As you know, the 'Alawis are backward. They live under a feudal regime and submit to it. Sulayman al-Murshid's leadership is not disputed all the more so because it relies on the religious character that many 'Alawis attribute to this leader.

This state of affairs governs our attitude toward Sulayman al-Murshid. He is obeyed, he is feared, he has many supporters and he has arms. It would be a grave political mistake on our part to alienate him and turn him into an enemy by taking a position against him in his disputes with the peasants and above all by taking stern measures against him.

In more practical terms Catroux argued that from a security point of view it was more important to cultivate the goodwill of the powerful Murshid than to alienate him in favor of 'some villagers who can do nothing for or against us'. Murshid had been loyal to France, and would be loyal to her ally Britain if the latter's agents did not threaten him and his position. From this perspective the activities of Captain Evans-Pritchard, Catroux added, were 'inopportune and abusive' and he demanded his immediate removal from the territory.[13]

The next month was spent in British-French arguments over the question of the proper mechanism through which the Bab Jenneh incident could be investigated, and Franco-British differences of opinion over the issue were aired, The Free French wanted a joint Anglo-French Committee formed according to an earlier precedent. General Holmes agreed but on condition that the Committee be given a wide scope and examine the issue in its full context. This was not acceptable to Catroux who insisted that the investigation be limited to the conduct of Captain Evans-Pritchard. To end the stalemate General Holmes appointed a British court of enquiry whose work began on 24 September in Latakia.

The enquiry proved to be a relatively simple matter. The court had before it a complaint cum report by Capitaine Lavarde, the *Services Spéciaux* inspector in Latakia. In his own testimony Evans-Pritchard did not dispute the essence of Lavarde's report. With a great deal of confidence and conviction he argued before the Court of Inquiry that the details of the allegations against him were unimportant. Furthermore, he felt that his actions 'were entirely justified and I should feel bound to act in precisely the same manner were similar circumstances to occur in the future'.

Evans-Pritchard justified his conduct on several grounds. It was a 'paramount duty' of a political officer to maintain public order. From a moral point of view he could not stand by 'watching the poor and weak being plundered by the rich and powerful without making some effort to stop them'. He then added that the goodwill of the general 'Alawi population was essential for the success of the 'post occupational' guerrilla activities which he was asked to prepare. Evans-Pritchard felt also that since the French délégué adjoint in Latakia (General Monclar) was hostile to the British, he could not be relied upon 'in maintaining our prestige and the interests of our army in the territory' so that direct British action had to be taken. Most important he felt that he had acted with the support and implied authorization of his superior, General Spears. If, however, the Court were to decide that Evans-Pritchard had exceeded his instructions, 'I shall be content with that decision because I believe that I was right in acting as I acted.'[14]

As has already been described above, the Court of Inquiry found Evans-Pritchard guilty of a technical infraction of his written instructions, but given Spears' contradictory instructions it took a very light view of the matter. General Holmes, however, thought otherwise and saw to Evans-Pritchard's swift removal from the territory. The General's real anger, however, was directed at Spears and not at his subordinate. In a letter to Spears written on 30 September, he stated that to his mind 'the case is all the more regrettable in that it could have been avoided'. If this jibe was too subtle, the General proceeded to state that the prevailing state of affairs, in which the status of the Military as 'the final responsible authority' was not sufficiently clear, had to be ended. He took on the Spears Mission by complaining that 'at the present time there are too many organizations resulting in too much overlap and insufficient coordination' all the more so since in certain instances unsuitable personnel were being employed.[15]

Interestingly enough, General Monclar, too, was transferred to another post at the end of September. But the Spears Mission came to the conclusion that this was the result of a personal dispute with Catroux that had nothing to do with the Bab Jenneh incident. In fact General Monclar from his new post, continued to deal on occasion with the affairs of the 'Alawi region.

The September 1942 Court of Inquiry and Evans-Pritchard's removal from Latakia had little effect on the underlying conflicts affecting the politics of the 'Alawi community – British vs French, the Arab nationalists of the interior vs 'Alawi separatists, internecine conflicts among the British in the Levant and Murshid's and other 'Alawi landlords' continued efforts to expand their domain at the expense of the 'Alawi peasants. Thus in February 1943 another incident developed in Bab Jenneh which led to violence and subsequently to adjudication.[16] As the July 1943 Syrian and Lebanese parliamentary elections indicated, the British increased their pressure on the Free French to make concessions to the Arab nationalists. In British bureaucratic terms it represented a victory for Spears over his critics, particularly Gilbert MacKereth. Spears, though, overplayed his hand and both he and MacKereth were recalled in 1944. But by then Sulayman al-Murshid had felt the impact of the new circumstances when he was picked up in Beirut in June 1944 by the Lebanese government and handed over to the Nationalist Government in Damascus where he was held under house arrest. The issue of 'Alawi separatism remained, though, as an important bone of contention between British and French and was to explode in full force in 1945. Murshid himself was hanged by the Nationalists after the French evacuation. His followers still constitute a small sub-sect in the 'Alawi region.

Within this train of events the Bab Jenneh incident of August 1942 and its sequel constitutes one important link. Its significance lies primarily in the particularly revealing light it throws on the principal actors in the Syrian scene during the Second World War. Evans-Pritchard's role in this episode is of special interest to social scientists familiar with his contribution to social anthropology and to students of Middle Eastern history who hold his work on the Sanusis in high regard. It is interesting to note that in contradiction to the Sudanese tribes of his early work and the Bedouin of Cyrenaica, 'Alawi society did not arouse his professional interest. Soon after leaving Latakia he wrote a general paper on the 'Alawis (whom he correctly called Nusairies) as a guide for other British officers. It is a rather routine piece of writing in which, interestingly again, greater emphasis was laid on the origins and history of the 'Alawi region rather than on 'Alawi social organization.

From the minutes of the Court of Inquiry and from the brief reference to the incident in his autobiographical note Evans-Pritchard's role in the incident appeared as a combination of bemused flippancy and a sense of mission and moral rectitude. But it would be a mistake to contrast, in this case, British moral rectitude with French cynicism. The British exerted moral pressure selectively. They positioned themselves on the side of the exploited peasants when a French protégé was the villain but failed to apply the same criteria in other parts of Syria where their friends were the landlords.

As an episode in the history of the Levant during the Second World War and in Evans-Pritchard's development as an anthropologist his conflict with Sulayman al-Murshid and the French authorities was not very significant. But it certainly throws an interesting light on the personality of a major anthropologist, and adds raw material to the heart-searching and internal debates among contemporary anthropologists.

In fact, one such debate has been started off by another episode connected with Evans-Pritchard's wartime career. In 1973, the last year of his life, and the one during which his 'autobiographical note' was published, Evans-Pritchard contributed also a piece to The Army Quarterly, a British military journal under the title 'Operations on the Akobo and Gila Rivers, 1940–1941'. In it Evans-Pritchard described his exploits as a bush irregular in the Sudan. The piece was used by Clifford Geertz as the basis for an essay titled 'Slide Show, Evans-Pritchard's African Transparencies'.[17] As he put it, Geertz set out to analyse Evans-Pritchard's 'mode of discourse' not according to one of his 350 anthropological works but according to excerpts from 'a fugitive, out of category, little noticed piece of his, describing his activities as a bush irregular in the Sudan'. He went on to explain that:

> I do this not just to be perverse or cute nor to unmask him as possessed as he certainly was and even defiantly possessed of a colonial mentality – let he who writes free of his time's misgivings cast the first stone, but because the piece ... displays virtually all the characteristics of Evans-Pritchard's way with discourse in a text which his substantive and methodological arguments as an anthropologist do not, save glancingly, figure. Nevertheless, 'Operation on the Okobo' [sic] gives a nutshell image of the limits of Evans-Pritchard discourse that are, as anyone's, the Wittgensteinian limits of the world.

If Geertz used a marginal piece by Evans-Pritchard in order to point out the 'limits of his world', another anthropologist, Ernest Gellner, used Geertz's article in order to express his own opinion on 'the American version of the hermeneutic trend' of which, he says, Geertz is 'a brilliant and distinguished representative'.[18] 'A position,' argues Gellner, 'can perhaps be best understood by seeing what it attacks, and above all, what it attacks with glee.'

Before proceeding to state his views on the 'hermeneutic school' of anthropology, Gellner expressed his opinion on Evans-Pritchard's exploits in wartime Sudan. 'I have no access to evidence about what really happened in 1940–1941', he wrote, 'but I can only say that anthropologists are often uncharitable if not malicious about each other: had Evans-Pritchard been caught out in exaggeration, one would quite probably have heard of it. I have heard stories of that kind about other anthropologists, but none has reached me about Evans-Pritchard ... Evans-Pritchard's war record is not really to our purpose ... What is at issue is his anthropological style, and its weaknesses as corroborated by his reminiscences ...'

Evans-Pritchard's less successful activities in the 'Alawi Mountains and the written record he left in their wake represent the man and his work from a different perspective. The anthropological debate concerning his work and its larger context may well be enriched by a closer look at that episode.

NOTES

1. This article was published in Haim Shamir (ed.), *France and Germany in an Age of Crisis 1900–1960* (Leiden: E.J. Brill, 1990).

2. E. Evans-Pritchard, 'Genesis of a Social Anthropologist – an Autobiographical Note', *The New Diffusionist*, 3, 10 (January 1973), pp.17–23.

3. Ibid., p.20.

4. Lt General W.G. Holmes, General Officer Commanding, Ninth Army, 'Opinion and Recommendation' (August 1942), FO226/238/836.

5. For the history of Anglo-French rivalry in the Levant during the Second World War and the Spears Mission, see A. Roswald, 'The Spears Mission in the Levant: 1941–1944', *The Historical Journal*, 29, 4 (1986), pp.897–919; A. Susser, *Western Power Rivalry and Its Interaction with Local Politics in the Levant, 1941–1946* (Unpublished PhD Dissertation, Tel Aviv University, 1986).

6. See in this volume I. Rabinovich 'The Compact Minorities and the Syrian State, 1918–1945'; M. Kramer, 'Syria's 'Alawis and Shi'ism', in M. Kramer (ed.), *Shi'ism, Resistance and Revolution* (Boulder, CO: Westview Press, 1987), pp.237–54.

7. The best summary of Murshid's career can be found in the seven-page despatch, no. 45 (68/96/45), by the British Minister in Beirut, Terence Shone, to Anthony Eden. FO371/45562/7505 [E2235], 19 March 1945.

8. Telegram no. 269 to Ministate (repeated to FO, no. 419) from Prodrome Beirut, 19 August 1942. FO226/238/836.

9. Memorandum by Captain E. Evans-Pritchard, 19 August 1942. FO226/238/836.

10. FO Telegram no. 381 to British Legation, Beirut. 24 August 1942. F.G. 226/238/836.

11. Telegram no. 288 to Ministate Cairo (repeated to FO, no. 448) from H.M. Minister, Beirut, 27 August 1942. FO226/238/836. In this telegram, a conversation between Army Commander and Deputy Head of Mission is reported.

12. Minute by Gilbert MacKereth, 21 August, 1942. FO371/31474/7617.

13. G. Catroux to W.G. Holmes, Beirut, 26 August 1942. FO226/238/836.

14. Evans-Pritchard's statement before the Court of Inquiry, p.3, ch.6. FO226/238/836.

15. Lt Gen. Holmes to Maj. Gen. E.L. Spears. Ref. 9A/31/ADC. Main HQ Ninth Army, 30 September 1942. FO226/238/836.

16. Spears Mission, Beirut, Weekly Political Summaries no. 47, 24 February 1943, FO371/35175/7658, and no. 49, 10 March 1943, FO371/35176/7658.

17. Clifford Geertz, 'Slide Show, Evans-Pritchard's African Transparencies', *Raritan Quarterly*, Fall 1983, pp.62–80.

18. Ernest Gellner, 'The Stakes in Anthropology', *The American Scholar*, Winter 1988, pp.17–30.

II

ETHNICITY AND POLITICS

8

The Compact Minorities and the Syrian State, 1918–1945[1]

Historians of the modern Arab world tend to emphasize the elements of novelty and discontinuity that were introduced by the period of the First World War and the ensuing Peace Settlement. This perspective stresses such aspects as the dismemberment of the Ottoman Empire, the formation of the Arab states, the establishment of a direct European rule and the replacement of traditional loyal ties by the supremacy of Arab nationalism. A different perspective underlines the importance of patterns and processes, which were transmitted often in a modified form from the late Ottoman period to the Empire's Arab successor states.

One such facet of the transition from Ottoman to Arab rule concerns the dominant role played in the government of the new states by members of the notable families, which had emerged in the eighteenth and nineteenth centuries as a new, local elite in the Arab provinces of the Ottoman Empire.[2] This element of continuity also had an important impact on the relations between the communities, which formed the heterogeneous population of the new states of the Fertile Crescent. Thus, for the sizeable Shi'i communities of Syria and Iraq the Arab governments installed in Damascus and Baghdad represented a perpetuation of the Sunni predominance and hegemony of the Ottoman period.[3]

In this context the relationship which developed between the embryonic Syrian state and the 'Alawi and Druze Communities is of particular interest to the study of both the Ottoman legacy and the issue of inter-communal relations in the Arab successor states of the Ottoman Empire. The two 'compact minorities'[4] shared a number of common characteristics: both were Arabic speaking, closely knit communities based on the solidarity of persecuted Shi'i sects. Both inhabited mountainous areas on the fringes of Syria in which the majority of the community was concentrated and in which that community constituted an absolute majority.

These characteristics had shaped one major aspect of the Ottoman Empire's attitude to the 'Alawis in Jabal Ansariyya and the Druzes in Jabal al-Duruz since the sixteenth and eighteenth centuries, respectively. The Empire was a Sunni state, the upholder and presumably the enforcer of Islamic orthodoxy. Inherent in this fact were tension and conflict with Shi'i communities seeking to preserve their autonomy and separate identities.

In its other aspects this conflict was similar to the conflicts between the Ottoman state and other groups in remote and mountainous areas. The Ottomans and their Syrian governors repeatedly tried to impose their authority in and collect revenue from the 'Alawi and Druze areas. At other times they sent punitive expeditions in the wake of 'Alawi depredations in Western Syria or of Druze interference with the Hajj.

The antagonism was blunted to some extent by the limited scope of Ottoman government and administration, and even more by their growing weakness in the period of Ottoman decline. The 'Alawis and Druzes were not endowed with the status of millets but during much of the Ottoman period they enjoyed virtual autonomy – and the freedom to practise their own religion.

This began to change in the nineteenth century. Like other autonomous sectors in Ottoman Syria, the Druze and 'Alawi communities were confronted with the effective military power and centralizing policies of a modernized state during the Egyptian occupation in the 1830s. The experience was too brief to leave a lasting mark, but the Ottoman state during the final decades of its history demonstrated a tendency and an ability to conduct similar policies. The efforts, which the Ottomans directed at the Druzes, were relatively well documented. Their strategy combined military pressure with a more subtle use of political methods. Militarily the Ottomans were able in 1910 to suppress a Druze revolt (generated by their centralizing policy) and to subdue the entire territory of the Druze Mountain. An interesting feature of their political strategy was the attempt to draw the Druze 'uqqal (spiritual leaders) closer to Islamic orthodoxy.[5]

The destruction of the Ottoman Empire saved the 'Alawi and Druze communities from the full impact of its new might and policies. But the passing of the old order meant that an adaptation had to be made to a new order. The preservation of the community's identity and autonomy now had to be reconciled with new powers, some of which had been marginally relevant in this respect before the First World War. Since 1918 it was evident that a Syrian state would be established. But the nature and boundaries of that state and the status of the Druze and 'Alawi communities within it remained open questions until well into the Second World War. Between 1918 and 1945 the process of establishing a Syrian state and defining the status of the compact minorities underwent six distinct phases:

1) Between October 1918 and July 1920 the Hashemite Amir Faysal, with British help, headed an Arab government in Damascus. While his actual control and British endorsement of it were limited to parts of the Syrian interior, his more radical supporters claimed sovereignty over geographic Syria and in March 1920 proclaimed him King of Syria. Faysal was defeated and evicted from Damascus in July 1920 by the French, who established their rule in those parts of Syria, assigned to them, first by their agreements with Britain and eventually as a League of Nations mandate.

2) In August 1920 the French created the state of Greater Lebanon and, for reasons which are explained below, divided the rest of the area into a number of small states. These included (under a variety of names) a Druze and an 'Alawi state (a state signifying in this context a separate, semi-autonomous entity).

3) Only in January 1925 was a Syrian state reestablished by a merger of the states of Damascus and Aleppo. The 'Alawi and Druze areas remained separated from this state until 1936.

4) In 1936 a treaty was signed (but not ratified) which granted Syria limited independence from French tutelage. It provided also for an incorporation of the Druze and 'Alawi areas into the Syrian state under a special status. This was implemented in 1936 but the process of integration met with great difficulties until its suspension in 1939.

5) Between 1939 and 1943 the two areas remained detached from the state of Syria and were governed by the French with the aid of local separatist elements. In 1941 the Vichy French were replaced by the Free French, whose authority was restricted by Britain, the source of ultimate power in Syria since 1941.

6) In 1943 elections were held and a nationalist government returned to power in Damascus. Gradually with British support it imposed its authority over the Druze and 'Alawi areas and during 1944 and 1945 integrated them fully into the state of Syria.

Syria's repeated oscillation between unity and fragmentation left an obvious mark on the relationship between the 'compact minorities' and the Syrian state as it finally emerged in 1945. Small minorities that have practised and developed the art of survival dread the need to choose between conflicting demands for their loyalty and commitment. In this case the choices had to be made several times within a short span of time and in uncertain circumstances. The nature of the dilemmas which confronted the Druze and 'Alawi communities and their response to them were also determined by

French policy, the outlook and conduct of the nationalist movement in Syria and by developments within the two communities.

The struggle between France and the nationalist movement, which governed Syria's political history throughout the Mandate involved a clash of interests as well as a conflict between two divergent concepts of Syria's essence and future. France's decision in the summer of 1920 to carve the territory of Syria into several units rather than form a single Syrian state marked the triumph of a policy line, which had been advocated since the final stages of First World War. This policy, whose most prominent advocate was Robert de Caix, sought to acquire for France a maximal degree of control and influence in the Syrian littoral and interior in accordance with the Sykes-Picot Agreement. The implementation of this goal was threatened by three chief obstacles: 1) The hostility of Arab nationalism which under the leadership of the Amir Faysal viewed Syria as an Arab country; 2) American advocacy of the idea of national self-determination; 3) A British policy which relied on and supported the Amir Faysal and which viewed French ambitions in the Syrian interior with an indifference tinged with hostility.

In order to overcome this political and ideological challenge a school of thought and an argumentation were developed which claimed that Syria was not a distinct and coherent entity, let alone a national one.[6] The arguments that were used for this purpose ranged from the general to the very specific. Thus, at the end of 1918 l'*Asie Francaise*, the bulletin edited by De Caix, explained that in the Arabic speaking countries there were no 'nationalities' but only religious groups.[7] On several other occasions De Caix explained that Syria was a heterogeneous country, both in religious and ethnic terms and that its political structure should reflect this pluralism. The solution would be a federal organization, which gradually under French supervision and guidance should mature toward unity.

Still, De Caix and like-minded Frenchmen were fully aware of the fact that France's traditional Christian Catholic allies were concentrated in Lebanon and that the Sunni Muslims, the great majority in the rest of Syria, were under the spell of Arab nationalism. Here, the non-Sunni territorially concentrated minorities assumed a great importance for a French policy, which sought to partition Syria and to justify its action in the fashionable terminology of the day. Thus, in October 1918 Foreign Minister Pichon instructed his ambassador in Washington to explain France's position to President Wilson. The President was to be told that the Druze population and the tribes of the Ansariyya in the Syrian littoral should not be subordinated to an Arab-Muslim government of a theocratic nature.[8]

This line was not unopposed within the French government where it was also argued that the (Sunni) Muslims constituted the majority in Syria and that France should come to terms with them, rather than antagonize them.[9] The conflict between these two approaches was still evident in the instructions which General Gouraud, the first High Commissioner, issued to his generals on the eve of Faysal's eviction from Damascus in July 1920.[10] But by the end of August the policy advocated by De Caix, then Secretary General of the Mandatory Government, had won.

It has been pointed out[11] that the mandatory administration in Syria was influenced by and bore resemblance to the model of 'native administration' that had been developed by Marshal Lyautey in Morocco. Lyautey's method was based on indirect rule oriented primarily toward the rural population and based on the promotion of rural and conservative elements, the preservation of traditional society and its protection from rapid change and modernization and reliance on local troops and administrators. Gouraud's approach and that of his advisors was undoubtedly influenced by their own and France's general experience in North Africa, but Lautey's impact on the organization of Syria should not be exaggerated.[12] The decision to partition Syria seems to have been shaped primarily by the antagonism to Arab nationalism and the specific conditions prevailing in Syria, one of which was the existence of the 'compact minorities'. The influence of Lyautey's North African legacy seems to have been mere important in determining the local policy conducted in the Druze and particularly the 'Alawi areas.

'La Politique Minoritaire' which France implemented in Syria has been the subject of an acute controversy. Its critics denounced it as a policy of divide and rule while its defenders claimed that it was a policy suited for the conditions of a heterogeneous country. But even sympathetic observers[13] could not deny a fundamental flaw in the policy which led to the creation of separate Druze and 'Alawi states. Robert de Caix had explained that the federal system created in Syria should eventually lead to a unitary state. But the manner in which France conducted its policy led to the elevation rather than to the removal of the partitions between the political centre and the autonomous states in Syria's outlying areas. When the Syrian state was thus established and given a measure of autonomy in 1936 it had to contend with the difficult task of integrating into its body politic two powerful autonomous communities among whom separatist tendencies had been encouraged during the previous fifteen years.

The task was not rendered easier by the orientation and policies of the Syrian Arab nationalists, most of whom came to be centered in the early and mid-1930s around the Nationalist Bloc. It has been noted above that the social origins of the Nationalist leaders tended to present their government as a continuation of the Sunni hegemony of Ottoman times. This tendency was accentuated by the assimilationist policies of Syria's Arab nationalist leaders and by their attachment to a pan-Arab ideology.

The first exponents of Arab nationalism in the latter half of the nineteenth century, most of whom were Syrian and Lebanese Christians, had a secular conception of a political community in which they could participate on an equal footing. Later a change occurred when the movement was espoused and taken over by Sunni Muslims. The mainstream of Arab nationalism came to be intimately linked to Sunni Islam and acquired a Sunni tincture. Christian and Shi'i Arabs were implicitly (sometimes explicitly) expected to assimilate into the dominant majority but their acceptance not guaranteed.[14]

In that respect, the insistence of the Damascus nationalists on the unification of Syria under their hegemony and their intolerance of local particularism and autonomy was also construed as an attempt to subordinate the non-Sunni communities to their rule. The 'Alawis and the Druzes would have been suspicious of any Damascus government in the 1920s. Still, it would have been easier for them to accept a government upholding a secular-territorial concept of a Syrian state and indicating its awareness and tolerance of Syrian society's pluralistic nature.

Furthermore, the nationalist leaders were pan-Arab nationalists. Ideologically they saw Arab Syria as an ephemeral state pending the creation of a larger Arab one. For minority communities, which constituted a sizeable power in Syria, the prospect of becoming negligible minorities in a large Arab entity was discouraging.

Both the assimilatory and pan-Arab proclivities of Syria's Arab nationalists were given a clear expression in an illuminating book *Unite Syrienne et Devenir Arabe* by Edmond Rabbath. The book, an intellectual platform of pan-Arab nationalism in its Syrian version, addressed itself directly to the problem of the 'Alawis and the Druzes. The solution it offered was simple: the heterodox communities are not different, they simply lag behind: 'En vérité', he adds, 'Aloovites et Druses ne se separent des Sunnites que par les années. Une politique appropriée, servie par des conditions favorables, faciletraient leur rapprochement rapide'. Himself a Christian who immersed himself in political Arabism Edmond Rabbath chose to rely on the example of the Lebanese Druze Amir Shakib Arslan 'qui s'assimile la culture arabe et s'en nourrit de facon si merveilleuse, se retrouve musulman de gout et de cœur'.[15]

But when Rabbath's book was written, the 'favorable' conditions he postulated did not exist. Nationalism in Syria became more pronouncedly integral and the mood of the nationalist leaders less tolerant of differences within Syrian society and of the anxieties and concerns of minority groups. The outlook of the National Bloc was coloured by the activity of several ultra-nationalist active factions in its fringes and in its ranks. Their view of the 'compact minorities' was also influenced by the direction of French policy since 1920. If their autonomy had been fostered by the French as an attempt to break Syrian unity then there was something innately wrong in that autonomy.

These trends were reinforced by another process – the crystallization of Syrian statehood in the territory allocated to the Syrian state by the French. When they signed the 1936 treaty with France the leaders of the National Bloc made a dual concession: they settled formally on a state that was only a fraction of Greater Syria and they accepted in fact the existence of Greater Lebanon. It was a natural corollary of these concessions that their concern with the Arabism of their truncated Syrian state and with their control over it became more intense.

These developments go a long way in explaining the conduct of the National Bloc government in the Druze and 'Alawi areas when the 1936 treaty was partially implemented (though not ratified). The treaty provided for a special regime for the Druze and 'Alawi areas but the Damascus government chose to appoint Sunni nationalist figures as provincial governors in Suwaida and Latakia and, we are told 'filled all the important offices with Damascus Sunnis'.[16] The 'Alawi and the Druze response to their policy was influenced by continued French encouragement on a local level of separatist tendencies and by developments that had taken place within the two communities. The latter will be explained in some detail.

In both communities attitudes toward the Syrian state were closely linked to their own domestic politics and both shared an important pattern: behind a wall of solidarity and cohesion directed against external challengers they were deeply divided into groups and factions. In the Druze mountain the Atrash clan was the paramount local force and until well after the Second World War it continued to exercise a decisive influence on the community's external orientation. Its influence was manifold. The Turshan were themselves sub-divided into factions which formed according to lineage, personality, standing and policy line. It was only rarely that the majority of the clan was united around the leadership and policy of one chief. Also, that policy was likely to be opposed by other clans, fearing Atrash domination and seeking an enhancement of their own position. Thus while the Turshan were as a rule considered pro-British the rival Banu 'Amer were considered pro-French. But in periods of fierce Druze particularism with Atrash domination of an autonomous mountain as a corollary, the Banu 'Amer would shift their own orientation and draw closer to the Sunni nationalists in Damascus. These dynamics were illustrated in the retrospective analysis of the French failure in their relations with the Druze that the former Governor of the Druze mountain Capitain Carbillet wrote in February 1926: 'La famille Halabi ... était hostile au principe même de l'accord, qui créait un état indépendant Druze. Elle eut préféré un rattachement a l'Etat de Damas, parcequ'elle savait qu'avec les Atraches, maîtres du Djebel, les Halabis seraient tenus a l'écart, et auraient peu de functions, malgré la supériorité intellectuelle indéniable de cette famille sur les autres familles du Djebel.'[17]

After the establishment of their rule in Syria the French succeeded in forming a working relationship with part of the Turshan and on that basis signed an agreement, which created the autonomous Druze state. But a series of grave French errors estranged and antagonized the majority of the Druze leadership, which rallied behind Sultan al-Atrash. Sultan was consistently anti-French and had a long-standing relationship with several Arab nationalist leaders in Damascus. His posture vis-à-vis the French and the Damascus nationalists was improved by the option open to him and to other Druze leaders to cross the border and join the Amir 'Abdallah who had his own designs on the Syrian state.

Finally a Druze revolt led by Sultan al-Atrash broke out in 1925 and lingered into 1927. During this period a close alliance was created by Sultan al-Atrash and his followers and a group of Syrian Arab nationalists headed by Dr 'Abd al-Rahman Shahbandar. This alliance enabled the latter to graft the political super-structure of a Syrian nationalist revolt on a military effort invested primarily by the Druze community. The political programme of the Druze Revolt was couched in Syrian and Arab nationalist terms, but this should not be taken to mean that the Druze community or even an important segment of its leadership sought to amalgamate themselves into the Syrian state. The alliance was forged primarily by common hostility to French rule which in 1924 and 1925 appeared to the Druzes as more centralizing and ominous than the Damascus nationalists. Since the revolt ended in defeat the divergence of Druze and nationalist outlooks was not clearly spelt out and was later further obfuscated by a tendentious historiography.[18]

After the suppression of the revolt and until the 1936 Treaty the Druze Mountain remained squarely under French control thinly disguised as Druze autonomy. This was acceptable to a majority of the Druze chiefs who saw no better alternative in the prevailing circumstances. The opposition to this policy line was led by Sultan al-Atrash from his haven in Transjordan and by a group of lesser chiefs in the Druze Mountain. But these traditional elements were supplemented by a new social stratum: a group of younger educated Druze. For them the endorsement of a unionist policy involved two interrelated aspects. One was a new way for manifesting their opposition to the hegemony of the predominant chiefs and families. Another was their expectation that their higher level of education would facilitate assimilation into a Syrian-Arab political community.[19]

In the 1930s, though, politics in Jabal al-Duruz were still conducted along traditional channels and this new stratum was significant as an indication of future trends rather than as an influential political force. The policy of the nationalist government encountered the united opposition of the Turshan and the Banu 'Amer. Their opposition coupled with its own errors obstructed the policies of the Damascus government. Eventually, it had to recall Nasib al-Bakri, the provincial governor, and to replace him with Hasan al-Atrash, the leader of the Druze separatists. The implications of his appointment were not limited to the trilateral relationship between Druzes, French and Syrian nationalists. Hasan al-Atrash had ties to the Amir 'Abdallah who in the more fluid situation which obtained in the Fertile Crescent after 1936 conducted his efforts to extend his rule into Syria in a rather overt fashion.[20]

The political history of the 'Alawi community in the inter-war period was shaped by forces and processes which were in part common to Syria's two 'compact minorities'. But several aspects were unique to Jabal Ansariyya and coloured its relationship with the French Mandatory Authorities and the Syrian nationalists:

1) Unlike the small Christian and Bedouin minorities within the Druze Mountain, there were sizeable Sunni and Christian minorities in the 'Alawite territory. Many of the latter, moreover, were concentrated in the city of Latakia. Latakia had been the seat of the Ottoman local governor and many of its Sunni inhabitants served as landlords to 'Alawi sharecroppers. The 'Alawis in the area, to use Weulersse's elegant phrase were 'a numerical majority but a political minority'. The same relationship existed in a still more acute form between the city of Hama and its largely 'Alawi hinterland. Anti-Sunni feeling among the 'Alawis was therefore not an abstract resentment of a remote political centre but a very concrete grudge.

2) 'Alawi society was deeply divided. The 'Alawi peasant was intensely individualistic and his allegiance was claimed by distinct spiritual and tribal leaders and often by a landlord as well.

3) Its isolation, poverty and social structure inflicted backwardness on the 'Alawi area. This coexisted with a strong feeling of solidarity with and attachment to the community and a sense of exclusiveness and mission.[21]

During the transitional period which followed the end of the First World War various 'Alawi chiefs pursued policies which were oriented towards the French, the British, the Sharifian government in Damascus and the Turkish nationalists in the north. These multifarious policies reflected the diversity and disunity of the 'Alawi community but were also the result of an attempt to uphold its autonomy in a state of confusion and uncertainty. The efforts of the French to improve their authority encountered stiff resistance by an 'Alawi chieftain, Sheikh Saleh al-'Ali, whose revolt was portrayed by later historiography as a (modest) forerunner of the 1925 Druze revolt. Al-'Ali did have ties with Faysal and with Ibrahim Hananu, the nationalist leader in the Aleppo area but was very much preoccupied with internecine 'Alawi quarrels and had no real attachment to Arabism or to the cause of Syrian unity.[22]

When the French consolidated their hold over Syria in 1921 they established their direct rule over the 'Alawi area and administered it as a separate autonomous state. In its technical aspects French policy toward the 'Alawis was very successful. The French Administration was orderly and efficient, enjoyed local cooperation and the reforms it introduced resulted in a noticeable improvement of the standard of living. Even less sympathetic observers had to concede that due to these improvements French rule was popular among the 'Alawis.[23] During the period 1921–36 separatism was predominant among the 'Alawis who appreciated the advantages of French Administration and preferential treatment, their insulation from Damascus and Hamah and their share of government positions in their own territory. The unionist elements were mostly Sunnis and to a lesser extent Christians, the latter resentful of what they regarded as 'Alawi over-representation in the local government.

The availability for the first time in a long period of orderly and benign government and its grafting on the traditional social structure had diverse repercussions on 'Alawi society. The ferment and the quest for social advancement at least for their offspring prompted numerous 'Alawi families to invest in education or to have a son enlisted in the French *troupes spéciales*.[24] A more traditional manifestation of existing agitation and expectations was the rallying of thousands around the person of Sulayman al-Murshid. Murshid, a young shepherd suffering from epileptic fits, began his career in 1923 as a soothsayer and thaumaturge and acquired within a short span of time a fortune and a political following. Murshid became a power in the land and but for his humble origins was hardly different from the veteran tribal leaders and feudatories who came from such families as Kanj and 'Abbas. The later phases of Murshid's rise to power lend themselves to a cynical interpretation, but the millenarian aspects involved in his early career are unmistakable. When the first, more unruly, stage of Murshid's career was over, he became acceptable to the French authorities who sanctioned his new status. This suited a general French policy of encouraging the diffusion of power among the 'Alawi chieftains so as to prevent the emergence of an all-powerful source of local power.[25]

Sulayman al-Murshid's political standing ceased to be a local matter and assumed an all-Syrian importance in 1936 when the 'Alawite territory became part of the Syrian state. Murshid and other 'Alawi leaders vacillated between cooperation with and opposition to the new authorities. His considerations were clearly of a pragmatic order. Unlike the Druzes who constituted about 3 per cent of Syria's population the 'Alawis accounted for over 10 per cent of the population and their impact on national politics in a unified Syrian state could be considerable. For a time, Murshid, who was elected to the Syrian Parliament, and other traditional 'Alawi leaders seemed to have hoped to retain and even enhance their position in a unified Syria. Broader regional developments – the weakening of British and French positions, the gains made by various nationalist movements – reinforced this trend. But later the tide turned. France failed to ratify the treaty with Syria and at least part of the French personnel stationed in the area encouraged separatist tendencies among the 'Alawis.

The Unionist Party in the 'Alawi territory continued in the late 1930s to draw most of its strength from the Sunni urban population. But it attracted also an increasing number of 'Alawis who saw Syrian unity as inevitable. It is significant that like other Arabic speaking non-Sunni minorities before them these 'Alawis concluded that assimilation was a prerequisite for successful integration. Thus, in July 1936 a group of pro-unionist religious and political leaders met in the small town of Kardaha and published two separate manifests in the Damascus press. They argued that the 'Alawis were true Arabs and true Muslims. The arguments as well as the evidence brought forth to support them are most illuminating.[26]

As in the case of the Druzes, unionist trends among the 'Alawis were facilitated by the spread of education. The same process led also to the appearance of a novel form of political organization – the ideological party. In the late 1930s it was primarily the PPS (acronym for the French language name of the Syrian Social Nationalist Party).[27] The PPS expounded a doctrine of secular territorial pan-Syrian nationalism and appealed to several young educated 'Alawis. Like their Christian forerunners in the nineteenth century these recruits were seeking to form a new political community in which they could participate as equal members. The idea of a secular territorial Syrian nationhood and statehood was an anathema to Arab nationalists and never struck roots in Syria. But the appearance of the PPS and, a few years later, of its rival the Ba'th, in the 'Alawi area had momentous consequences for the eventual history of the 'Alawi community and the Syrian state.

It was during the Second World War that the future of the Syrian state and its constituent parts was finally decided. The most important changes affecting Syria which occurred during the war were the fall of France and the invasion and conquest of Syria in 1941 by a British army supported by auxiliary Free French Forces. Ultimate power and authority now rested with Britain (but a vague division of responsibilities with the Free French contributed to the creation of an ambiguous political situation).

When Britain invaded Syria several fundamental questions regarding its future had yet to be resolved by the British government. The fluidity of the situation was reflected by Churchill when he wrote that he was not 'sufficiently acquainted with Syrian affairs to be able to formulate a plan for the creation of the Syrian state'.[28] At that time the British were preoccupied with the immediate wartime considerations and their order of priorities was clear: to guarantee the cooperation first of the French troops in the Levant, then of Turkey and only as a third alternative to mobilize the support of the Syrian Arab nationalists. So loose was the notion of Syrian statehood at the time that the British offered the area of Aleppo to Turkey and seriously considered Syria's inclusion in a larger Arab federation.[29]

By 1943 a different and a more coherent British policy crystallized. It favoured the creation of a unified independent Syrian state under the leadership of the National Bloc. Britain's Syrian policy was formulated and conducted on different levels by a number of military and civilian agencies, but a particularly important role was played by the Spears Mission. A typical product of wartime conditions, the Spears Mission originated as a liaison unit with the Free French forces and developed into a chief instrument of British policy in the Levant.

As interpreted and executed by Sir Edward Spears until his recall in 1944 this policy viewed De Gaulle's efforts to preserve France's position in the Levant as injurious to Britain's immediate and post-war interests. From the same vantage point separatist tendencies in the 'Alawi and Druze areas and even insistence on a special status or guarantees were perceived as French-inspired attempts to obstruct the formation of a united and independent Syria. Thus the political officer stationed by the Spears Mission in Latakia wrote in June 1942 about the 'Alawis that: 'This compact minority in addition to being well-armed and tenacious as fighters controls the whole coastline of Syria and could under French pressure put separatist claims backed by breaches of public order giving the French an excuse to impose direct rule again in Syria.'[30]

Britain's support inspired the National Bloc's leaders with certainty that following their return to power in 1943 Syria's independence and unity were inevitable. Self-confidence also bred obtuseness to the anxieties of the minorities and underlay a policy which sought to integrate and fully assimilate the Druze and 'Alawi areas into the Syrian state.

The leadership of the Druze community in Jabal al-Duruz was quick to perceive the practical political implications of the changes which had taken place in Syria. With France weakened, the traditional policy of preserving Druze autonomy by playing the French and the nationalists one against the other was no longer viable. Britain, the traditional friend of the Druzes, acquired a predominant position in Syria, but chose to exercise its influence in order to enforce Syrian unity rather than promote Druze particularism. The one alternative option which seemed open to Druze leaders seeking to secede from Syria or to acquire leverage vis-à-vis Damascus was to flirt with the Amir 'Abdallah. The Amir was trying to exploit the wartime state of flux in order to pursue his plan to establish a Greater Syrian state under his rule. Malcontent Druzes across his northern border were one natural target of his efforts. Several of them, including Hasan al-Atrash maintained their contacts with 'Abdallah throughout the Second World War (and later as well), but these contacts led to no sustained or effective political action.[31]

The Amir Hasan's flirting with 'Abdallah represented, moreover, an exception rather than the rule. The Atrash family as a whole reached the conclusion that the cause of Druze autonomy was lost. They decided, therefore, to ride the tide of unity and anticipate the Damascus government, their rival clans and the unionist party in the Jabal. The Turshan approached the National Bloc government of their own initiative and proposed to abolish the autonomy of the Jabal and incorporate it fully into the Syrian state. Aware of their motives the nationalists were slow to respond. Once they did, early in 1944, the process of unification was carried out with great fanfare. But the British political officer who observed and recorded this process remained disillusioned: 'The enthusiasm which this event aroused throughout the Jabal', he wrote, 'cannot, however, be taken as a true measure of the satisfaction of the population ... it is always easy to get the Druze to demonstrate for or against anything if given the lead by their chiefs.'[32]

Conditions in the 'Alawi area were different and by far more complicated than in the Druze Mountain. For one thing, France was much more deeply entrenched among the 'Alawis and her commitment to their autonomy was a matter of sentiment as well as of political calculation. 'Alawi fear and distrust of the Damascus nationalists, the existence of a nationalist Sunni minority among them and the authoritarian proclivities of the nationalist leaders were all bound to make the incorporation of the 'Alawi territory into the Syrian state a lengthy and painful process.

This process was then given a peculiar twist by the policy of Sir Edward Spears. Spears and other British officers in Syria shared the suspicions of the political officer in Latakia, that the French were encouraging 'Alawi separatism as an artifice designed to obstruct the course of Syrian independence and to perpetuate their own influence. They saw French support of Sulayman al-Murshid and their efforts to harmonize his relations with other senior traditional 'Alawi leaders as well as a variety of other measures taken by the French as confirming their suspicions.[33]

Their suspicions were not entirely unfounded, but long before they could be verified Spears deliberately chose to challenge the French on the 'Alawi issue. By so doing he tried in the summer of 1942 to forestall their alleged plans. But he also sought to demonstrate to all concerned – France, Syrian nationalists and 'Alawis – the frailty of France's position and Britain's supremacy in the Levant. Spears based his tactics on the allegation that Sulayman al-Murshid was a brigand, that he had accumulated his landed wealth by extortion, that his conduct threatened to undermine public order in a sensitive area and that Murshid endangered the security of British troops. At that time Spears' efforts were foiled by watchful British officials in Cairo and London who wanted to avoid an unnecessary confrontation with the Free French, understood the slenderness of Britain's case and the implications of British involvement in the social structure and the domestic politics of the 'Alawi community.[34]

But the line advocated by Spears in 1942 finally triumphed in 1944. Murshid, who had been elected to the Syrian parliament in 1943, was seized in Beirut and held in an illegal house arrest in Damascus for several months.[35] His arrest was part of a firm and uncompromising attitude that the Syrian government displayed with regard to the 'Alawi area. Other manifestations of the same attitude were the appointment of a Sunni nationalist as provincial governor and the 'Sunnification' of the local government and administration.

This policy encountered some 'Alawi resistance, part of it fomented by zealous French officers. But on the whole the 'Alawis like the Druzes fully grasped the new reality. In February 1945 the British minister, Terrence Shore, quoted the opinion of 'competent British observers' who believed that 'the 'Alawis would not have acquiesced in the extension of Syrian government control during the past year if they had not believed that this was in accordance with the wishes of the British authorities.'[36]

The nature of the available sources tends to present the problem of the 'Alawi area during the Second World War primarily through the prism of Anglo-French rivalry in the Levant. But the issue had several other intriguing aspects. One was the interaction between the 'Alawi community and the political system of the nascent Syrian state part of which it was becoming. Thus, as a sizeable minority the 'Alawis controlled ten seats in the Syrian parliament and could decide the fate of political factions and individual

politicians. The National Bloc was torn by internecine strife and as a consequence simultaneously with the process of amalgamating the 'Alawi area
various nationalist leaders were trying to recruit 'Alawi supporters in
1943–45 against their own partners.[37] The Bloc's leaders also found it difficult to undermine the political position of Sulayman al-Murshid in the
'Alawi area. His landed wealth was an important source of his political
power and any attempt to confiscate his lands was bound to have repercussions in other parts of Syria. The nationalist leaders whose own power
derived from similar sources were understandably reluctant to open an
agrarian Pandora's Box.[38] In 1945, then, the Syrian state and the 'Alawi
community were not two solid and coherent entities clashing with each
other but heterogeneous systems interlaced with one another.

The assimilation of the Druze and 'Alawi areas into the Syrian state was
completed during the first years of Syrian independence. In both areas the
military power of the state had to be exercised against the opposition of
traditional upholders of local autonomy. Murshid was executed by the
Syrian government soon after independence while the conflict with the
traditional Druze leadership occurred under the authoritarian regime of
Adib Shishakli. But these traditional patterns of the state's relations with the
compact minorities were of marginal importance in independent Syria.
The significant fact was that as a result of the social and political developments of the previous decades, large numbers of Druzes and 'Alawis were
concentrated in the ranks of the Syrian army and ideological parties – the
Ba'th and the PPS. Consequently they were catapulted into the centre of
Syrian politics in the 1950s and 1960s with far-reaching repercussions for
both state and community.

NOTES

1. This article was published in *Journal of Contemporary History*, 14, 4 (1979), pp.693–712. Research for this
   paper was facilitated by a Ford Foundation grant, administered through Israel's Foundations Trustees.
2. Cf. C.E. Dawn, 'The Rise of Arabism in Syria', *Middle East Journal*, 16 (1962), pp.145–68, and A.H.
   Hourani, 'Ottoman Reform and the Politics of Notables', in W.R. Polk and R.L. Chambers, *Beginnings of
   Modernization in the Middle East* (Chicago: University of Chicago Press, 1968), pp.51–68.
3. See A. Kelidar, 'Religion and State in Syria', *Asian Affairs*, 61 (New Series, Vol. V), (1974), pp.16–22.
4. The term was coined and made current by P. Rondot and A.H. Hourani.
5. J. Weulersse, *Le Pays de Allouwites* (Tours: Arrault, 1940), pp.113–16. First part of D. McDowall, 'The Druze
   Revolt 1925–1927 and its Background in the Late Ottoman Period' (B. Litt thesis, St John's College,
   Oxford, 1972), as well as chapter 8 of M. Ma'oz, *Ottoman Reform in Syria and Palestine 1840–1861* (Oxford:
   Clarendon Press: 1968).
6. This marked a departure from a French line of thinking, which claimed that Syria was a distinct, non-
   Arab entity. See Kamal Salibi, 'Islam and Syria in the Writing of Henri Lammens', in B. Lewis and P.M.
   Holt (eds), *Historians of the Middle East* (London: Oxford University Press, 1962), pp.330–42.
7. Quoted in D. Eldar, 'France's Policy in the Levant and French Attitudes to Arab Nationalism and
   Zionism, 1914–1920' (PhD Dissertation, Tel Aviv University, 1978) [in Hebrew].
8. France MAE (Ministere des Affaires Etrangeres). Levant, Syrie-Liban, Dossier General, Vol. 3, quoted by
   Eldar, 'France's Policy in the Levant and French Attitudes to Arab Nationalism and Zionism,
   1914–1920'.

9. Ibid.

10. See Gouraud's 'Directives Politiques' in file 6 B3, Commandant Superieur des Troupes du Levant, 1917–1939 in the French Military Archives.

11. E. Burke III, 'A Comparative View of French Native Policy in Morocco and Syria, 1912–1925', *Middle Eastern Studies*, 9, 2 (1973), pp.175–86.

12. For the difference between Gouraud's methods of ruling Syria and Lyautey's original model in north Africa, see Burke, 'A Comparative View of French Native Policy in Morocco and Syria', p.179.

13. Weulersse, *Le Pays de Allouwites*, pp.119–21.

14. See R. Haddad, *Syrian Christians in Muslim Society: An Interpretation* (Princeton, NJ: Princeton University Press, 1970), pp.70–98.

15. E. Rabbath, *Unité Syrienne et Devenir Arabe* (Paris: Marcel Riviere, 1937), pp.200–210.

16. Public Record Office, FO371 31472, Weekly Political Summary of the Spears Mission, 1 June 1942. The mistakes committed by the Nationalists in the Druze Mountain are described in M. Homet, *L'Histoire Secrete du Traite Franco-Syrien* (Paris: J. Peyronnet, 1938), pp.247–58.

17. See Carbillet's memorandum 'La Paix avec les Druzes', in MAE, Dossier General, Vol. 193. A considerable portion of the documents available on Mandatory Syria in the French diplomatic archives deal with the Druze Revolt. Of particular interest are the perceptive instructions with which Colonel Catroux (then the delegue in Damascus), provided his emissary, Trenga upon his departure for Suwaida on 1 July 1921. These are available in file 3 B3 in the papers of the Commandant Superieur quoted above.

18. McDowall, 'The Druze Revolt 1925–1927 and its Background in the Late Ottoman Period', pp.377–84; see also in this volume I. Rabinovich, 'Historiography and Politics in Syria'.

19. Shibli al-'Aysami, Dawd Nimr and Mahmud al-Shufi, *Muhafazat al-Suwayda* (Damascus, 1963), pp.187–92.

20. One episode during which part of the Turshan tried to involve the British Consul in Damascus in their dealings with 'Abdallah took place in December 1938 and January 1939. See FO371 23276.

21. Weulersse, *Le Pays de Allouwites*, pp.199–21 and *Paysans de Syrie et du Proche Orient* (Paris: Gallimard, 1946), pp.87, 270–8.

22. Weulersse, *Paysans*, p. 118 and 'Abd al-Latif Yunis, *Thaurat al-Shaykh Salih al-'Ali* (Damascus, ND).

23. Report by Captain Mott Radcliffe on the situation in the 'Alawi area written at the end of 1941, FO371 27319 and a review of political events in Iraq, Syria and Lebanon by an unnamed British analyst in the Spears Papers, St Antony's College, Box II, File IV.

24. For an analysis of the social changes which occurred during this and the somewhat later period see M. Van Dusen, 'Intra and Inter Generational Conflict in the Syrian Army' (Unpublished PhD Dissertation, Johns Hopkins University, 1971), pp.314–19.

25. For a description of Murshid's career see Weulersse, *Paysans*, pp.275–8, and the lengthy memorandum by Terence Shoe, the British Minister in Beirut, FO371 45562, 25 March 1945.

26. The activities of this group and excerpts from the manifestos were recorded by one of its members Munir Sharif in his *al-'Alawiyyun min hum wa-ayna hum* (Damascus, 1946). The date of publication is significant.

27. Van Dusen, 'Intra and Inter Generational Conflict in the Syrian Army'.

28. Churchill's memorandum, 'Our Syrian Policy', 19 May 1941, reproduced in G. Cohen, *Churchill and Palestine* 1939–1942 (Jerusalem: Yad Izhaq Ben-Zvi, 1976), pp.82–4 [in Hebrew].

29. Eden memorandum, 'Our Arab Policy', 27 May 1941 reproduced in Cohen, *Churchill and Palestine* 1939–1942, pp.85–8. The British government's attitude to Syria's place in a prospective Arab federation is discussed on pp.30–51 in the Hebrew language section of Cohen's book.

30. Weekly Political Summary of the Spears Mission, 1 June 1942. FO371 31472.

31. Weekly Political Summary of the Spears Mission, 15 September 1943. FO371 35182.

32. Report by the British Political Officer in Suwaida, 28 October 1944. FO371 40306.

33. See for instance the Weekly Political Summaries of the Spears Mission for 9 and 16 February 1944. FO371 40300 and 371 40299.

34. Several telegrams were exchanged between Beirut, Cairo and Damascus in August 1942, which dealt with this issue. FO371 31474.

35. During October 1944 Murshid was again the subject of an acrimonious debate within the British government. See FO371 40318. In March Robin Hankey of the Foreign Office noted in a minute on Shone's memorandum (see n.34) that 'the Syrians took action against Sulayman al-Murshid at Sir E. Spears' instigation'.

36. Memorandum by Terence Shone, 25 March 1945. FO371 45562.

37. Weekly Political Summaries of the Spears Mission, 16 and 23 June 1943. FO371 35177.

38. Beirut Telegrams of 9–12 March 1945. FO371 45553.

9

Syria: *A Case of Minority Might*[1]

The Gulf crisis and the Gulf War as the key issues of international politics during the latter part of 1990 and the early months of 1991 generated considerable, albeit superficial, interest in Iraq's politics. While it was mentioned but not sufficiently recorded, the fact was that Saddam Husayn and the core group of his regime came from a minority community representing some 20 per cent of Iraq's population. This is not only a key factor in Iraqi politics, but also one clue to the complexity of ethnic relations in the Middle East. It is easy to assume that in the Middle East, majorities invariably dominate minorities, but as this chapter will show, this is not always the case. Furthermore, Saddam Husayn and the Sunni community's supremacy in Iraq is not the most significant case of minority rule in the Middle East. It is the 'Alawi community's control of Syrian politics that provides the most intriguing exception to the common pattern of majority rule and the attendant need to protect the minority or minorities' rights.

The Middle East is an area rich in ethnic diversity and the twenty-odd states that inhabit it offer a rich variety of relationships between the communities of which their populations are comprised. At one end of the spectrum stands Egypt, with a majority of about 90 per cent Muslims and a Coptic-Christian minority of up to 10 per cent. At the other end of the spectrum is Lebanon, a true mosaic composed of several communities, while the other states of the region are ranged in between. Thus, Saudi Arabia has a rather homogeneous Arab Sunni population but also a sizable Arab Shi'i minority in its eastern province; Jordan is divided along the line separating the East Bankers from Palestinians; and Turkey, comprised of an overwhelming Turkish Muslim majority, contains within its territory a concentrated Kurdish minority as well as the legacy of the Armenian and Greek minorities problems.[2]

It is difficult to generalize against this diverse background. But all the same, it is clear that minorities do not enjoy full rights and proper protection in the Middle East. The failure of the constitutional and the democratic experiments in the Middle East, the Islamic tradition of acceptance and recognition of minorities, albeit as inferior in status, and the structure and political dynamics of most states in the region have resulted in a situation whereby the majority (or the grouping in power) shaped the state according to its own lights and relegated the minorities, or other excluded groups, to a subordinate position. The one effort to form a pluralistic political system in the region (Lebanon) collapsed in the mid-1970s.

Mention has already been made above of the contrast between Egypt and Lebanon in terms of their ethnic composition. This comparison can be expanded in order to illustrate some of the major elements in the relationship between majorities and minorities in the Arab world.

Egypt has been Muslim since the seventh century. Most Islamic states did not seek to force the conversion of the non-Muslim subjects – a policy continuing that of earlier empires, and resulting also from an obvious unwillingness to lose a major source of income – the poll tax imposed on non-Muslims. However, given the centralized nature of the Egyptian State and government and the country's topography, a gradual process of conversion took place through the centuries that resulted in the present proportional division of the population between Muslims and Christians. In the 1930s a process began that culminated in the 1950s and led Egypt to embrace Arab nationalism as its national ideology. But Arab nationalism never held complete sway over Egypt, and a sense of a distinct Egyptian nationalism buttressed by the powerful Egyptian state sometimes waned and sometimes thrived. Thus, despite Muslim-Coptic tensions exacerbated by the agitation of large fundamentalist Muslim groups, Muslims and Copts in Egypt are also united by a bond that is often absent in the Arab states of the Fertile Crescent.[3]

The Fertile Crescent is the term denoting the area presently occupied by the states of Syria, Lebanon, Israel, Jordan, Iraq and the Palestinian Authority. It is in this region that Arab nationalism was born in the late nineteenth century and has been particularly strong and influential. The Arab states in this region are characterized by ethnic and communal diversity, if not fragmentation. Mention has already been made of Lebanon as a mosaic society. Syria's population can be divided into an Arab Sunni Muslim majority of roughly 60 per cent and several minorities that comprise the other 40 per cent. Among these minorities the two schismatic Shi'i sects, the 'Alawis (about 11 per cent) and the Druze (about 3 per cent), as well as the Kurds (Muslim Sunni but not Arab, about 10 per cent), and the Christians (about 10 per cent), should be mentioned. Iraq's population is divided into three major blocs and a host of small minorities. The Shi'i Arabs are the single largest community and in all probability constitute an absolute majority of over 50 per cent. The Sunni Arabs comprise some 20 per cent, as do the Kurds.

Earlier in this century in the territory of British Mandatory Palestine, the lines of division were quite simple: there was a significant Palestinian Christian minority but Palestinian society was dominated by an overwhelming Muslim-Sunni majority whose hegemony was reinforced, as elsewhere in the region, by a long tradition of Sunni domination that was manifested in the Ottoman State. Likewise, the Bedouin tribes and small urban population east of the Jordan were overwhelmingly Sunni. But the political turmoil, particularly in 1948 and its immediate aftermath, confused the situation and resulted in the transformation of the Jordanian Emirate into the Hashemite Kingdom of Jordan. That state, having annexed the West Bank, came to have a Palestinian majority, so much so that this has remained the case even after the loss of the West Bank in 1967. All percentages and proportions that have been cited above are based on evaluation rather than hard statistics or the findings of a census. As we shall see presently, these issues are sensitive in all states of the region, and the Arab states whose official credos maintain that their population is simply Arab ignore or suppress ethnic and communal lines in any project concerned with demography. This is also true of Jordan, where both the regime and the Palestinians are not eager to establish what may very well be a Palestinian majority east of the river. The regime would like to maintain the essence of a Hashemite rule resting on a Jordanian entity and East Bank loyalism, while the Palestinians are wary of playing into the hands of Israeli ultra-nationalists who claim that Jordan is Palestine.[4]

Before turning to an analysis of the ethnic politics of Syria and Iraq, the issue of Sunni-Shi'i relations in Islam should be briefly explored. The break between Sunni (Orthodox) and Shi'i (Heterodox) is the single most important schism in the history of Islam. The largest Shi'i communities developed outside the confines of the Arab world (Iran and India), but important Shi'i communities can be found in Iraq, Lebanon, Syria, Yemen and the Arabian Peninsula. The Shi'a are divided among themselves into the Imami group, the Twelvers (Iran, Iraq, Lebanon, etc.) and the more radical Isma'ilis. The 'Alawis and the Druze are regarded as sectarian offshoots of the radical Shi'a. Islam was never as preoccupied with Orthodoxy as was Christianity, but under close scrutiny the 'Alawis and the Druze would fall outside the pale. In recent decades, the historic conflict between Sunnis and Shi'is in the Arab world has manifested itself either in a competition for power in specific States (Iraq, Lebanon) or as a subtler struggle over the nature of Arab nationalism. Two passages written by astute Arab intellectuals of Shi'i extraction are illustrative and significant in the context of the present article.

Thus, complained 'Abbas Kelidar: 'The collapse of the Ottoman Empire was to offer the [Arab Sunni] leaders the opportunity to assert the position of their community, a position of primacy in Islam. They came to the conclusion that they had a divine right, almost a God-given right, to lead the new community, now called a nation.' Fouad 'Ajami, in a very personal piece, wrote in a similar vein that the Shi'ites were the 'stepchildren' of the

Arab world. As 'Ajami put it, 'in the principal cities they were strangers, a people of the countryside. To its Sunni Orthodox, they were sectarians. Modern Arab nationalism never quite accommodated them.'[5] In the past few years the relationship between Sunnis and Shi'is has been transformed by the Islamic Revolution in Iran in 1979, the build up of Iran's position as a regional power, Iran's cultivation of Shi'i groups in several Arab countries as a constituency and, more recently, the American war in Iraq, the toppling of Saddam Husayn's regime and the shift of power in Iraq to the Shi'i community. The Sunnis states' anxiety and response have become a key issue in the politics of the region.

When the British founded the state of Iraq, they made two significant decisions that had a decisive influence on the course of Iraqi political history for the rest of the century. First, they added the province of Mosul to the provinces of Baghdad and Basra thereby including a Kurdish minority of 20 per cent in an otherwise Arab state. Second, they installed King Faysal and an Arab nationalist Sunni establishment in power. By so doing, they perpetuated the Ottoman policy of relying on the Sunni minority in an area bordering on the rival Shi'i state of Iran. For the Iraqi state, this has meant a virtual disenfranchisement of the single largest group in the country.

The significance of this British choice was enhanced and exacerbated by the Sunni bias and tincture of Arab nationalism. Arab Christians in the Levant played an important role in the genesis of Arab nationalism in the nineteenth century. But the idea, and subsequently the movement, were taken over by members of the Sunni majority. The bond between Arabism and Islam has been one of the cardinal elements in Arab nationalist thought as it developed in the twentieth century. Several interesting attempts were made by Christian Arabs to formulate a secular doctrine of Arab nationalism or to replace Arab nationalism with a territorial alternative, but during the half century of Arab nationalism's ideological domination (1920–70), they were all defeated. In the context of Syrian politics, the single most important effort of this kind was invested by Michel 'Aflaq, one of the founding fathers of the Ba'th. The address he gave in 1943 at the University of Damascus on the occasion of the Prophet's birthday, illustrated the difficulty faced by a Christian-Syrian Arab who sought to reconcile Islam's preponderant role in the formation of the Arab nation with his quest for equal status in a Syrian-Arab political community. It is against this background that the spectacular transformation of the 'Alawi community from a backward and downtrodden group to the dominant element in the Syrian State should be described and analysed.

As a geographic term, Syria had traditionally referred to the territory of geographic Syria or the Syrian lands. The modern state of Syria is a product of the wartime agreements made between France and Britain during the First World War, the politics of the ensuing peace conference, and subsequent French policy in the 1920s and 1930s. In that state, Arab nationalism was the dominant ideological force, and urban notables subscribing to it were the preponderant political force. These notables dominated the Syrian state when it became independent in 1945.[6]

During Syria's early years of independence, relations between majority and minorities developed along familiar lines. The country's ruling elite, drawn mostly from notable Sunni families from Syria's four largest cities, took their primacy for granted. Not only did it perpetuate the pattern of earlier centuries, but for most Arab Sunnis Arabism and Islam were to be largely overlapping and complementary. Upon obtaining independence, Syria faced minority problems resulting both from the country's ethnic composition and from the French policy of encouraging minority separatism as an instrument designed to help the French in their conflict with the urban Sunni leadership. At first the political leadership of the young Syrian State sought to solve the problem by a mixed policy of dealing gently with non-problematic minorities and harshly with the difficult ones.

Thus, following a time-honoured Middle Eastern practice, they gave the country's Christians a small guaranteed representation in parliament, but the 'Alawis and Druze, the 'compact' territorially concentrated minorities, who had enjoyed autonomy under the French, were confronted with the might (such as it was) of the Syrian state and its army.[7] All traces of territorial autonomy were eradicated, and the 'Alawi separatist leader Sulayman al-Murshid was hanged by the Damascus government.[8]

Less perceptibly, Syrian politics were infused by an ethos of Arab nationalist and Muslim Sunni hegemony, and all other groups were implicitly expected to conform. The tensions generated by this atmosphere burst out into the open in 1950, when the Constitution was drafted by the regime of Adib Shishakly. Following the nearly universal practice in the Arab world, the draft text of the Constitution stated that Islam was the religion of the state. This brought forth a stream of protests by Christian leaders, who argued that they were being relegated to the status of second-class citizens. Their campaign was supported by a small group of secularists. The controversy ended with a compromise: Islam was not proclaimed the state religion, and the Constitution stipulated instead that the President of the state must be Muslim and that Islamic jurisprudence shall be a chief source of legislation.[9]

While this controversy was raging, a process of change had already begun in Syria that in the 1960s would transform the relationship between majority and minorities. Adib Shishakly was the country's third military dictator. Unlike his two predecessors, he was not a mere power-hungry army officer but the product of the ideological movements of the 1930s and 1940s. These parties had failed to acquire any real political power but came to have an enormous influence by instilling ideas of radical nationalism, secularism and socialism in important segments of Syria's youth, including a large proportion of cadets in the country's new military academy.

It was this twin process that in the 1950s brought army officers to power, led several of the country's radical ideological parties at least to the fringes of power, and consequently contributed more than anything else to the spectacular rise of the 'Alawi community.

The 'Alawis were concentrated in the province of Latakia, along the coast in north-western Syria. During the Ottoman period, they were a marginal, backward and down-trodden community. The Ottoman state did not seek to enforce its authority in this remote region and during most periods was satisfied with the collection of taxes and the maintenance of a minimal degree of public order. The population, mountainous and rural, was divided along tribal and denominational lines. It was exploited by its own chiefs and by the Sunni landlords residing in the cities of Hama and Latakia.[10]

Important changes came with French mandatory rule. The French created an 'Alawi territorial autonomy, modernized the area to some extent and attracted a fairly large number of young 'Alawi men to their auxiliary forces in the Levant. Two new avenues were thus opened for the region's youth: military service and education. Education entailed politicization, which led in turn to participation in radical ideological politics. 'Alawi young men were attracted primarily by two ideological parties: the Syrian Social Nationalist Party (advocating a radical form of Greater Syrian nationalism) and the Ba'th. It is the Ba'th's influence among the 'Alawi youth of the 1940s that is of particular interest in the context of this article.

Of the three founding fathers of the Ba'th party preaching a blend of secular Arab nationalism and socialism two came from minority communities – Michel 'Aflaq was a Greek Orthodox Christian and Zaki Arsuzi was an 'Alawi, while Salah al-Bitar was a Sunni-Muslim. It is hardly surprising that members of minority communities would formulate a secular nationalist ideology designed to obliterate their minority status and that such an ideology would appeal to the educated youth of minority communities.

By the 1950s, the politicization of the Syrian military and the militarization of Syrian politics, coupled with the high proportion of 'Alawis in the ranks of the Syrian army, brought a sizable number of 'Alawi officers into Syria's political arena. The country's stormy history during the decade lasting from 1954 to 1963, culminating in the establishment of the Ba'th regime in March of that year, accelerated the process.

It so happened that most of the members of the small nucleus that planned and staged the Ba'thi *coup d'état* of 8 March 1963 in Syria were members of minority communities – 'Alawi, Druze and Isma'ili. Much ink has been spilled in Syria and elsewhere by critics and enemies of the Ba'th regime in an effort to argue and prove by virtue of this fact that the March coup and the regime that emerged from it were the product of a 'minority plot'. The accusation is false. But there is no denying the fact that the preponderant role played by officers from the minority communities in the establishment of the Ba'th regime launched processes that (a) gave both military and civilian members of these minority communities the decisive role in the Ba'th and its Syrian politics after 1963, at the expense of the previous urban Sunni governing elite; (b) catapulted the 'Alawi community from marginality and obscurity to the center of Syrian politics; and (c) turned the question of inter-communal relations in Syria into one of the key issues in the Syrian political arena.[11]

Following the brief discussion of these three consequences, this chapter will address in some detail the relationship between the present Syrian regime and the country's Sunni majority.

During the Ba'th's first three years in power (March 1963–February 1966), several conflicts among its constituent factions were played out: the party's founding fathers against its young guard, supporters of Egypt's 'Abd al-Nasir and his foes, radical revolutionary socialists against pragmatic moderates, civilians against the military, and a host of individual leaders and personal factions against other blocs. Eventually all factions coalesced into two large coalitions. The final showdown took place on 23 February 1966, when the coalition headed by Salah Jadid and Hafiz al-Asad defeated its rival and established the second phase of the Ba'th regime (February 1966–November 1970).

Both Jadid and Asad were 'Alawis, and the communal factor played an important role in the conflict that culminated in the February 1966 coup. Again, many attempts were made to reduce Ba'thi politics in the years 1963–66 to a conflict between the 'Alawis and their sectarian allies, on the one hand, and the Sunnis on the other, but this is a simplistic explanation. As we have seen, many forces were at work during that period, communal solidarities and animosities being but one of them in a society where primordial loyalties play an important role. It was natural for officers and politicians fighting for survival to rely on family members, neighbours and others who also happened to be members of the same community.[12]

At some point, the issue was also introduced explicitly into the political arena, in all likelihood by Sunnis who tried to reinforce their position by working against a 'minority takeover'. The latter's response must have been a greater show of solidarity. Indeed, in the final analysis, when the lines were drawn for the confrontation of February 1966, communal solidarity was in many cases the overriding consideration in many officers' decisions to throw in their lot with Jadid and Asad.

In any event, in the aftermath of the February 1966 victory, the proportion of 'Alawi, Druze and Isma'ili officers in the core of the regime became even higher. Then came the conflict between the 'Alawi and Druze officers and the elimination of the Isma'ili faction which left the 'Alawis as the one minority community at the centre of Syrian politics. The fact that the next round of the conflict took place between two 'Alawi officers and their factions (Jadid versus Asad) had little impact on the Syrian public's perception that it was ruled by 'Alawis.

So far, we have dealt mostly with the process that led army officers, members of the 'Alawi community, to the centre and summit of Syrian politics. But these developments obviously had a great impact on the community as a whole. Hafiz al-Asad and the other army officers and party militants who went into politics were never emissaries or representatives of their community, but when Asad's regime was established in November 1970, it had an 'Alawi colouring and Asad relied, and has continued to do so, on the 'Alawi community as one of the foundations of his regime. In practical political terms, it makes little difference that Asad came to power at the end of an unplanned process. The important fact is that he and his community found themselves in power and realized that the regime's fall would have enormous negative repercussions for the whole community. There is, thus, a great degree of identification between Asad's regime and the 'Alawi community, although for obvious reasons considerable efforts are invested in limiting, disguising and denying this bond. Entailed in this course of events were important gains for the community, as well as for many of its individual members. Large investments were made in the 'Alawi region, and many 'Alawis moved to Damascus and other cities to occupy positions in politics, the governmental bureaucracy and the public sector.

To what extent, then, can Hafiz al-Asad's regime be defined as an 'Alawi regime? The regime possesses an impressive array of political institutions designed to create the impression that it is a Ba'th Party regime enhanced by popular representation and partnership with other 'progressive' forces. There is a grain of truth in all of this, but, in the final analysis, political power in Syria resides in the hands of Hafiz al-Asad and the small group of trusted confidants which constitutes the core of his regime. Within this group and among the trusted officers who command the important units of army forces and intelligence services, the number of 'Alawis is very high, out of any proportion to their share in the general Syrian population.[13]

In any event, in the Sunni public's perception the country is governed by an 'Alawi regime, a social and political revolution it has found difficult to accept, particularly in the major cities of the country. For one thing, the rise of the 'Alawis and the dispossession of the traditional elite reversed an order that had existed for a very long time. Furthermore, not only political power was taken away from the Sunnis, but the nationalization and the agrarian reforms of the 1960s transferred Sunni property directly and indirectly into 'Alawi and other rural hands. The fact that the 'Alawis had been a despised lot in Syria in earlier decades and centuries added insult to injury. The transfer of power in Syria had been made all the more acute by the authoritarian nature of the Ba'th regime since 1963. Not only did the Sunnis lose power but they had few channels and arenas in which to articulate or present their grievances, wishes and interests.

There is also an important religious dimension to this antagonism and conflict. As stated, most Sunnis do not accept the 'Alawis as proper Muslims. As early as 1964, the Muslim Brotherhood and other Orthodox groups and members of the religious hierarchy played a leading role in articulating and expressing the urban Sunni opposition to the Ba'th regime. This role is to be explained by more than one factor. Resentment of the Ba'th as a secularist party, socio-economic grievances and the availability of a communications and recruitment network through the mosques all converged to emphasize the role of religion and religious men in leading the opposition to the Ba'th regime. Thus, in the spring of 1967, a mass protest was organized in Damascus and other Syrian cities when it became known that a Syrian army journal had published a piece written by an 'Alawi junior officer who denied God's existence. Many Sunnis refused to live under the rule of the regime they regarded as un-Islamic and irreligious but they did not possess nor could they marshal the resources necessary for overthrowing the Ba'th.

The issue of the Ba'th regime's denominational affiliation and identity came to a new head after November 1970 when Hafiz al-Asad established his regime and made public his intention of assuming the presidency of the state. For many Sunnis it was one thing to have an essentially 'Alawi regime disguised by most of its institutions and another to live in a state formally ruled by a President regarded as less than a full Muslim. The question had a formal aspect, as well, that was embedded in the constitutional compromise of 1950. If the President of the state was supposed to be a Muslim, then, in their eyes, Hafiz al-Asad could not be the President of Syria. When Asad released a draft of his first Constitution in February 1973, it generated a wave of demonstrations and protests which forced him to back down and reinstate the original formulation of 1950 which he had sought to delete.[14]

Asad had the power necessary to quash the opposition with force. But this would have gone against his fundamental strategy – appeasement of the urban Sunnis. Asad, in fact, offered the Sunnis an entente of sorts – they would relinquish all pretence and aspiration to political power and he, in turn, would moderate the radical socio-economic policies of the 1960s, enable them to thrive and would not interfere with their lives as long as they did not dabble in politics.

For several years this policy seemed to work. But in 1976–77 it collapsed and an offensive by radical Muslim groups against the Asad regime was launched which culminated in an open revolt that raged in several Syrian cities in 1979–80. The best-known and most terrible events of this revolt happened two years later when a final assault against the regime was launched in the city of Hama and was put down with unprecedented brutality.[15]

The Syrian crisis of the late 1970s derived from numerous sources but the fundamentalist Muslim offensive against Asad's regime was its single most important dimension.[16] It should be seen as part of the larger wave of Islamic fundamentalism that swept the Middle East in the late 1970s though in Syria it acquired a distinct local character. If in Egypt Muslim fundamentalists sought to topple a regime they saw as secular and un-Islamic, then in Syria the cutting edge of their wrath was directed at the 'Alawis. They saw and presented themselves as acting in the name of Islam but also in the name of the disenfranchised Sunni majority which they claimed to represent. This comes out clearly in their various manifestos. Thus, a publication directed at western audiences argued that:

> From an Islamic standpoint, then, the religious beliefs and practices of the Nusairis set them off as a distinct religion, neither Islamic, nor Christian, nor Jewish, and it has always been the consensus of the Muslim 'ulama', both Sunni and Shi'i, that the Nusairis are kuffar (disbelievers, rejecters of faith) and idolaters (mushrikun) ... Furthermore nine or ten per cent of the population cannot be allowed to dominate the majority because that is against the logic of things, and we are quite sure that the wise men of the sect agree with us that neither we nor they are obliged to support the empire of Hafiz and Rif'at Asad. In our case, the sectarian war was not waged by the majority trying to protect itself against the domination of the minority. It is definitely the minority that forgot itself and took no notice of the facts of history

and its strict logic in its unsuccessful attempt to force its oppressive domination over the great majority of the population.[17]

The Sunni revolt against Asad's regime during the years 1977–82 had far-reaching consequences for the relations between the minority and majority in Syria. Asad was forced to relinquish his original strategy of appeasing the Sunni majority. The fundamentalist revolt could not be 'surgically' eliminated. The rebels found harbour and refuge in sympathetic Sunni quarters and in order to eliminate them large segments of the Sunni population of such cities as Aleppo and Hama had to be brutalized and even killed. A new balance of terror was struck between the regime and the Sunnis. Special forces including the elite unit composed largely of 'Alawis and commanded by the President's brother were used against the Sunni population. The regime made it abundantly clear that it was willing to go to any length in order to protect itself and survive. Hafiz al-Asad is not the Shah of Iran. The Sunnis did not and do not have the means of contending with the force, power and political sophistication of Asad and his regime. They also learned the lesson of the abortive revolt and allowed no new opposition to plant itself in their midst.

In the decade since 1982, the Asad regime has not faced any serious opposition from outside its own ranks. But the antagonism of the silent Sunni majority lingers on. Asad is aware of it and takes it into consideration. It has affected his conduct in Lebanon and his policy toward the Palestinians. One reason for the caution with which Asad treads in Lebanon is his anxiety that his Lebanese policy not be seen in Syria as a partisan and sectarian promotion of 'Alawi interests. Likewise, his personal animosity toward Yasir 'Arafat has been moderated by his awareness of the degree to which many Syrians view the Palestinian leader as a Sunni figure. But perhaps the most interesting recent manifestation of Sunni-'Alawi tensions in Syria occurred in the summer of 1990 after Saddam Husayn's invasion of Kuwait and Asad's participation in the coalition led by the US. There was opposition to and criticism of Asad's policy on Iraq which reflected to some extent support and admiration for Saddam Husayn and his message. It is difficult to document but there is a clear sense that many in Syria sympathized with Saddam Husayn as a Sunni leader, thereby also expressing their disenchantment and unhappiness with the nature of Hafiz al-Asad's regime. It is only one of the many ironies of contemporary Middle Eastern politics that the idol of many Syrian Sunnis was himself a representative of a minority ruling over an unhappy majority in his own country.

NOTES

1. This article was published in the *Israel Yearbook on Human Rights*, 21 (1992), pp.1–13. Research for this article has been supported by a research grant from the German-Israeli Binational Research Foundation (GIF).

2. For a general survey of Middle Eastern communities and communal structure of the Arab states, see G. Baer, *Population and Society in the Arab East* (New York, NY: F.A. Praeger, 1964); see also in this volume Itamar Rabinovich, 'Arab Political Parties: Ideology and Ethnicity'. The classic work dealing with the relationship between majority and minorities in the Arab world is Albert Hourani's *Minorities in the Arab World* (London: Oxford University Press, 1947). Baer's book brought Hourani's work and data up to date. The volume, edited by J. Esman and I. Rabinovich, drew on a conference that sought to recast the issue in concepts and terminology developed by the social sciences in the intervening period.

3. See N. Safran, *Egypt in Search of Political Community Community: An Analysis of the Intellectual and Political Evolution of Egypt, 1804-1952* (Cambridge, MA: Harvard University Press, 1961); I. Gershoni and J.P. Jankowski, *Egypt, Islam and the Arabs: The Search of Egyptian Nationhood, 1900–1930* (New York, NY: Oxford University Press, 1986).

4. For an original and interesting analysis by an Arab scholar of the complex relationship between Jordanians and Palestinians in the Jordanian State, see the review essay by A. Kelidar in *Middle Eastern Survey* (1987), pp.382–5. See also U. Dann, 'The "Jordanian Entity" in Changing Circumstances', in I. Rabinovich and H. Shaked (eds), *From June to October* (New Brunswick, NJ: Transaction Books, 1978), pp.231–41; also by the same author, 'Regime and Opposition in Jordan since 1949', in M. Milson (ed), *Society and Political Structure in the Arab World* (New York, NY: Humanities Press, 1973), pp.146–81.

5. See A.R. Kelidar, 'Religion and State in Syria', *Asian Affairs*, 16–22 (1974). See also Fuad 'Ajami, *The Dream Palace of the Arabs: a Generation's Odyssey* (New York, NY: Pantheon Books, 1998), and his article in the *Wall Street Journal*, 28 September 2005.

6. See, in this volume, I. Rabinovich, 'Syria and the Syrian Land: The Nineteenth-Century Roots of Twentieth-Century Developments'.

7. See, in this volume, I. Rabinovich, 'The Compact Minorities and the Syrian State, 1918–45'.

8. Kelidar, 'Religion and State in Syria', n.4.

9. B. Winder, 'Islam as the State Religion, A Muslim Brotherhood View in Syria', *The Muslim World*, 49 (1954), pp.215–26.

10. The classic work on the 'Alawis in Syria is Jacques Weulersse's book, *Le Pays des Alaouites* (Tours: Arrault, 1940).

11. By now a thoroughly rich literature has been published dealing with the rise of the 'Alawis in contemporary Syria. Among the major works dealing with this issue mention should be made of Nikolaos van Dam, 'Middle Eastern Political Clichés: 'Takriti' and 'Sunni Rule' in Iraq; "Alawi Rule" in Syria, A Critical Appraisal', *Orient*, 21 (January 1980), pp.42–57; N. van Dam, *The Struggle for Power in Syria: Sectarianism, Regionalism and Tribalism in Politics, 1961–1980* (London: Croom Helm, 1981); Hanna Batatu, 'Some Observations on the Social Roots of Syria's Ruling Military Group and the Causes for Its Dominance', *The Middle East Journal*, 35, 3 (1981), pp.331–44.

12. For a sophisticated analysis of the various factors at work in Syrian politics of the mid-1960s, see M. Seymour, 'The Dynamics of Power in Syria since the Break with Egypt', *Middle East Survey*, 6, 1 (1970), pp.35–47.

13. The question is dealt with extensively in two biographies of Asad. P. Seale, *The Sphinx of Damascus: The Struggle for the Middle East* (London. I.B. Tauris,1988); M. Ma'oz, *The Sphinx of Damascus – A Political Biography* (London: Weidenfeld and Nicolson, 1988). Seale's book, written on the basis of unusual access to Asad, is of particular interest in reflecting the regime's apologetic arguments in this and other sensitive spheres.

14. For a full treatment, see Kelidar, 'Religion and State in Syria', n.4.

15. See the different treatment of this question by Ma'oz, *The Sphinx of Damascus* and Seale, *The Sphinx of Damascus*, n.13.

16. For a sophisticated analysis of the root causes of the crisis of Asad's regime, see Yahya Sadowski, 'Ba'thist Ethics and the Spirit of State Capitalism: Patronage and the Party in Contemporary Syria', in P.J. Chelkowski and R.J. Pranger (eds), *Ideology and Power in the Middle East* (Durham, NC: Duke University Press, 1988).

17. Umar F. Abdallah, *The Islamic Struggle in Syria* (Berkeley, CA: Mizan Press, 1983), pp.48, 211. See also M. Kramer, 'Syria's 'Alawis and Shi'ism', in M. Kramer (ed.), *Shi'ism, Resistance and Revolution* (Boulder, CO: Westview Press, 1987), pp.237, 254. Nusairis is another term used to denote the 'Alawis, a term the 'Alawis themselves regard as pejorative.

10

Arab Political Parties: Ideology and Ethnicity[1]

In May 1976 Karim Pakradouni, a Lebanese of Armenian extraction, a lead-ing member of the Lebanese *Kata'ib* Party (the Phalanges), and a confidant of President-elect Elyas Sarkis, was sent by the latter to Damascus with a message to Syria's President Hafiz al-Asad. In the course of their lengthy dis-cussion, Asad told his visitor how he had explained the complexities of Lebanese politics to an earlier visitor, Libya's prime minister, 'Abd al-Salam Jallud. 'One should begin', Asad said to the prime minister, 'by defining such words as 'nationalism' and 'isolationism.' If the *Kata'ib* are considered 'isolationists' because they want to keep the Lebanese entity outside the orbit of Arab unity, what should one call those like Kamal Junblat, who want to keep half the Lebanese isolated in Lebanon's very interior?' Asad contin-ued with an invective against Junblat, the most important leader of both the Lebanese Left and the Druze community, and leader of the Progressive Socialist Party. Asad too was critical of the traditional Lebanese system and its failure to reform itself, but, he argued, 'A distinction should be made ... between true national reforms and the sectarian demands of the national movement'. He charged, 'According to his attitude, Junblat is conducting a religious war against the Christians. In this there lies a danger for Arabism.'[2]

This conversation between the disillusioned 'Alawi leader of the Syrian Ba'th Party and the doctrinaire Sunni prime minister of Libya, as reported to the Christian Phalangist emissary, is but one of the numerous ironies produced and insights afforded by Syria's intervention in the Lebanese Civil War. It can also serve as an excellent introduction to the study of the relationship between Arab ideological parties and the ethnic structure and problems in an important part of the Arab world.

It is difficult to speak in sweeping terms about ethnic politics in the Arab world as a whole. There is an especially marked difference between Egypt, which is closest to the West European model of a nation-state, and the states of the Fertile Crescent, where the definition of the political community is still contested and the population is divided along religious, communal, and ethnic lines. Ethnicity is a factor in Egyptian politics, but a minor one. It is a cardinal and sometimes a governing factor in the political life of Syria, Lebanon, Iraq, Jordan and the Palestinian Arabs.

This divergence is naturally reflected in the orientation, structure, and ideology of the political movements and parties that grew up in Egypt and in the Fertile Crescent. Ethnicity played an important role in the formation and subsequent development of the Egyptian Communist Party, but not in those of the more central *Wafd, Misr al-Fatat* and the Muslim Brotherhood. This is clearly not the case with a large number of parties and movements in the Fertile Crescent, five of which – the Syrian Social Nationalist Party, the Ba'th Party, the Lebanese *Kata'ib* Party, the Muslim Brethren in Syria, and the Communist Party we will look at below.

It is almost banal to point to the relationship between any of these parties and particular ethnic groups or problems. But other issues should be explored too. How did a party's ethnic roots or composition affect the formulation of its doctrine? How important was the ethnic factor in comparison with the other elements that shaped a movement? What relationship was there between the party and the state or states in which it operated, and between it and the community with which it has been identified or affiliated? How was the party's development affected by differences and divisions within that community? And finally, what transformations have these parties and movements undergone since they were founded in the 1920s and 1930s?

These five parties and movements were chosen for practical reasons. They offer a gamut wide enough for illustrating the complexity and richness of the subject, yet they are sufficiently circumscribed to be manageable.

THE SYRIAN SOCIAL NATIONALIST PARTY

The Syrian Social Nationalist Party (the PPS, according to the acronym of its French name) was founded secretly in Beirut in 1932 by Antun Sa'adeh, a Greek Orthodox Lebanese who spent his formative years in Brazil and returned to Lebanon in 1929.[3] Sa'adeh formulated and expounded a doctrine of secular territorial Greater Syrian nationalism. Geographic Syria (present-day Syria, Lebanon, Israel, the Palestinian Authority and Jordan, to which at a later stage Iraq and Cyprus were added) was defined as a national entity. According to Sa'adeh, nations were formed by countries, and a Syrian entity and a Syrian nation were formed in the land of Syria. But Syria and the Syrian nation were dismembered by the peace settlement of 1918–20, and that settlement had to be undone. A Greater Syrian state, in which the Syrian nation would be reunited, should be established. The enemies of Sa'adeh's ideas and party were the defenders of the territorial status quo – France and the Lebanese state – and the other contenders for the same territory or parts of it, Arabism and Zionism.

Sa'adeh's ideas had numerous roots – secular notions of territorial nationalism that arose in Ottoman Syria and Lebanon in the late nineteenth century, Christian and French-inspired concepts of a Syrian, non-Arab entity, and general dissatisfaction with the dismemberment that resulted from the post-First World War settlement in the Levant.[4] But Sa'adeh reflected also the dissatisfaction of the Greek Orthodox community with the Lebanese state. It was a state dominated by the Maronites and protected by the French. The Greek Orthodox, a large though diffuse group in Greater Syria, were relegated to a secondary position in Lebanon. As we shall see below, the Greek Orthodox community in the Levant has been an effervescent group, closer to Arab nationalism than other Christian communities, and active in several ideological parties. In Lebanon the PPS became the chief conduit for the community's disenchantment with the existing order and its aspirations for transforming and transcending it.

In the 1940s the party spread to Mandatory Palestine and Syria. While some of its important members were in Palestinian, the PPS never became a significant actor in Palestinian politics. But its impact on Syrian politics was powerful. A number of important Syrian politicians – Akram Hourani and Adib Shishakly, to name two – received part of their political schooling in the ranks of the PPS, and it was one of the first parties in Syria to understand the importance of cultivating a following in the army's officer corps.[5] In the early 1950s the party emerged as the rear guard of the Syrian Right, but it was defeated by the Ba'th and the Communists and disappeared from the scene as an effective political force.

Authoritative data are not available, but it is possible to characterize the communal appeal of the three main branches of the PPS. In Lebanon the party attracted mostly members of the Greek Orthodox community, and to a lesser extent members of other communities who were dissatisfied with the Lebanese political order – Sunnis and Druzes. In Syria the impact of Sa'adeh's personality was not so strong, and in the 1940s it was primarily the party's doctrine of secular territorial nationalism that attracted members of the minority communities – heterodox Muslims and Christians – who felt that they could not become full members in a polity defined explicitly or implicitly on the basis of Sunni Islam. The notion of secular Syrian or Arab nationalism had originally been formulated by Syrian and Lebanese Christians in the second half of the nineteenth century. For later generations in a different political configuration, the same underlying problem still presented itself. In Syria of the 1940s, the politicized youth of the 'compact' heterodox Muslim communities – the 'Alawis and the Druzes – were added to the Christian minorities as seekers of a secular political community. Among these communities, the PPS and the Ba'th

(with its doctrine of secular Arabism) were the principal competitors for
the hearts and minds of the ideologically bent youth. It is in the 'Alawi
region that this conflict has been best documented. The line would sometimes divide a single family. One telling example is the Jadid family. Two
brothers, Ghassan and Fu'ad, became army officers and PPS members and
were implicated in the 1955 assassination of 'Adnan al-Maliki, the last-
ditch effort by the PPS to check the Ba'th. A third brother, Salah, was a
Ba'thi officer and from 1963 to 1970 was one of the Ba'th regime's principal leaders.

Among the party's Palestinian members, communal origins appear to
have been a secondary issue – the Sayyigh brothers were Christian, and
Hisham Sharabi was a Muslim. Judging by Sharabi's memoirs, they were
attracted by Sa'adeh's personality and by the atmosphere and the intellectual stimulation that the PPS generated in the early phases of its history.
They may also have felt that the party's doctrine was a more sophisticated
way of mobilizing support against the Zionists than the Arab nationalist
short-lived effort in the early 1920s to define Palestine as 'Southern Syria'.
Since the mid-1950s, the PPS has been for all practical purposes a Lebanese
party, and it was in Lebanon that the party underwent further changes and
transformations. While Sa'adeh was absent from Lebanon during the
Second World War, a pragmatic trend seeking to operate within the
Lebanese state appeared, but was quashed by Sa'adeh upon his return.
Following Sa'adeh's execution in 1949, the party entered a lengthy period
of ideological and political confusion. Its activity as a pro-western force in
Syria of the 1950s was matched by close cooperation with President
Camille Chamoun in Lebanon. An effort to mend fences with the apparently victorious doctrine of pan-Arab nationalism in 1961 was contradict-
ed by participation in an abortive *coup d'état* against President Fu'ad Shihab
in December of the same year.[6]

In the late 1960s the party's legacy among its former Palestinian member was manifested through the Palestine Liberation Organization's (PLO)
adoption of the notion, or slogan, of 'a secular democratic state' in
Palestine.

In the early 1970s a new phase in the party's history in Lebanon began
with consolidation of Hafiz al-Asad's Syrian Ba'th regime and the related,
gradual disintegration of the Lebanese political system. The PPS became a
pro-Syrian force and in a sense completed a circle, because it was working
at the service of a force seeking hegemony in the area of Greater Syria and
fighting for a transformation of the existing order in Lebanon.

Authoritative data concerning the communal composition of the PPS
are not available, but certain general trends can be observed. The party still

draws a large part of its membership from the Greek Orthodox community and is still seen to some extent as a representative and defender of that community's interest. But during the last decades the party has recruited heavily, or at least tried to recruit, among other communities – Shi'ites, Druze and Sunnis. For them the PPS was one of the revisionist parties identified more closely with Syrian policy.

It is interesting that most of the party's achievements among the Shi'ites were erased by the rise and development of *Amal. Amal* was a genuine expression of the Shi'a community, and once it acquired legitimacy and effectiveness it could easily displace the PPS. But some of the party's losses among the Shi'ites were made up for by recruitment among Walid Junblat's Druze rivals in Southern Lebanon. In the absence of state authority, protection of party and militia became even more crucial. As opponents of the Junblats and their party, the PSP, these Druze have tended to join the PPS.

THE BA'TH PARTY

The Ba'th Party was founded in the 1940s, but its origins can be traced to the 1930s – Michel 'Aflaq's and Salah al-Bitar's flirtation and subsequent conflict with communism, Akram Hourani's activity in Hama, Zaki al-Arsuzi's activity in Alexandretta and Damascus, and the short-lived career of an important but little-known party, the League of Nationalist Action.[7] Like the PPS, the Ba'th attracted a generation that was dissatisfied with the social and political order, impatient with the traditional leadership and its style, and seeking a comprehensive ideology and all-embracing organizational framework. And also like the PPS, the doctrine and the party appealed to people from several countries – Syrians, Lebanese, Iraqis, and Palestinians. But while the PPS became a party of the Radical Right, the Ba'th placed itself on the leftist side of the Arab ideological spectrum.

The original doctrine of the Ba'th sought to combine a secular formulation of pan-Arab nationalism and a non-Marxist approach to socialism and social reform. These elements proved attractive to different groups. In Syria the party drew many Christians and heterodox Muslims who (like Michel 'Aflaq, one of the party's founders and the principal formulator of its ideology) saw a secular definition of Arabism as a solution to their problem. But though it had a disproportionately large number of members from the minority communities, the Ba'th was not a minoritarian party; Sunni Muslim Syrians were attracted by the elaboration of a pan-Arab nationalist ideology, or in other cases by the vision of a humane Arab socialism that was different from the materialism and internationalism of the Communist movement.

In other parts of the Fertile Crescent, the Arabism of the Ba'th proved to be more appealing than its socialism and secularism. In Lebanon the party attracted members from communities that were hostile to the Lebanese state, particularly Sunnis and Greek Orthodox. In Iraq it was a small party until the early 1960s, when it transpired that a powerful party organization had been developed clandestinely. The pre-1963 Iraq Ba'th did not have a particular appeal to either Sunni or Shi'ite Arabs and was indeed described as 'a genuine partnership between Sunnis and Shi'a 'poor Arab' youth'. They were attracted by the party's socialism and pan-Arabism – many of them saw 'Abd al-Karim Qasim's regime as a deviation from the Arab mainstream but were reluctant to join an outright Nasserite organization.[8]

The Ba'th's capture of power in Syria and Iraq, particularly in the former, and its success in building unusually durable regimes, turned it into a party identified with ethnic politics and minoritarian rule. To a large extent the Ba'th was a victim of its own success. During its first years in power the party was a complex entity, representing numerous social groups and ideas. Its regime consolidated the existence of an independent Syrian state and effected a social and economic revolution in Syria. But in later years, when these driving forces had been spent, the regime became preoccupied with power and survival. As we shall see below, because power was concentrated in the hands of one ethnic group, the 'Alawis, Syrian politics since the late 1960s has been increasingly identified with the conflict between those seeking to preserve and those seeking to topple the power of the 'Alawis.[9]

When the Ba'th came to power in Syria in 1963, the ethnic or communal issue was but one of the dividing lines in Syrian politics. Alliances, rivalries, and factions were formed along personal, ideological, regional, and generational lines, along the line separating the military from the civilian and according to communal affiliation.

The increasing importance of the communal issue derived originally from the over-representation of the minorities (Christians and heterodox Muslims, 'Alawis, Druze, and Isma'ilis) in the ranks of the Ba'th, particularly its military wing. This contributed to the antagonism between the regime and the predominantly Sunni population of Syria's large cities. For the latter, the Ba'th was a radical and irreligious regime that stripped Syria's traditional elite of its political power and part of its social and economic power and planned to continue along the same lines. That Syria's new rulers were, or were perceived to be, largely or predominantly minoritarian added insult to injury.

In the internecine conflicts of the Ba'th regime, communal solidarity and communal suspicion and hostility proved more powerful than other factors. Furthermore, once this element was introduced it acquired a dynamic of its own. 'Alawi, Druze, and Isma'ili officers congregated against Sunnis in February 1966. Later, the Druze and the Isma'ilis were purged and the 'Alawis remained paramount. Within the regime other issues predominated, but in the relationship between regime and population the communal factor became overriding.

The establishment of Hafiz al-Asad's regime in November 1970 contributed both to an exacerbation of the problem and a temporary attenuation of it. Asad's presidency aggravated the challenge to devout Muslims, who as we shall see do not view the 'Alawis as proper Muslims and who regard a regime headed by an 'Alawi as illegitimate. During his first six years in power, Asad pursued a successful strategy that sought to conceal the regime's 'Alawi inner core and to mitigate the conflict with the urban Sunni population.

This strategy collapsed in 1977. The regime quashed the challenge presented by the opposition in the years 1977–80, but its continued existence has since depended on power and deterrence, rather than on the more subtle strategy of earlier years. Furthermore, Asad's illness and the beginning of a war of succession has underlined two interesting aspects of Syria's ethnopolitics.

One concerns the relations between 'Alawis and Sunnis in the regime, the party, and the army. 'Alawi predominance never meant exclusive rule and control. 'Alawis constitute some 12 per cent of the population, and over-represented as they might be, they could not hope – and indeed wisely never tried – to hold even a plurality of the political and military positions within the regime. Instead, 'Alawi predominance meant that 'Alawis had been nimbly placed in many key positions. The power struggle now adumbrated in Syria will not necessarily be conducted along communal lines, but it is possible that fear of their collective downfall and its consequences is already having a restraining effect on the 'Alawi officers.

The question has been raised in the past and is made all the more acute by the present circumstances with regard to the relationship between the members of the 'Alawi community who led the Ba'th regime and the 'Alawi community. Bits of reliable evidence point to a contemporary intra-'Alawi power structure and to the influence it has on decisions made by 'Alawi leaders of the regime. How precisely the two groups function and interact remains a mystery. Little is known about the 'Alawi community and its structure since it was studied in the 1940s by the French social geographer Jacques Weulersse. Most of his findings must have been outdated by the community's modernization and politicization during the past few decades and by its spectacular rise from the fringes of Syrian public life to a position of power and dominance. This must therefore remain an area for further study, which current research and future developments are likely to illuminate.[10]

The political history of Iraq during the same twenty years can be described as, literally, a mirror image of the processes that took place in Syria. In Iraq the Sunni Arabs are a minority of some 20 per cent that – as a result of four centuries of Ottoman rule and the policies of the British Mandatory – had enjoyed a lengthy pre-eminence in the country and the state. Such was the evolution of the Ba'th regime, particularly in its second (post-1968) phase, that power came to be monopolized by the Tikritis (natives of Tikrit) and their Sunni allies.

As in the case of the Syrian 'Alawis, the original choices were not confessional in nature. One joined a faction, made a commitment, and pledged allegiance on the basis of personal and family ties or common regional origins. These all implied affiliation with the same community, and so in time the regime found itself in the role of yet another upholder of the traditional Sunni hegemony. Until the late 1970s, the personal and regional factions within the regime tended to overshadow this fact. It was perceived in terms of primordial ties – the 'regime of the Tikritis' rather than 'the regime of the Sunnis'. But the rise of Khomeini's regime in Iran shifted the emphasis, and the cleavage between the Sunnis and the Shi'ites became paramount.[11]

THE LEBANESE *KATA'IB* PARTY

The Lebanese *Kata'ib* Party, the other historical rival of the PPS, was founded in 1936 as a militant youth movement designed to protect the interests of the Maronite community and the Christian-dominated state of Greater Lebanon against the challenge of the PPS Arab nationalists and the Sunni community. To its adherents the organization offered more than the sense of fulfillment and gratification generated by participation in the defense of community and state. Like other radical parties and organizations of the period, it offered a charismatic leader, a demanding, all-encompassing framework, uniforms, discipline, dynamism, and a form of protest and rebellion against the traditional communal leadership.[12]

It was a distinctive characteristic of the *Kata'ib* that since its inception the organization had a dual character – a vigilante organization and a fairly pragmatic political party. Having contributed its share to the formation of an independent Greater Lebanese state, the *Kata'ib* attenuated its militia-like features and immersed itself as a political party in the Lebanese political system. But under the surface of a genuine and very successful political party, the other face of the *Kata'ib* was retained – a militant militia ready to use its power to defend the state, the political system, and the Maronite-Christian community. This it did in 1958 and in the early 1970s.[13]

The interplay between these two aspects of the *Kata'ib* has been manifested by the three phases through which its ideology and orientation have gone since 1936. During its first years, the *Kata'ib* was a Maronite-Christian political organization seeking to protect and perpetuate a territorial and political status quo considered vital for the survival and well-being of the community. The very term Maronite-Christian reflects a deliberate ambiguity. The Maronite community clearly meets the criteria by which a national group is defined, but even the radical Maronites who demanded a state, and subsequently a Greater Lebanese state, spoke of a Christian rather than a Maronite entity. They must have felt that the Maronites were too few to sustain a state. Instead, Lebanon was seen and presented as a Christian homeland, fortress, and haven for the Christians of Lebanon and sometimes for the whole region. There had to be one state in the region in which Arabic-speaking Christians could live as free and full members of the body politic. Such were the arguments raised at the end of the First World War by the spokespersons of the Maronite community – both clerics and political leaders – when they demanded a separate state with expanded borders under French protection.[14] In its early years the *Kata'ib* was a successor to this tradition and upheld it and lent it the support of its power. It was one among several Maronite groups belonging to this orientation, coupled by growing antagonism to the French authorities.

In the 1950s and 1960s, when the *Kata'ib* operated as a political party within Lebanon's pluralistic political system, it was no longer formally identified with a distinctively Christian, let alone Maronite, orientation. The party now became an advocate of Lebanonism, an ideology that argued that there had been and certainly was a Lebanese entity transcending the constituent communities. This notion had been put forth and elaborated in earlier decades by such people as Michel Chiha, Charles Corm, and Sa'id 'Aql, either to bind the Lebanese together or to present a counterpole to Arabism.[15]

The idea of a Lebanese entity, rooted in a historic tradition and serving as a bridge between East and West, though apparently secular, was perceived, certainly by its opponents, as Christian in orientation. Indeed, the Lebanonism of the *Kata'ib*, despite much elaboration and sophistication, was ultimately Maronite-Christian. This was clearly reflected in the party's communal make-up. Despite a serious effort to diversify it, the party's membership remained Christian and Maronite. Some members were recruited among the Druzes and the Shi'ites, but Sunni and Greek Orthodox Lebanese persisted in their reluctance and opposition.[16]

The party's ideological development during these years was not limited to its preoccupation with definition of the state and the political community. Much thought was given to social and economic reforms, which some of the leaders argued were necessary if the system was to be preserved. The internal debate on these issues resulted in crystallization of the conservative and radical wings in the party. The *Kata'ib*'s distinctive ideology, large membership, and elaborate structure set it apart from the other Maronite political parties and factions as well as from the community's religious establishment.[17]

These trends began to wane in the late 1960s as the domestic and external challenges to the status quo in Lebanon became more ominous. The *Kata'ib* became more distinctively Maronite. In 1968 the *Kata'ib*, together with Chamoun's National Liberals, and Raymond Eddé's National Bloc formed the essentially Maronite Tripartite Alliance. In the early 1970s, particularly after the Lebanese army's failure to check the PLO in May 1973, the original outlook of the vigilante organization was fully revived. The state occupied an important place in the party's thinking, but the community was more important than the state. If the Lebanese could not defend the community's existence and way of life, the party should undertake the task.

The trend was accelerated and accentuated by the civil war of 1975–76 and by the continuing Lebanese crisis. The Phalangist militia was the single largest force fighting on behalf of the status quo coalition, and the *Kata'ib* was an important component of the Lebanese Front, an umbrella organization formed in 1976 to coordinate the policies of the Christian community. The Front's leadership included Camille Chamoun (as chairman), Pierre Jumayyil, Sharbal Qassis (head of the Federation of Maronite Orders), and other politicians and intellectuals (including the Greek Orthodox Charles Malik). The Front's outlook was expounded in a platform it published in 1980 under the title 'The Lebanon We Want to Build'. The platform demanded a special position for the Christians in Lebanon based not on their relative numerical strength, but on their role in the creation of Lebanon and on their objective needs.[18]

The civil war of 1975–76 threatened the very existence of the Lebanese state and in any event signified the demise of the Lebanese political system as it had existed between 1943 and 1975. Several potential alternatives presented themselves – Syrian hegemony, partition and the establishment of a smaller Christian state, cantonization, preservation of Maronite-Christian hegemony over Greater Lebanon through an alliance with Israel, and a restructuring of the Lebanese political system through new communal alignments.

The *Kata'ib* were divided over these matters, and the division can be seen as a reincarnation of the party's original dualism. The party's leader, Pierre Jumayyil, and his elder son Amin, never quite relinquished the hope of reviving the traditional Lebanese system based on a slightly readjusted partnership with the other communities in Lebanon and on a *modus vivendi* with Lebanon's Arab environment. Jumayyil's younger son Bashir pursued a more militant line and developed an autonomous power base, affiliated with the *Kata'ib* but distinct from them. The Lebanese Forces developed as a militia organization based on a partnership between the militias of the *Kata'ib*, the National Liberals, and two smaller groups – the *Tanzim* and the Guardians of the Cedar. The Forces were affiliated with the Lebanese Front but were not its military arm. The *Kata'ib* militia provided the Forces, at least originally, with the bulk of its men, but the Forces should not be confused (as they often are) with the *Kata'ib*.[19]

Like the *Kata'ib* in their early days, the Lebanese Forces began as a militia and developed into a political movement, with its bureaucracy and an intellectual cadre and milieu. Until 1982 the tension between the new organization and the *Kata'ib* remained latent.

The Lebanese Forces began and developed as an uninhibited Maronite-Christian organization. Its first leader sought to impose for the first time a single effective leadership on the community and was willing to use force to achieve his purpose. He had partial success with the National Liberals and failed in North Lebanon. It is idle to speculate on the policy that Bashir Jumayyil would have pursued as president of Lebanon had he not been assassinated, but it is instructive to read the last speech he delivered a few hours before his death. It was the statement of a Christian leader about to become president of a state that he viewed as a Christian homeland.[20]

Bashir Jumayyil's assassination, Amin Jumayyil's election to the presidency, and the other developments of the years 1982–84 further confounded the relationship between the *Kata'ib*, the Lebanese Forces, and the larger Maronite community. These developments cannot be analysed here in detail, but the following statement made by Karim Pakradouni, now the political adviser to the Forces, in a press interview given in March 1984 reflects the Lebanese Forces' view of itself as a protector of the Lebanese Christians.

> The Lebanese Forces are drawing up a political program based on three main points:
> 1) The defense of Christian regions by establishing 'Red Lines'

around these areas. These 'Red Lines' are both military and political –
the military lines being mobilization of the Christian population to
defend these regions, and the political ones being the contacts,
which the Lebanese Forces are undertaking at the regional and international levels. ...

2) Proposing, at the national level, a plan for a federal republic with
a view to achieving a comprehensive settlement of the Lebanese
problem ... The Christians see reforms as forced concessions, while
the Muslims consider them inadequate. This is why we believe the
logic of reforms is not enough.

3) Whereas the 1943 National Pact was based on an agreement
between the Maronites and the Sunnites, we are becoming more and
more convinced that the new National Pact will have to come about
through an agreement between the Maronites and the Shi'ites ...[21]

Since the publication of this statement, the Lebanese Forces have been torn
apart by internecine conflicts, and their posture and effectiveness as
defenders of the Maronite-Christian cause have been seriously compromised.

THE MUSLIM BROTHERHOOD IN SYRIA

In the span of some thirty years, the Syrian branch of the Muslim
Brotherhood underwent a transformation from a movement reflecting the
complacency of a confident majority to the militant representative of a
beleaguered community. In the early years of Syrian independence, it
would have seemed odd to examine the Muslim Brotherhood in the context of ethnic politics. The movement's leaders saw themselves as standing
above such matters; they were spokesmen of the community and nation of
Islam for Sunni universalism. Syria, to them, was an Islamic-Arab country
inhabited by a large Sunni Muslim majority, and the Syrian state should
have an Islamic government shaped by the Shari'a. Syria's non-Muslim citizens, be they Christian or heterodox Muslim Arabs, would have to adapt
themselves to that projected reality.

The Brotherhood's position was articulated eloquently during the constitutional debate of 1950 by its leader, Mustafa al-Siba'i, who argued that
Islam should be made the state religion. 'In every state', wrote al-Siba'i,
'there is a majority and a minority in religion'. The minority, he implied,
should resign itself to the supremacy of the majority, particularly because
Islam recognized and respected the rights of the adherents of Christianity
and Judaism.[22] The 1950 debate ended with a compromise: Islam was not

declared the state religion, but it was specified that the president of the state must be a Muslim and that Islamic jurisprudence should be the major source of legislation. This became a standard formula in Syrian constitutions until the late 1960s.

The position taken by the Muslim Brotherhood in the 1950 debate mirrored a frame of mind current among Sunni Arabs, who tended to see themselves as the only full-blooded Arabs and who expected others to adjust to that state of affairs. Christian, Shi'ite, and heterodox Muslim Arabs have responded to this attitude with varying degrees of resentment, envy, or resignation. Thus, one Arab student of Arab politics wrote bitterly about the Sunni Muslim leaders in the twentieth-century Arab world: 'They came to the conclusion that they had a divine right, almost a God-given right, to lead the new community, now called a nation ... The implication of this was the Sunni community had a divine right to rule over Arabs. This right has now been enhanced by the fact that the new political elite was not only Muslim and Sunni Muslim but Arab too.'[23]

During the first twenty years of Syrian independence, the Muslim Brotherhood was one of several parties and movements contending for power or influence in Syria. Its views on government and society likewise constituted one ideological current, with lesser impact than, say, Nasserism and Ba'thism. But Syria's ruling establishment, the traditional nationalists, and their immediate radical successors were Sunni Muslims. It was only in the 1960s that power shifted to an entirely different social group as the heterodox Muslims and Christians became pre-eminent in the upper echelons of the Ba'th regime.

The traditional roles were thus reversed. The Sunnis now felt dispossessed and humiliated. In the past they had not thought in ethnic terms, because their community's supremacy could be taken for granted; now they began to do so. In the circumstances obtaining in Syria, the Sunni religious establishment and the Muslim Brotherhood became the chief vehicles for transmitting the grievances of the large and diffuse Sunni community.[24] Social and political strife were blended with religious objection to domination by members of a sect (the 'Alawis) that strict Muslims regarded as lying beyond the pale. The Muslim fundamentalists came to represent a large group, many of whose members did not necessarily accept the movement's fundamentalism but saw it as the only authentic and effective defender of the Sunni majority.

For about a decade the Brotherhood and its allies conducted their struggle against the regime along conventional lines – trying to bring it down, to force it to change certain policies, or just expressing their frustration through strikes and demonstrations. In the mid-1970s it became clear that such traditional methods, while publicizing the opposition of a significant portion of the population to the regime, were futile as a strategy designed to bring it down. The stalemate was symbolized by the constitutional controversy of 1973. The devout Sunni demonstrators forced the regime to reinsert the compromise formula of 1950 it had tried to rescind. But an 'Alawi, Hafiz al-Asad, remained head of state.[25]

It was against this background that radical elements within the Muslim Brotherhood rejected the leadership of 'Isam al-'Attar, whom they regarded as too timid. Organizationally, the movement lost its unity and coherence. In operative terms, its radical wing (or fringes) sought to bring the regime down through a strategy of terror and to exacerbate Sunni-'Alawi tensions. During the 1973 constitutional controversy, the opposition's manifestos suggested cautiously that the regime was dominated by 'Alawis and that the 'Alawis were not proper Muslims. A few years later this was stated explicitly. Terrorist attacks were directed at 'Alawis as individuals and as a group. The massacre of some sixty 'Alawi artillery cadets in Aleppo in June 1979 was clearly intended to draw the 'Alawis to react and to bring about open warfare between Sunnis and 'Alawis. In the eyes of the radical Brotherhood this was preferable to the continued subjugation of the majority by the minority and to the rule of a secular and (in their view) a non-Muslim government.[26]

Politically, the radical wing of the Brotherhood succeeded in broadening its base by becoming the chief element in the Syrian Islamic Front in which its leaders were joined by well-known 'ulama' (Muslim men of religion) who had not previously been affiliated or identified with the Brotherhood. The Front has devoted considerable effort to expounding its line in Syria and abroad. Its comprehensive programme is an excellent guide to the movement's outlook and views. It includes a 'call' and an 'appeal' to the 'Alawis that seems to continue Siba'i's argument of 1950: '9 or 10 per cent of the population cannot be allowed to dominate the majority, because it is against the logic of things ... In our case the sectarian war was not waged by the majority trying to protect itself against the domination of the minority. It is definitely the minority that forgot itself.' Along with assurances for the 'Alawi community once it decided 'to shake off the guardianship of the corrupt elements which drove them to this dangerous predicament', it included a vow: 'We shall continue in our course, disregarding dangers and obstacles until this oppressive regime has fallen and gone for ever.'[27]

The Brotherhood's offensive against the regime was broken, first in 1980 in Aleppo and then at a terrible price in Hama in February 1982. The brutal suppression of the opposition and the indiscriminate punishment of the environment in which it operated lent a new acuteness to the question of the Brotherhood's relationship with the larger Sunni community. Political attitudes could not, of course, be measured in Ba'thist Syria. It could be assumed that the Brotherhood had the sympathy and, to a lesser extent, the passive support of a considerable segment of the Sunni community. The latter, while not necessarily subscribing to the fundamentalists' views on Islamic government, would see them as the genuine expression of the majority's resentment against the regime. But the 'environmental' punishment imposed by the authorities proved effective in forcing the Brotherhood's sympathizers to draw away from it in practice. Political conduct had to be divorced from political sentiment. It was a new reality that the Brotherhood had difficulty contending with.

THE COMMUNIST PARTY

The record left by some sixty years of Communist activity in the Arab world bears ample testimony to the complex interplay between the party and the region's ethnic structure. It would be impossible within the scope of this chapter to examine the interplay as it had unfolded in several countries and branches, but its contours can be characterized in general terms.[28]

Communism was propagated in the post-First World War Middle East as a doctrine, as a disciplined and often secretive revolutionary organization, and as the arm of an international movement based in Moscow. Individuals were attracted to the party as leaders and members for a variety of reasons, but its main appeal on the 1920s and 1930s was to national and ethnic groups seeking a total transformation of their societies. This was true of Armenians in Syria and Lebanon, Kurds in Iraq and Syria, Greeks in Egypt, and Jews in Egypt, Iraq, and Mandatory Palestine.[29] Consequently, all Communist parties in the region had a disproportionate number of leaders and members from minority communities, particularly 'harder' minorities that were not so easy to assimilate.

Herein lay an important difference between the Communists and parties like the PPS and the Ba'th. To the extent that they attracted members of minority communities, the latter two tended to appeal to 'softer' groups, such as Greek Orthodox Christians or 'Alawis, who could hope to find an equal status in a redefined political community. The anticipated radical levelling consequences of a Communist revolution appealled to groups that were separated from the bulk of society by higher and thicker walls or placed across lines of national rather than ethnic or communal divisions. Communism's appeal to groups preoccupied with national conflicts was enhanced by the Soviet Union's attempt to cope with the national question

within its own territory and by the fact that several national groups –
Armenians, Jews, Kurds – were represented in both the Soviet Union and
the Middle East. This pattern of recruitment provided Communist parties
in the inter-war Arab world with cadres of leadership and membership.
But in later years the over-representation of the minorities, together with
the internationalism and secularism of the party and the Soviet-
Communist support for the establishment of Israel, militated against the
party's spread among the Arab-Muslim majority.

Communists and Communist parties contributed their share to the revolutionary phase of Arab politics in the 1950s and 1960s. But as close as
they seemed to be to seizing power on several occasions, they were ultimately defeated by nationalist elements. The ensuing disappointment (and
Moscow's advice) led them to accept the suzerainty of the victorious
nationalist elements, but it also led to heart-searching and schisms. The
Syrian case is instructive and well documented. The brochure entitled 'The
Problems of the Conflict in the Syrian Communist Party' provides a
detailed account of the rebellion against Khalid Bakdash, the party's historic leader and the best-known Communist in the Arab world (himself of
Kurdish extraction). The rebels argued that the Syrian Communist Party
must join the mainstream of Arab leftist politics and acquire a more
nationalist coloring. In concrete terms the argument focused on the party's
position in the Arab-Israeli conflict. The opposition to Bakdash believed
that by endorsing Soviet acceptance of the legitimacy of Israel's existence
the party was perpetuating its stigmatized position in Arab politics.

These reservations were stated explicitly and answered by a Soviet party
delegation that tried to settle the controversy. But the text of the debate also
reflects unstated tensions. The impatience of the opposition with the
party's place in the periphery of Arab politics and its desire to join the
'majority' was evident. Implied in this feeling was also the notion that the
party should shed its minoritarian heritage and join the majority in that
sense as well.[30] A similar trend in an entirely different context can be
observed among Israel's Arab Communists. As an Israeli researcher has
clearly shown, the history of Israel's Communist parties and of their predecessors in Mandatory Palestine has been shaped to a large extent by
national as well as ethnic factors. Their efforts to transcend the Arab-Jewish
conflict attracted some and repelled many in both communities.[31] Among
the Arabs, as in other parts of the region, it has attracted more Christians
than Muslims.

Two inter-related trends recently became apparent. In the absence of a
legal Arab national party in Israel, Rakah (the New Communist Party)
became the principal outlet for expressing the political sentiments of

Israel's Arab minority. And as the party became more nationalist in character, the discrepancy between a largely Christian-Arab leadership and
Muslim-Arab voters became more pronounced and politically more significant. Ironically, then, it is a predominantly Arab Communist party in a
Jewish state that has been the only effective Communist party in the region
in recent years. But effectiveness exacted an ideological price. In order to
represent the nationalism of Israel's Arabs, the party had to shed most of
its Marxist attributes.

This state of affairs raises two related questions. One concerns the Arab
world's failure to produce a new ideological framework that would play a
role similar to that played until the 1970s by pan-Arabism. The vacuum has
been filled to some extent by the new salience and intensity of Islamic loyalties, but one still expects a fresh set of ideological formulations addressing the profound changes of the past fifteen years or so. The other draws
on the crucial role played by ethnic and communal tensions in the inter-
war period in producing the ideologies that predominated in the 1950s
and 1960s. During that phase, members of minority groups had sought to
transform their status and predicament by transcending the political units
created by the 1919–21 peace settlement. These states have so far survived,
but all are scenes of bitter inter-communal conflict. It is still an open question whether these conflicts will be conducted essentially as power struggles or whether some of them will give birth to new ideologies affecting
the whole region.

NOTES

1. This article was published in J. Milton Esman and Itamar Rabinovich (eds), *Ethnicity, Pluralism and the State in the Middle East* (Ithaca. NY: Cornell University Press, 1988), pp.155–72.
2. Karim Pakradouni, *La Paix Manquée: Le Mandat d'Elias Sarkis, 1976-1982* [in Arabic, French and English] (Beirut: Ed. FMA, 1984), pp.6–8.
3. For the history and ideology of the PPS, see L.Z. Yamak, *The Syrian Social Nationalist Party* (Cambridge, MA: Harvard University Press, 1966). For a portrait of Sa'adeh, see Eliyahu Eylath, 'Antun Sa'adeh – Portrait of an Arab Revolutionary', in *Zionism and the Arabs* (Tel Aviv: Devir, 1974), pp.372–86 [Hebrew], and Hisham Sharabi's memoirs, *Al-Jamr wal-Ramad* (*Embers and Ashes*) (Beirut, 1978) [in Arabic].
4. A.H. Hourani 'Ideologies of the Mountain and the City', in R. Owen (ed.), *Essays on the Crisis in Lebanon* (London: Ithaca, 1976), pp.33–41.
5. M. van Dusen, 'Political Integration and Regionalism in Syria', *Middle East Journal*, 26, 2 (1972), pp.123–36.
6. For a description and analysis of the coup, see 'The Attempted NSP Coup' in Y. Oron (ed.), *Middle East Record, 1961* (Jerusalem: Israel Program for Scientific Translations, 1966), pp.398–404.
7. J. Devlin, *The Ba'th Party: A History from its Origins to 1966* (Stanford, CA: Hoover Institution Press, 1976), pp.1–22.
8. H. Batatu, *The Old Social Classes and the Revolutionary Movements in Iraq* (Princeton, NJ: Princeton University Press, 1979), pp.1077–93.
9. N. van Dam, *The Struggle for Power in Syria: Sectarianism, Regionalism and Tribalism in Politics, 1961-1980*

(London: Croom-Helm, 1981), and H. Batatu, 'Some Observations on the Social Roots of Syria's Ruling Military Group', *Middle East Journal*, 35, 3 (1981), pp.331–44.

10. Batatu, 'Some Observations on the Social Roots of Syria's Ruling Military Group', pp.331–44.

11. N. van Dam, 'Middle Eastern Political Clichés: "Takriti", and "sunni Rule" in Iraq; "'Alawi Rule" in Syria', *Orient*, 21 (January 1980), pp.42–57.

12. J. Entelis, *Pluralism and Party Transformation in Lebanon: Al-Kata'ib, 1936–1970* (Leiden: E.J. Brill, 1974).

13. F. Stoakes, 'The Supervigilantes: The Lebanese Kata'ib Party as Builder Surrogate and Defender of the State', *Middle Eastern Studies*, 11, 3 (October 1975), pp.215–36.

14. The fullest and best-documented study of Maronite political attitudes in the late nineteenth and early twentieth centuries and the establishment of Greater Lebanon is Meir Zamir's *The Formation of Modern Lebanon* (London: Croom-Helm, 1985). Part of Zamir's findings were published in his 'Smaller and Greater Lebanon: The Squaring of a Circle', *Jerusalem Quarterly*, 23 (Spring 1982), pp.215–36.

15. Kamal Salibi, 'The Lebanese Identity', *Journal of Contemporary History*, 6, 1 (1971), pp.76–86.

16. Entelis, *Pluralism*, pp.101–24.

17. Stoakes, 'The Supervigilantes', passim.

18. 'The Lebanon We Want to Build', December 1980.

19. L.W. Snider 'The Lebanese Forces: Their Origins and Role in Lebanon's Politics', *Middle East Journal*, 38 (Winter 1984), pp.1–33.

20 The text of this speech is included in a collection published on the first anniversary of Bashir Jumayyil's death.

21 *Monday Morning* (Beirut), 5–11 March 1984.

22. R.B. Winder, 'Islam as the State Religion: A Muslim Brotherhood View in Syria', *Muslim World*, 49 (July and October 1954), pp.215–26.

23. A.R. Kelidar, 'Religion and State in Syria', *Asian Affairs*, 61, 5 (February 1974), pp.16–22. See also F. 'Ajami, *The Vanished Imam: Musa al-Sadr and the Shi'a of Lebanon* (London: I.B. Tauris, 1986).

24. T. Mayer, 'The Islamic Opposition in Syria, 1961–1982', *Orient*, 24 (December 1983), pp.589–609, and E. Sivan, *Radical Islam, Medieval Theology and Modern Politics* (New Haven, CT: Yale University Press, 1985).

25. Kelidar, 'Religion and State', and I. Rabinovich, 'The Islamic Wave', *Washington Quarterly*, 2 (1979), pp.139–43.

26. Mayer, 'Islamic Opposition'.

27. A translation of the programme, appended with an elaborate introduction and apparatus, was published in book form by the sympathetic Mizan Press, as Dr 'Umar F. 'Abdallah, *The Islamic Struggle in Syria* (Berkeley, CA: Mizan, 1983). Nothing is known about the author, but the book includes a foreword and a postscript by Professor Hamid Algar of the University of California at Berkeley.

28. For general studies and surveys of communism in the region, see W.Z. Laqueur, *Communism and Nationalism in the Middle East* (New York, NY: Praeger, 1956), and E. Marqus, *Ta'rikh al-Ahzab al-Shiyu'iyya fi-l-wataqn al-Arabi* (History of the Communist Parties in the Arab Homeland) (Beirut: Dar al-Tali'a, 1964).

29. Batatu, *Old Social Classes*, and A. Flores, 'The Early History of Lebanese Communism Reconsidered', *Khamsin*, 7 (1981–2), pp.7–19.

30. Extracts in English from this publication are published in the *Journal of Palestine Studies*, 2 (October 1972), pp.187–212.

31. Elie Rekhes, 'Jews and Arabs in the Israeli Communist Party', in Esman J. Milton and Itamar Rabinovich (eds), *Ethnicity, Pluralism and the State in the Middle East* (Ithaca, NY: Cornell University Press, 1988), pp.121–39.

III

THE BA'TH REGIME

11

Historiography and Politics in Syria[1]

The 'decolonization of history' or the rewriting of a country's national history after achieving independence or overthrowing the old order is a familiar phenomenon of third-world intellectual life and politics.[2] This process provides in most cases a revealing testimony of a new regime's self-view and of some of the fundamental issues with which it is confronted and preoccupied. The most comprehensive and far-reaching attempt at reshaping the past of a Middle Eastern nation was made in Ataturk's Turkey. It was part of a broader effort to create a secular territorial nationalism to replace the Imperial Ottoman and Islamic loyalties. In the Arab part of the Middle East the best-known effort at historiographic revision was invested by the Nasserite regime which sought in the early 1960s to sponsor the rewriting of Egypt's modern history from a 'socialist' perspective.[3] Most recently a committee headed by Husni Mubarak, first deputy to President Sadat, was formed to supervise, probably from a rather different perspective, a project dealing with Egypt's history since 1919. Ba'thi Syria did not witness such sweeping experiments at historical rewriting, but it seems to provide a much more intricate instance of the relationship between an Arab regime's political and ideological concerns and its approach to history writing.

The Ba'th came to power in Syria in March 1963. The first phase of the Ba'th regime's history lasted from that time to February 1966. It was a dramatic and eventful period during which Syria and the Ba'th Party underwent a transformation. The Ba'th became the sole effective political force in the country. Then the military who staged the original coup and their civilian clients ousted the Ba'th's 'founding fathers' and acquired full control of the party. During the years 1966–70 the major issue in Syrian domestic politics was the struggle between the two rival factions headed by Generals Salah Jadid and Hafiz al-Asad. The third phase of the regime's history began with the latter's triumph in November 1970. Asad formed his own regime and has been successful in building one that has been remarkably free of internecine conflict. He has been less successful in eliminating the urban public's hostility to the Ba'th regime and to the ideas and social groups it has come to represent.

A recognition of the importance of history and the historical explanation were inherent in the ideological concerns of the Ba'th party. The Ba'th
left its distinctive mark on Arab nationalism and on the political scene of
the Fertile Crescent in the 1940s primarily by offering the educated Arab
youth of that region a doctrine of secular Arab nationalism and Arab socialism couched in appealing modern terms. In order to establish this doctrine
Michel 'Aflaq, the party's founder, had to rely on reinterpretation of the
course of Arab history so crafted as to prove the independent existence of
an Arab entity that had been deeply influenced by Islam but had pre-dated
it and acquired a standing in its own right. 'Aflaq presented this interpretation in its fullest form in a lecture delivered in 1943 at the University of
Damascus under the title 'The memory of the Arab Prophet'.[4] This is the
best-known but naturally not the only example of reliance on a historic
interpretation in presenting a new self-image and a new programme of
action in that formative phase in the history of the Ba'th party.

The focus of the Ba'thi interest in history shifted in later years. As the
party became an effective political force, particularly after its rise to power
in Syria and Iraq in 1963, its leaders became more interested in the immediate rather than in the remote past. It was the issues of the recent past
which nourished the polemics between the Ba'th and its rivals, and this
was the period within which the party's political career has taken place.
After 1963 another shift occurred as the Ba'th regime in Syria became preoccupied with the party's own history. This trend was affected by the continuous struggle during the years 1963–71 between rival party factions for
hegemony within the regime and over the right to represent the party's
legacy. These were essentially struggles for power, but they were accompanied by ideological and historical debates in which the respective factions
and contending leaders sought to establish their legitimacy. A telling example of such polemics was the argument raised by Michel 'Aflaq's rivals that
it was not he but rather Zaki al-Arsuzi who founded the Ba'th party in the
early 1940s and developed its ideology. After the coup of 23 February
1966, which resulted in 'Aflaq's being ousted from the party's ranks, the
authors of the coup tried to draw a line linking Zaki al-Arsuzi's early career
to that event, in order to prove that they actually continued an original orientation in the Ba'thi tradition that had been obscured during the hegemony of 'Aflaq and his associates.[5]

The process of establishing its rule and the bitter conflicts within its
own ranks delayed but did not altogether prevent the Ba'th regime from
reconsidering and subsequently undertaking a partial revision of Syrian
historiography. As far as can be determined on the basis of indirect evidence this initiative was generated by a variety of motives. The overthrow

of the old order had to be justified, among other things, by disparaging the historic record of the rulers who bad been ousted. Then there were practical considerations which emerged as the new regime consolidated its hold. Governmental and administrative routine must have raised questions such as the adaptation of textbooks of various levels to the doctrines accepted by the regime, or the attitude to events, anniversaries and personalities cherished by previous regimes or by opposition groups. Beyond these issue, questions had to be answered which concerned the regime's very essence as the embodiment in power of an ideological party. Ought the Ba'thi leaders to be satisfied with maintaining themselves in power, or should they try to mould the Syrian public in their own image, and instil into it a corrected version of Syria's history?

Awareness of these problems and the various approaches to them within the Ba'th regime are illuminated by the proceedings of a symposium held in 1965 by al-Ma'rifa, a periodical issued by the Ministry of Culture and National Guidance, which dealt with the question 'How shall we write our national history?' The participants were presented with seven questions, central among which were the following: (1) What is your opinion on the sources now available for the study of Arab history? (2) What are the flaws which blemish our history and should be got rid of? (3) What is your opinion of the view which holds that current historiography is interested only in the history of kings, not in that of the people? (4) In many countries attempts are being made at rewriting history according to changes of outlook, which have taken place in society … Do you not see a need to do so with regard to our own Arab history?

The presentation of these questions and their phrasing were significant. Implicit in them were the assumptions that rewriting the national history was a necessary task and that the task should be done in a manner that would glorify Arab and Syrian history and reflect the new ideas and values which had to become dominant in regimes such as the Ba'th regime in Syria.

The participants in the symposium included non-Ba'thi Syrian historians and intellectuals from other Arab countries. But we are primarily interested in the Ba'thi participants: Zaki al-Arsuzi, Shibly al-Aysami, Yasin al-Hafiz and Sulayman al-Khish. Zaki al-Arsuzi was not at that time directly associated with intra-Ba'thi struggles, but the last three represented the principal trends in the ideological conflicts, which had taken place within the Syrian Ba'th in the years 1963–66. Shibli al-Aysami, a Druze, was a supporter of 'Aflaq and an exponent of the party's original ideology. Yasin al-Hafiz, together with Elyas Murqus and Jurj Taribishi, was a member of a radical faction which sought to replace that ideology with a Marxist doctrine adapted to the conditions of the Arab world. Members of this faction were ousted from the Ba'th in

1964 but remained for a while in Syria before moving their activities to Lebanon. Sulayman al- Khish, a future Minister of Education, was also regarded as a member of the party's radical wing. But, unlike Yasin al-Hafiz, he was among those who restrained their radicalism and accepted the authority of the military, the dominant element in the Ba'th regime.

Shibli al-Aysami's short response to the questions posed by the organizers[6] focused on a subject considered by other participants as well – history textbooks, which, he argued, should be 'scientific, guided and the product of a collective effort'. In keeping with the party's secularist conception of Arab nationalism, Aysami criticized the negative portrayal of the Jahiliyya (pre-Islamic) period in these books. The textbooks currently in use, he said, neglected also the role of the people and underplayed the importance of social, economic and ideological issues 'which are the source and the chief moving force of historic events'. These textbooks should therefore be re-examined. The researcher and the university student should be allowed 'to study the details and the parts and to delve beyond the abstract scientific truth' but 'It is not useful, in our mind, to allow this to authors of history taught at the primary, intermediate and high school levels, since the value of the historic facts in the textbooks is linked to the goal one aims at, and not to the abstract truth they carry'. The conclusion which follows is that we are not required to falsify but merely 'to distil the facts and events and present them in a correct scholarly fashion'.[7]

The most comprehensive and coherent view was presented by Yasin al-Hafiz.[8] He came out with a scathing criticism of the ultra-nationalistic proclivities of Arab historians and with a more implicit criticism of similar tendencies that were reflected in the question presented by al-Ma'rifa. The available books on Arab history were lagging not only behind the progressive method of historical analysis, he argued, but even behind 'bourgeois objectivity' in the West. The great majority of history books offered to the Arab public were written from a medieval standpoint, this being supplemented by narrow-minded and arbitrary bourgeois nationalist effort to 'inflate' Arab history. Nor was Hafiz in favour of glossing over shameful aspects of the Arab past, even if these were being exploited by western imperialism, since this very way of looking at history indicated a conservative view and a lack of a proper understanding of the laws of historic development. Similarly, he rejected the simplistic view, which advocated the obliteration of the role of kings and rulers – which indeed had previously been overplayed because of class-related considerations. This role existed and could not be abolished, but the role of the masses should be illuminated as well. This latter role, in fact, he said, only becomes prominent in periods of transition, and the 'progressive historian' is called upon to shed light on these periods.

Such strictures are characteristic of the radical criticism of Arab society by the group of which Yasin al-Hafiz is a member. But he had positive proposals as well. The writing of history should be undertaken from a progressive point of view: this is an important task since the traditional history books reflect part of the ideological structure of the old Arab society. But in any case, rather than indulge in the past, one should focus one's attention on the present and the future. Without explicitly saying so, Hafiz follows the Marxist line. He registered his reservations with regard to the historiographical falsifications of the Stalinist period but did not deviate from the fundamental principles: 'The progressive historian should focus his attention on the dialectical contradiction within the movement of history ... historical dialectics is the most scientific instrument for the study of history.'

The position taken by Sulayman al-Khish,[9] a spokesman for the non-Marxist Ba'thi radicals, was in sharp contrast to those of Hafiz. Khish stated 'we are primarily nationalists, and this very fact contradicts the communist world view'. In his view, the implementation of socialism in the Arab world does not rest on a belief in dialectics and historical materialism but is a practical approach seeking to fortify Arab society in its struggle for unity and liberation. It would therefore be artificial for an Arab society treading the path of socialism to formulate its historiography in a Marxist fashion since this would divert it from the road of national struggle.

Khish also expressed the very same ultra-nationalist tendencies that Hafiz had denounced. Zaki al-Arsuzi, in his contribution to the discussion, recommended that the new history books should emphasize the Arab nation's closeness to the cultures of the peoples called Semites such as the Chaldeans, Assyrians, Aramaics and Hebrews, since Arabic, as he said, was the mother language of the Semitic peoples. This, Arsuzi thought, would be of use by drawing attention to 'the bolstering of the potential inherent in the Arab soul'.[10]

Arsuzi, possibly influenced by the Iraqi historian Jawad Ali's series of books on the pre-Islamic history of the Arabs, mentioned this point in passing. Sulayman al-Khish took it and developed it to grotesque proportions. He used it first in order to distinguish – in the best Ba'thi tradition – between Arabism and Islam and to underline the former's existence as a separate and secular entity. But Khish sought also to adopt the whole cultural legacy of the ancient Near East and to make it part of the Arab legacy. Thus he asserted that the ancient history of the Middle East is part of Arab history. Babylon, Nineveh, Tyre and Carthage were cities 'inspired by the spirit of Arabism'. The misleading nomenclature of western scholars who called the peoples of the area Semites should be abandoned since they ought to be called 'Arab peoples' (Aqwam 'Arabiyya).[11]

While not operative statements, these selections from the symposium indicate the importance attributed by the Ba'th regime to the rewriting of Syrian history and represent the attitudes of the major currents within it to the subject. But the regime's actual approach and activity can best be examined through history textbooks used in the various phases of its development. While affording only a partial picture this is the only source rich enough to allow for systematic comparison. The importance of this source, it should furthermore be recalled, was often mentioned in the symposium.[12]

The period to be examined extends from the end of the First World War to Syria's establishment as an independent State in the aftermath of the Second World War. The regime's attitude to cardinal issues in Arab history, interesting and significant in itself, could thus not be considered. But in terms of the specific problems of the Ba'th regime the period under consideration presents a number of interesting questions: how could textbooks used in State schools present the career of the Ba'th party, which surfaced as a political movement during the Second World War? What treatment would be given to the period of Faysal's regime in Damascus, being a member of the Hashemite family, a bitter enemy of the Ba'th in the 1960s, but also a representative of a nationalist struggle for independence at a period in which, at least in theory, there existed a greater Syria? How would schoolchildren in Ba'thi Syria be introduced to a party like the National Bloc, which led the nationalist struggle against the French but had also been the home of the leaders of the *ancient regime*, the social and political rivals of the Ba'th? How would the Druze Revolt of 1925 be discussed, when issues of 'confessionalism'[13] were matters of particular sensitivity in the Ba'th regime?

The treatment of these and related questions in the available Syrian textbooks suggests three different stages in the Ba'th regime's approach to the rewriting of history.

The first book[14] was designated for 1965/6, the year of the *al-Ma'rifa* symposium, and it is clear that no, or at most very superficial, changes were introduced in it. The Ba'th Party and regime are never mentioned in the book. Faysal is portrayed as the head of a nationalist Syrian regime in Damascus, though his policy toward the French is occasionally criticized.[15]

The 1925 revolt is described, in the tradition of Syrian historiography,[16] not as a single episode but as the culmination of a series of anti-French revolts, which began in 1919.[17] It is interesting that throughout the description of the 1925 revolt the word Druze is never mentioned. But at this point the Ba'th was not required to introduce any changes, as it had already been the tendency of traditional historiography to glorify the

Syrian nationalist resistance to the French and to obscure the special significance of the 'confessional' problem in the history of Syria.

The National Bloc and the struggle for independence are presented briefly, in an informative manner and without comment. The ideological movements which appeared in Syria during the 1930s as an opposition to the first National Bloc are not mentioned. Reference is not made to the social composition of the Bloc's leadership nor to its domestic policies.

The next book[18] was prepared for 1968/9 but was still in use at least two years later and represents an interesting transitional phase. The chronological pages narrating the period 1918–45 remained essentially unchanged except for Ba'thi slogans added at the end of each chapter as a historical lesson for the students. The novel element in this edition was provided by the addition of two new chapters. One was entitled 'The Arab Socialist Revolution in Syria and the Arab Countries' and describes the Ba'thi revolution and regime in laudatory terms. Still more interesting is the next chapter, called 'The Socialist Movement in the Arab World'. Its analysis goes back to the mandatory period and explains the rise of socialism as a reaction against cooperation between Western imperialism and 'the treacherous factions of capitalists and feudatories'.[19] 'Under the influence of popular resistance and struggle', the authors say, 'imperialism handed the reins of power to these factions'. But it retained its economic, political and military interests, 'which means that the bad conditions remained even if the ruling bands were replaced by Arab hands and the Arabic language'.

Without saying so explicitly, the post-1936 treaty situation is described again in this chapter. The 'Nationalist Bloc', described in an earlier chapter of the same book as the government 'of the first nationalist period',[20] is now presented as being 'subservient to western imperialism'. The emergence of the Ba'th and its doctrine are described as the reaction to this state of affairs. The drive to replace the previous school of thought with a socialist doctrine, it was explained, was motivated by a belief in two factors: (1) that the toiling masses are the true force in the struggle; (2) the need to continue the struggle against 'deplorable social conditions ...' Syria as a country was the heart of Arabism and the focus of anti-imperialist struggle, and the Ba'th party raised the banner of revolutionary socialist thinking more than twenty years ago. 'To that banner rallied first the 'educated class' and then the toiling masses, who possess the true interest in struggle and revolution.'[21]

This book, then, seems to represent a hybrid stage. The 1968/69 additions to the text of the mid-1960s clearly reflect the ideas and attitudes which appeared in the al-Ma'rifa symposium, as well as an attempt to glorify the Ba'th party and its role in modern Syrian history. Still this was an addition superimposed on an existing text and not an actual revision.

The marks of such a revision are evident in the next textbook we have. This was originally printed for 1967/68; was radically revised, so it is stated, for the year 1969/70, and radically revised again for 1971/72.[22] It would have been most interesting to compare the three versions of this same book, but the first two versions, unfortunately, are not available. Still, a comparison of the latest version with the previous textbook is highly instructive as well.

The major change in 1971/72 seems to be the percolation of terminology and motifs that are either Ba'thi or in line with the trend of the *al-Ma'rifa* symposium into the chronological chapter. Thus the description of the 1925 revolt emphasizes the role of Hasan al-Kharat, who in an earlier version was described as a *shahid* (martyr for the faith) and in the new version is depicted as a 'popular militant' (*Munadil Sha'bi*).[23] Of greater significance seems to be the addition dealing with the loss of Alexandretta in the late 1930s. The description of 'the nationalist movement in the province' underlines the role of the League of Nationalist Action, a precursor of the Ba'th, and eulogizes Zaki al-Arsuzi, 'the great nationalist fighter'. Arsuzi had indeed played an important role in resisting the Turks, but the description offered to the students is a reconstruction fitting the conceptions of the Ba'th regime thirty years later. Arsuzi, we are told, succeeded in generating a movement that 'resembled the greatest nationalist movements in the modern world'. This movement 'rallied the masses, among them students, labourers, peasants, small merchants and craftsmen ... and put forth slogans which represented the interests of the masses and their inspirations'.[24]

Still the attitude toward the leadership of the nationalist leadership during the French mandate remained ambivalent. Shukri al-Quwatli and his government are commended in one chapter for their 'patriotic stand' against the French in the 1945 crisis while a subsequent chapter chides the selfishness of the old ruling elite.[25]

This ambivalence becomes all the more pronounced when the version above is compared with the description of a Ba'thi text, prepared at about the same time and published for the first time in April 1972. This is an official history of the Ba'th, distributed both by the party's national leadership and the Political Directorate of the Syrian army.[26]

This work, as might have been expected, emphasizes the decisive historic role played by the Ba'th party as a culmination of the Arab nationalist struggle, which began at the twilight of the Ottoman period. Contrary to the school textbooks version, the Great Arab Revolt of 1916–18 and the Arab nationalist leadership that it produced receive a critical treatment: 'but the Arab revolt failed to achieve any of its goals, and, furthermore, many of those called to lead it became, in the wake of its failure, rulers collaborating with the new imperialist rule in the various Arab countries'.[27]

The forces of independence in Syria during the inter-war period were mainly represented by the mass of peasants in the countryside and by urban masses: labourers, craftsmen, tradesmen, students, professionals and intellectuals. This nationalist struggle was led by feudalist, tribal and 'confessional' leaderships.[28]

That leadership achieved its utmost in the 1936 treaties but soon wasted its achievements as a result of incompetence and selfishness. The Second World War enriched the landowners and contributed also to the development of the urban commercial bourgeoisie. The alliance between feudalism and the commercial bourgeoisie was embodied in the first National Bloc, which was willing to play that part in government that had been allocated to it by the occupation authorities. The National Bloc shunned a confrontation with the French and preferred to suppress the Nationalist movement rather than to rely on it in order to achieve complete independence.[29]

It is against this background that the particular contribution of the Ba'th is described. The Ba'th represented the continuation of the original Arab struggle and the essence of the experience that had been accumulated during this struggle. The Ba'thi movement crystallized comprehensive principles for the Arab revolution and formulated them with the utmost simplicity and clarity. The Ba'th fought against the three major deviations of the period, represented by the Communist party, the Syrian Social Nationalist party and the Muslim Brethren, and goaded a hesitant National Bloc to struggle for full independence.[30]

A comparison of this relatively coherent and clear version with the latest textbook available raises the question as to why an effort was not made to achieve similar results with textbooks whose importance for the purposes of the regime was so widely recognized. The 1971/72 books are clearly different from those of 1965/66, yet it is evident that no full-fledged effort was made to rewrite history textbooks in order to bring them completely into line with the version of history acceptable to the regime.

It seems that part of the explanation lies in considerations of priorities. After all, it took the regime nine years to publish an officially inspired history of the Ba'th party itself. The effort required for a radical rewriting of textbooks had to wait until this and other tasks were completed.

This order of priorities should perhaps be seen in relation to the distinction made by the Ba'th regime since its inception between party and State and between *Khassa* and *'Ammah*, namely party members and non-partisans, and between various ranks of membership within the party.

Information in Syria has been and still is divulged and distributed according to these categories. According to this line of thinking, preference in
expounding the correct image of the past should have been given to members and associates of the party, while the rest could wait for their turn.

The process of rewriting history books should also be seen in the context of the factional and ideological strife which took place within the Ba'th
regime during these years. Yasin al-Hafiz, who was quoted extensively
above, and his associates, preached a radical rewriting of Syria's history as
part of a total transformation of Syrian society. The ousting of this faction
was an expression of the opposition of the regime's military leaders to
such aspirations, and contributed in turn to their further weakening. Later,
in November 1970, the Asad regime came to power, representing a more
pragmatic and less doctrinaire approach. To this regime the rewriting of
history textbooks would seem a less urgent task than it would have
appeared to Asad's predecessors.

Of particular importance would have been the question of the relationship between the Ba'th regime and the urban population in Syria. In 1972,
after nine years of Ba'thi rule, the regime was not confronted with serious
rivals, but it had failed to win the support of broad strata in Syria and, as
the events of February–March 1973 showed, it had to contend with the
hostility of the urban middle classes (in the loosest sense of the term).
These groups usually remained passively hostile, but when their fundamental values were challenged in 1967 (when an atheistic article was published in a military periodical) or in 1973 (when the role of Islam in the
constitution was diminished) they tended to react violently.[31] Asad's regime
may have seen history textbooks as pertaining to a sphere where it was
wise to tread carefully. They ought to be rewritten and brought into line
with the regime's general orientation, but this should be done gradually
and carefully in order not to arouse the urban public.

The approach to history writing in Ba'thi Syria appears, then, to be primarily a function of factional balance within the regime of the tenuous relationship between state and society. Ideologically inclined Ba'this and other
leftist critics of the Asad regime would argue, in line with the broader criticism of the military-based Arab regimes, that the failure to bring about a
radical ideological transformation perpetuates this tenuous relationship. But
this would not suit the political style of Hafiz al-Asad, a style vindicated by
an unprecedented period of over seven years of power in Syria.

At the time of writing and given Syria's earlier political history, seven
years looked like a long period. Asad in fact ruled Syria for over thirty years.

NOTES

1. This article was published in *Asian Affairs*, 9 (1978), pp.57–66.
2. B. Lewis, *Islam in History* (London, 1972), pp.51–6.
3. See N. Rejwan, *Nasserist Ideology: Its Exponents and Critics* (New York: J. Wiley, 1974), pp.11–28.
4. The text of the lecture was reprinted in M. 'Aflaq, *Fi sabil al Ba'th* (Beirut: Dar al-Tali'ah, 1959), pp.51–60.
5. See I. Rabinovich, *Syria under the Ba'th 1963–1966: The Army-Party Symbiosis* (Jerusalem and New York: Israel Universities Press, 1972), pp.7, 21, and 22.
6. 'Kayfa naktubu tarikhana al-qawmi', Tahqiq Majallat *al-Ma'rifa* (Damascus: Ministry of Culture and National Guidance, 1966), pp.49–54.
7. A similar distinction between history writing for adults and history writing for schoolchildren was made by another participant in the symposium, the Palestinian historian M. Darwaza, 'Izzat. *Al-Wahda al-'Arabiyya* (Cairo: al-Maktab al-Tijari lil-Tiba'ah wal-Tawzi'i wal-Nashr, 1957) [in Arabic], pp.40–1.
8. Ibid., pp.82–9.
9. Ibid., pp.18–34.
10. Ibid., p.68.
11. Ibid., pp.5–26. For similar views in Egypt see Rejwan, *Nasserist Ideology*, p.18.
12. For a brief study of history textbooks in Syria, see D. Gordon, 'History and Identity in Arab Textbooks: Four Cases', *Princeton Near Eastern Paper*, 13 (1971).
13. Confessionalism is a somewhat awkward application of a French term, the equivalent of the Arabic term *tai'fiyya* which denotes the uniquely Middle Eastern phenomenon of attitudes and relationships emanating from the Ottoman Millet system. See Esman, J. Milton and Itamar Rabinovich (eds), *Ethnicity, Pluralism and the State in the Middle East* (Ithaca, NY: Cornell University Press, 1988).
14. *Tarikh al-arab al-hadith min al-ghazu al-'uthmani hata al-waqt al hadir* (al-saff al-thalith al-I'dadi) *Ta'lif Fi'ah min al-Mu'aliffin* (Damascus, 1965/6).
15. Ibid., pp.111–12.
16. Cf. Salamah 'Ubaid, *Al-thawrah al-suriyya al-kubra* (Beirut, 1971).
17. *Tarikh al-'arab*, pp.115–16.
18. Samih al-Imam, Suleiman al-Khuri and Ahmad Bitar, *Ta'rikh al-'arab al hadith* (al-saff al-sadis al-ibtida'i) (Damascus 1971/2, first printed in 1968/9). This book was prepared for a lower grade but the level of presentation is essentially the same.
19. Ibid., p.112.
20. Ibid., p.96.
21. Ibid., pp.112–13.
22. Tawfiq Baru, Ahmad Ibrahim 'Ibad and Mahmud 'Abduh, *Ta'rikh al-'arab al-hadith al-mu'asir* (al-jiz' aththan, ath-thalith, ath-thanawi, al-adabi) (Damascus, 1971/2).
23. Ibid., pp.9–10.
24. Ibid., p.20.
25. Ibid., pp.28, 129–30.
26. *Dirasa ta'rikhiyya tahliliyya muwajjaza li-nidal hizb al-Ba'th al-'arabi al-ishtiraki 1943–1971* (Damascus, 1972).
27. Ibid., pp.2–6.
28. Ibid.
29. Ibid., pp.9, 15.
30. Ibid., pp.6, 12–13, 15, 18.
31. Several years after the publication of this essay the Islamic opposition to the Ba'thi regime staged a full-blown rebellion in such cities as Aleppo and Hamah. The rebellion was finally brutally crushed by the regime in 1982.

12

Syria's Quest for a Regional Role[1]

Syria's quest for an influential role has been an important dimension of the regional politics of the Middle East since 1974. The persistence of this quest in the present Middle Eastern context is, therefore, hardly innovative. The novel elements in the present situation derive from the fact that following a period of unusual success in the years 1983–84 Syria's foreign policy has during the last two years encountered increasing difficulties. This paper seeks to explain the transition from earlier success to current adversity and to assess its repercussions for the region and the larger international arena. It will do so against the background of the Asad regime's foreign policy as it had evolved since the early 1970s.

A NEW SYRIAN FOREIGN POLICY

The first three years in the history of Hafiz al-Asad's regime (November 1970–October 1973) can be seen as a gestation period during which he formed and consolidated his regime and took Syria out of the isolation of the 1960s. Domestic stability and external success turned out to have been two mutually reinforcing pillars of his regime. The emergence for the first time in independent Syria of a comparatively stable regime enabled it to formulate and carry out a systematic foreign policy. In turn, the success of that policy had an important legitimizing effect within Syria.[2]

The policy of cooperation with Egypt that Asad initiated upon seizing power culminated in the joint launching of the October War. The war's course and outcome played a crucial role in the shaping of Asad's new foreign policy. Syria's treatment as a junior actor by the Soviet Union and Egypt and Asad's appreciation of the new circumstances and opportunities in the post October 1973 Middle East motivated him to seek a hitherto unfamiliar role of regional influence.

The first manifestations of the new policy were in evidence in 1974 but it became fully developed in 1975. As a full-blown policy it sought to turn Syria into a front row Arab and regional power, on par with Egypt, dealing with the two superpowers from a position of strength. That position was to rest on the domestic stability of Asad's regime, on Syria's military power and on its ability to control its immediate Arab environment – Lebanon, Jordan and the Palestinians. No regional policy should be allowed to unfold without Syria's participation or support particularly when issues concerning Syria's direct sphere of influence were concerned. Conversely, Syria should be able to implement within that sphere such policies deriving from its claim to an effective regional role.

Tensions and contradictions were inherent in Syria's new position and policies. Asad did build an effective and powerful regime but it remained a thinly disguised minoritarian government resting on unstable foundations. Asad wanted to develop and maintain a dialogue with the United States, whom he viewed as the key to developments in the Middle East, but he remained the head of a radical regime relying primarily on the Soviet Union. He joined the Arab-Israeli diplomatic process that Henry Kissinger began in December 1973 but he remained dubious of the process and its prospects. It was the mark of Asad's success that in the years 1975–77 he formulated and conducted an integrated policy, which harmonized these different elements and occasionally excelled in capitalizing on this very diversity. Asad could be doctrinare or pragmatic and could either harness or unleash the violent side of his regime.

In the spring of 1977 Asad reached the zenith of his success. His intervention in Lebanon resulted in a hegemonial position there recognized by the Arab world. He had a close working alliance with Jordan while the PLO, though inimical, had been brought under Syrian influence. When the Carter Administration launched its effort to bring about a comprehensive Arab-Israeli settlement it recognized and gave due consideration to Syria's and Asad's crucial and indispensable role in the successful implementation of its plan.

Asad had already demonstrated in 1976 that he was capable of standing on his own against the Soviet Union when the latter took exception to the direction of Syrian policy in Lebanon.

CRISIS AND RECOVERY, 1977–82

But later in 1977 success was replaced by failure and a regime crisis developed that lasted to the end of 1980.[3] The crisis affected domestic politics as well as foreign policy. At home the intervention in Lebanon proved to have been the catalyst of a wave of opposition that nearly brought the regime down. Externally Asad overplayed his hand against Egypt and the United States and Sadat's decision to open direct negotiations with Israel and Washington's subsequent endorsement of his decision left Syria without an effective response. There were two important lessons to be drawn

from this turn of events. The Baʿth regime, despite the impressive successes of the early 1970s, did not provide a domestic base firm enough for the
conduct of an ambitious regional policy. Nor could Asad's regional policy,
drawing as it did on skilful manipulation and balancing rather than on
Syria's intrinsic power and weight, compete with the power of Egypt when
the latter harnessed its power in the service of a well-defined regional policy.

Asad's difficulties came to a head in the spring and early summer of
1980, but he weathered the crisis and by the end of 1980 his position at
home and in the region had improved considerably. Having broken the
backbone of the radical Islamic opposition he could devote greater attention to foreign policy. Hence, the cumulative effect of Syria's military
build-up, the signing of a formal treaty with the Soviet Union, the new
cooperation with Iran and the difficulties of his chief Arab rivals, Egypt and
Iraq, combined to alleviate the pressure on Syria and to enhance its standing in the region. This was demonstrated in November 1980 when Syria
threatened war in order to disrupt an Arab Summit in Amman and again in
November 1981 when it foiled a Saudi effort to reformulate the Arab consensus on the question of settlement with Israel at the Fez Arab Summit.
The minutes of that meeting as published in the Lebanese press portray
Syria's Foreign Minister, ʿAbd al-Halim Khaddam, as the dominant figure,
lecturing his colleagues and upholding the cause of pan-Arab nationalism.
It was more difficult to contend with Israel's power and with the policies
of Menachem Begin's second government. Syria emerged triumphant from
the Lebanese 'missile crisis' of April 1981 but when Israeli law was extended to the Golan, Syria was hard put to respond nor could it marshall Arab
support. In 1982 it became increasingly clear that Israel was preparing a
large-scale operation in Lebanon and that Asad was seeking a way to avoid
a large-scale conflict with the Israel Defence Forces in Lebanon.

Asad failed. Israel fought him in Lebanon in June 1982 and defeated
him in the air and on the ground. The relatively good performance by
Syria's troops on the ground and the fact that considerable Syrian forces
remained in Eastern and Northern Lebanon offered little consolation in the
summer of 1982. By early September 1982 Bashir Jumayyil, an ally of the
US and Israel, had been elected president of Lebanon, the PLO had evacu-
ated Beirut and the Soviet Union had failed to provide Syria with any effective support. The Reagan Administration issued its plan for a revival of the
Arab-Israeli peace process that completely ignored Syria. It was a dark
hour. Against this background Asad's successes during the next two years
seem all the more impressive.[4]

A NEW REGIONAL EMINENCE, 1982–84

The assassination of Bashir Jumayyil in mid-September 1982 marked the transition to a dynamic Syrian drive to undo the consequences of the 1982 war in Lebanon and to rebuild Syria's hegemony across its western border. Almost from the outset, but more clearly after its initial successes, Syria sought to use its position in Lebanon to promote its broader regional policy.

The new configuration in Lebanon after Bashir Jumayyil's assassination confronted Syria with three principal adversaries in the Lebanese arena: (1) the new president, Amin Jumayyil, and his Maronite supporters; (2) the United States, Amin Jumayyil's chief supporter; and (3) Israel, whose relationship with Amin Jumayyil was complex and problematic.

In its conflict with these adversaries, Syria's greatest asset was its ability to perceive and take advantage of the tensions and contradictions, which militated against effective cooperation between its adversaries. Thus while the US lent its support to the Jumayyil Administration on the understanding that it would sponsor political reform in Lebanon and help formulate a new national consensus, the new president saw American support as an asset that would enable him to eschew reform and concessions and one that could be used in order to rid Lebanon of both Syria and Israel. But the United States was not in a position nor did the Reagan Administration desire to commit troops over time or to sustain casualties in order to support such policies. Israeli policy in Lebanon was still conducted by Ariel Sharon but the domestic political basis of that policy that had been contested during the summer was completely eroded by the massacre in Sabra and Shatila. Nor was Israel inclined to sustain casualties on behalf of a Lebanese president who opposed a direct and open relationship with it. Israel's alliance with other Maronites, the Lebanese Forces militia in particular, was shaken by other developments during the same period.

Under these circumstances it was relatively easy for Syria to organize a Lebanese coalition directed against one or all three of Syria's rivals. Shi'is, Palestinians and radical Lebanese were activated against Israel, radical Shi'is were used against the United States and a large group of Lebanese communities, parties and leaders was assembled against Amin Jumayyil. Asad was very skilful in patiently building and using these ad hoc coalitions, always working through proxy, always testing the limits to which he could push his stronger adversaries without exposing himself to a costly retaliation. His efforts were facilitated by the Soviet Union's decision at the end of 1982 to rebuild and improve Syria's air-defence system and by the numerous errors that his adversaries committed. As of May 1983 the conflict focused on the May 17 Agreement that was signed between the Lebanese and Israeli governments under American auspices.

Though not a peace treaty, it was, on paper, quite an impressive political document designed to regulate Israeli-Lebanese relations and to provide security arrangements in the south in return for which Israel was to withdraw from Lebanon. The US was led to believe that Syria would accept the agreement.

In the event Syria stepped up the campaign against the agreement and the Lebanese government had signed it. It won in the winter of 1984 when the United States decided to withdraw its troops from Beirut and Amin Jumayyil travelled to Damascus to capitulate, annulled the May 17 Agreement and asked the Israeli legation in the Beirut area to leave. Israel had already withdrawn its troops from the Beirut area to the Awali River in September 1983 and was clearly on its way further south. Syria was once more paramount in Lebanon.

Well before the final victory in 1984 it had become clear that the Lebanese arena had become the focal point of regional developments. This was primarily a result of the fact that the US committed its own troops to Lebanon in the service of a specific policy. The success or failure of that policy and of the US troops were bound to have important ramifications on the international scene and on the domestic American scene; all the more so in a year of presidential elections. As it transpired that Asad held the key to developments in Lebanon, it followed that he held an equally important key to American success or failure. This had been a traditional objective of Asad's policy but he was aware that the potential risks were as high as the potential rewards. As in 1977, the American-Syrian dialogue proved to be sterile and collapsed, but Asad managed to emerge practically unscathed from the confrontation.

The Lebanese arena during these years became also the central stage on which Arab-Israeli affairs were played out. Asad took advantage of the Palestine Liberation Organization's predicament after the evacuation of Beirut and sought to settle old scores with Yasir 'Arafat and to bring the organization under Syrian authority. His emissaries fomented Abu Musa's rebellion against 'Arafat and drove him out of the Baqa' Valley and eventually (in December 1983) from Tripoli. Earlier, in April 1983, Syria used its increased leverage on the PLO in order to obstruct its negotiations with Jordan's King Husayn. A Jordanian-Palestinian agreement was deemed necessary for King Husayn to respond to President Reagan's initiative of 1 September 1982. In this fashion, then, Syria contributed to another American failure in the region and demonstrated that it could not be easily ignored or outskirted.

But there were other messages in the Arab-Israeli context that Syria was sending through Lebanon. By taking indirect responsibility for Shi'i and Palestinian attacks against Israeli troops in Lebanon Syria was positioning itself as the leader of Arab resistance to Israel, an antithesis to Egypt and 'the Camp David road'. Since Israel was in retreat and seeking a way out of Lebanon Syria kept arguing that its line was being vindicated, that Israel could be defeated by a popular war of liberation and that all political bargaining with and concessions to Israel were gratuitous. In the same context it became ever more important to undo the May 17 Agreement. That agreement could be presented as a replica of the Camp David Accords, an Arab-Israeli political agreement negotiated under American auspices. If the replica could be destroyed the lessons could be applied to the original.[5]

A LOSS OF DIRECTION, 1984–86

This phase in the conduct of Syria's regional policy, marked as it was by clear sense of aim and direction, single-minded drive, effective management and orchestration and, of course, success ended in the spring of 1984 as many of these features disappeared. To some extent Syrian policy was the victim of its own success. This is particularly true of the Lebanese arena. Amin Jumayyil's capitulation, the departure of American troops and Israel's subsequent withdrawal (June 1985) transformed the situation. Syria was now hegemonial and had to shift from the relatively easy task of building a hostile coalition against an unpopular president and his external allies to the far more difficult task of building and maintaining a friendly coalition aiming at pacification, normalization, a new political consensus and, never to be forgotten, consolidation and formalization of Syria's own position.[6]

Related to these developments was the decline of Lebanon's centrality in the region. The focus of regional political activity shifted to other arenas: the renewal of Egyptian-Jordanian relations, the Egyptian-Iraqi rapprochement and Jordan's rapprochement with the PLO. Syria failed in its efforts to prevent 'Arafat from convening the Palestinian National Council in Amman or from signing the 11 February 1985 agreement with King Husayn, a measure designed to enable Jordan to negotiate the future of the West Bank with Israel.

The effectiveness of Syria's foreign policy during this period was clearly diminished by the deterioration, in November 1983, of Hafiz al-Asad's health and by the power struggle which erupted in 1984 between the president's brother, Rif'at, and the latter's rivals. In May 1984 Hafiz al-Asad reasserted his position and sent his brother and two of the latter's rivals out of the country in order to defuse the crisis. The power struggle has continued in a more subdued form but it and Asad's state of health have had their effect. It thus seems impossible to separate the fact that several of the heads of Syria's intelligence services were participants in the power struggle from the apparent loss of control over their activities in 1986.[7]

But the most striking change seems to have been the loss of a sense of purpose and direction. In the mid-1970s, as we saw, Syria was engaged in a sustained effort to build its power in the region and then to demonstrate it. In 1982–84 it conducted a specific drive against well-defined targets and rivals and demonstrated once again that it could not be ignored. It was to a large extent a reactive policy – a series of responses to a challenge in Lebanon and to the attempts to revive the Arab-Israeli peace process in ways unacceptable to Syria. The success of that policy left Syria without a regional policy. It has discrete policies on most regional questions but not an integrated regional strategy. It is to these discrete policies that attention should now be turned.

THE ARAB-ISRAELI CONFLICT

Syria's policy in the Arab-Israeli conflict is conducted under the doctrine and slogan of 'strategic parity with Israel'. The doctrine holds that Syria should have sufficient military strength to stand on its own against Israel in a future confrontation. Under that doctrine an impressive build up took place that turned Syria's armed forces into a large and well-equipped military machine. This machine does not have 'strategic parity' with Israel, but the Syrian leadership's perception of the balance of forces with Israel remains a subjective matter.

It is debated in Israel and elsewhere whether the doctrine of 'strategic parity' has an offensive or defensive edge or, in other words, whether it is designed to provide Syria with the capacity to launch on its own a full or limited war against Israel or whether it merely seeks to give Syria the power to oppose Israeli policies it would deem unacceptable. A good example of the latter is the second 'missile crisis' of November 1985–January 1986. Following an aerial battle above the Syrian-Lebanese border and the shooting down of two Syrian planes by Israeli planes over Syrian territory, Syria deployed ground to air missiles along its border with Lebanon and inside Lebanon's territory. Asad knew that Israel may act against the missiles but he obviously thought that this was an issue over which he wanted to take a stand and he also believed that this was a confrontation he could sustain. This particular crisis was resolved in January 1986 but a pattern was established.

The 'offensive school' interpretation of 'strategic parity' holds that Syria is planning and may well be on the verge of launching at least a limited attack in the Golan Heights or through Eastern Lebanon in order to seize some territory and to force Israel to make the concessions it did not make in the Golan Heights in 1973–74. Such interpretations of Syria's intentions appeared occasionally in the Israeli and international press and were from time to time reinforced by statements of Israeli military and political leaders. In February and March 1986 speculation concerning a planned Syrian attack on Israel was fuelled by two speeches in which Hafiz al-Asad spoke about 'strategic parity' and used threatening language towards Israel. A close reading of the same speeches revealed that Asad was actually telling his people that 'strategic parity' had yet to be achieved and was in fact a long-range goal. In any event, public speeches are not necessarily a good source for gauging operational plans and intentions. The wave of speculation and statements, which emanated from Israel, had, though, a curious mirror image effect on Syria. Since Syria did not, in fact, plan an attack at that time, its leaders tended to interpret the Israeli statements as the preparatory political groundwork for an attack on Syria.

The American raid on Libya in April and a visit by the Israeli Defence Minister to Washington exacerbated Syrian anxiety in the spring of 1986 that the US and Israel were planning an attack on Syria.[8]

Syria and Israel thus continue to deploy large armies along the Golan front and to monitor each other's movements and intentions with anxiety and suspicion. They continue to operate at cross-purposes in Lebanon and the danger of an unintended escalation is at least as acute as that of a calculated attack.

The other pole of Israeli-Arab relations, the diplomatic process, has not represented a real policy option for Syria for several years now. Syria's concept of a possible settlement with Israel is incompatible with the standards established in 1977 and has not, for different reasons, been acceptable to the United States and Israel. Syria has treated all diplomatic initiatives since 1975 as likely if not designed to exclude and isolate it and has fought against them with varying degrees of success. Asad and Syria do not reject the notion of settlement as such but their advocacy of Arab resilience against the 'capitulationist' road represented by Anwar al-Sadat or King Husayn and Yasir 'Arafat has tended in recent years to obscure the fine distinctions.

In the absence of either a war or a settlement option Syria's activity in the Arab-Israeli conflict continued to focus on South Lebanon. In 1986 it was also implicated in a series of terrorist attacks on Israeli and Israeli-related targets outside the Middle East.

From Syria's point of view Israel's concept of 'security zone' in South Lebanon and its continued activity there remained unacceptable even after the completion of its withdrawal plan in June 1985. Asad's point of departure has been that all gains accruing to Israel as a result of the 1982 war had to be eliminated. These included the South Lebanese Army under General Lahad (the upgraded version of Major S'ad Haddad's original militia), its Druze component and presence in Jizzin, the Christian town on the southern slopes of Mount Lebanon. Implicit in this rejection of the post-1982 innovation is the possibility of compliance with the pre-1982 elements of Israel's security plan in South Lebanon, but the political context for exploring the potential flexibility that this afforded did not exist in 1986. Syria fought Israel's presence and influence in South Lebanon by proxy, supporting attacks by Shi'ite, Palestinian and sundry Lebanese groups on the South Lebanese Army, on Israeli troops and, on a few occasions, on targets in Israel proper.

During the past few months all other aspects of Syria's foreign policy have been overshadowed by the fallout from the discovery of direct Syrian implication in terrorist activities. Only some of these were directed at Israeli or Israeli-related targets. This pattern is not new; Syria had engaged, directly and indirectly, in what can be defined as anti-Israeli terrorist acts and other forms of political violence for years now. The same organizations had been used against Israeli, Arab and even Syrian targets. The recent wave had been distinguished by heavy-handed direct involvement and by the absence of a reasonable comprehensive framework. The attempt to plant a bomb on an EL-AL plane in London may have been designed to punish Israel for the interception of a Libyan plane that carried an important Syrian politician. Even if this explanation is accepted, important questions linger about subsequent events. In May and June President Asad was clearly worried by the prospects of an Israeli or American-Israeli attack and invested considerable efforts in denouncing terrorism and in disassociating his regime from terrorist acts. How is, then, one to explain the attempt to plant another bomb in an EL-AL plane in Madrid in late June (an Israeli target) and the terrorist wave in Paris in September (non-Israel related) in which Syria was once again implicated.[9]

SYRIA AND THE LEBANESE CRISIS

Since its victory in Lebanon in the winter of 1984, Syrian policy there has been concerned with four main interests: pacification and normalization, consolidation and formalization of its own position and the conflicts with the PLO and Israel.

As has already been mentioned, Syria has encountered serious difficulties in Lebanon since, and to some extent because of, its victory. The underlying goals as set in the latter half of the 1970s have not changed. Syria wants control of Lebanese affairs without formal annexation and without having to maintain a large army across its western border. It seeks to base this control on its paramount influence over the central political institutions and the security forces, on its relationships with and influence over a whole spectrum of political forces and leaders in Lebanon, on some military presence and on the ability to project force and influence across a long border. It would like to formalize this paramount position, or hegemony, by signing a defence pact with Lebanon.

The pursuit of Syria's goals in Lebanon has been hampered by Asad's decision not to engage his troops in the quicksand of Lebanese politics. This was a lesson of the developments which nearly brought his regime down in the late 1970s. Syria's military forces thus remained mostly in the background while an intricate policy seeking to manipulate and operate through local forces and actors was carried out. It turned out to have been a policy full of flaws and contradictions that failed to overcome the complexities of Lebanese politics. Nor were Syria's policy makers in Lebanon, despite their proximity and experience, free from grave errors of judgement.

This was illustrated by the Syrian effort in December 1985 to accomplish Syria's two main aims through an agreement between the three most prominent militia leaders in Lebanon – Nabih Berri, the leader of *Amal*, the Shi'ite militia, the Druze leader, Walid Junblat, and Elie Hobeika, the new leader of the Maronite Lebanese Forces, who had recently taken over that militia after successive power struggles. The three were brought to Damascus to sign an agreement arranging for political reform and compromise and formalizing Syria's dominant position in Lebanon. The Syrians resorted to this strategy after a long series of attempts to act through the president and the traditional leaders of the large communities. The absence of a consensus militated against the normalization of public and political life and contributed to the persistence of violence. This state of affairs reflected on Syria whose supremacy made it responsible for the lingering crisis.

But the agreement signed in December 1985 collapsed in January 1986. Syria's mistake was to view Elie Hobeika as a reliable instrument representing the Maronite community and the important complex of East Beirut and its outlying areas. His position had been fragile to begin with and was completely undermined by his willingness to sign away some of the Maronites' traditional privileges. He was ousted and replaced by his rival Samir Ja'ja. Hobeika went first to Europe and then to Damascus where he tried to prepare a comeback with Syrian help. One such effort was made last August and failed.

Hobeika's downfall left Syria without a comprehensive policy in Lebanon. It has tried a variety of approaches – encouraging its proxies to shell East Beirut, drawing a 'security plan' for Beirut and even, in a clear departure from its original policy, dispatching several hundred Syrian troops and intelligence agents to West Beirut.

Syria is clearly obstructed in Lebanon not only by the complexity of Lebanese politics and its own inhibitions and vulnerability but also by the continued involvement of external actors, particularly the PLO, Iran and Israel.

We have seen how in 1982 and 1983 Syria used the PLO's predicament in Lebanon in an attempt to bring the organization under its own influence. The PLO had indeed been greatly weakened by the war and by Syria's pressure but it survived the crisis. Yasir 'Arafat defeated the Syrian effort to unseat him and remained the recognized leader of the mainstream PLO. He has been also quite successful in reestablishing presence in Beirut and South Lebanon. In so doing he has relied on his financial resources, the support of the Sunni community and his skill in exploiting the nuances of Lebanese politics. Syria has relied primarily on *Amal* in its efforts to dislodge the PLO from its remaining positions in West Beirut and to prevent it from establishing new ones there and in the south. But *Amal* has so far failed in its drive. The PLO, in turn, has struck an alliance with Hizballah, *Amal*'s radical rival. In return for Hizballah's shelter the PLO has provided personnel, materiel and money for operations designed to embarrass common rivals – Israel, *Amal* and Syria. Asad's decision to dispatch Syrian troops to West Beirut in July 1986 was influenced by his realization that the indirect efforts to stop the PLO had failed.

Hizballah's cooperation with the PLO is but one element in the complex trilateral relationship between Syria, Iran and the radical Shi'a in Lebanon. Syria's main ally in the Shi'ite community is *Amal*, though in characteristic fashion Asad's regime cultivates more than a single channel of contact and influence. Syria and Hizballah had a close cooperation when the joint drive against the US presence so required during the years 1982–84. But presently Hizballah, as a radical Muslim organization insisting on its independence from Syria, and its right and ability to maintain relations with other patrons presents a challenge to Syrian policy in Lebanon. Conceivably Syria could use its power against Hizballah in the Baqa' Valley more so than in Beirut but it knows full well that this would mean a breakdown in relations with Iran that broader considerations of Syria's regional interests rule out as a possibility.[10]

SYRIA IN INTER-ARAB RELATIONS

Syria's position in Arab politics is based on its power but also on an Arab nationalist prestige of sorts. Despite the decline of pan-Arab nationalism in the recent decade and despite much criticism and reserve directed at Asad's regime, he also draws some grudging admiration from Arabs impressed by the fact that he stands up to the United States and Israel. During his more successful periods the aura of success was an added asset.

Its influence in Arab politics has given Syria a blocking power. It has not been able to impose its views on many issues – if an Arab Summit were to be held Syria would be isolated in its efforts against the PLO. But it has succeeded in preventing such a Summit from being held and in obstructing Egypt's return to the Arab fold despite Egypt's and most Arabs' wishes.

But the radical alliance had been a problematic partnership in other respects too. Syria's relationships with both Libya and Iran have remained uncomfortable. Asad thus needs Mu'ammar Qadhdhafi's support and resources, but he resents the latter's proclivity to confront him with faits accomplis on sensitive issues, and as a leader mindful of his international reputation and standing he often tries to distance himself from his Libyan ally.

The relationship with Iran is still more complex. Since 1979, Iran has been an important ally against the common Iraqi rival. The implicit endorsement by the Ayatollah Ruhallah Khumeini has been an important legitimizing factor for a regime attacked by a radical Islamic opposition. More recently, against the background of persistent economic difficulties, direct and indirect economic aid from Iran has grown in significance. But there is less than complete confidence between the two regimes. The Iranian regime has avoided an explicit endorsement of Asad's regime and, as we saw, its cultivation of the radical Shi'a in Lebanon has often embarrassed the Syrian leadership.

It is difficult to support the following argument with evidence but it would seem that during the past year Syria, too, became worried by estimates that Iran was about to defeat Iraq militarily. It was one thing to support Iran when it had been invaded by Iraq or even when it succeeded in shifting the war to Iraq's territory. But an Iraqi defeat would bring Iranian presence and a galvanizing radical religious order far too close to the home front.

Earlier in the year it seemed for a while that the Jordanian-Syrian rapprochement and Jordanian mediation might result in a *renversement des alliances* and a Syrian-Iraqi mending of fences. It later transpired that Asad did not seriously contemplate a change in his relations with Iran and Iraq and may have used the occasion to exert some pressure on his Iranian allies.

The rapprochement with Jordan, though, is a more serious and durable matter. It began in 1985 and has continued to the present. It has not restored the Syrian-Jordanian relationship to the level of intimate alliance on which it had been in the mid 1970s. The active hostility of the late 1970s and early 1980s may have destroyed the possibility of all genuine cooperation between President Asad and King Husayn. But it suited both parties to end their active hostility and to normalize their relations. From Syria's perspective it has been a successful maneouver that neutralized some of the negative effects of the decline in the importance of the Lebanese arena. In the latter part of 1984 and in 1985 Asad felt relegated to the margins of Arab politics, unable to affect moves by Egypt, Jordan and the PLO except, possibly, by threatening to use force. The normalization of relations with Jordan, which coincided with the collapse of Jordan's dialogue with the PLO, was, in that respect, a most successful move. There is also a security dimension to the Syrian-Jordanian rapprochement. Syria wants closer coordination with Jordan assuming that Israel might seek to use Jordanian airspace in a future war. But so far the degree of confidence necessary for such coordination does not seem to have been restored.

SYRIA AND THE SOVIET UNION

After sixteen years of cooperation and six years of formal alliance the Soviet Union and Hafiz al-Asad's regime are fully aware of the advantages and drawbacks of their relationship. For both parties it is a utilitarian relationship devoid of sentiment and ideological zeal. For the Soviet Union, Syria is its one ally in the core area of the Middle East, the key to influence over the Arab-Israeli conflict and other important regional issues. The Soviets know by now that Asad guards his independence, would like to have a dialogue with the United States and is liable to become embroiled in a war with Israel that would confront them with odious policy choices. But these are problems they can live with and can hope to minimize. They provide Syria with sophisticated weapon systems and maintain a studied ambiguity with regard to their actions in case of war. The ambiguity is directed both at Syria and Israel. Syria is to be kept in the dark so as not to embolden it to go to war on the assumption that a Soviet safety net is guaranteed. Israel is to be deterred by the notion that a major Syrian defeat could bring about Soviet intervention.[11]

In 1984 Asad tried to expand the terms of the Soviet-Syrian relationship. He wanted a strategic 'cooperation' and 'dialogue' comparable to the American Israeli one and designed to neutralize its effects. He also wanted to become Moscow's 'super-client' in the region, a broker of its regional policies. Both demands were rejected by the Soviets. The relationship was strained at the end of 1984 by other policy differences. The Soviets objected, as they had done in the past, to Asad's campaign against 'Arafat; they also engaged for a brief period in an effort to develop relations with the conservative Arab states of the Gulf region with a view to diversifying their Middle Eastern policy. It was a passing episode and in 1985 Soviet-Syrian relations were back on their familiar course.

On 14 November 1986 the White House announced the imposition of sanctions on Syria 'in response to Syria's continued support for international terrorism' and more specifically as a punitive measure occasioned by Syria's role in the attempt to plant a bomb aboard an EL-AL airliner in London on 17 April 1986. The verdict in the trial of the man who actually tried to plant the bomb, the evidence presented at the trial and additional evidence had already led the British government to sever diplomatic relations with Syria, the American and Canadian governments to recall their ambassadors from Damascus and the European Economic Community to impose (mild) sanctions on Syria. Later in November the Federal Republic of Germany imposed its own sanctions on Syria after a court in Berlin had established that Syrian diplomats played a role in the bombing in March 1986 of an Arab club in West Berlin.

The White House's announcement was clearly timed for the British Prime Minister's visit to Washington. The sanctions imposed by the US were not particularly severe, but the statement contained a very specific warning. It explained that 'these measures are intended to convince the Syrian government that state support of terrorism will not be tolerated by the civilized world. We will continue to closely monitor the situation and take additional steps as necessary'.

The episode and the chain of events of which it formed a part must have been very embarrassing and unsettling to Hafiz al-Asad. As a ruler sensitive to his international standing and reputation and eager to maintain a dialogue with the United States, he undoubtedly realized the danger entailed by the recent turn of events. But he could also derive some satisfaction from the fact that the United States and its European allies were quite reluctant to impose sanctions on Syria and, except for Britain, settled on fairly mild ones. The White House statement of 14 November ended, in the same vein, with a revealing sentence. 'Syria', it read, 'can play an important role in a key region of the world but it cannot expect to be accepted as a responsible power or treated as one as long as it continues to use terrorism as an instrument of its foreign policy'. This was the other side of the threat mentioned earlier – should Syria change its ways, an American-Syrian dialogue could be renewed that would recognize and possibly enhance Syria's regional role.

The theme itself is hardly new. During the past thirteen years, since Henry Kissinger's first visit to Damascus in December 1973, Asad had tried

to persuade successive US Administrations that Syria was an important
regional power and that if the US wanted to conduct an effective Middle
Eastern policy it had to acknowledge and accept that role. Over the years
Asad's willingness to shape his policies so as to accommodate American
views and interests and Syria's perception by different American
Administrations varied considerably. In the 1974–76 period Henry Kissinger
cooperated successfully with Hafiz al-Asad in the context of the Arab-Israeli
settlement process and in Lebanon, but their cooperation was limited and
American-Syrian relations remained partly adversarial. Asad did obstruct
Kissinger's efforts to include Jordan in the diplomatic process and when he
arranged for a separate Israeli-Egyptian agreement over the Sinai Syria conducted a political offensive designed to isolate Egypt and render the agreement useless.[12]

The Carter Administration tried to coopt Asad and Syria into its effort
to bring about a comprehensive Arab-Israeli agreement but failed. Syria's
subsequent effort to undermine the Camp David Accord and the Israeli-
Egyptian peace treaty failed too. It did, however, contribute to the contro-
versiality of these agreements and to the failure of the autonomy plan.[13]

The Reagan Administration, during Alexander Haig's tenure at the State
Department adopted a hostile attitude toward Syria. Syria was to be isolated and weakened rather than courted. It could be brought into the context
of an American sponsored settlement but only after it will have been weakened and mellowed.[14] This changed after the 1982 war in Lebanon and
Haig's departure. The following period, September 1982 to February 1984,
constituted the most intricate phase in American-Syrian relations. The US
tried to revive the Arab-Israeli peace process through a plan excluding and
unacceptable to Syria, to install in Lebanon an Administration not acceptable to Syria and to regulate Lebanese-Israeli relations through an agreement that Syria saw as anathema. Throughout this period it communicated
with Syria through a number of senior emissaries and was fully aware of
Syria's role in orchestrating the opposition to its policies in Lebanon. It
suspected Syria of having a role in the attacks on the US embassy and the
US marines in Beirut and occasionally resorted to using limited force
against Syria. The Reagan Administration was also apparently led to believe
that Syria would endorse the 17 May Lebanese-Israeli agreement.

Asad, as we saw, conducted this complex dialogue with great skill,
probing the limits of American tolerance and not exceeding them. In
February 1984 he registered a victory over the US and a vindication of his
assertion that Washington could not successfully pursue a policy that he
found unacceptable at least not in his part of the region.

One of the limiting effects of this phase has been the Reagan

Administration's reluctance to sponsor new regional initiatives. The only such initiative it supported – the effort to bring about Israeli-Jordanian-Palestinian negotiations – never gathered sufficient momentum to become the object of serious Syrian opposition. In the absence of American initiatives Syria's claim to indispensability has not been tested. The relative decline in Syria's standing during the same period had a similar effect.

An American-Syrian muted dialogue of sorts continued. It dealt with a fairly limited bilateral relationship and the US was also able to exert some moderating influence over the Syrian-Israeli rivalry in Lebanon. In this context issues which come under the loose heading of terrorism came to play an unusually prominent role in American-Syrian relations. This new form of dialogue was predicated on Syria's hegemonial role in Lebanon and on Lebanon's centrality to this issue – either as the arena in which hostages were taken and hijacked planes landed or as the base from which terrorist acts in other parts of the world are launched.

As a rule, Asad's regime artfully straddled the line – supporting some Palestinian and Shi'i organizations, opposing others and having a measure of influence over some. It was helpful during the hijacking of a TWA airliner in June 1985 but in the final analysis could not obtain release of all the passengers without turning to Tehran. In October of the same year Syria was clearly interested for its own reasons to obstruct and embarrass Yasir 'Arafat. On other occasions, particularly those involving Abu Nidal and his organization, suspicions of Syrian involvement were raised but not backed by clear public evidence.

Getting credit for helpfulness in this matter from the Reagan Administration was a diluted version of earlier policies which capitalized on the Asad regime's ability to harness the darker side of Middle Eastern politics, including its own. In any event, that policy ran its course and began to backfire in the spring of 1986. A satisfactory explanation for this turn of events has yet to be provided, but it seems to be related to Hafiz al-Asad's state of health, to the power struggle within his regime and to the participation in that struggle of the heads of several of Syria's intelligence services.

The impact of these events has been blunted by revelations concerning the US government's dealings with Iran. It is curious to note that the story was first made public by a pro-Syrian newspaper in Beirut. This may have been done in coordination with the Iranian regime (or part of it) or without such coordination, but the short-term effect has clearly benefited the Syrian Ba'th regime. Still, Syria's immediate gain is marred by the recurrence of a familiar theme: it is the real sources of power in the region, states like Iran and Egypt, that the superpowers are ultimately interested in. Syria has not been able to exceed the limits of an intermediate regional power.

CONCLUSION

A number of patterns and characteristics emerge from the foregoing examination of Syria's twelve-year quest for a regional role:

1) An almost rhythmic oscillation between phases of success and
retreat. Syria's inability to sustain its regional success over time
seems to be the product of its limited intrinsic power and
resources, the underlying weakness of the regime's political base
and the shifting nature of Middle Eastern regional politics. Syria
has been at once part of the regional political system and an actor
seeking to shape it to its own liking. Its ability to do so has naturally depended on the attitudes and relative strength of the other
actors.

2) A particularly close relationship between domestic politics and the
conduct of foreign policy. During the formative years of the Asad
regime its own relative stability and its external exploits were
mutually reinforcing determinants of its political success. Later the
negative effects of this close relationship became evident when
domestic problems hampered the regime's performance in the
region and foreign policy set-backs contributed to the erosion of
the regime's legitimacy. Asad's illness may well have introduced a
permanent uncertainty into Syrian politics with an attendant
impact on the country's regional role. Here the repercussions of
Asad's failure to place his regime on a solid institutional basis are
felt quite acutely. To this Syria's current economic difficulties must
be added as a political constraint. Economists agree that these difficulties are not likely to be resolved soon and that they will
continue to affect the regime's political and military capabilities in
the foreseeable future.

3) A pragmatic approach to foreign policy. There is an ideological
dimension to Asad's foreign policy. He is a Ba'thi of long standing
and despite the fact that power is ultimately in military hands, the
party plays an important role in Asad's regime. It is difficult to
envisage Asad reorienting his international or regional policies in
a fashion reminiscent of Sadat. But short of radical reorientations,
Asad's record points to a willingness and ability to follow
geo-political and pragmatic considerations.[15]

4) On the whole, Asad's foreign and regional policies have been
reactive. There has been a deliberate and conscious drive on Asad's
part to build a power base and a regional role for his regime and

country. It has sometimes been suggested that he was motivated by a vision. The notion of Greater Syria is often suggested as the core of such a vision. This interpretation has some merit but cannot be accepted as the key to Asad's and Syria's conduct in the region. It is intellectually less exciting but probably more correct to view Asad as a man of both ambitions and anxieties who developed a powerful machine which he has since used mostly to respond to threats, less so to opportunities in the region.

It is against this background that the significance of the present phase in the development of Syria's regional policies should be examined. The decline in Syria's regional influence has coincided with a passive period in regional politics. Syria still has the capacity to end this passivity by taking the initiative vis-á-vis Israel, in the Lebanese arena or in the context of the war between Iran and Iraq. But it is difficult to see the attraction that an initiative in any of these arenas holds for Syria in the present circumstances. Syria's own reaction to the sanctions imposed by the US and its European allies suggests a cautious approach, hardly a surprise given Asad's record. American and international preoccupation with the fallout from a political scandal arising from a different Middle Eastern issue may well vindicate this approach.

It is difficult, for the same reason, to envisage the Reagan Administration embarking on a major new initiative in the Middle East. It has been its policy during the past two years, and recent experience must have reinforced these trends. The absence of initiatives removes potential pressures from Syria but also reduces Syria's importance as a state whose objection must be neutralized or whose goodwill and services must be secured. This state of affairs may suit Asad now but may prove difficult for him to sustain over time. A regional role is important to the regime's self view and may prove to be an urgent necessity for a regime seeking financial aid from the richer states of the region. Given the nature of regional politics in the Middle East the opportunity or the need for Syria to take a more active role may arise. Even in a period of retreat Syria's military power and its influence in Lebanon are significant assets and they could be brought to bear as they were, for example, in 1976.

A different approach to the same set of data would seek to take advantage of Syria's embarrassment in order to offer it a positive role in a larger Middle Eastern context. A fresh effort to revive the Arab-Israeli peace process does not seem feasible now. But Syria has the potential and may have the motivation to contribute to a stabilization of South Lebanon. Of the various difficulties which militate against the successful pursuit of such an effort, one inherent contradiction could be the most serious. In 1976 a tacit and indirect understanding was worked out between Syria and Israel through the US. It was successful because Asad saw an overriding necessity and because it was kept tacit. The overriding necessity may be there, though it would be very difficult to keep a calming Syrian role in South Lebanon tacit now. But it is still a worthwhile effort.

NOTES

1. Research for this article was completed under a Fellowship at the Woodrow Wilson Center and pre-pared for presentation at a colloquium, Woodrow Wilson International Center for Scholars, Smithsonian Institution, 11 December 1986. It was published as a Working Paper 79, International Security Studies Program, Woodrow Wilson International Center for Scholars, 1986.

2. On Asad's foreign policy see, among other works, Raymond A. Hinnebusch 'The Foreign Policy of Syria', in Bahgat Korany and Ali E. Hillal Desouki (eds), The Foreign Policy of Arab States (Boulder, CO: Westview Press, 1984), pp.283–322 and I. Rabinovich, 'Syria', in Colin Legum and Haim Shaked (eds), Middle East Contemporary Survey, Vol. I, 1976–1977, New York, NY: Holmes and Meier Publishers, 1978, pp.604–18.

3. On the crisis of the late 1970s in Syria see Stanley F. Reed III, 'Dateline Syria: Fin de Regime?', Foreign Policy, 39 (Summer 1980), pp.176–90.

4. See Itamar Rabinovich, The War for Lebanon, 1970–1985 (Ithaca, NY: Cornell University Press, 1985).

5. Ibid. and in Moshe Maoz and Avner Yaniv (eds), Syria under Asad: Domestic Constraints and Regional Risks (London: Croom Helm, 1986), passim.

6. For an excellent analysis of recent Syrian policies in Lebanon see William Harris, 'Beirut: the Battle to Come', The Middle East, 140 (June 1986), pp.10–11 and 'Syria Rides the Tiger', The Middle East, 144 (October 1986), pp.8–9.

7. See Alasdair Drysdale 'The Succession Question in Syria', The Middle East Journal, 39, 2 (Spring 1985), pp.246–57.

8. For an outsider's summary of Israeli views see Leslie H. Gelb 'Israelis Say Syria Might Seek a War', The New York Times (14 July 1986). For articles in the Syrian press in 1986 warning against an Israeli or an American-Israeli attack on Syria see Tishrin (25 and 30 March), al-Ba'th (8 May 1986), al-Ba'th (18 March 1986) as typical examples. For a semi-official Israeli view, see 'Syria: The Strategic Threat', IDF Journal (Fall 1985), pp.73–6.

9. On 14 November 1986 the State Department distributed a list of terrorist incidents in which Syria has been implicated. The list was distributed along with the White House's statement.

10. On Syria's relationship with Iran see Rouhullah Ramazani, Revolutionary Iran: Challenge and Response in the Middle East (Baltimore, MD: Johns Hopkins University Press 1986).

11. For recent works on Soviet-Syrian relations see Pedro Ramet, 'The Soviet-Syrian Relationship', Problems of Communism, 35 (September–October 1986) and the sources cited there.

12. For that period see Henry Kissinger, Years of Upheaval (Boston, MA: Little Brown, 1982), pp.760–1 and onwards.

13. Jimmy Carter, Keeping Faith: Memoirs of a President (Toronto, ON: Bantam Books, 1982), p. 286 and William Quandt, Camp David, Peacemaking and Politics (Washington, DC: Brookings Institution, 1986), passim.

14. Alexander Haig, Caveat: Realism, Reagan and Foreign Policy (New York, NY: Macmillan, 1984), p.342.

15. Some of the best insights into Asad's conduct of foreign policy and examples of his pragmatism are provided by a Lebanese Phalangist politician who had served as liaison with the Syrians in the late 1970s and early 1980s; see Karim Pakradouni, La paix manquée (Beirut, 1984), passim.

IV
SYRIA AND ISRAEL

13

Syria, Israel and the Palestine Question, 1945–1977[1]

During his Revolution Day address on 8 March 1974, President Hafiz al-Asad of Syria made a rather startling statement: 'Palestine,' he said, 'was indeed the major part of Southern Syria.'[2] This was apparently a response to a declaration by Golda Meir that the Golan Heights formed an indivisible part of the state of Israel. But the claim implied in Asad's statement and the very use of the term 'Southern Syria' indicated that more was meant than just a forceful reply to an Israeli contention.

In fact, during the next three years several writers and spokesmen enlarged on this idea. The Syrian state, headed by Asad, it was suggested, was seeking to implement King Faysal's unsuccessful scheme of 1918–20 and to establish a Greater Syrian state centered in Damascus.[3] This (possibly organized on a federal basis) was to comprise the existing states of Syria, Jordan and Lebanon, and eventually whichever parts of Palestine were to be freed or received back from Israel. As recently as August 1977, a Syrian-inspired report on Radio Beirut claimed that Syria and the PLO had agreed that 'there shall be no links between the [Palestinian] state and Jordan before the Geneva Conference ... moreover, any links with Jordan later on should be in the form of a confederation between Syria, Palestine and Jordan'.[4]

Underlying this scheme is the notion that Greater Syria is a natural entity which should have been made into one Arab state after the destruction and partition of the Ottoman Empire. In 1918–20, King Faysal made a feeble attempt to assert this idea during his brief reign and the term Southern Syria comes from that period. A group of Palestinian Arab nationalists seeking support against the Zionist Movement were willing to submerge Palestine into a Greater Syrian entity under the name of Southern Syria. This was a short-lived episode but the term survived to be picked up for its own purposes by the Syrian regime of the mid-1970s.

It is significant that during the fifty-odd years which separated Faysal's fall from the mid-1970s, no Syrian government tried to promote the idea of a Greater Syria. In the 1930s and 1940s, King 'Abdallah of Transjordan and the Syrian Social Nationalist Party made some attempts in this vein, but they were strongly resisted by the Arab Nationalist governments in Damascus

President Asad and other members of his entourage joined the Ba'th Party as adolescents in the 1940s; they were, however, probably also influenced to some degree by the rival doctrine of the Syrian Social Nationalist Party. Nevertheless, the present regime's allusions to the existence of a Greater Syrian entity and its contingent claim to a special and direct relationship between Syria and Palestine do not represent a continuous policy line, but rather, novel elements in a new policy. This new policy was shaped by the changes in Syria's position in inter-Arab affairs and in the Arab-Israeli conflict in the early 1970s, particularly after the 1973 War. These changes can be fully appreciated against the background of earlier phases of Syrian policy towards Israel (1945–49, 1949–61, 1961–67, 1967–73), each dominated by one particular element. It was only after the 1973 War that Syria's claim to a direct link with Palestine became an important part of her policy.

Two major factors accounted for Syrian participation in the Arab-Israeli War of 1948–49: emotional and ideological identification with the Palestinian Arabs and the dynamics of inter-Arab relations. Syrian Arab nationalists felt a sense of particular closeness and attachment to the Palestinians; their support was also rooted in a broader Arab nationalist perspective and they regarded active support for the Arabs in Palestine as a national duty, comparable to the anti-colonial struggle against the French in Syria itself.

Damascus, during the late 1930s, under the autonomous government of the National Bloc, had served as the political and operational centre of the Arab Revolt in Palestine. In the late 1940s several civilian and military leaders of the younger generation of Syrian nationalists such as Akram Hourani and Adib Shishakli volunteered to fight as irregulars in Palestine.[5] There were those more calculating nationalist leaders and politicians in Syria whose interest was motivated by a desire to bring the Palestinian Arabs under the hegemony of Damascus, but this does not appear to have been an important factor.[6]

Of far greater significance for Syrian policy makers was the network of inter-Arab rivalries and alliances which by the mid-1940s had already taken a clear shape. Syrian governments at that time tended to side with Egypt and Saudi Arabia against the Hashemite regimes in Iraq and Transjordan, the latter two having ambitions in Syria and Palestine. The participation in the Palestine War of 1948–49 was designed to obstruct

Hashemite expansionist plans quite as much as to support the Palestinian Arabs or promote direct Syrian interests.

After the 1948–49 War and the establishment of the state or Israel, another important dimension was added to the Palestinian and Arab nationalist aspects of the conflict: there arose a series of bilateral confrontations between Israel and her Arab neighbours, of which the Syrian-Israeli dispute became the most acrimonious.[7] Its intensity was influenced by the inherited traditions of Syria's rulers during the 1950s: a particular attachment to the territory and people of Arab Palestine, a deep identification with pan-Arab nationalism and heavy involvement in pan-Arab issues. A series of new factors was added to these emotions.

For example, the armistice agreements signed between Israel and most Arab participants in the 1948–49 War were envisaged as only a temporary measure, not intended for long-term regulation of complicated questions, such as those along the Syrian-Israeli frontier: the demilitarized zones, the al-Hammah enclave, disputed border properties, etc.[8] Such a cluster of problems would be sufficient to spoil relations between potentially good neighbours; it could certainly not be controlled by two bitter rivals.

Moreover, unlike the Egyptian army, the Syrians emerged from the 1948–49 War in full control of their national territory as well as some slices of Palestine. Although the war had been lost, the Syrian army considered itself undefeated and perfectly capable of holding its own against the Israelis. Reinforced by topographic superiority in the frontier areas, this feeling prompted several Syrian army commanders to adopt a bellicose attitude towards Israel.

The assumption by the military of an increasingly important role in Arab politics exacerbated the Arab-Israeli conflict, contributing to an arms build-up and creating complex linkages between military performance and political fortunes. In Syria, where such involvement in politics began early and remained a consistent feature, this issue assumed a particular importance.[9]

Similarly, the early and significant role of ideological movements and parties in Syrian politics tended to exacerbate the confrontation with Israel. Whereas a policy based on interests and ambition may be conducive to compromise and settlement, these become more difficult when the conflict and the opponent are construed in ideological terms.

In February 1958 Syria gave up her independent existence as a state and merged into the United Arab Republic, and until 1961 had no independent foreign policy. However, the traumatic break-up of the UAR and the ensuing animosity towards Egypt deeply affected the new Syrian state, whose legitimacy 'Abd al-Nasir refused to recognize. He attempted to topple its

government and the effectiveness of his assault derived from Syria's singu-
lar commitment to Arabism and from his own position as the leader and
spokesman par excellence for Arab nationalism. If he maintained that the
Syrian regime was inimical to the true interests of Arabism, then good Arab
nationalists everywhere were bound to oppose it. This was the chief cause
of the domestic instability and external isolation of the new Syrian regime.
In self-defence, its leaders had to show that 'Abd al-Nasir was not the
mighty Arab nationalist leader he claimed to be. Or, in a different vein, they
could assert that their unique contribution to Arab nationalism justified
Syria's independent existence. In both cases, Palestine and the Arab-Israeli
conflict provided the best arena for their efforts. In 1962, therefore, the
Syrian leaders, headed by Akram Hourani, launched a campaign designed
to show that 'Abd al-Nasir had sold out to the United States on the issue of
Palestine.[10]

Later, when in March 1963 the Ba'th replaced the 'separatist' regime,
new elements were added. The Ba'th was, in ideology and organization, a
pan-Arab party and must therefore have, and be seen to have, a policy of
its own in the Arab-Israeli conflict. One radical wing genuinely sought to
develop a new Arab strategy against Israel. Finally, the Ba'th embroiled itself
in factionalism and the regime's policy towards Israel became an instrument in domestic power struggles.[11]

As a result, in 1963 and even more so in 1966, Syria's attitude in the
Arab-Israeli conflict changed to one of provocation. Often calculated to
embarrass Egypt (or Jordan), the policy at times got out of hand and at
other times was the manifestation of a genuine belief in its merits. A party
congress convened by the radical authors of the 23 February 1966 coup d'é-
tat resolved that: 'The Congress views the Palestine Problem as the main axis
of our domestic, Arab and international policies. It believes that the traditional policy with regard to the liberation of Palestine has always been and
remained [a stratagem] designed to obliterate the line distinguishing the
progressive from the reactionary forces.'[12]

Syrian-Egyptian rivalry led directly to the convening of the first Arab
Summit Conference in January 1964, at which it was decided among other
things to establish the PLO. In retrospect the consequences of this decision
seem very significant, greater perhaps than was intended at the time. In more
immediate terms it led to the institutionalization of the notion of a Palestinian
entity, to the revival of inter-Arab bickering concerned directly with the
Palestine issue and to the surfacing of such 'anti-establishment' organizations
as the al-Fath. The Ba'th regime in Syria extended occasional support to these
organizations for three major reasons: as part of the feud with Egypt, to
whom the PLO and its head Ahmad Shuqayri were accountable; as a means

of subverting the Hashemite regime in Jordan; as a propaganda weapon, since the activities of the Palestinian organizations could be depicted as the implementation of the 'popular war of liberation'. The Ba'th asserted this doctrine to be its unique contribution to the Arab struggle against Israel, and made much of the contrast between this 'fresh' and 'revolutionary' approach, and Egypt's 'routine' and 'traditionalist' reliance on regular armies and conventional warfare.[13]

The Palestinian issue, submerged in earlier years by other aspects of the Arab-Israeli conflict, in the mid-1960s regained some of its original prominence, although its contribution to the outbreak of the June 1967 War should not be exaggerated. The immediate conflict between Israel and three of its Arab neighbours (and the relations between them) was chiefly responsible for generating the process which led to war. It was ironic that Syria, having played such a prominent role in this process, made a comparatively small contribution to the Arab war effort. Embarrassed by the loss of the Golan Heights, the regime, which had claimed to possess the key to the liberation of Palestine, now had to explain its failure to defend its own national territory.

One result of the Six Day War was that the Golan Heights now became the crucial issue in Syria's policy in the Arab-Israeli conflict. The Ba'th regime survived the immediate crisis, but now had to regain the Golan or at least show that it was doing its best to accomplish this goal. In the period 1967–73 it formulated two distinct strategies in response to this challenge.

The policy adopted in the summer of 1967 (and pursued until the end of 1970) rested on the assumption, or rather assertion, that the line chosen by the party had been correct; that the armed struggle and the 'popular war of liberation' were still the best means of achieving a fundamental solution of the 'Palestine problem'. The liberation of the Golan Heights was construed as part of the greater aim so that there was no need to concede Arab rights in Palestine in order to regain territories lost in 1967. A political and diplomatic struggle against Israel was not reprehensible as such, but it had to be part of a combined military and political strategy and should not involve any concessions. The most complete and authoritative presentation of Syria's policy was made in the communique published at the end of the Ninth National Congress of the Ba'th Party on 17 September 1967.[14]

This policy line enabled the Ba'th regime to avoid the contradiction, which, it asserted, was inherent in Egypt's policy. Egypt, according to its own concept, sought to regain the Sinai through a political settlement. But in Syria's view any such settlement was bound in practice to entail some concessions, which must erode the fundamental Arab positions. In theory, the Syrian approach was diametrically opposed to Egyptian policy, but in practice certain options were left open. For example, Egypt's definition of a settlement ruled out any essential concessions to Israel. Syria, in turn, did not object to a diplomatic solution as such, so that while criticizing Egypt's policy and refusing to accept Security Council Resolution 242, she refrained from out-and-out condemnation, in case Egypt's approach should prove vindicated.

The one major flaw in this policy was that it left the Ba'th regime open to the charge that it was doing nothing to regain the Golan Heights: it was not conducting any diplomatic activity and the war it preached appeared vague and remote. The solution to that problem had already been sketched in 1967 when the regime openly supported Palestinian activities against Israel conducted through the territories of Jordan and Lebanon. This enabled the Syrian Ba'th to claim credit for activity which could be presented as the implementation of 'a popular war of liberation' whilst running a minimal risk of Israel retaliation.

The policy collapsed with the Jordanian Civil War of 1970. The Syrian government had to choose between support of the Palestinians and criticism of its failure to live up to the expectations it had created. Syrian decision making in this matter was also affected by the conflict between the factions of Salah Jadid and Hafiz al-Asad. The recriminations which followed Syria's eventual abortive intervention in Jordan resulted in Hafiz al-Asad's seizure of power in November 1970.

Among the many changes introduced by the Asad regime was the formulation of a new Syrian policy towards Israel, which was instrumental in preparing the ground for the October War three years later. Even before November 1970, Asad had advocated political and military cooperation with other Arab countries irrespective of ideological differences. He reasserted and began to apply this policy immediately after coming to power. Other changes surfaced during the Ba'th Fifth Regional Congress of May 1971. It was then determined that a distinction should be drawn between the two major components of the conflict with Israel: the national rights of the Palestine Arabs, and the necessity of achieving complete Israel withdrawal from its 1967 gains. It was clearly implied that priority should be given to the latter. The rejection of Resolution 242 was reaffirmed but a more flexible political line was recommended. The congress criticized the Palestinian organizations and singled out Syria and Egypt as the two Arab countries genuinely confronting Israel.

The new line preparing the ground for Syria's military alliance with Egypt was further developed in Asad's Revolution Day address of 8 March 1972. The regime was now determined to endorse the Egyptian strategy advocating the use of continued military and political efforts to force Israel to withdraw from the territories captured in 1967. Consequently in 1972 Syria was confronted with the situation that Egypt had been facing since 1967: how to separate the 'problem of 1967' (the Golan Heights) from the 'problem of 1948' (Palestine). In other words, how could Syria regain territories lost in 1967 without offering recognition of Israel's legitimate existence within her pre-1967 borders? The Ba'th regime thought this to be insoluble: however, Asad was now willing to set out his position in positive rather than negative terms. Accordingly, he announced Syria's interpretation and acceptance of Resolution 242 in these words: 'When the Security Council Resolution [242] is interpreted as expressing the enemy's withdrawal from the Arab territory occupied since 1967 and as expressing the consolidation affirmation and implementation of the Palestinian people's rights, I am for that resolution.'[15]

Apparently, Asad's statements were aimed at a closer Syro-Egyptian cooperation rather than at a more specific policy goal. But they assumed considerable operative importance once Egypt decided – probably in late 1972 or early 1973 – to launch war against Israel. Syria had drawn closer to Egypt's position in the Arab-Israel conflict, but fundamental differences remained. Egypt went to war in order to impose a settlement on Israel, which would be essentially based on Israeli concessions but would include some compromise on the Arab side. As yet, little is known about the political preparations made by the two Arab states before the October War but it seems that Syria did not agree even to such minor Arab concessions. The full significance of their differences did not become apparent until the end of the October War, whose course and outcome had by that time magnified their points of disagreement.

In the three and a half years following the October War, Syria's policy in the Arab-Israeli conflict underwent a number of important changes, brought about by the combined impact of two inter-related but distinct processes: the efforts to arrive at a political settlement of the conflict, and the gradual development of the Syrian leadership's ambition to acquire a prominent position in the system of inter-Arab relations.

The weakness inherent in the Syrian-Egyptian alliance were exposed and exacerbated by the war and its consequences. Between November 1973 and May 1974, Syria's efforts were primarily directed at regaining the additional territory lost to Israel in October, and she had strong reservations with regard to the policy pursued by Egypt after war. Opposition to the policy itself was intermixed with growing suspicion of Egypt's true intentions. But the Ba'th regime in Syria realized that Egypt's policy was the only viable option. The radical alternative advocated by Libya, Iraq and part of the PLO was not likely to regain the territories lost in 1967 and 1973, certainly not in the near future.

Syria thus made an important decision – to participate in the so-called 'political process', the effort initiated under American auspices to reach a political settlement of the Middle East conflict. While Damascus agreed to the Arab policy line adopted at the Algiers Summit Conference as well as to the principle of 'interim agreements' with Israel, it was vehemently opposed to the preference given to Egyptian over Syrian interests.

This phase, dealing primarily with the immediate problems occasioned by the October War, ended with the Syrian-Israeli Disengagement Agreement in June 1974. In the next phase of efforts to reach a second series of interim agreements between Israel and its Arab neighbours, there were two important developments in Syria's policy. The first was the formation of a new Syrian strategy, which would accommodate the cumulative changes of the post-1973 period into a comprehensive framework. This was adopted at the twelfth Ba'th National Congress, which met in Damascus in July 1975. The relevant resolutions were not published, but their general direction was alluded to in a statement in August of the same year. The ultimate goal of the Syrian policy, as reflected in the statement, was still 'the liberation of all Palestinian soil'. But, in line with the principle of 'revolutionary realism' the 'interim targets' of the struggle were to be defined. These included the 'establishment of an independent national authority in the liberated parts of Palestine' and could be achieved through interim and partial settlements, which should not, however, affect the struggle for the final goal. Syria thus endorsed the Arab consensus put together at the Algiers and Rabat conferences, whilst carefully expressing reservations with regard to Egypt's position and to emphasizing the distinctive features of her own policy.[16]

The second development was the crystallization during 1974 and 1975 of a new regional policy, with obvious repercussions on the Syrian attitude towards Israel. Though never put into words by any Syrian leader, the new strategy was alluded to by a number of Syrian spokesmen and was fully described by Patrick Seale, a British journalist and Asad's biographer, after a revealing interview with President Asad in March 1977:

> His current unionist campaign is two-pronged: first he sees Syria's immediate neighbours, Lebanon and Jordan, as a natural extension of its territory, vital to its defence. This three-nation grouping is already a *fait accompli* – although in the low profile Asad manner, without fanfare. Asad now rules by proxy in Lebanon, while the progressive integration with Jordan is well advanced. If the Palestinians ever

recover a West Bank homeland they too will inevitably join this complex. The second prong of the policy is directed at Egypt, enfeebled and with Arab leadership slipping from its grasp.[17]

It seems that a number of developments combined to produce the new strategy. One was the vacuum created by the decline of Egyptian hegemony in Arab politics. This had been noticeable since the later 1960s, but at that time Syria was in no position to exploit it. Not until the mid-1970s, having for the first time enjoyed a few years of comparatively stable and effective government, could Syria conduct a more ambitious foreign policy.

The Ba'th regime was prompted to embark on such a line as a result of its experience in 1973 and 1974, which had emphasized the importance of the US position in the Middle East and the unreliability of the Egyptian alliance. It was important for Syria to build a power position from which she could conduct a more autonomous policy. With little or no dependence upon Egypt, she could initiate warlike or peaceful measures and could negotiate directly with the US or Saudi Arabia.

Politically, Syria's power position was to rest on her close relations with Jordan, on her growing influence in Lebanon and on the special relationship, which she was trying to forge with the PLO, the latter being of prime importance. Control of the PLO could make Syria the arbiter of a crucial question: a Palestinian decision – given or withheld – that 'the problem of 1948' had been resolved. For these purposes the concept of Greater Syria was found extremely useful since, as has been seen, it provides the state of Syria with a claim to a special relationship with Jordan, Lebanon and Palestine.

These ideas were given further impetus by the outbreak of the Lebanese Civil War in April 1975, and again early in 1976. Syria's attitude to the Civil War and the decision to intervene were governed by several considerations, some of which were related to her direct interests in Lebanon and others to domestic politics. Lebanon was the obvious area for Syria to demonstrate that she was the predominant power in her immediate environment and that she could exercise her power effectively and judiciously. Moreover, in the wake of the second Sinai agreement, the Lebanese Civil War provided an excellent opportunity to demonstrate Egypt's impotence in Arab politics.

But Syria's efforts to stabilize the situation in Lebanon by imposing a comparatively moderate reform plan brought her into direct conflict with those who sought to overturn the status quo, among them a section of the Palestinians. Others, including the PLO, were horrified by the notion of Syrian control in Lebanon. Syria had already sent troops there and if she were to impose a political settlement, then surely she would perpetuate her pre-eminence in Lebanon, the last autonomous Palestinian base. In that case, the Palestinians would become subservient to Syrian policy. The PLO leaders, fully aware of Syria's claims to a special relationship with Palestine and the Palestinians, rejected in the spring of 1975 her offer to unite Syrian and Palestinian military and political commands.

Consequently, in the late winter and spring of 1976 the PLO spear-headed the struggle against Syria's tactics in the Lebanon. It became very important to Syria that her policy should be successfully implemented and for this purpose she was even prepared to engage her army against the PLO and the Lebanese left. When half-measures proved ineffective, she found it necessary to launch a full-fledged invasion of Lebanon on 1 June 1976. The invading armoured column encountered stiff Palestinian resistance, and a wave of criticism was generated in Syria and throughout the Arab world. This turn of events further reinforced the trends, which had already appeared in Syrian policy in 1974. Her rulers were seeking a means of legitimizing their presence and activities in Lebanon. To this end, the notion of Greater Syria proved useful. Indeed, during the summer of 1976, this idea was frequently expounded, often with reference to Syria's policy in Lebanon. For example, in early September, a group of Lebanese politicians returning from a visit to Damascus probably reflected the Syrian line when they explained how their country stood to gain from the establishment of a Greater Syrian federation: 'The Palestinian concentration in Lebanon will shrink after the establishment of a federation that will also include the West Bank when this is returned to her own sons.'[18]

Syria's involvement in Lebanon also brought its latent conflict with the PLO to the surface. The debate was no longer concerned with policies but went right to the heart of the matter: who was the true custodian of the Palestinian cause? The PLO leaders suspected that Syria intended to claim such custodianship and then to submerge the Palestinian entity in a broader entity dominated by Damascus. Syria contested the PLO's claim to be the sole spokesman for the Palestinian cause and to decide on the right policy for its advancement. While not actually arrogating her own right to such a position, this was vaguely implied in President Asad's speech of 20 July 1976.

The Riad and Cairo conferences of October 1976, which temporarily put an end to the active fighting in the Lebanese Civil War, also blunted the clash between Syria and the PLO. As part of the settlement Syria ceased to campaign against the PLO leadership, who in return accepted Syrian hegemony in Lebanon. This settlement was achieved largely because Saudi Arabia, Egypt and Syria decided that the Lebanese Civil War had to end so that the Arabs could prepare for the expected renewal of the American effort to settle the Arab-Israeli conflict. Syria's role in these and later developments has reflected the changes in her position after the 1973 War. The Palestinian dimension in her regional and Israeli policies has grown in importance. Her own standing as a power seeking regional influence has been improved by the influence acquired over the PLO and in other Palestinian issues. But these developments are only elements in an ever-changing situation whose future twists and turns are unpredictable.

The main theme of this chapter – the effort invested by Hafiz al-Asad's regime to justify and rationalize his quest to dominate his Arab environment by invoking the notion of a Greater Syria – declined in importance during the past two decades. The SSNP, the party founded in the 1930s by Antun Sa'adeh in order to promote and implement the idea and ideology of a Greater, secular, Syrian state is active in Syria as an ally of sorts of the ruling Ba'th Party. But the efforts and references made by Asad and other Syrian spokesmen to Greater Syria in the mid 1970s proved to be a temporary expediency. His efforts to impose his hegemony over Lebanon and the Palestinians persisted.

Syria's investment in Lebanon continued to go through dramatic ups and downs. It survived the 1982 War and the Israeli, American and French effort to dislodge it. In 1989 the Taif Agreement, put together by the Arab consensus of the time, sought to limit Syrian control in Lebanon but in fact legitimized it. Syria then took advantage of the diplomatic opportunities provided by the Gulf Crisis and War of 1990–91 and tightened its hold over Lebanon. In 2005, after the assassination of Lebanon's former Prime Minister, Rafiq al-Hariri, it was confronted by the combined opposition of a large domestic Lebanese coalition, the US and France. Syria was forced to withdraw its forces from Lebanon but fought to retain its influence through other means and assets. This was the Syria of Bashar, not Hafiz, al-Asad and it conceded much of its influence to its two chief partners in Lebanon, Iran and Hizballah.

Syria remained hostile to Yasir 'Arafat and the PLO. In the early 1980s it tried to set one of its Palestinian Lieutenants, Abu Musa, as an alternative to 'Arafat. The Palestinian 'rejectionist' organizations, who refused to endorse 'Arafat's acceptance, meek as it was, of a two-state solution, have been hosted in Damascus in order to fight both Israel and the PLO.

Syria's decision in 1991 to join the Madrid Peace Process added a new, often ironic, twist. Syria and the PLO were now partners in the same peace process. For nearly two years Syria acted as a committed custodian of the Palestinian cause and compounded its own negotiation by refusing to tell Israel that it will sign a 'self-standing' agreement with Israel. In September 1993 Syria was surprised and stunned by the fact that the PLO had made its own deal with Israel. It subsequently conveyed to Israel that from that point on 'a comprehensive agreement' with Israel meant an agreement concerning Syria and Lebanon.

The deaths of Hafiz al-Asad and Yasir 'Arafat removed their personal hostility from the Syrian-Palestinian relationship. But Syria continued its campaign against the PLO and the Palestinian Authority, a product of the Oslo Accords, an anathema for Syria. It continues to host *Hamas* and the Islamic *Jihad* in Damascus and to promote its own Palestinian agenda.

NOTES

1. This article was published in the *Wiener Library Bulletin*, 31, New Series, 47/8 (1978), pp.135–41.
2. Radio Damascus, 8 March 1974.
3. See in this volume I. Rabinovich, 'The Greater Syria Plan and the Palestinian Problem: Historical Roots, 1919–39'.
4. Radio Beirut, 2 August 1977.
5. Patrick Seale, *The Struggle for Syria: A Study of Post-War Arab Politics, 1945–1958* (London: Oxford University Press, 1965), p.86.
6. For details see Eliyahu Eylath, *Zionism and the Arabs* (Tel Aviv: Devir, 1974) in particular p.286 [Hebrew].
7. Cf. S. Shamir, 'The Arab-Israeli Conflict', in A.L. Udovitch (ed.), *The Middle East: Oil, Conflict and Hope* (Lexington, MA: D.C. Heath, 1976), pp.195–230.
8. N. Bar-Ya'acov, *The Israel-Syrian Armistice Problems of Implementation, 1949–1966* (Jerusalem: Magnes Press, Hebrew University, 1967) [in Hebrew].
9. The initiative taken by Syria's first military dictator, Husni Za'im, vis-à-vis Israel should be seen as a unique episode, not representative of the dominant trends in Syria's attitude and portrayal of Israel in the late 1940s and 1950s. See in this volume I. Rabinovich, 'Israel and Husni Za'im'.
10. For an analysis of Syrian-Egyptian rivalries in the early 1960s, see Malcolm Kerr, *The Arab Cold War: A Study of Ideology in Politics* (London: Oxford University Press, 1965).
11. For details see Itamar Rabinovich, *Syria under the Ba'th, 1963–1966* (Jerusalem and New York, NY: Israel Universities Press, 1972), pp.102–3, 167–71.
12. *Al-Thawra*, Damascus, 1966, Cf. F. Jabber 'The Palestinian Resistance and Inter-Arab Politics', in W.B. Quandt, F. Jabber and A. Mosley Lesch, *The Politics of Palestinian Nationalism* (Berkeley, CA: University of California Press, 1973), pp.166–7.
13. D. Dishon (ed.), *Middle East Record, 1967* (Tel Aviv: Israel Universities Press, 1971), pp.159–62. For a comprehensive study of the Palestinian Entity, see M. Shemesh, *The Palestinian Entity 1959–1974, Arab Politics and the PLO* (London: Frank Cass, 1988), pp.37–94, 97–181.
14. Dishon (ed.), *Middle East Record, 1967*, pp.491–2.
15. See I. Rabinovich, 'The Impact of the October War in Syria's Position and Policy in the Conflict with Israel', in A. Cohen and E. Karmon (eds), *In the Aftermath of the October War* (Haifa: University of Haifa, 1976) [in Hebrew].
16. The text of the statement was distributed by the German News Agency on 14 August 1976.
17. *The Observer*, London, 6 March 1977.
18. *Al-Sayyad*, Beirut, 9 September 1976.

14

Israel and Husni Za'im[1]

Among the various attempts that were made after the 1948 War to reach an Arab-Israeli agreement, the brief quest for a comprehensive Syrian-Israeli accord stands out as an especially intriguing episode. There was nothing in the earlier history of Syrian-Zionist relations to suggest that the head of Syria's government might take the initiative in proposing that Syria and Israel plunge directly into peace negotiations. Discussions had taken place between Syrian political leaders and emissaries of the Jewish Agency in the 1930s and 1940s, but they had failed to produce even a broad agreement. Syria was particularly committed to Arab nationalism and to the Arab cause in Palestine, and so an understanding similar to those reached in 1946 with 'Abdallah and Isma'il Siqdi was impossible in the case of Syria.[2] Unlike the case with Egypt and Jordan, contacts with Israel were not established during the war's final phases, and it was quite difficult to get the Syrian government in the winter and early spring of 1949 to agree to begin armistice negotiations. The abrupt transition from this negative position to the language of peace and comprehensive settlement, therefore, was most dramatic.[3]

Likewise, there is little in the subsequent course of Syrian-Israeli relations that seems to be contingent on this overture. The Syrian-Israeli conflict has been the most bitter of Israel's bilateral conflicts with its Arab neighbours. To those accustomed to the acrimony of nearly four decades, therefore, it is surprising to discover that the notion of reconciliation was on the agenda of the two countries' relationship, albeit briefly and unclearly. Given the isolated nature of the episode there is a natural tendency either to dismiss it or to build it into a tantalizing 'missed opportunity'. The need for a historian's sober and detached judgement is felt.

An examination of Israel's encounter with Syria's Husni Za'im throws an interesting light on the interplay between the Arab-Israeli conflict and other aspects of Middle Eastern politics. Husni Za'im was the first military dictator in the post-Second World War Arab world, and his conduct displayed some of the advantages and disadvantages of dealing with a military regime. Za'im could act swiftly and decisively, or so it seemed, free from the confusion and paralysis of Syria's weak parliamentary governments. But his style was characterized by whim and levity, and his legitimacy and durability were questionable.

Syria's domestic politics in the spring of 1949 and later provided the arena in which inter-Arab and international rivalries were played out. The fluidity produced by the 30 March coup d'état exacerbated the familiar rivalries between the Hashemite and Egyptian-Saudi blocs and, on a different level, between Britain and France. The novel element was the intercession of the United States in an effort to shape the politics of a Middle Eastern country.

There is, finally, an instructive lesson concerning sources. The recent interest in Husni Za'im's relationship with Israel has been to a considerable extent the result of the newly opened diplomatic archives. But as we shall see later, much is still unknown, and most of what we do know comes from the Israeli and American archives. But the core of this story has been available all along, as it was published in 1949 in one of the most underrated sources for the region's history – the contemporary Arab press. Additional details were revealed over the years with the publication of several memoirs.

But it was only the authoritative material released by the opening of the archives and the consequent fresh review of the 1948–49 period that drew attention to this intriguing episode.

HUSNI ZA'IM AND ISRAEL: 30 MARCH–14 AUGUST 1949

Husni Za'im, the commander in chief of the Syrian army, staged his coup on 30 March 1949, and ruled Syria until 14 August, when a group of army officers led by Sami al-Hinawi deposed and killed him.

On 5 April 1949, armistice negotiations commenced between Syria and Israel, although they had been agreed to in March, before the coup, so that they were one of the new regime's first undertakings and, from an international point of view, a significant act of early recognition. It was the Soviet government that raised this issue with the Israelis: on 8 April the Soviet minister, Pavel Yershov, asked Walter Eytan: 'Why is it that Israel was negotiating with the new Syrian government when no Arab state has recognized it? Have you given sufficient thought to the fact that your willingness to sit with this government constitutes an act of recognition of the Syrian government, so that you appear to be the first to recognize it?'[4]

Yershov's criticism reflected his government's belief at that time that Za'im had acted in league with 'Abdallah and thus was an instrument of British policy in the region.

Syria had not taken part in the Rhodes negotiations, and so its negotiations with Israel were conducted against the background of the three armistice agreements signed earlier in the year with Egypt, Lebanon, and Jordan. The Syrian-Israeli talks were held under UN auspices in the no-man's land near the Israeli village of Mishmar Hayarden. Not surprisingly, the effort to conclude a Syrian-Israeli armistice agreement proved to be the most protracted of these agreements. The major stumbling bloc was Israel's insistence that Syria, which had ended the war still occupying some territory west of the international boundary with Mandatory Palestine, withdraw its forces to the international border as part of the armistice agreement, and Syria's refusal to accede to this demand.

Several issues were involved in this debate. For the Syrians, ending the war in possession of territory west of the international border would be a considerable achievement, as they would be in a position to claim that they had ended the war with a concrete gain in hand. There also were points of principle: the Syrians had argued against the legitimacy of their border with Palestine, which, they claimed, had been drawn to Syria's disadvantage by two colonial powers. In addition, there was a vague Syrian claim to parts of Galilee and a more explicit argument that Israel had no right to hold on to those parts of Galilee not assigned to it by the UN partition resolution of 1947. More concretely, Syria sought to exploit its advantageous position on the ground, in order to obtain a better hold over two important keys to the region's scarce water resources – the Jordan River and Lake Tiberias.

From the Israeli perspective, the principle of adhering to Palestine's international borders had been established earlier when Israel withdrew from Egyptian and Lebanese territory, and so Israel felt that this principle should also be respected when Israel was at a disadvantage. Israel was as acutely aware as Syria was of the strategic importance of water resources, and so Syria's attempt to acquire new leverage only stiffened Israel's resolve to hold on to the established international frontier. There also were more immediate, as well as contradictory, considerations: on the one hand, a strong urge to end the war, consolidate the existence of the state, and normalize life, and, on the other, a sense that there was no point in making concessions on important issues when Israel enjoyed an overwhelming advantage over a weak Syria practically devoid of Arab support.

The armistice agreement, nonetheless, was finally signed on 20 July 1949. At the time of the negotiations Syria and Israel also were participating in the Lausanne Conference organized by the PCC.[5] Because there were no bilateral contacts between the Syrian and Israeli delegations in Lausanne, other channels were used throughout the period to exchange messages between Husni Za'im's government and Israel. Through these channels Za'im expressed his willingness to meet with Ben-Gurion, to enter into peace negotiations with Israel, and to settle 250,000 or 300,000 Palestinian refugees in north-eastern Syria. This series of informal contacts and exchange of messages between Husni Za'im's regime and Israel unfolded in three phases.

APRIL TO LATE MAY

On 16 April, eleven days after the armistice negotiations began, David Ben-Gurion noted in his diary:

> Mordechai (Makleff) and Josh (Palmon) spoke with Za'im's representatives without the UN's participation. The Syrians proposed a separate peace with Israel, cooperation, and a common army. But they want a border change ... half of Lake Tiberias ... I told them to inform the Syrians in clear language that first of all [there would be] the signing of an armistice on the basis of the previous international border, and then [there would be a] discussion of peace and alliance. We will be ready for maximal cooperation.[6]

At the same time, in view of the stalemate in the formal armistice talks, Ben-Gurion was considering military action if the negotiations failed. On 22 April he wrote in his diary: 'refusal to meet with Syria and to accept its participation in Lausanne if an armistice agreement is not signed and preparation for expelling the Syrians from the state's territory'.[7]

On 28 April Za'im met with James Keeley, the US minister in Damascus. According to Keeley's report, Za'im 'had intimated willingness as part general settlement including realistic frontier adjustments, accept quarter million refugees if given substantial development aid in addition to compensation for refugee losses'. Later in the same conversation Za'im 'reiterated his willingness to resolve the Palestinian problem by pursuing henceforth a policy of give and take, provided that he [Yadin] not be asked to give all while other side takes all'.[8] A more elaborate version of the discussion between Makleff and Palmon and Za'im's representatives was supplied by Yigael Yadin during the consultation on 19 April in preparation for the Lausanne Conference:

> A meeting with the Syrians. They came full of admiration for Za'im. They want to sign immediate peace rather than armistice and to exchange immediately ambassadors, etc ... [G]enerally speaking, Za'im wants to fight for control of the Middle East, and he calculated that

Israel and Syria together can reach the number of 500,000 soldiers, who, when appearing as a unified bloc, can obtain control of the Middle East. Because they speak of peace, the border line should be adjusted. They want the border line to cross Lake Tiberias and then go down along the Jordan ...

I had a meeting with the prime minister, to which I also invited Makleff and Palmon. The prime minister said that if we do not reach an armistice with the Syrians before Lausanne, he doubts whether we would be able to sit with them in Lausanne. With regard to the border, we would agree either to changes in our favor or to an international border, and the Syrians said that they will communicate that to Za'im. I proposed one more thing – a direct meeting between ourselves and Za'im in order to clarify matters – and emphasized that this would not constitute a precedent. The meeting took place yesterday, and we stated our position in no uncertain terms. When we asked them what about Degania, they did not know what to say precisely about its fate. They proposed that the eastern half of Lake Tiberias be given to Syria and that north of the lake the Jordan line be followed. They say this is convenient.[9]

On 1 May Keeley met again with Za'im and reported that he [Za'im] reminded me that several days ago he had expressed his desire for a speedy solution to Palestinian problem and had stated his willingness to accept as part of a comprehensive settlement of the conflict a quarter-million or more Arab refugees for resettlement in Syria, provided that Syria is compensated for its losses and is given adequate financial aid to resettle the refugees. He reiterated his sincere desire for prompt agreement with Israel and his desire to enter direct negotiations with Israel to that end. Za'im went on to say that because Syria, Transjordan, and Egypt are the Arab states most directly concerned with the Palestinian problem, he would meet with 'Abdallah and Farouk in order to decide on a common basis for their approach to Israel.[10] Although Za'im was eager to give concrete proof of his sincerity – already evidenced by his proffered concessions – he emphasized that 'unless Israel also manifested a spirit of compromise, the stalemate would continue, as the Arab states cannot be expected to make all the concessions'.

Two days earlier, after the 29 April meeting between the Syrian and Israeli delegations, one of the Syrian delegates, Major Muhammad Nasir, met with Josh Palmon 'privately, in order to reach an agreement'. According to Ben-Gurion's diary:

The Syrian proposed that the political boundary be agreed on only in the negotiations for peace and not those for armistice. Josh informed him that he would communicate this to his own government, provided that we agree on a two-month period at the end of which the international border be restored, whether or not peace had been reached. Nasir proposed this after meeting with Za'im. We looked into the possibility of [military] action ... [F]or the time being we are putting Bunche and the Americans to work. It was agreed that they meet with Za'im and propose Reuven [Shiloah] and Yigael [Yadin], but Za'im might insist on the prime minister or the foreign minister. Moshe is willing to meet, but not this week.[11]

A few days later the US government and the UN mediator Ralph Bunche – both of whom were mystified by Ben-Gurion's refusal to meet with the leader of an important Arab state who had proposed the meeting – began to exert pressure on the Israeli government. On 8 May, Ben-Gurion met with the US ambassador to Israel, James McDonald. The prime minister demanded 'pressure on Za'im to evacuate the territories, just as pressure had been exerted on us to evacuate Lebanon's territory. If we sign with Syria, a de facto peace will be reached'. For his part, McDonald told Ben-Gurion, as the latter wrote in his diary, that 'Za'im and [the US] ambassador in Damascus demand that I meet with Za'im. The State Department did not accept. I said that if Za'im made a prior commitment to evacuate our territory and withdraw to the international border, I shall be ready to meet with him'.[12] When McDonald spoke to Ben-Gurion, be was unaware that the State Department had instructed him by cable to find out whether Ben-Gurion had indeed been informed by his own people of Za'im's willingness to meet with him.[13]

On 10 May Ralph Bunche, worried by the deadlock in the armistice negotiations, approached Ben-Gurion through his (Bunche's) personal representative, the Swedish diplomat Paul Mohn, requesting that he agree to an early meeting with Za'im 'to discuss the armistice lines and any other matters relating to the peace between your two countries that you may mutually agree to discuss'. Ben-Gurion replied two days later through Shiloah: 'I am quite prepared to meet Colonel Za'im in order to promote peace between the two countries, but I see no purpose in any such meeting as long as the representatives of Syria in the armistice negotiations do not declare unequivocally that their forces will withdraw to their prewar territory.'[14]

On 2 May the political adviser of the UN observers' headquarters, the French diplomat Henri Vigier, transmitted a message to Moshe Sharett stating that Colonel Za'im had invited Mr Ben-Gurion or Mr Sharett to a meeting. As an internal memorandum of the Israeli Foreign Ministry put it,

'Because Mr Sharett thought that the time, at that stage of the armistice negotiations between Syria and Israel, was not suitable for such a high-level meeting, Vigier suggested that Shiloah and Yadin be dispatched for "clarification talks"'. On 5 May they met with the two representatives of Husni Za'im (whose identity could not be established) for what was defined as a 'secret session'.

At the end of the meeting they agreed that the Syrian delegation to the armistice talks would bring new proposals to the next day's meeting. This meeting took place on 6 May and was brief and unimportant. Rather, the important discussion that day took place between the Israeli delegation, on the one hand, and between Brigadier General William E. Riley, the American chief of the UN observers, and Vigier, the other. Vigier was full of complaints about the Israelis: in his opinion Sharett should have represented Israel in the 5 May meeting, and by insisting on the international border rather than the water line, the Israelis missed 'a unique opportunity to come to a long-term agreement with the Syrians'. The Israelis left with the impression that when Vigier invited Za'im to take part in the discussion, he 'presented it as our initiative, even though a week ago we had emphasized that if we wanted the private talks to break the deadlock, it was necessary that he should present them as his own idea'. Riley, in turn, made it clear to the Israelis that the US government (and apparently he personally) thought 'that the water line made more sense militarily and politically than did the present international border'. The Israelis stressed that from their point of view, the water question was a fundamental economic and social matter.[15]

On 11 May Keeley met with Za'im, who complained that the meeting 'on the diplomatic level between Syria and Israel was fruitless and blamed the failure on the Israeli insistence that Syria withdraw to the international border'. When Keeley asked whether Za'im was still ready for direct negotiations with Ben-Gurion on a comprehensive settlement with Israel, Za'im replied affirmatively, although he was less enthusiastic about it than on earlier occasions. He added that if Ben-Gurion 'were to take the same tough position held by earlier Israeli negotiators', little could be expected from such a meeting. But if he were to meet with him 'in a candid spirit of compromise based on give and take', mutual advantages could be agreed on swiftly. Za'im stated his general outlook on negotiations between leaders: 'It was natural in negotiations, particularly among juniors, to demand more than was expected and to make minimal concessions, but when candid men with the authority to settle things met, an agreement became feasible if they presented to one another reasonable requests that cannot be rejected.' Za'im also told Keeley that he sincerely wanted peace with Israel but was ready to fight if Israel tried to take by force whatever he refused to give. As Za'im put it, 'The Syrian army was never defeated during the Palestine war, and Israel would be mistaken if it treated Syria as a vanquished enemy.'[16]

On 17 May the armistice talks were suspended for a whole month. In an apparent attempt to prevent their collapse, General Riley, at the end of that day's meeting, started a conversation with the Israeli delegate Shabtai Rosenne, the Foreign Ministry's legal adviser. Using information obtained from 'informal' sources in Damascus, Riley briefed Rosenne on Za'im's intentions. This was the first time that Za'im's willingness to settle Palestinian refugees in Syria was communicated to the Israeli government. Rosenne reported:

> According to him [Riley], Husni Za'im wants to resolve the Syrian Israeli problem in an honorable and peaceful way, in order to devote himself fully to the goals of Syria's revival and advancement. On the other hand, he is afraid that a coup could occur one day in Syria that would restore to power the politicians who would critically scrutinize Za'im's activities, including his negotiations with Israel. He thus is anxious that we help him emerge honorably from his dilemma. For this reason Riley wanted to know how the Israeli government would respond to the following proposal:
>
> In the framework of the Lausanne negotiations Syria would agree to receive and settle within its boundaries 300,000 Arab refugees. Likewise, in the framework of the same conference the problem of frontiers would be resolved, and Riley believes, but is not fully certain, that the Palestine Conciliation Commission would have no choice but to pressure Syria to withdraw to the international frontier as it had existed before the invasion. As a quid pro quo, an armistice agreement between Israel and Syria would be signed now on the basis of the present cease-fire lines and with clear provisions for mutual troop reduction in order to dispel the mutual fear and suspicion that currently exist between the two countries. This agreement would remain valid for a maximum of three months and would contain a clause alluding to Israel's firm insistence on its demand for a Syrian withdrawal to the previous international border[17]

A brief exchange followed between Rosenne and Riley that resulted in the introduction of minor changes in the draft proposal. Rosenne told Riley that he believed that Ben-Gurion would reject the proposal and gave him his reasons for this conclusion. Indeed Ben-Gurion's reaction was negative, but

he determined to delay his final decision until Sharett returned from the
United States.

At the UN in New York Abba Eban must have felt Bunche's pressure
more directly, for on 18 May he cabled the Foreign Ministry asking for 'further clarifications why we unimpressed with prospect Syria absorb
300,000 fact he made proposal through Riley with consequent transmis-
sion Washington of readiness accept large-scale resettlement seems to me
of great importance.'[18] To this Sharett replied on 25 May:

> Have informed Vigier am ready to meet Za'im soonest. For your
> information: intend to try to cut Gordian knot armistice and explore
> reality his alleged proposal resettle 300,000. Attach tremendous
> importance latter point, was greatly impressed by it when first
> learned it Geneva. In talk with Za'im intend to brandish stick Moabit
> [UN Security Council] must know Bunche's latest firm stand. Believe
> our position inside UN can only be strengthened by this initiative on
> my part.

Sharett also made a similar, more detailed statement in a meeting held on
the same day with the Foreign Ministry's departmental directors.[19]

LATE MAY TO EARLY JUNE

Sharett's reply to Eban can also be seen in the context of the effort made
in late May and early June by the UN's mediators, headed by Bunche, to
break the deadlock in the armistice negotiations, through a high-level
Syrian-Israeli meeting. This episode illustrates the UN mediation team's
modus operandi, as well as additional aspects of Israel's relationship with
Husni Za'im's regime.

In his discussions with Israel's representatives, Bunche appeared supportive of their demand for Syria's withdrawal to the international border
and was generally more sympathetic than Vigier was, whom the Israelis
perceived as leaning toward the Syrians and their position. But both
Bunche and Vigier were disappointed in Ben-Gurion's unwillingness to
meet with Za'im earlier. Implicit in their disappointment was their feeling
that such a meeting could have achieved a breakthrough and prevented the
mid-May deadlock. In any event they now tried to arrange a meeting
between Sharett and the Syrians.

But their effort failed. Za'im refused to see Sharett, whom he regarded
as too junior to meet on an equal footing. Sharett did not contest the point
but believed that his own willingness to meet Za'im on the latter's own
ground was appropriate compensation for the difference in their respective

positions in their countries' formal hierarchies. Sharett was also willing, however, to meet with 'Adel Arslan, Za'im's foreign minister. But on 30 May the Syrians proposed through Vigier a meeting between a delegation headed by Ibrahim Istiwani, deputy secretary-general of the Syrian Foreign Ministry, and an Israeli delegation headed by Sharett. The Israelis understood at that point that Bunche was acting on the assumption that his (Bunche's) compromise proposals were bound to be rejected by the Syrians and that for this reason, he chose not to present them but to organize first a high-level Syrian-Israeli meeting. Ben-Gurion would have preferred that Bunche show his own hand first, but he agreed to wait for the results of Sharett's attempt to meet with Arslan. Indeed, Sharett proposed to the UN staff that he go to Syria and, at their request, suggested also an agenda for the prospective meeting, to include a discussion of the armistice problems and the problems concerning the future peace relations.[20]

On 8 June Vigier brought the Syrian government's negative reply, and so both Husni Za'im and 'Adel Arslan refused to meet. As for the armistice problems, they were tied to the armistice negotiations, and 'the question of future peace relations can be discussed only together with the other Arab states'. Sharett felt deceived and humiliated and responded sarcastically: 'They probably assumed that we would put on the agenda such topics as medieval Arabic poetry or Bedouin tradition ... This impertinent affront by a self-styled Syrian government is decisive proof ... [that we have witnessed] ... a series of evasions and deceptions.' Implied here was Sharett's contempt for the dubious legitimacy of a military dictatorship.[21] Sharett and his Israeli colleagues were apparently unaware of the debate on these very issues that had taken place between Za'im and his foreign minister.

Za'im was of Kurdish extraction and quite remote from Arab nationalism. He had no ideological commitments and apparently few principles. The members of Za'im's generation who joined and were commissioned in the Troupes Spéciales, France's colonial auxiliary force in the Levant were men desiring to serve the Mandatory Government against the Arab nationalist opposition. It was only later that younger men like Adib Shishakly went to the military academy in order to provide a nucleus for a national and nationalist army.

'Adel Arslan came from an entirely different tradition. He was a member of a princely Druze Lebanese family and, like his brother Shakib, had played a prominent role in the politics of pan-Arab nationalism between the two world wars. He was fully committed to the Arab cause in Palestine and was opposed to Za'im's policy toward Israel, on grounds of both principle and tactics. Arslan's position in the spring of 1949 is recorded in both his published diaries and foreign diplomatic dispatches, and both sources reflect the depth of his opposition to direct negotiations with Israel and to the notion of settling Palestinian refugees in Syria.

On 31 May Arslan paid a visit to P.M. Broadmead, Britain's minister in Damascus, and told him in confidence that during the past few days, Vigier had been exerting pressure on Za'im, in Bunche's name, to meet with Sharett. He himself, Arslan said, refused to meet with Sharett, and he had warned Za'im of a trap. At the same time the US minister urged Za'im to accept Bunche's offer. Arslan told Broadmead that if the Israelis had anything to offer, they could do it in the armistice talks or at the Lausanne Conference. In his opinion Israel was motivated by its economic difficulties and by its desire to release those forces currently stationed in the north in order to attack the Old City in Jerusalem. Arslan, who liked to take advantage of the competition among the western powers, explained to the British minister that the US government was an 'agent' of its Israeli counterpart. Broadmead, for his part, characterized Arslan as a 'diehard' on the 'Jewish question.'[22]

Arslan's diary is full of details concerning his opposition to Za'im's Israeli policy. He thus tells that in the Syrian cabinet's meeting on 25 May Za'im announced that Sharett was scheduled to arrive by plane in Quneitra for a meeting with Arslan. Arslan responded by stating that he would not recognize the state of Israel, would not meet its foreign minister, and would not allow any employee of his own Foreign Ministry to meet with him.[23]

Shortly thereafter Za'im made some changes in his government. He had himself elected president in a referendum and appointed his confidant, Muhsin Barazi, as both prime minister and foreign minister. Arslan was ousted from the government. These changes were hardly a surprise, however, for when he had staged his coup Za'im needed well-known civilian politicians in order to give his regime a measure of respectability and legitimacy. At the time, Muhsin Barazi was closely identified with the ousted civilian regime. But after three months, this changed: Za'im, whose personal ambitions had become quite grandiose, wanted to be president; Barazi had become his confidant and special emissary; and Arslan had proved to be too difficult and independent. In any case Arslan was lucky that he was not part of the regime when Za'im was toppled on 14 August. After Za'im's downfall Arslan settled his score with his former chief by publishing, in the Lebanese press, a derogatory account of this period.[24]

JULY TO AUGUST

After a month's suspension the Syrian-Israeli armistice negotiations were renewed in mid-June. Bunche's diplomatic ability plus the US government's pressure helped achieve a breakthrough even without a high-level Syrian-Israeli meeting. The compromise was based on the demilitarization of the territory held by Syria west of the international border. The armistice agreement was signed on 20 July, but its imminence was sensed earlier that month. On 9 July Ben-Gurion wrote in his diary:

> Za'im stated in a discussion with a Swiss journalist that he wants peace with us. In my opinion we should hold on to this statement. The very fact that Za'im is ready to accept a cease-fire that requires full withdrawal to the border proves that for some reason he wants good relations with us. Is it because of the conflict with Iraq? Also, the interests of France – Za'im friend – require peace between Syria and Israel. And should the cease-fire agreement between us and Syria be signed this week, as Makleff believes, it would be desirable for Sasson to go to Damascus to examine the lay of the land.[25]

A similar approach, arguing that upon the signing of the armistice agreement it would be possible to test Syria's willingness to settle in a more serious and relaxed fashion, was evident in the 'guidelines to the legations' issued by Moshe Sharett on 25 July:

> To the extent that matters depend on our own initiative, the possibility of direct negotiations and separate peace with Egypt should be reexamined, and we should especially concentrate on establishing contact and exploring the possibility of peace with Syria. The changes that took place in the Syrian delegation [to Lausanne] could prove helpful. In negotiations with Syria, any promise or hint of possible promise on our part of a change in the border between Palestine and Syria and along the Jordan and the lakes should be avoided. On the contrary, it should be clear to the other side that under no circumstances can such a change be contemplated. On the other hand, the Syrian delegation should be encouraged to think about a large-scale absorption of refugees that would be combined with Syria's own rehabilitation and the possibility of financial and technical aid by us for the implementation of this scheme.[26]

On 6 August Eliyahu Sasson began acting according to his government's new line toward Syria. From Lausanne he sent a letter to Muhsin Barazi proposing that 'direct and informal' talks be opened with Israel. He also suggested three alternative venues – the dispatching of a Syrian emissary to Europe, a meeting on the border, or a trip by himself to Damascus.[27] But this initiative came too late, not merely because Za'im and Barazi were killed eight days later, but also because Za'im had lost any real enthusiasm for a separate settlement with

Israel. Za'im had continued to speak to American and French diplomats and to UN mediators about his desire for a settlement with Israel, but he now sounded more reserved and was clearly in no hurry.[28] Hardly less important was the fact that the US government had changed its own attitude. Now that the signing of an armistice agreement had removed the immediate danger of renewed hostilities, the State Department was no longer eager for a Syrian-Israeli Summit. Washington now gave priority to the Lausanne Conference. On 26 July the State Department explained to McDonald, in Tel Aviv, that it understood that Ben-Gurion was now interested in meeting Za'im but that the United States preferred the 'Lausanne format'. A few days earlier the US legation in Damascus had asked Washington what it was that Damascus should do specifically in order to advance a solution to the refugee problem. The answer was: 'It will be of considerable value if Za'im would authorize Syrian delegation [to Lausanne] inform PCC officially of its willingness coop erate in facilitating solution of refugee problem by accepting substantial num ber of refugees for permanent settlement Syria.'[29]

The foregoing sequence raises a number of questions: What motivated Za'im to launch his far-reaching initiative vis-à-vis Israel? How could 'Adel Arslan, a foreign minister with no political power, have stood up to a military dictator like Husni Za'im? Why did Ben-Gurion refuse to meet Za'im, and how did Israel perceive Za'im and his initiative? And how serious and politically viable was Za'im's overture?

Za'im undoubtedly wanted to end the active conflict and confrontation with Israel following the 1948 War. For this he had several good reasons, first and foremost among them his fear of renewed fighting in the face of Israel's overwhelming military superiority. Although Za'im did tell Keeley that he was not worried by the prospect of fighting the IDF, he must have realized that he could not stand up to the Israelis when all the other Arab states had signed armistice agreements and the IDF's full might could be directed against the Syrian army alone. Furthermore, the army was the mainstay of Za'im's regime, and as such its primary task was to protect the regime against domestic rivals and external foes, the Hashemites in partic-ular. During his first weeks in power Za'im was seriously interested in an ambitious programme of social and economic reform, and he surely want-ed to remove the Israeli issue from the top of his country's national agenda. Moreover, Za'im was remarkably free from ideological commitments and sensibilities and so was outside the pale of Arab nationalism. As we noted earlier, members of his age group who joined the French auxiliary troops in the Levant served as an instrument of the Mandatory Government against the Arab nationalist opposition. In later years younger men joined the *Troupes Spéciales* with a nationalist motivation, seeking to form the nucleus of a

Syrian national army. Adib al-Shishakly belonged to this group, but not so the older Za'im.

Za'im and his colleagues found themselves in a state of conflict with the patrician leaders of the Arab nationalist movement, who became the country's leaders when independence had been achieved. The latter viewed Za'im not only as a collaborator with the French but also as a social climber. He, in turn, was full of contempt for a privileged group that, as he saw it, had failed in its struggle against the French, had failed to form a stable and effective government, and had been forced to call on the army for protection against the demonstrators who had threatened to topple its regime in the early years of independence. This conflict between the two groups was further embittered by the debate over responsibility for the Palestine debacle.[30]

As a ruler, Za'im was indeed glad to break all the taboos of the Syrian Arab nationalists. He drew close to France, which had just been driven out of Syria and was still viewed by most Syrians as a hostile colonizer. He likewise improved relations with Turkey, which a decade earlier had annexed the province of Alexandretta. And shortly after taking power Za'im ratified the Tapline Agreement, providing for the laying of an American oil pipeline from Saudi Arabia to Tripoli through Syrian territory, an agreement that his predecessors had found difficult to enact. Za'im was surrounded by other army officers from a minority background (the French had deliberately recruited into their auxiliary forces a disproportionate number of minorities), and in July he appointed Muhsin Barazi (of Kurdish extraction like himself) as prime minister.[31] Against this background it is evident that from Za'im's personal perspective the conflict with Israel could be terminated with a reasonable compromise.

In early March 1949, on the eve of his coup, Za'im, in his preparatory talks with the US diplomats (the importance of which will be clarified later) stated that he intended to offer Israel more reasonable demands than those presented by the civilian politicians. He was especially adamant about his demand for modification of the border line between Syria and Israel, insisting that it run through Lake Tiberias. Za'im's insistence on this matter is explained in the memoirs of the civilian prime minister ousted by his coup, Khalid al-'Azm. Al-'Azm admitted that it was his regime that had accepted the principle of armistice negotiations with Israel, but he pointed a barb at Za'im by claiming that his own government had stood firm on the principle of holding on to the positions held by the Syrian army at the end of fighting and shifting the border line to the middle of Lake Tiberias. This is an extended illustration of the mechanism of political overbidding (*muzayadah*), about which 'Azm himself complained elsewhere in his memoirs. In this and other cases, Arab politicians sought to raise their political stock by portraying themselves as advocates of a political position more radical and pure than that of their competitors. The practical outcome of these dynamics was a radicalization of the Arab side's position and conduct.[32]

These were all important considerations, but Za'im's reform and economic development plans and his bold initiative vis-à-vis Israel cannot be understood except in the context of a less familiar dimension of his regime – his close relationship with the United States.

HUSNI ZA'IM AND THE UNITED STATES

On 18 August 1949, four days after Za'im's downfall and death, the *New York Times*'s correspondent, Albion Ross, filed a story from Damascus entitled 'End of Za'im Rule Perils Peace Plan'. Probably after having been briefed by a member of the US legation in Damascus, Ross wrote that 'the deaths of President Husni Za'im and Premier Muhsin al-Barazi and the apparent restoration of Republican government in Syria have, ironically, wrecked the basis of existing plans for a solution of the Palestine problem and the restoration of peace in the Middle East'.[33]

The tension between the dictatorial character of Za'im's regime and his willingness to pursue policies that the United States favoured, alluded to in the article's first paragraph, was the thesis of the article. Ross explained that the regime as represented by Prime Minister Barazi was willing to go a long way in settling Palestinian refugees in Syria with American and international support and that Syria was about to take the initiative at the Lausanne Conference and in the Arab League's Political Committee in order to have the other Arab states endorse that plan. In a similar vein, Za'im's regime had been 'pushing hard a program of cooperation with Turkey and the formation of some sort of a Middle Eastern defense system based on alliance with the Western powers'. But, wrote Ross, Americans and other Westerners were aware and supportive of Barazi's policies, 'while in principle they could not approve the circumstance that its rapid realization was based on the existence of a dictatorship'. The impression now is that there was little chance that the programme could have been carried out effectively and rapidly under a genuinely democratic government.

Whoever thought that Sami al-Hinawi's coup signified a return to a genuine parliamentary regime did not understand the political realities of Syria, but the arguments that Ross used in his story indicate that in addition to his conversation with Muhsin al-Barazi in July,[34] he must have spent time with a member, or members, of the US legation.

Some twenty years later, in 1969, a former Central Intelligence Agency (CIA) agent in the Middle East, Miles Copeland, published *The Game of Nations*[35] in which he described the attempts made by the American intelligence community in the late 1940s and early 1950s to reshape the politics of Egypt and Syria. Copeland, who had served in the American legation in Damascus, explained that the United States was worried that the narrow-mindedness of Syria's traditional ruling elite and its refusal to permit any social, economic, and political reforms were bound to end in a volcanic eruption that would put the radical elements in power and play into the Soviet Union's hands. Having failed in their efforts to generate change in Syrian politics by intervening in the 1947 election, Copeland tells us, a 'political action task force' operating out of the US legation in Damascus under Major Stephen Meade, the assistant military attaché, set to work. Meade established contact with Husni Za'im, then the chief of the General Staff of the Syrian army, brought up the idea of a coup, and advised him on the complex preparations for its execution.[36]

As Copeland describes it, there were strong disagreements in the US mission in Damascus over encouraging a military dictatorship, even a temporary one. One young diplomat, Deane Hinton, was vehemently opposed to the idea, whereas Keeley and the State Department came to accept it but 'without enthusiasm'. Keeley believed that after a brief transitional period of military dictatorship Syria could return to the path of democracy and reform. But the truth of the matter, according to Copeland, was that Za'im had made it clear to the Americans that he was not aiming at an early restoration of democracy. Instead, the four main elements of his programme were (1) to put the corrupt politicians in jail; (2) to reorganize the government to be more efficient; (3) to institute much needed social and economic reforms, and; (4) to 'do something constructive about the Arab-Israel problem'.[37]

Although the somewhat pretentious framework into which Copeland fits his story and his condescending and facile tone tended at first to undermine his credibility, the documents now available in the American diplomatic archives at least partially support his version. These documents show that Major Stephen Meade and his superior officer, Colonel Lawrence Mitchell, knew in advance of Za'im's plans and that Major Meade continued to meet with Za'im after the coup and had discussions with him in an atmosphere of intimacy and familiarity not typical of talks between a country's ruler and head of state and an assistant military attaché, albeit of a superpower. In these conversations, issues were raised that were not being discussed between Za'im and Keeley who, in fact, used Meade as a vehicle for transmitting messages to Za'im. He thus asked him to make it clear to

Za'im that the United States wanted him to act with moderation toward Lebanon. On another occasion Meade simply asked Za'im for Syria's order of battle.[38]

During the weeks that preceded his coup, Za'im met at least six times with Meade and briefed him in great detail about his plans. He also advised the British military attaché (rather cryptically) of his plans and apparently did the same with the French military attaché.[39] In turn, Meade briefed Mitchell and G2 headquarters about his conversations with Za'im. Meade's comprehensive account of his discussions with Za'im on 3 and 7 March clearly shows that Za'im was willing to go to great lengths to obtain (direct or indirect) American support for his coup and even more so for his future regime and policies. Given the fact that reliable records of pre-coup conversations between Arab army officers and Western diplomats are rare, as well as the extraordinary nature of Za'im's statements and their relevance to our subject, it seems worthwhile to examine this document quite carefully.

Za'im began by stressing the secret nature of his statements but asked that they nevertheless be communicated to the US government. He explained that 'he wants to see his country militarily allied with the United States' and proceeded to elaborate on the advantages to the United States that such an 'alliance' with his regime and the United States' provision of 'military aid' to Syria were bound to produce. 'A strong and stable government', in his words a 'dictatorship', would give the United States 'a reliable and permanent authority with whom to deal in Syria'. Moreover, the 'United States' approval of his plan and subsequent action in accordance therewith would result in Turkey's greater strength, a potential holding force against Russian aggression, and the immediate suppression of the Communist fifth column in Syria'.

Za'im then outlined a four-phase plan of action: First, a 'seizure of power in Syria that he will ensure'. Za'im planned to take advantage of the unrest and disturbances in his country and take over smoothly, preferably in response to the government's own request. He then thought of installing 'a selected political figure' as head of state while exercising real power from the Ministry of Defense. Far from being a passive listener to all of this, Meade asked him about his choice for his own replacement as army commander and about the reaction Za'im expected from the gendarmerie's commander: 'Concomitant with the execution of the first phase would be a general Communist round-up and internment, together with 'weak' politicians in desert concentration camps for which he has already made plans.' At this point Za'im and Meade exchanged information 'regarding Communist personalities and their activities', and Mitchell, impressed that Za'im was so well informed, made sure that Za'im would take 'the necessary precautions for his personal safety at all times'.

'Second and closely following the completion of his first phase Za'im hopes to receive US aid in the form of military material.' Za'im listed his priorities and explained the importance of such prospective aid's arriving during his tenure of power (and not earlier).

'The third phase envisages US technical and training missions, particularly in the fields of aviation and armor.'

The fourth phase would include the mobilization of the entire country under military supervision, expansion of the army, and the enforcement of social reforms. Citing Kemal Ataturk as his model, Za'im enumerated the reforms he had in mind: breaking the existing 'feudal power' of the tribal chiefs and landowners, instituting agrarian reforms, modernizing the medical and judicial systems, and in a more general way, 'educating' and 'disciplining' the population. Za'im 'claimed that there is only one way to start the Syrian people along the road to progress and democracy and that is with the whip, adding emphasis to this statement by striking the desk with his riding crop'. Za'im felt that 'three to five years will be required to obtain satisfactory results from his program, and following this he plans a gradual lessening of the regimentation of the population over a ten-year period'. He contended that 'he would be able to develop, with the aforementioned aid and missions, an effective fighting force of 40,000 within one to one and a half years' time'. As it turned out, the American military advisers were supposed to replace a group of former German and Austrian army officers who had arrived in Syria after the Second World War.

Finally, Za'im and Meade discussed Syria's relationship with Israel. Meade had been authorized by the US chief of mission in Damascus to brief Za'im on the state of the Israeli-Lebanese armistice negotiations. Za'im was critical of his own government's approach to Syria's eventual negotiations with Israel. The president and the prime minister, he complained, were going to demand Galilee. His own idea was 'to permit the Israelis to keep Galilee, to cede the recently occupied Mishmar Hayarden salient, but to demand that the present frontier be modified to give Syria all territory on the east bank of Lake Tiberias from al-Kursi to Samakh'. He would also demand that Lake Tiberias be internationalized: the eastern half to Syria and the western half to Israel. But he felt that such revision, would result in a peaceful future between Syria and Israel.

The US Foreign Service's bureaucratic procedures required that the reporting officer's account be concluded with his own evaluation and comment. Meade's analysis was that 'although unscrupulous, bombastic and a complete egoist, it must be admitted that he [Za'im] has a strong personality, unlimited ambition and the backing of the Syrian army. If the ever-present element of fate happens to be in his favor, Za'im may realize his desire to be dictator in Syria'.[40] Meade added that Za'im's confidence in him 'was at least partially induced through recent efforts by Amir Farid Shihab, Director of Lebanese Sûreté, with whom I have worked for the past two years and who knows Za'im intimately'.

Meade and Za'im had another meeting on 14 March, and this, time Za'im requested specifically that US agents 'provoke and abet' internal disturbances 'essential for coup d'état' or that US funds be given him for this purpose.[41] There is no evidence that the United States supported Za'im in his coup. It was not really necessary but Meade's reports clearly indicate that he made no effort to dissuade Za'im but, rather, gave him every reason to believe that the United States was sympathetic to his ideas.

The similarity between the four-phase plan reported by Meade and the four points enumerated by Copeland is readily apparent and enhances the latter's credibility. But it is difficult to accept Copeland's version in full and thus to believe that Meade's encouragement was necessary to prompt Za'im to stage a coup when, since 1946, there had been persistent reports of Za'im's intention to seize power, first in conjunction with 'Abdallah and later unrelated to the Greater Syria plan.[42] Nor do Za'im's conversations with Meade in early March point in this direction, unless one assumes that Za'im maintained a whole network of parallel contacts and spoke differently with his various contacts.

ZA'IM'S OTHER US CONTACTS

This network of contacts could have included the State Department and its representatives in the Damascus legation, military attachés and members of the intelligence community, and oil executives. The military attaché's dispatches from Damascus in March 1949 clearly point to the centrality of the oil issue in American-Syrian relations at that time and to the effort to mobilize the political system to ratify the Tapline Agreement and to neutralize the opposition to it by nationalist opinion. On the basis of the available source material, it is difficult to reconstruct the relationship among the US legation, the American intelligence community, the oil companies, and the Syrian army's officer corps, but a memorandum written later in 1949 by Colonel Mitchell to the US minister, Keeley, offers a glimpse into the unorthodox relationship between Tapline and some of the Syrian officers. On 1 November 1949, Mitchell told Keeley:

Last evening I called on Lt. Colonel Mohamed Nasir, G3, Syrian Army by prior appointment, to arrange the conduct of official business ... Colonel Nasir is my regularly assigned contact for the negotiation of military business. Colonel Nasir was most cordial. The office was filled with other officers, also Mr. Ashley of Tapline, and it was impossible for me to obtain confidential information.[43]

In fact, Za'im ratified the Tapline Agreement shortly after seizing power.[44]

The Syrian army officers probably discussed with Tapline's representative issues of oil and oil pipelines, but it appears that regarding bilateral Syrian-American questions and Arab-Israeli affairs, Za'im dealt with the United States through two parallel channels – Keeley and the State Department on the one hand and the intelligence community on the other. Nonetheless, it is difficult on the basis of the available evidence to establish precisely how the two channels functioned and the degree of coordination between them. And so we also do not know to what extent Za'im's ideas were originally his or whether at least some of them had been planted through the 'parallel channel' with or without the State Department's knowledge. More specifically, we do not know whether Za'im's offer to Keeley on 28 April, as reported by the latter, to settle 250,000 Palestinian refugees in Syria in return for American aid was the Syrian ruler's idea or whether it had been suggested by his American contacts and was subsequently shifted, in the conversation with Keeley, to a formal level. Copeland asserted that Za'im promised on the eve of his coup to 'do something constructive' about the Arab-Israeli problem, which 'neutralized any inclination the Department might have had to give us explicit instructions to lay off.'[45]

In any case, in Washington's relationship with Za'im, two central themes of the United States' Middle Eastern policy coalesced: the effort to preempt domestic upheavals by encouraging reforms and the effort to settle the Arab-Israeli conflict. Both efforts derived from the underlying fear that instability in the Middle East would play into the Soviet Union's drive to acquire a presence and influence in the region. Washington's endeavours to persuade Syria to accept a political solution to the conflict with Israel and, more concretely, to join in the armistice negotiations had predated Za'im's coup. Thus, in a conversation with Za'im's successor, President Shukri al-Quwatli, and Prime Minister Khalid al-'Azm, Keeley acknowledged that 'given evidence of Syrian goodwill of which [the] Palestine settlement [was the] first step, it was my personal belief that the United States would increasingly give Syria evidence of its friendship'.[46]

From this perspective, Za'im displayed an immense amount of goodwill. Although the principle of opening armistice negotiations with Israel had been established by his predecessors, he not only continued that policy but also proposed to advance the negotiations to a compromise settlement. Furthermore, his willingness to discuss the settlement of 250,000 Palestinian refugees in Syria gave new life to the 'McGhee plan' – the State Department's main effort to resolve the Arab-Israeli conflict in the spring of 1949. The McGhee plan called for about half of the Palestinian refugees to be resettled in the Arab states and for the other half, or at least 200,000, to be taken in by Israel and for this scheme to be part of an impressive regional development project. Then, according to this plan, a political solution would be achieved at the Lausanne Conference.[47] In addition, the massive American aid package that would accompany the resettlement effort in Syria would not merely make it more palatable to public opinion but would also generate economic activities and development schemes and give substance to the model presumably represented by Za'im – an autocratic reformer improving the lot of his country with American support. The two pillars of US policy in the region would thus become mutually supporting and would ensure the policy's success.

The prospect of success on such a large scale aroused among the American diplomats an urgency and an eagerness that are reflected in their own dispatches,[48] as well as in more sober reports by their British colleagues. When the British Foreign Office found out that the Americans had told the Syrians about their intention to raise $200 million for the project (a huge sum of money in 1949), it was remarked in London 'that the State Department and the US Minister in Damascus were exerting heavy pressure on the Syrians with regard to the resettlement of the Palestinian refugees to the point of risking the prospects of their own plan'.[49]

The degree to which Za'im's agreement to cooperate was seen as essential to the State Department's larger plans is evidenced by the telegram from Washington to Keeley on 13 May 1949. Secretary of State Dean Acheson wrote:

> Dept notes with interest marked progress you report re Za'im's attitude resettlement Arab refugees. This is first concrete evidence Syrian willingness take large number refugees and is particular importance since Syria only Arab country except already willing Transjordan which can assimilate such number within reasonable limit. If this opportunity can be exploited back of refugee problem can be broken. You should take early opportunity discuss matter further with Za'im giving appropriate emphasis his expression of willingness accept quarter million refugees, which Dept regards as humane and statesmanlike contribution to solution this problem.

Express hope Za'im will use his influence with other Arab states adopt similarly constructive attitude towards problem, within limits their absorptive capacity, in order assist PCC in permanent liquidation problem. Emphasize steps USA is taking to persuade Israel make appropriate concessions re repatriation.[50]

In Za'im's mind, in any event, there was a clear linkage between his willingness to resettle the Palestinian refugees and the expectation of vast American aid. But when time went by and nothing happened. Za'im met with Keeley on 14 July and warned him of the dangers inherent in a continued stalemate. He explained that he himself 'could not openly take [the] initiative because powerful opposition would attack him for selling out to [the] Jews and their backers'. But Za'im pledged his 'wholehearted cooperation if the United States would take [the] lead'. Later in their conversation, Za'im spoke of 'numerous economic development projects which Syria is anxious to implement' and 'pleaded for necessary funds and technical assistance promptly'.[51] Later, when time was running out, Za'im apparently lost hope of obtaining American financial aid in this fashion and proposed a different kind of linkage. During the farewell visit paid to him by Major Meade, Za'im told his visitor that he was planning to ask the United States for a loan of $100 million to be used strictly for his economic and social program. Meade wrote, 'Za'im asked me to have our government make a formal request for air bases in Syria, which request he promised he would grant'.[52]

HUSNI ZA'IM AND 'ADEL ARSLAN

As we have already seen, the attempt to promote Syrian-Israeli negotiations in late May and early June had failed. When this issue was raised in the Syrian cabinet's meeting on 24 May, Foreign Minister 'Adel Arslan, after announcing his refusal to meet Sharett, stated categorically that he had ordered all Foreign Ministry staff not to take part in such meetings with Israelis. Arslan left two detailed versions of this episode, in a series of articles published in the Beiruti paper *al-Hayat* in August 1949 and in his diaries cum memoirs.[53] Arslan's version can be compared with reports sent at the time by Western diplomats, and it has been, on the whole, confirmed by their accounts. Arslan, it seems, knew nothing about the ideas and initiatives raised by Za'im's emissaries in their conversations with the Israelis in April or about Za'im's discussions with Keeley in April and early May. All he knew at that time, he wrote, was that Za'im was very eager to reach an agreement with Israel and that he would make considerable concessions to that end.

Arslan was particularly perturbed by Za'im's willingness to recognize Israel's borders, even implicitly (and thus to recognize Israel's legitimacy as well). According to his account, Arslan had a direct link to Colonel Fawzi Selu, a member of the Syrian delegation to the armistice talks, and extended support to Selu and to the legal adviser of the Syrian Foreign Ministry, Salih Tarazi, against Za'im's pressures.

In the cabinet meeting on 24 May, when Za'im raised the idea of a meeting between Arslan and Sharett and tried to present it as a fait accompli, Arslan indignantly refused to comply. Za'im then argued that heavy external pressure was being exerted on him and hinted that it was mostly American pressure. Arslan, who did not realize the depth of Za'im's relationship with the United States, arranged to see Keeley and learned from him that the initiative was Za'im's. But he decided not to resign, so as to be able to fight against Za'im's policy from a position of some influence. Accordingly, he asked the Saudi minister to have King Ibn Sa'ud use his influence with the Americans to give up their plans, and he himself sent Vigier a formal letter of rejection designed to serve as a coup de grace. And indeed, he writes, after 6 June, Za'im no longer raised the issue.[54]

Arslan's version of this issue raises the question as to why Za'im failed to act decisively against a reluctant foreign minister. True, he ousted him from his government in July, but in a matter of such importance to him he could have exerted heavy pressure on a minister who enjoyed status and prestige but had no real political constituents in Syria. After all, when Za'im disagreed with Michel 'Aflaq, the leader of the Ba'th party, he did not hesitate to have him jailed and tortured until 'Aflaq signed an embarrassing statement. This question throws an interesting light on Za'im's regime and on the domestic context in which he conducted his policy toward Israel. Let us now take a brief look at Za'im's career and personality.

A BRIEF BIOGRAPHY OF HUSNI ZA'IM

Husni Za'im was born in 1889 in Aleppo to a family of Kurdish extraction. He went through the Ottoman educational system to become a junior officer in the Ottoman army and was captured by the British during the Ottoman offensive against Egypt in the First World War. In 1920, after the French capture of Syria, he attended a French military college and became an officer in the Troupes Spéciales, the French auxiliary force in the Levant, and rose to the rank of colonel. In the Second World War Za'im chose to fight on the side of the Vichy forces against the British and the French and was sentenced by the victors to ten years in jail.

In 1946 when Syria won its independence from France, Za'im managed to become a senior officer in the Syrian army, and by lobbying among his politician friends he managed to obtain from President Shukri al-Quwatli the posts of director of internal security and commander of the army. He held these posts during the 1948 War and so was able to lead the army that clashed with civilian politicians over responsibility for the debacle. The memoirs of Syrian politicians and various diplomatic dispatches between 1946 and 1949 portray a corrupt officer in the middle of political intrigues cultivating ties with politicians inside and outside Syria. Za'im seemed to stand permanently on the thin line separating the prospect of expulsion from the army from the temptation to seize power.

Za'im seems to have been a person of many contradictions. He radiated power and leadership but apparently was not very clever. He saw himself as a Syrian version of Ataturk, as a man who would take his country forward, but he was bogged down by his involvements and corruption and his lack of consistency and persistence, and it is not at all clear how he envisaged the country he wanted to lead. Furthermore, while oozing self-confidence he was full of anxiety and insecurity. The foreign diplomats in Damascus who evaluated him on the eve of his coup were clearly not enamoured of the man who was to act in league with their governments. Major Stephen Meade depicted him 'as a 'banana republic' dictator type', and Deane Hinton thought that he 'did not have the competence of a French corporal'.

The political establishment that Za'im overthrew in March 1949 was mostly made up of the Syrian Arab nationalist movement's veteran leaders. Between the two world wars, most of them had gathered within the loose framework of the National Bloc, but when Syria became fully independent, the bloc had already disintegrated into several parties and factions. During the 1948 War, Shukri al-Quwatli and Jamil Mardam Bey, two of the bloc's leaders, served as president and prime minister, respectively. But Mardam Bey was forced to resign following the domestic political turmoil in December 1948 and was replaced by Khalid al-'Azm, scion of one of Syria's most distinguished families and an independent politician who had not been associated with the National Bloc.

The main opposition to the government from within the ruling establishment came during that period from the People's party – an Aleppo group representing that city's interests, with a fresher, commercially oriented perspective and a pro-Iraqi orientation. Outside the establishment a series of radical ideological parties and movements – the Ba'th party, the Parti Populaire Syrien, the Communists, the Muslim Brotherhood, and Akram Hourani's party – proclaimed their alternatives to the prevailing order.

As Za'im explained to his American contacts in early March, his original

plan was not to assume the premiership but to place at the head of the government a public figure and to exercise power from the Ministry of
Defense. His was the first coup in post-Second World War Arab politics, and
Za'im was very unsure of himself and of the policies he should pursue. His
pre-coup conversations with the military attachés of all three Western powers were a manifestation of this lack of confidence. In any event, Za'im was
unable to find a respectable public figure to head the government under
mutually acceptable conditions.

Za'im did, at first, have the support of the People's party and some of
the radical parties and movements, either because they were pleased that
he was undermining their nationalist foes or because they were still hoping to promote their own reforms, unionist programmes, or personal
careers. But all of this was not enough to give the regime a civilian base of
support or even a respectable facade. 'Adel Arslan was not Za'im's first
choice for foreign minister, but his role was, anyway, to give the regime
(albeit as a minister and not as prime minister) at least some political legitimacy. By June, Za'im had concluded that his regime's political structure
was inadequate, and so in July he made two major changes: He had himself elected president by a referendum and entrusted Muhsin al-Barazi (not
to be confused with Husni al-Barazi) with the formation of a new government. Husni al-Barazi was a second-tier nationalist politician, from an
Arab-Kurdish family in Hama, who had served as a minister in several earlier governments and had been considered close to Quwatli and Mardam
Bey. Because of this he was jailed briefly by Za'im in the aftermath of his
coup but, in a swift and remarkable about-face, became his confidant and
special emissary to the Arab world. Al-Barazi was believed to have great
influence over Za'im and even was called by one observer 'the evil genius'
of Za'im's regime.

As Za'im drew further away from the Hashemites and closer to the
Egyptian-Saudi axis, the gap between him and the People's party grew
wider. And as the ethos of reform that seemed to have marked his early days
in power dissipated, Za'im became, instead of a Syrian Ataturk, an apparently corrupt, megalomaniac, and volatile dictator. Although he lost the
support of the radical ideological parties, most crucial was the estrange-
ment of the younger officers led by Adib al-Shishakly, who staged the 14
August countercoup under the direction of Colonel Sami al-Hinawi.[55]

It is against this backdrop that 'Adel Arslan was able to stand up to
Za'im on an issue that he considered important. Arslan came from a
princely Lebanese-Druze family and, like his more famous brother Shakib,
embraced Sunni Islam and became a prominent leader of the Arab nationalist movement in the inter-war period. For Za'im, Arslan was a civilian

and political 'fig leaf'. Arslan did not have a political base in Syria, but he did have a good public and political reputation and a network of political connections in the Arab world. (When Za'im had a falling-out with the Ba'th party's leader, he had him jailed and tortured.) Michael 'Aflaq in 1949 was a practically anonymous leader of a new and weak political movement and Za'im assumed that he was free to treat him as he wished, but Arslan enjoyed a considerable degree of immunity. Furthermore, as he himself tells it, Arslan had a direct relationship with Fawzi Selu and apparently with other army officers as well, thus reinforcing his position in the regime. Therefore, although Arslan could not prevent Za'im from pursuing an Israeli policy that he opposed, he could withdraw his cooperation and show him the degree of resistance he should expect from the Arab nationalists.

ISRAEL AND HUSNI ZA'IM

Israel's response to Husni Za'im's initiatives was puzzling in 1949, and it still raises questions, albeit different ones. As we saw, the State Department, other American officials, and even Abba Eban could not understand why Ben-Gurion refused to meet with Za'im and at least put to the test his willingness to conclude an agreement with Israel. Sharett, however, had consented to meet Za'im, but he seemed to be taking his time, and when Arslan refused to see Sharett, Sharett's angry response focused, strangely, on matters of status and procedure. Because the Israeli Foreign Ministry was aware of the UN and US criticism of Israel's conduct in this matter, it accordingly prepared a background paper to refute it.

On 2 May 1949, Moshe Sharett presented the Knesset's Foreign and Security Affairs Committee with a survey of Israel's political position:

> As has been published we stated that we will not negotiate with Syria until an armistice has been signed. We decided not to sign an armistice agreement with Syria unless it evacuates the strip of [Mandatory] Palestine's territory that it is presently holding. The territory's importance does not derive from its size, which in fact is negligible. Rather, what is at stake is the water's edge, the shore of Lake Tiberias, the East Bank of the Jordan River, and Mey Marom. We regard this as Syria's expressing its intention to adjust the border, and we are opposed to it for this reason. We want to keep these waters within the state's territory and not to make Syria a partner ... Our statement creates a certain pressure on Syria and makes it in advance responsible for the failure of the Lausanne discussions.[56]

Sharett stated also that for Israel, peace was desirable with Egypt and 'likewise with Lebanon and possibly with Syria, bearing in mind the reservations concerning the new regime'.[57]

Some three weeks later, on 25 May, Sharett addressed a forum composed of his ministry's department heads. When he reached the subject of Syria, he commented:

> A difficult problem with regard to which we should clarify our thinking is Syria. We will obviously not agree that any part of [Mandatory] Palestine be given to Syria, as control of the water sources is at stake. There was a proposal by Za'im to meet, but that meeting did not materialize. He thought that the prime minister or at least I would come. We sent distinguished persons, Shiloah and Yadin, but he considered them below his own rank and so sent people without standing, and the meeting did not take place, of course. In the meantime General Riley, whom we have no reason to distrust, has communicated to us that Za'im is willing to discuss the absorption of 300,000 refugees into Syria. If it is true, it is purely to Za'im's credit. It would mean that he has greater vision than the others do, is more daring, and understands the advantages that may accrue to him from it – the income for the state and the fact that everybody could do well on these monies ...
>
> For us this is something tremendous; it means that he is willing to absorb three times the number of refugees who are currently in Syria and Lebanon. In any event, if there is a state prepared for something of this nature, the [unified Arab] front will be broken. I think it is worth our while to meet with Za'im, particularly in order to clarify the issue of refugee absorption.[58]

If Sharett really considered Za'im's initiatives 'tremendous', regarded him as 'more daring' than the others, and attributed to him 'greater vision', his policy lagged behind his analysis. In this case it was not sufficient to observe that 'it would be worth our while to meet with him'. The same Israel that conceived the idea of annexing Gaza in order to cope with the pressures anticipated in Lausanne could have taken much greater advantage of the opening provided by Za'im, at least in tactical terms. How, then, can Israel's policy toward Za'im be explained?

Part of the explanation is to be found in Ben-Gurion's and Sharett's own statements. They gave priority to obtaining an armistice on the basis of the international frontier and thought, correctly, that Za'im wanted to adjust the border, particularly in the sensitive area of Lake Tiberias and the Jordan River. The Israeli leaders knew that the lake's basin was the key to all of

Israel's future national irrigation schemes and to the development of the Negev and so were not willing to give up full Israeli control of and sovereignty over the lake. The Israelis found out from Riley that the United States in fact supported Za'im's demand for an armistice not based on the international border line, in recognition of his goodwill, and estimated, again correctly, that the failure of a prospective meeting with Za'im would be blamed on Israel. The importance of these considerations to Ben-Gurion's position in April and May 1949 is revealed by the fact that in July, when the armistice agreement was about to be signed on the basis of full Syrian evacuation, Ben-Gurion changed his mind and wanted a meeting and negotiations with Husni Za'im after all.

The fluid state of Syrian policies at the time, the uncertainty regarding the stability of the new regime, and the new phenomenon of military coups and regimes and questions regarding Za'im himself all contributed to Israel's hesitation. On 2 April, immediately after Za'im's coup, Ben-Gurion told the American consul in Jerusalem that 'Israel must always ask itself whether the representatives of an Arab state really represent their country. Farouk is apparently Egypt, but who is Za'im?'[59]

Incensed by the cancellation of Za'im's meeting with him in May, Sharett expressed his disdain for a military dictatorship that he regarded as illegitimate. In his presentation to the department heads in his ministry, Sharett alluded to his suspicion that Za'im expected to profit personally from the forthcoming American aid ('everybody could do well on these monies'). In early April 1949 Israel had information that Za'im was in league with 'Abdallah and more reliable information that 'Abdallah was considering taking advantage of the Syrian coup in order to try to seize control in Damascus. Some in Israel argued that it would be to their country's advantage to channel the Jordanian king's ambitions northward. And those who did not agree could assume that a period of change and uncertainty lay ahead for Syria.

THE REASONS FOR ISRAEL'S HESITATIOn

It can be assumed the Israeli leadership did not take Husni Za'im seriously but viewed him as an ambitious adventurer. Nonetheless, despite the extent of the Israeli archives, I could not find an explicit expression of such a view. Rather, my suspicion that this was the Israeli leadership's view of Za'im is based on two facts.

First, in 1948 Israel's intelligence services maintained at least an indirect contact with Za'im and viewed him as a candidate for staging a coup in Syria aided by Israel and designed to promote Israel's aims. Some writers have argued that there was a direct relationship between Za'im and Israeli intelligence agents. Although this cannot be proved, there is reliable evidence that when the Israeli Foreign Ministry's Middle East Department contemplated in the summer of 1948 a coup in Syria that would take it out of the war, they regarded Za'im as the chief candidate to lead it.

Behind that scheme was the fear that the war might drag on without a definitive terminal point and that Israel might be worn out by the protracted effort. On 21 September 1948, Ezra Danin wrote to Tuvia Arazi in Paris:

> Without knowing exactly what you had initiated regarding a rebellion-revolution in Syria, we have given it a lot of thought here as the only means of ending the war here and opening a way for peace. The assumption was that only if 'a respectable show were held' in one of the Arab countries that would attract the attention of the Arabs and divert it away from Israel could we make some progress toward ordinary peace relations. The assumption is that the rebellious government would need our aid and support, would recognize us, and would cooperate with us ... Last week we raised this problem for discussion with the foreign minister. We assumed that for the preliminary exploration we may need ten thousand pounds, for the preliminary examination a hundred thousand pounds, and for execution a sum of over five hundred thousand pounds ...
>
> We emphasized this estimate of ours because our cause is in a bind: Breaking the cease-fire and continuing the war by one of the parties out of the war will not bring us to either decision or solution; on the other hand, the discussions of peace proceed very slowly and do not promise a near solution visible on our misty horizon.

Sharett responded with a great deal of scepticism. He did not believe in political changes initiated from the outside but, instead, in 'self [authentic] action' and did not think that even much less money could be allocated to 'explorations and examinations'. But he 'was not opposed and even suggested that we check what is at stake concretely, listen to what the Druzes or others propose, and discuss it again when we have understood the real intentions'. Danin then suggested to Arazi that he 'get Josh [Palmon] interested in this proposal so that he too could try to confirm it. After all, he was the last to have explored this area and had even had some success'.[60]

Arazi and Palmon operated vis-à-vis Syria through a number of channels. At least some of their activities were conducted through middlemen who promised 'to deliver' army officers, politicians, tribes, and minority communities that would carry out the actual operation. That is, not every

name mentioned in their correspondence necessarily had a direct contact
with the Israelis. In August 1948 Danin managed, after strenuous effort, to
meet with Ben-Gurion and told him in detail about the Middle East
Department's plans to stage a coup in Syria and to encourage Palestinian
autonomy as an alternative to 'Abdallah's rule. But Ben-Gurion dismissed
these ideas and stated that 'we will not enter into new adventures.'[61] On 2
November Ya'acov Shimoni wrote to Arazi in Paris that

> in the meantime I have received your telegram, informing me that
> you have not spoken to Moshe (Sharett) about the proposal to invite
> Husayn Za'im [sic] and Husayn Barazi [sic]. In fact our suggestion that
> you raise it with Moshe was made in a tone of bitter irony: We have
> no doubt that Moshe will not agree to invite these men and will not
> be in a position to allocate the appropriate budget for such an oper-
> ation. Our intention ... was to tell you: Because you know that Moshe
> rejected all our broad and practical plans regarding Syria and the
> Druzes, how is it that you ask us whether you should invite these two
> persons to Paris?[62]

The fact that Shimoni spoke in his letter about Husni Za'im and Muhsin
al-Barazi (both given names were given incorrectly), who were of Kurdish
descent, reinforces the assumption that this was an attempt to take advantage
of a connection established in 1948 between Sasson and Palmon and a group
of Kurdish activists in Paris through the Israeli diplomat Maurice Fischer.
Fischer had served during the Second World War with French intelligence
in the Levant and had at that time cultivated contacts with various groups,
some of which he introduced to Israel's Foreign Ministry and intelligence
community. It thus seems that the Kurdish activists told their Israeli contacts
in 1948 that they could persuade Za'im to stage a coup in Syria.

In the Israeli correspondence and other records from the spring of 1949
available in the archives, this episode is not mentioned. But it stands to reason
that those involved in it in the summer of 1948, who continued to hold senior positions in Israel's Foreign Ministry and intelligence community in 1949,
made sure to tell or remind their superiors soon after Za'im's coup that less
than a year earlier Syria's new ruler had been a candidate to stage a coup in
Syria with Israel's support and financial aid. As we shall see, the Israeli connection was not mentioned in the Foreign Ministry's first evaluations of
Za'im's coup and regime. But this may not be significant, because in the Israeli
system, as in other foreign offices and intelligence services, there was a clear
distinction between operations and evaluations.

The Israeli Foreign Ministry's archive contains an interesting illustration
of the ministry's ambivalent attitude toward those Arab politicians who

had accepted financial aid from Israel in return for their cooperation. In September 1951 Walter Eytan wrote to Tuvia Arazi, who was then stationed in the Israeli legation in Ankara. Arazi had earlier written to Eytan about a Syrian politician who had taken money from Israel in the late 1940s and had apparently offered his services again. Eytan responded:

> Our general attitude toward the specific question that you raise ... as well as other similar requests transmitted every so often is more or less the following: As a general rule we have no great confidence in the kind of person who shows up and says that in return for a thousand pounds sterling he will stage a coup in an Arab state and will put in power a government that will make a settlement with Israel. At the same time, we must pursue some Arab policy, and it is clear that we must take risks, including financial risks, and spend money quite lavishly, even if it is apparent that the prospects of success are poor and the money might be lost. It is a matter of cast thin bread upon the waters.[63]

Second, after his rise to power and at the same time as his political initiative toward Israel, Za'im and his men also made other moves that must have puzzled the Israelis. We mentioned earlier Yadin's description of the far-reaching and politically unrealistic proposals made by Za'im's officers to their Israeli contacts regarding joint hegemony in the Middle East. But these were not the only proposals they made. According to the authoritative and detailed testimony of Major Itzhak Spector, who was a member of the Israeli delegation to the armistice talks, during one of these meetings, Spector was approached by Colonel Muhammad Nasir[64] who said that with the permission of Husni Za'im he had proposed assassinating Ben-Gurion for 'millions'. Nasir promised to provide weapons and 'everything you may want, including [Syrian] people who will be loyal to you'. Spector reported this to General Mordechai Makleff, who ordered him to keep silent and said that he himself would report this to Yadin. Following a conversation with Yadin, Makleff ordered Spector to tell Nasir that Yadin too 'was in the business' and that he belonged to 'our gang'. Spector delivered the message, and in order to prove to Spector how serious 'the business' was, Nasir told him that he was 'willing to meet on your territory' at the Shulamit Hotel in the small town of Rosh Pina with Makleff, Yadin, and Spector. An agreement to meet was reached in principle, and the contact continued for months. One Saturday when Spector was home on leave, Nasir sent Makleff a note saying that 'if you want to meet today, I have final instructions from Husni Za'im'. Nasir asked that Spector take him over to Israeli territory. But because Spector could not be found, his deputy was sent instead and brought Nasir in an armored car to the military camp in Mahanayim. On the next day Makleff briefed Spector. According to Makleff, Nasir repeated his detailed proposal, and as Makleff told Spector, 'You missed the high point of your life.'[65]

Muhammad Nasir was one of the brigade commanders who took part in Za'im's coup and was considered a key figure in his regime. He survived Za'im's downfall and after Hinawi's coup was appointed head of operations on the Syrian army's General Staff. He has already been mentioned as the Syrian contact of the American military attaché Lawrence Mitchell, in November 1949. In this case there is no doubt that the proposed assassination of Ben-Gurion was reported, albeit indirectly, to Ben-Gurion himself. On 27 April Ben-Gurion noted in his diary that Makleff had told him that the Syrian officer 'proposed to him to expel the government and let the army take power, as in the case with them, to which Makleff responded, you had Quwatli but we have Ben-Gurion'. The text of the diary entry is somewhat puzzling, in that this sentence was inserted later, but in any case it is certain that at least the gist of the story was brought to Ben-Gurion's attention.[66]

A similar though far less dramatic effect must have been created in the latter half of June 1949, by the visit to Israel of Max Wolf, the emissary of the president of the International Red Cross. On 24 June Wolf met with the American ambassador James McDonald and told him, 'as someone unfolding a melodrama', of a statement attributed to Za'im a short time after seizing power that 'everything could be settled between Syria and Israel provided that Colonel Za'im's cousin, Ihsan Kamel Maz, be returned to Damascus'. According to the Red Cross's information, Maz was captured by the Israelis in May 1948, was wounded, was treated in a hospital in Haifa, and had since disappeared. The Israeli authorities had not responded to the Red Cross's queries in this matter. McDonald passed the story on to General William Riley, who must have raised the question with the Israelis.[67]

It is difficult to gauge the impact of these episodes on Israel's view of Husni Za'im and his regime, but the material available in the Israeli archives enables us to reconstruct several aspects of Israel's perception of the changes occurring in Syria during the spring of 1949.

First, we should stress that throughout Za'im's tenure of power, the Israelis failed to understand his relationship with the United States. They knew that the United States was interested in Syria and had good relations with Za'im but did not perceive the special bond between the US government and the Syrian dictator. As the Israelis saw it, France was the principal external supporter of Syria's new military regime.

In the immediate aftermath of Za'im's coup d'état, Eliyahu Sasson, who was then out of the country, assumed that it had been inspired by

'Abdallah, to promote his Greater Syrian plan, and that, in line with his general outlook on the region's politics, the changes in Syria were the result of yet another British design. On 4 April Sasson wired Sharett, who was then in New York, that he had had an exchange of telegrams with Eytan regarding the significance of Husni Za'im's coup. Eytan had told Sasson that the 'indications that the Syrian coup had been strongly sup-ported by Meir ['Abdallah's code name] but not necessarily by the British may be a step on road to greater Syria'.

To this and to Eytan's statements that if Bunche recognized the new regime, Israel would have no other choice but to enter into armistice nego-tiations with Syria, Sasson answered:

> Any strengthening of the Husni Za'im regime would have the fol-lowing consequences: (1) It would promote a union of Iraq, Trans-jordan, Syria, and Lebanon; (2) it would lead Egypt and Lebanon to sign defense and economic treaties with Britain; and (3) it would drag out the conflict between Israel and the Arab world and dis-courage real peace and sincere collaboration.[68]

Sasson's conclusion was undoubtedly reinforced by Walter Eytan's report on his trip back, early in the morning of 31 March, from Shuneh, where he had met with 'Abdallah. In the car 'Abdallah al-Tal told him that he was about to depart for Damascus to transmit the king's good wishes to Husni Za'im. As he told it, the king was to decide within the next two or three days whether to try to implement his plans. Al-Tal raised the possibility of Israel's helping 'Abdallah in this matter and asked what Israel would do if 'Abdallah sent his army north and exposed himself to the danger of an Israeli attack. Al-Tal was quite specific and explained that 'Abdallah planned to move to Damascus while Prince Talal would remain in Amman as the prince of Transjordan. Furthermore, al-Tal 'hinted that our air force might play a useful part. Nothing would be easier than to paint our aircraft with the colors and markings of Transjordan'. Eytan and Shiloah replied that 'Israel would not interfere'.[69]

Ben-Gurion, like Sasson, tended to view Britain's long arm behind many developments in the Middle East and thus noted in his diary on 3 April that he believed that Za'im's coup had been organized by Britain:

> We are informed from Paris that the coup in Syria is a British prod-uct General [Edward] Spears had arrived in Damascus two weeks ago. British agents bought the support of the Druze ... The revolution was directed against Shukri Quwatli and Khalid al-'Azm, who had obstructed the British ... Well, in Iraq, Nuri; and in Transjordan,

'Abdallah; and in Syria, Spears, and Azem [Za'im]. Bevin rules the Middle East.[70]

Ben-Gurion traced the information regarding the connection between Za'im, on the one hand, and the British and 'Abdallah, on the other, to a report from Paris. But the French themselves were not swayed by similar rumours. The first dispatches from the French mission in Damascus after Za'im's coup did reflect France's familiar preoccupation with Britain's quest for influence in Syria but they also portrayed Za'im's coup as the result of the conflict between him and the civilian government rather than as the result of external intervention.

The first account written in the Israeli Foreign Ministry, by Shmuel Ya'ari of the Middle East Department's Syrian desk, was quite perceptive. On 29 March Ya'ari issued a preliminary evaluation stating that 'the coup that took place in Syria at the dawn of 29.3 has a distinctive military character like the Bakr-Sidqi revolution in Iraq in the 1930s'. Ya'ari determined that Za'im was not connected to the large opposition People's party and that there was no reason to doubt his statement that he was not connected to the 'Greater Syria' plan. Rather, Ya'ari saw Za'im's move as a 'coup d'état of a purely military nature' and expressed his concern that armistice negotiations with Israel 'at least be postponed so as not to hurt the pride of the Syrian army'.[71]

Two days later, however, Ya'ari began to doubt his first interpretation and thus concluded, 'with all appropriate caution, that a certain connection existed between the authors of the coup in Damascus and those who pull the strings in Amman'. In time the Israelis became acquainted with Za'im's regime and the forces affecting it from within and without, as a Political Department paper on 'the new Syrian government' written on 6 July shows.[72] Still, Israel failed to understand the complex relationship between Za'im and the military and were completely surprised by the 14 August coup. On that date Ben-Gurion wrote in his diary:

> At 10 o'clock Elkana [Gali, his secretary] came in with a 'bombastic' piece of news: Za'im and Barazi had been assassinated by one of Za'im's senior officers. The assassin wants to return the regime to those elected by the people. Elkana added that the oriental [Orientalists] were not prepared for this action, which came by surprise. Za'im should have been prepared, and if he were not, it is not surprising that this thing happened.[73]

It was not the last time in Israel's history that prime ministers lambasted the intelligence community's experts for their failure to predict a dramatic change in the politics of an Arab state.

When Za'im's regime was toppled, the instigators of the coup published a statement that denounced his crimes and justified their actions. The principal themes in this first statement were repeated in greater detail in later statements and revelations: Za'im was accused of deviating from the aims of the original coup and, more specifically, of causing anarchy, wasting the people's money, disparaging the army's honour, exploiting his power for private ends and personal profit, harming the Islamic tradition, conducting unwise and treacherous foreign policy, and granting unwarranted concessions to French interests.

It is curious that the charge of treachery in Za'im's foreign policy was aimed at his relations with France. The ratification of the Tapline Agreement was mentioned, but the new regime, which refrained from adopting an anti-American policy, did not denigrate its predecessor on this issue. It is still more curious that his successors did not castigate Za'im for his relations with Israel, the fact that he had signed an armistice agreement with Israel, and the broad initiatives he had taken toward that country. As we mentioned, 'Adel Arslan did include Za'im's relations with Israel in the series of revelations he published in Beirut at this time. But his denunciation did not spread. The restraint that Za'im's successors displayed in this matter derived from several factors. First, some of them, led by Fawzi Selu – who was responsible for seizing power and assassinating Za'im and Barazi – had taken an active part in the armistice negotiations with Israel and so hurling accusations in this matter would have been hurting themselves. Nor were Syria's new rulers interested in exacerbating the conflict with Israel, and consequently they did not want to undermine the relations between the two countries during the months preceding the coup. Furthermore, the Syrian public in 1949 was preoccupied with issues other than the conflict with Israel. Accordingly, in his annual report summing up the year's events, the first secretary of Britain's embassy in Damascus wrote that 'the problem of Palestine was relegated to the background by Syrian internal affairs during the year. There were the usual storms in the press but after the conclusion of the Armistice agreement in July the public lost interest'.[74]

This comment does indeed point to the public's varying preoccupation with the question of Palestine and the conflict with Israel at different times, even in a nation so committed to the Palestinian cause as Syria was.

The most important question is whether Israel missed a historic opportunity in the spring of 1949 to come to an agreement with Syria and thereby change the course of the Arab-Israeli conflict, or to put it differently, was the Husni Za'im of 1949 an early version of the 1971 Anwar al-Sadat? The question cannot be answered definitively, as it is impossible to establish in

retrospect whether or not an opportunity has been missed, and yet historians, political scientists, and students of inter-Arab relations still debate this
question. But even if it cannot be answered with any certainty, anyone who
passes judgement or expresses an opinion on decisions made by leaders at
crucial turning points must deal with this question explicitly or implicitly
by stating that a certain decision was warranted or unwarranted. The historian implies that the choice underlying the decision was warranted. In
his important text on international relations Inis Claude offers an elegant
formulation of the problem:

> A major difficulty in the development of the 'science of peace' lies in
> the fact that we cannot really know when any technique for prevent-
> ing war works successfully. The evidence of failure is provided by the
> outbreak of war, but if the technique succeeds in averting hostilities
> the world may never know and scholars can never demonstrate that
> it was the effective cause of that negative result. In this as in many
> other realms disproving is more feasible than confirming.[75]

In any event, the options that confronted the decision makers and the
problems with which they had to contend can be analysed. From this point
of view and from the current perspective, it seems that Ben-Gurion's
refusal to meet Husni Za'im in April–May 1949 did not destroy the
prospect of reaching an agreement that would have transformed Arab-
Israeli relations, an assessment based on several considerations.

First, the premises of the two parties were so different and remote from
each other that it is difficult to believe that the gap between them could
have been bridged. Za'im viewed his meeting with Ben-Gurion as the
means to an agreement that would eliminate the Syrian-Israeli conflict in
one fell swoop. But Za'im also saw an Israeli territorial concession in the
area of Lake Tiberias and the Jordan River as enabling him to justify his
unorthodox conduct and to present himself as the victor in the 1948 War.
But such a concession was unacceptable to Israel, as it would spill over into
the conflict over the waters of the Jordan River.

Second, it is difficult to believe that Za'im would have survived in
power even if he had reached an agreement with Israel and enjoyed massive American aid. The man who appeared during his first days in power as
a popular reformer soon became a corrupt dictator who was consumed
with gaining prestige and status but who also had lost the support of his
original allies and thus was easily removed by the same military faction
that had put him in power. As has been shown, the Israeli leadership had
its own reasons for failing to take Za'im seriously.

Third, Za'im's willingness to enter into an agreement with Israel was completely divorced from the prevailing public opinion in Syria and the rest of the Arab world. True, the question of Israel had yet to occupy the position in Syrian public opinion that it came to have later when Arab-Israeli relations grew more bitter and Syria's politics became more radical and ideological, but the Syrian public commitment to pan-Arab national-ism and particularly the Palestine question could not be ignored. As we shall show, Syria might have been able to negotiate with Israel on a practi-cal level but not on a level that touched on values and symbols. Za'im tend-ed to dismiss this dimension of Syrian politics, and this tendency was, indeed, among the factors that led to his downfall. In regard to Israel, 'Adel Arslan was able to stand up to Za'im precisely because Arslan represented the attitude of most Syrians toward this component of the conflict with Israel. Against this background it seems that a far-reaching agreement between Israel and Husni Za'im in the spring of 1949 would have resem-bled the Lebanese-Israeli agreement of May 1983 more closely than the Camp David Accords.

NOTES

1. This article was published in Itamar Rabinovich, *The Road Not Taken – Early Arab-Israeli Negotiations* (New York: Oxford University Press, 1991), pp.65–110.

2. For details of the discussions and conversations between representatives of the Jewish Agency's political department and the Syrian leaders and politicians, see Eliyahu Eylath, *Zionism and the Arabs* (Tel Aviv: Devir, 1974) [in Hebrew]; and Eliyahu Sasson, *On the Road to Peace* (Tel Aviv: Am Oved, 1978) [(in Hebrew]. See also Philip Khoury, 'Divided Loyalties: Syria and the Question of Palestine, 1919–1939', *Middle Eastern Studies*, 21, 3 (July 1985), pp.324–48.

3. For Syria's role in the 1948 war and its position on the question of the war's termination, see Abraham Sela, 'Syria and the Palestinian Question from the Establishment of the Arab League to the Armistice Agreement, 1945–1949', *Dapei Elazar*, 6, 10 (Tel Aviv University 1987), pp.24–42 [in Hebrew]. An intriguing version by the Syrian prime minister in the first months of 1949 can be found in Khalid al-'Azm's *The Memoirs of Khalid al-'Azm* (Beirut: Al-Dar al-Taqadumiyya Lil-Nashir, 1973), vol. I, pp.379–90 [in Arabic].

4. The Soviet Union's attitude was determined by the fact that at this time it still believed that Husni Za'im was linked to 'Abdallah and the British. See Moshe Zak, *Israel and the Soviet Union – A Forty-Year Dialogue* (Tel Aviv: Ma'ariv, 1988), p.216 [in Hebrew].

5. An excellent background to and summary of the armistice negotiations between Israel and Syria can be found in the introduction written by Yemima Rosenthal to the third volume of Documents of the Foreign Policy of Israel (DFPI), *Armistice Talks with the Arab Countries*, ed. Yemima Rosenthal (Jerusalem: Israel State Archive, 1983) [in Hebrew], pp.11–12, 27–32. See also N. Bar-Ya'acov, *The Israeli-Syrian Armistice: Problems of Implementation, 1949–1966* (Jerusalem: Magnes Press, 1967) [in Hebrew]; Aryeh Shalev, *Cooperation in the Shadow of Conflict* (Tel Aviv: Ma'arachot, 1987) [in Hebrew]. Shalev was a member of the Israeli delegation to the Syrian-Israeli mixed armistice commission, and his book combines his memoirs with the fruits of archival research.

6. D. Ben-Gurion, *The War Diary: The War of Independence, 1948–1949*, vol. 1, p.34–5.

7. Ibid.

8. Israel State Archive, File 4373/13.

9. See FRUS, 1949, vol. 4, p.962, n.3.

10. Ibid., pp.965–6.

11. Ben-Gurion, *The War Diary*, vol. 2, p.436.

12. Ibid.

13. See FRUS, 1949, vol. 4, p.990.

14. DFPI, vol. 3, doc. 303, pp.562–3.

15. Shabtai Rosenne to Foreign Minister Sharett, 8 May 1949, Israel State Archive, File 2454/10. See also Shalev, *Cooperation*, pp.49–50.

16. Keeley to the secretary of state, 11 May 1949. National Archives 767, no. 90, D 15/5.

17. DFPI, doc. 310, pp.581–2.

18. DFPI, doc. 312, p.584.

19. DFPI, docs. 310, 320, 321, 323–7.

20. DFPI, docs. 332–7.

21. DFPI, doc. 328, p.597.

22. Broadmead to the Foreign Office, June 1949, FO371/E6804.

23. 'Adel Arslan, *The Memoirs of Emir 'Adel Arslan*, vol. 2, 1946–1950 (Beirut: Dar al-Taqadumiyya Lil-Nashir, 1983), pp. 839, 841–2, 844 [in Arabic].

24. For a summary of Arslan's articles in the Beiruti newspaper al-Hayat and their echoes in Damascus, see the report by the American Legation in Beirut on 31 August 1949, NA 890 D 00/8-3149, no. 217.

25. Ben-Gurion, *The War Diary*, vol. 2, p.445. Za'im indeed made his ideas public in an interview he granted to the correspondent of the *Gazette de Lausanne* in which he spoke broadly about his foreign policy. The Syrian newspaper *al-Inqilab* published a translation of the interview, according to the American legation in Damascus. Za'im said the following with regard to Israel: 'Syria and Israel are now bound by a cease-fire agreement. On my part I should like to conclude a permanent truce agreement, but if Israel does not abide by its pledges, I will proceed to take all the measures that the violation of these pledges might necessitate.'

26. M. Sharett's guidelines to Israel mission abroad, DFPI, vol. 4, doc. 146, pp.239–49.

27. DFPI, doc. 188, pp.300–1.

28. See FRUS, 1949, pp.1030–2; and Keeley to the secretary of state, 11 May and 19 May 1949, NA 767, N 90 D.

29. FRUS, 1949, pp.1245–6, 1256.

30. On the social and ideological differences among the various age groups in the Syrian officer corps during those years, see M. van Dusen, 'Intra and Inter-Generational Conflict in the Syrian Army' (Unpublished PhD dissertation, Johns Hopkins University, 1971). Za'im's lack of sensitivity with regard to the ideological sensibilities were analysed by Ya'acov Shimoni, 'Syria Between the Coups', *Hamizrah Hehadash*, 1 (October 1949–50), pp.7–21 [in Hebrew].

31. On 20 June 1949, the Israeli Foreign Ministry prepared a profile on Muhsin al-Barazi. See Israel State Archive, File 2565/13.

32. Khaled al-'Azm, *The Memoirs of Khaled al-'Azm* (Beirut: Al-Dar al-Taqadumiyya Lil-Nashir, 1973), vol. 2, p.380.

33. *New York Times*, 19 August 1949.

34. *New York Times*, 26 July 1949.

35. Miles Copeland, *The Game of Nations* (London: Weidenfeld & Nicholson, 1969), pp.60–6. In 1989 Copeland published a second biography, entitled *The Game Players* (London: Aurum Press, 1989). This book, too, includes a chapter dealing with the 'Syrian episode' of 1949, but it does not alter the main lines of the story told twenty years earlier. For a critical review of Copeland's first book, see E. Kedourie, 'The Sorcerer's Apprentice', in his *Arabic Political Memoirs and Other Studies* (London: Frank Cass, 1974), pp.170–6.

36. Copeland, *The Game of Nations*, p.42.

37. Ibid.

38. For Meade's reports to the State Department on his unusual discussions with Za'im, see, for instance, the memorandum he submitted to Minister Keeley on 11 August 1949. The report was released by the National Archives on 4 May 1984. For a summary of Meade's role in preparing for Za'im's coup, based on Meade's report to Washington, see Douglas Little, 'Cold War and Covert Action: The United States and Syria, 1945–1958', *Middle East Journal*, 44, 1 (Winter 1990), pp.51–75.

39. FO371/75529 E4-72, 28 March 1949.

40. NA, 350 Syria 3144.0501.

41. Integrated weekly report no. 60, 18 March 1949, Confidential File RG I30X.22.

42. FO371/68810 E 15669 and NA 800A Moose to Washington, March J2, r947.

43. See the report by the US military attaché, Lawrence Mitchell, on 1 November 1949 (no archival number).

44. For the role of the US oil companies in the formulation of US policy in the region, see Little, 'Cold War and Covert Action', pp. 53–4. The memoirs of Khalid al-'Azm and Nadhir Fansa echo the rumours current at the time that US oil executives were involved in staging Za'im's coup, in order to secure the ratification of the Tapline agreement. See Nadhir Fansa, *Days of Husni al-Za'im: 137 Days That Shook Up Syria* (Beirut: Manshurat Dar al-Afaq al-Jadida, 1982) [in Arabic], p.134. For 'Azm's insistence that during his period in power the Tapline agreement could not be ratified, see his memoirs, vol. 2, pp.373–6.

45. Copeland, *The Game of Nations*, pp.42–4.

46. For Keeley's discussions with the Syrian leadership regarding the termination of the war with Israel, see FRUS, 1949, pp.637–9, 796–8.

47. On George McGhee's plan, see his memoirs, *Envoy to the Middle World: Adventures and Diplomacy* (New York: Harper & Row, 1983); see also Cyrus Sulzberger, *New York Times*, 16 September 1949.

48. See Minister Keeley's report to Washington on 11 May 1949, for his discussion with Za'im and Arlsan on this matter. FRUS 890 D/0-02/5-1149.

49. FO371/75072 E702, 1949.

50. Acheson's cable to Keeley on 13 May 1949, FRUS, pp.1007–8.

51. See Keeley's report in FRUS, r949, pp.1226–8.

52. Meade's memorandum to the chargé d'affaires, 11 August 1949 (no archival number).

53. 'Adel Arslan, *The Memoirs of Amir 'Adel Arslan*, vol. 2 (Beirut: Al-Dar al-Taqadumiyya Lil-Nashir, 1983).

54. This description is based on Arslan's own version, as told in his memoirs and in al-Hayat. His version is confirmed by the dispatches sent at the time by British and American diplomats. See, for instance, the report by the British ambassador, Broadmead, on 1 June 1949, FO371 E6804.

55. See essay by Shimoni 'Syria Between the Coups', and the memoirs of Khalid al-'Azm and Nadhir Fansa. Fansa was Za'im's brother-in-law and private secretary, a fact that accounts for the book's advantages and shortcomings. Fansa was clearly familiar with the most intimate details of Za'im's regime and period, but he also is trying to defend Za'im's and his own records. 'Azm despised Za'im and held a grudge against him, but his memoirs abound in detail with regard to those months (see esp. vol. 2, pp.179ff).

56. Israel State Archive, File 2447/3.

57. Ibid.

58. Ben-Gurion, *The War Diary*, vol. 2, 2 April 1949.

59. Israel State Archive, File 33/II.

60. Israel State Archive, File 2570/II; Danin to Sasson, 24 August 1948.

61. Ibid.

62. Ibid.

63. Israel State Archive, File 130.02, file 22, box 2408.

64. Nasir was an 'Alawi officer, one of Za'im's brigade commanders and a key figure of his regime. See also the report by the US military attaché, Mitchell, 1 November 1949 (no archival number).

65. See the text of an interview conducted by Shabtai Teveth with Major Itzak Spector. I am grateful to Shabtai Teveth for making this available to me.

66. Ben-Gurion, *The War Diary*, p.463.

67. McDonald to secretary of state, 27 June 1947, FRUS 7767N-90D/6/2749.

68. Sasson's telegram to M. Sharett, 4 April 1949, DFPI, vol. 2, doc. 475, pp.547–8.

69. Eytan on discussion with 'Abdallah al-Tal, in DFPI, vol. 3, doc. 267, p.500, 3 April 1949.

70. Ben-Gurion, *The War Diary*, vol. 3, p. 984.

71. 'The Character of the Coup in Syria, Primary Comments', Israel State Archive, File AS/20/2408.

72. The New Syrian Government, Israel State Archive File AS/20/2408.

73. Ben-Gurion, *The War Diary*, vol. 2, 14 August 1949.

74. FO371/82782 EY/1011.

75. Inis Claude, *Swords into Plowshares* (New York: Random House, 1971), p.228. Claude relied here on Raymond Aron, *Peace and War* (Garden City, NY: Doubleday/Anchor, 1973), pp.116, 560.

15

Syria, Inter-Arab Relations and the Outbreak of the Six Day War[1]

Like a searchlight moving about as it is being carried forward illuminating parts of the dark environment from different vantage points, the very march of events, or the unfolding of our contemporary history alters the perspective from which patches of the past are seen and judged. In the immediate aftermath of the Six Day War its origins were debated in domestic political arenas – in Egypt, Syria and Israel – where credit for successes and blame for debacles were converted into positive and negative political assets. Later on, the debate over the nature of the war and the crisis which led to it were part of the diplomatic struggle between Israelis and Arabs and their respective international patrons.

Still later, the onset of an Arab-Israeli peace process brought yet another change. As Egypt and Israel were making peace in the 1970s, lessons of the 1967 crisis guided the leaders and experts who constructed the new political and security relationship between the two countries.

The Syrian perspective is different and, as usual, particularly interesting. For one thing, Syria played a major role, probably the major role, in bringing the 1967 crisis about. Of the many actors and forces at work who all had a part in leading Israel and the Arabs to their third war, the Syrian Ba'th regime which emerged from the coup of 23 February 1966 stands out as having conducted a deliberate policy of confrontation and provocation to the point of actually stating that it sought to carry the Arab world to a war with Israel.[2]

Second, the peace process between Syria and Israel developed two decades after the Egyptian-Israeli peace process. By that time Israel's attachment to the Golan Heights had become much firmer than the bonds that had tied it to the Sinai in the 1970s. Consequently, the outcome of the June War on the Syrian front, Israel's control of the Golan Heights, provided in the 1990s both the principal motivation for Syria's joining the peace talks and the major stumbling bloc obstructing their success.

It is important to note that the 1967 crisis was not seriously addressed by the parties in their peace negotiations. Responsibility for the 1967 War was fiercely debated during the early negotiating sessions, when the Shamir government was in power in Israel. Israel and Syria charged each other with aggression and responsibility for the war's outbreak but did not engage in a serious discussion of these issues. Nor did such a discussion become possible in the calmer atmosphere and tone of the new phase of the negotiations, which followed the formation of Yitzhak Rabin's government in the summer of 1992. Both parties held on to their immutable narratives. For Israel the war was brought about by Syria as a culmination of nineteen years of aggressive conduct and any settlement of the Israeli-Syrian conflict must take this backdrop and these facts into account. Only the establishment of genuine peace and an effective security regime could guarantee that a crisis and a deterioration to war like those of May–June 1967 do not repeat themselves at some future point. As Syria saw it, Israel captured the Golan in a war of aggression, characteristic of an inherently expansionist and aggressive state and the land should be returned to its rightful owners without any conditions. When Israel returned the Golan to Syria there would be no reason for future wars between them.[3]

It should also be noted that the passage of time added few fresh facts or insights to the actual account of Syrian policies prior to the May–June crisis. Access may now be available to some Soviet archives and officials and some access could probably be gained to US archives. But in the absence of fresh research drawing on such sources contemporary writing on this subject draws on more or less the same database that was available in the late 1960s and early 1970s.

Let us now consider three of the interpretations of Syrian policy put forth during the last decade.

Patrick Seale, the British commentator and journalist and Asad's biographer, offers a particular variety of a familiar Middle Eastern conspiracy theory. The crisis of May 1967, argues Seale, should be seen as a successful American-Israeli bid to bait 'Abd al-Nasir. Syria was then ruled by a young, inexperienced and amateurish group that unwittingly played into Israel's hands. As Seale's biography describes it, Hafiz al-Asad as we know him now, is a product of the 1967 crisis. Walking into the trap set up by the cunning Israelis and sustaining the military and political defeats of 1967 converted Asad from an inexperienced and amateurish member of an amateurish group into the seasoned politician and leader who understands the politics of his country and its region so well.

Seale recognizes, of course, that the trap was not laid in a void – there was a genuine conflict over the demilitarized zones – it was inflated by the weakness of Egypt, by the policies of 'Abd al-Nasir and by the appearance on the scene of the Palestinians – both the official PLO created by the Arab states, and authentic groups like al-Fath and The Arab Nationalist Movement. A crisis did develop but Israel set out to inflame it in order to lure Egypt into the Sinai. As Seale himself puts it:

> Such was the tinder waiting to be ignited. Nasir, at bay, casting about for some bold strike to raise him up again, an increasingly active Palestinian movement and Syria smarting over the loss of the DMZs and putting the guerrillas to use ... The point to be borne in mind is that, well into 1967, Asad and his colleagues conceived of the struggle with Israel in terms of greater or lesser border clashes ... a wider conflict was totally outside their experience and therefore unimaginable ... [On 7 April 1967] ... provoking Syrian fire the Israeli air force went into action ... in the ensuing air battle six Syrian MIGs were lost ... This was the most serious military reverse Syria had suffered since 1948 ... In baiting Syria, their real aim seems to have been to destroy Nasir. The importance of this moment of national ruin in Asad's career cannot be overestimated ... the defeat was the turning point in his life, jolting him into political maturity and spurring his ambition to rule Syria free from the constraints of colleagues and rivals who he felt had led the country to disaster.[4]

The conspiracy theory approach to the outbreak of the 1967 crisis has been dealt with effectively by Ambassador Richard Parker,[5] but it is probably not going to vanish altogether.

A second approach was offered in a fairly recent work by an American academic, Fred Lawson, who devoted a whole book to the subject of *Why Syria Goes to War – Thirty Years of Confrontation*. For Fred Lawson, Syria's conduct in 1967 is a classic case of external behavior shaped by domestic constraints and considerations. The Ba'th regime was unstable, it rested on a narrow, fragile basis and it saw confrontation with Israel, walking to the brink and mobilizing for war as means of survival. As Lawson himself sums it up:

> Under these circumstances, heightening the confrontation with Israel enabled Syria's rulers to reconsolidate the dominant social coalition, while at the same time attracting new resources from outside which greatly facilitated intra-regime coordination. Expanding the state-controlled Popular Defense Army, while simultaneously redirecting its activities toward Israel, sharply reduced the potential for open rebellion on the part of the craftspeople and traders in the larger cities and towns. Mobilizing radical workers and farm laborers into the Popular Defense Army in preparation for war also made it much easier for Syrian military commanders to integrate the country's increasingly restive paramilitary formations into the regular armed

forces' hierarchical command structure. And the regime's ability to achieve these domestic political objectives was compounded by the military and economic resources channeled to the central administration through the Syrian-Soviet alliance, which solidified as the confrontation with Israel escalated during the late spring of 1967.[6]

Moshe Ma'oz's book, *Israel and Syria*, deals mostly with the peace process between the two countries, but it deals also with their preceding conflict. Chapter 5 in the book is devoted to an explanation of how the war of 1967 came about. Unlike Lawson, who singles out domestic political considerations as the one factor governing Syrian behavior, Ma'oz offers a comprehensive set of explanations: the genuine radicalism of the Syrian regime, Israeli activism, the Soviet and Egyptian roles, mistaken Syrian assumptions about Israel's might and intentions and the impact of domestic political conflicts in Syria.[7]

Having considered three different attempts to account for the outbreak of the crisis and to explain Syria's role, I would now like to pick two strands – the dynamics of inter-Arab relations and rivalries in the mid-1960s and Syria's bilateral relationship with Egypt, follow their interplay between 1963 and 1967 and argue that in the complex set of developments which preceded and led to the Six Day War they stand out as particularly significant.

In the late summer of 1963 the leader of the Syrian Ba'th regime, General Amin al-Hafiz, threatened to go to war against Israel in order to prevent it from completing the construction of its overland water carrier designed to bring water from Lake Tiberias in the north to the country's southern, dry and sparsely populated areas.[8]

By threatening to go to war Amin al-Hafiz and his colleagues were seeking to deal with two different issues. One was a genuine concern with the imminent completion of Israel's water carrier. There was an earlier history to that concern. In the 1950s Syria together with other Arab countries objected to Israel's water development schemes. The Arab world saw these plans as a key to Israel's consolidation and growth. Syria of the 1950s played a prominent and successful role in thwarting Israel's plans at the time. Not only was Syria a particularly staunch enemy of Israel but the original Israeli plans – pumping the water out of the Jordan river – had a direct bearing on the already difficult border disputes between the two countries.[9]

Syria's rulers and leaders of the 1950s thus left a legacy to their radical successors of the 1960s. If they had been successful in blocking the original Israeli water development schemes, how could the revolutionary Ba'th regime accept the completion of the modified Israeli plan.

But there was another dimension to the dilemma. In the late summer of 1963, some six months after coming to power, the Ba'th regime was resting on very slender foundations, beleaguered and buffeted by a host of domestic and external foes. First and foremost among them was ʿAbd al-Nasir, who refused to accept Syria's secession from the union with Egypt (September 1961) and who continued to denounce the Baʿth leaders as illegitimate, parties to and beneficiaries of the break-up of the first union between two Arab states. These were Nasir's years of decline – indeed, the weakening of his grip on Arab politics was one of the more important contributing factors to the 1967 crisis – but even an enfeebled Nasir posed a significant threat to the unstable Baʿth regime. His refusal to renew diplomatic relations with Damascus sent a powerful message – Arab nationalism's great leader saw the Syrian government as an ephemeral, transitional and illegitimate entity. On 18 July 1963 Nasir's staunchest supporters in Syria staged an abortive coup and were quashed brutally. But his lingering hostility and refusal to recognize the legitimacy of the Syrian state and regime, most notably by declining to reestablish diplomatic relations with Damascus, continued to undermine their fragile existence.

Syria's ability to fight back and to exert counter-pressure was limited. It was against this background that the Baʿth regime's leadership decided to turn predicament to advantage and proclaimed its determination to launch war in order to prevent Israel from completing its overland water carrier. Syria could not realistically hope to win such a war but the import of the threat was quite clear. By launching a hopeless heroic war Syria would force other Arab states, first and foremost Egypt, to come to its aid. If ʿAbd al-Nasir did not wish to be drawn into a war – as was universally assumed, he would have to placate Syria by offering an all-Arab response to the fresh Israeli challenge and by resolving the bilateral Egyptian-Syrian feud.

ʿAbd al-Nasir's response on the first level was immediate. He invited all Arab heads of state to come to Cairo for the first Arab Summit of the period. A new phase in the evolution of both inter-Arab relations and the Arab-Israeli conflict was thereby inaugurated. Arab Summit meetings replaced the Arab League as the significant all-Arab forum. The first Arab Summit formulated a new comprehensive policy toward Israel. The water issue was fitted into a new and larger context. Israel's overland carrier would be made useless by diverting the tributaries of the Jordan. An Arab 'Diversion Authority' would plan the diversion works and a 'Unified Arab Command' would plan and provide defence for the frontline countries whose task would be to implement them. The Unified Arab Command would also plan the Arab armies' build-up and preparation for the inevitable military showdown with Israel. The oil-producing countries would foot the bill for the massive build-up. And in order to restore the conflict with Israel to its original paradigm the notion and essence of a Palestinian entity should be restored through the creation of the PLO.

If Syria's leaders sought to challenge Egypt on a specific issue they discovered that the Arab world's leading state had a more complex agenda and the capacity to formulate an equally complex policy designed to address it. Egypt was not willing to fray the political cost of restraining Syria; it would rather have the whole Arab state system do it. And if Syria unleashed the tiger of a prospective war with Israel Egypt was quite willing to ride it in order to resolve its most difficult problem of the day – an apparently hopeless military entanglement in the civil war in Yemen. If military backing was required for the diversion works in Syria, Lebanon or Jordan let Saudi Arabia release its grip on Egypt in Yemen so that the Arab world's strongest army could be brought up north to face Israel.

And there was more. The formation of the PLO was not merely directed against Israel. It also posed a direct threat to the stability, indeed very existence, of Jordan. The mid-1960s saw a stiff escalation of the cold war in the Middle East. By pitting the PLO against the Hashemite regime in Jordan 'Abd al-Nasir was not only assailing a personal political foe but he was also challenging the conservative Arab regimes.

Through all of this the bilateral Egyptian-Syrian relationship was not attenuated but in fact exacerbated. Syria and Egypt were vying for control of the revived arena of Palestinian politics. Syria's zealous implementation of its share of the diversion plan exposed it to Israeli military punishment. Syria demanded Egyptian military support and was told that Egypt would not underwrite Syria's policy without participating in formulating it. When Syria demanded Egyptian air cover, Egypt asserted that it would not send airplanes to Syria without the support of Egyptian ground troops. The Syrian Ba'th regime saw that as an attempt to create the infrastructure for a pro-Egyptian coup. Throughout this period (1964–66) Egypt persisted in its refusal to establish diplomatic relations with Syria.

In February 1966 the radical wing of the Syrian Ba'th finally ousted its more pragmatic rivals. Syria was now governed by a radical group, resting on a very narrow basis and haunted by a self-fulfilling sense of persecution. The policy of trying to frighten Egypt into recognizing Syria was stepped up. A demand for a security guarantee was added. The Soviet Union fearful of a pro-Western takeover in Damascus exerted its own influence in Cairo on Syria's behalf. In November 1966 'Abd al-Nasir finally agreed – diplomatic relations were reestablished with Syria and an Egyptian-Syrian defence pact was signed.

In the event this was to no avail. The vicious cycle of Syrian action and Israeli retaliation continued. Israel reached the conclusion that there was no hope of coming to some *modus vivendi* with the radical regime in Damascus while the regime itself, its Soviet patrons and its new grudging partner, Egypt, concluded in turn that Israel was determined to bring the Syrian government down through massive military action.

The issue was compounded by the radical conservative rift in Arab politics. Syria sought patronage over several Palestinian factions and used some of them against Israel. This was a method of striking at a militarily superior enemy but also a way of demonstrating that there was substance to the Ba'th regime's doctrine of 'popular war' as a fresh strategy for the liberation of Palestine. As a rule the Syrians dispatched their Palestinian proxies to act against Israel through the territory of Lebanon and Jordan. This made Israeli retaliation against Syria harder and had the additional merit of embroiling the conservative governments of two neighbouring states that were friendly to the West and hostile to Damascus.

This policy came to a head in November 1966. Four Israeli soldiers were killed in southern Israel when their vehicle was hit by a mine. The mine had been laid by a Palestinian squad that came from Jordan but had originated in Syria. The Israeli government, familiar with these facts, decided to act against Jordan. It is easy to trace the evolution of Israel's miscalculation. The doctrine of reprisal had been developed in the 1950s and maintained that Israel's neighbours were responsible for policing their territory. If the Palestinian squad could penetrate through Jordan it was clear that Jordan was not investing a sufficient effort at preventing such activity. Rather than add yet another item to the cluttered Israeli-Syrian agenda, Israel decided to act against Jordan and raided the village of Samu' near Hebron.

The punitive raid did play into the hands of Jordan's radical Arab foes. Samu' was a Palestinian village and the Hashemite regime was castigated for failing to offer protection to the West Bank population it had annexed. King Husayn and his men did not have to wait long in order to settle that score. Fighting along the Israeli-Syrian border continued. In April 1967 it escalated to dog fights over Damascus. Six Syrian fighter planes were shot down by the Israeli air force. The Jordanians lost no time in denigrating Syria's military impotence and Egypt's failure to meet the terms of its recent security pact with Syria and come to its aid. It was one thing, said the Jordanians, to build up an army for parades and another to build it for actually going to war.

We can now fully appreciate the impact of this Jordanian scorn on the evolution of the 1967 crisis. At the time it was not known how frustrated the Egyptian army was with the limitations imposed by it by the post-1956 arrangements and by 'Abd al-Nasir's comparative restraint. As the post-1967 court procedures and several memoirs reveal, 'Abd al-Nasir's direct access to the Egyptian armed forces was blocked by his deputy 'Abd al-Hakim 'Amer. 'Amer represented the army's unhappiness with the President's caution, wanted Egypt to abrogate the 1957 security regime in the Sinai and assured 'Abd al-Nasir that it could stand up to an Israeli attack. Against this background, Jordan's denigration of the Egyptian army's passive stance and apparent of impotence was particularly painful and effective.

The next phase is quite well known. Fearful of an Israeli attempt to topple the Syrian regime, the Soviets advised Egypt of a massive Israeli build-up in the north. Egypt sought to repeat the success of a 1960 episode and deter Israel by remilitarizing the Sinai. This time it was done in an almost ostentatious fashion. By the time Egypt had established that there was no Israeli military build-up for an attack on Syria, the genie was out of the bottle. Israel, the United States and the UN responded meekly. 'Abd al-Nasir's stature as the great messianic leader of Arab nationalism was revived. At stake was no longer the prospect of an Israeli attack on Syria but Egypt's return to the heyday of its regional and international influence and the establishment of a new equation and new rules of the game in Arab-Israeli relations. Egypt mounted a course that made war practically inevitable. The Red Line was crossed on 23 May when 'Abd al-Nasir closed the Straits of Tiran and announced Egyptian readiness to sustain an Israeli attack.

This set of events transformed Syria's calculus. For one thing, the threat posed to the Ba'th regime by a resurrected 'Abd al-Nasir was far greater. The Syrian Ba'this also felt that he had overplayed his hand. It was one thing to bring matters to the brink of war in the service of one's political aims, but crossing the brink was another matter. They did not plan to go to war and did not think that they were obliged by the terms of the November 1966 defence pact to join Egypt in war. If both parties were committed to each other by the agreement why did Egypt not bother to consult with Syria before providing Israel with a *casus belli*?

It was this frame of mind that accounted for Syria's conduct during the war's first day. The Syrian army shelled Israeli territory and staged one ground attack. Technically speaking, Syria attacked first and provided Israel with a reason or an excuse to launch an offensive. But in reality the Syrian attack was little more than an effort to go through the motions of paying one's dues. For a country that had played such a prominent role in the genesis of the crisis this was precious little.

Ironically, Syria's attempt to stay essentially out of the war was nearly successful. This falls outside the scope of the present paper but it should be mentioned briefly that Israel's Minister of Defence Moshe Dayan, for reasons of his own, did not want to launch an attack on Syria and capture the Golan Heights. He changed his mind on the night of 8 June and instructed the General Officer Commanding of the Northern Command, over the head of the Chief of Staff, Yitzhak Rabin, to mount an offensive and capture the heights. But for this change of mind on the eleventh hour, Syria that had played such a prominent role in prompting the War of 1967 – would have emerged from it practically unscathed.[10]

The duel between Yitzhak Rabin and Hafiz al-Asad that was at the core of the Israeli-Syrian negotiations of the 1990s can be seen from more than one perspective. It can legitimately be seen as a negotiation between the Chief of Staff whose troops had captured the Golan Heights and the Minister of Defence whose army had failed to defend them. Twenty-five years later the two men were groping for a formula resting on the fine balance that would give Israel peace and security and offer Syria land and dignity.

There was a great deal of drama in this encounter but also a measure of irony. Rabin himself was quite aware of it. In October 1995 on the eve of his assassination, he met with the editorial board of Time Magazine in New York. Rabin spoke in great detail about the Syrian and Palestinian tracks of the peace process. At this point one of the editors addressed a direct question to the Prime Minister: did he think that Israel could give up the Golan Heights for a peace treaty with Syria. Rather than offer a direct response, Rabin told the story of Dayan's initial reluctance to capture the Golan Heights and his subsequent change of mind. On the face of it the message was clear: had Dayan not changed his mind, Israel would have lived for the previous twenty-eight years without the Golan Heights. But upon reflection there was an additional, more ambiguous dimension – had Dayan not changed his mind, would there be a Syrian-Israeli peace process?

NOTES

1. Paper delivered at a colloquium held in Tel-Aviv University in 1998.
2. For direct quotations of Syria's statements of that time see: Itamar Rabinovich, 'Continuity and change in the Ba'th regime in Syria, 1967–1973', in I. Rabinovich and H. Shaked (eds), From June to October (New Brunswick, NJ: Transaction Books, 1978), pp.219–28. For the classic analysis of the deterioration to the Six Day War in June 1967, see S. Shamir, 'The Middle East Crisis: on the Brink of War', in D. Dishon (ed.), Middle East Record, 1967 (Tel Aviv: Israel Universities Press, 1971), pp.183–204. See also E. Dawn, 'The Egyptian Remilitarization of Sinai, May 1967', Journal of Contemporary History, 3, 3 (July 1968), pp.201–24. For a more recent analysis built on fresh archival research, see M. Oren, Six Days of War: June 1967 and the Making of the Modern Middle East (Oxford: Oxford University Press, 2002), pp.18–60.
3. Itamar Rabinovich, The Brink of Peace: The Israeli-Syrian Negotiations (Princeton, NJ: Princeton University Press, 1998).
4. Patrick Seale, Asad of Syria (London: I.B. Tauris, 1988), pp.126–7, 143.
5. Richard Parker, The Politics of Miscalculation in the Middle East (Bloomington, IN: Indiana University Press, 1993).
6. H. Lawson, Why Syria Goes to War (Ithaca, NY: Cornell University Press, 1996), p.51.
7. Moshe Ma'oz, Syria and Israel - From War to Peacemaking (Oxford: Clarendon Press, 1995), pp.79–111.
8. Itamar Rabinovich, Syria under the Ba'th, 1963–1966: The Army-Party Symbiosis (Jerusalem and New York, NY: Israel Universities Press, 1972), pp.183–204.
9. Ibid.
10. See Yitzhak Rabin, The Rabin Memoirs (Berkley, CA: University of California Press, 1996), pp.100–21 and Moshe Dayan, The Story of my Life (New York, NY: Warner Books, 1976), pp.361–457.

16

Israel, Syria and Lebanon[1]

Studies in the regional politics of the Middle East tend to deal with whole systems (inter-Arab relations, the Arab-Israeli conflict), bilateral relationships (Egyptian-Libyan, Israeli-Jordanian), or single issues (the Lebanese crisis, the Gulf War). The trilateral relationship between Israel, Syria, and Lebanon deviates from this pattern. Yet, during the past fifteen years the affairs of these three countries have become so closely intertwined that it is practically impossible to deal with the relationship between any two of them without taking the third into account. In geometric terms, the cluster of issues and problems comprised in this relationship can be described as two overlapping circles. The Syrian-Israeli relationship forms one circle and Israel's interests and policies in Lebanon the second while the overlapping area is defined by the Syrian-Israeli encounter in the Lebanese arena.

Following a brief survey of the principal problems involved in these clusters, this essay will examine their significance for the current phase of Arab-Israeli relations. Four main questions will be addressed:

1) the prospects for a comprehensive Syrian-Israeli settlement;
2) the prospects for a partial or interim Syrian-Israeli settlement;
3) the danger of another Syrian-Israeli military conflict; and
4) the Syrian and Israeli dimensions of potential efforts to resolve the Lebanese crisis.

THE SYRIAN-ISRAELI RELATIONSHIP

To the student of international conflict and to those specializing in Middle Eastern and Arab-Israeli affairs, the Syrian-Israeli dimension of the Arab-Israeli conflict is a particularly interesting case-study.[2] It is a deep and complex dispute full of genuine problems and mutual demonization. During the past forty years Syria and Israel have waged three full-fledged Wars (1948, 1967, 1973) and two limited ones (1969–70, 1982) and have engaged in various other forms of violent and political conflict. On several other occasions military conflict was narrowly avoided. The respective concepts of settlement held by Syria and Israel seem, at first sight at least, mutually exclusive, and both suspect the other of preparing for another round of fighting. And yet the ceasefire line in the Golan Heights is calm in an exemplary way, and the two antagonists have found ways of avoiding a clash in Lebanon during most of the period of their mutual involvement in the Lebanese crisis. Indeed, many Middle Easterners (and others) fond of conspiracy theories suspect that there is some sort of secret Syrian-Israeli understanding or coordination at work.

In a less fanciful vein, I view the Syrian-Israeli conflict as a composite of four sub-conflicts which focus on the following issues: the future of the Golan Heights; Syria's position and role as a leading Arab state and as a leading exponent of Arab nationalism demanding that any Arab-Israeli settlement be shaped to suit its status and outlook; Syria's specific outlook on the Palestinian issue as a function both of its larger view of the Arab-Israeli conflict and of its claim to a special status as a custodian of the Palestinian cause; and the Syrian-Israeli competition in Lebanon.

During the last fifteen years, Syria and Israel have made one formal and direct agreement (the Disengagement Agreement of May–June 1974) and one informal and indirect arrangement (the 'Red Line' agreement in Lebanon in early 1976). Several other attempts were made to bring about a comprehensive or partial agreement between the two states, and Syria's role in or attitude towards a comprehensive Arab-Israeli settlement has been explored on several other occasions. The issue is often addressed by the leaders and other spokesmen from both states. From these activities and statements, the positions of Syria and Israel on the question of a settlement can be distilled.

SYRIA AND THE QUESTION OF A SETTLEMENT

Syria's position on the question of a settlement with Israel has changed several times since 1967. The rejectionist position of the radical neo-Ba'th was moderated following Hafiz al-Asad's seizure of power in November 1970. Asad drew closer to Egypt, and in March 1972 issued a qualified acceptance of Security Council Resolution 242.[3] In the aftermath of the October War of 1973, Security Council Resolution 338 was likewise accepted in a qualified fashion and Syria joined in the 'diplomatic process' that was managed by the United States. In June 1975 the Ba'th party formally endorsed the acceptance of a 'phased settlement' as a compromise between the willingness to enjoy the potential benefits of a prospective settlement and the unwillingness to give up the goals of the radical Arab position.

The Carter Administration's quest for a comprehensive settlement of the Arab-Israeli conflict forced Syria to undertake a subtle shift in its position and to take practical steps in response to an apparently imminent international conference that was to shape the settlement. Asad's position was nominally positive, but highly qualified, and Syria's actual conduct led many to believe that it was not really interested in the conference. In fact Syria played a major role in obstructing the Carter Administration's original policy, thereby persuading President Anwar al-Sadat of Egypt to make his journey to Jerusalem.[4] The subsequent signing of the Camp David Accords and the Egyptian-Israeli Peace Treaty of 1979 led Syria to define its concept of a settlement in contradistinction to the Egyptian model. Syria's model was a clear antithesis to the Camp David pattern: a comprehensive solution, based on complete Israeli withdrawal and full restoration of Palestinian rights, offering Israel less than a full peace, and reached through an international conference in which the Soviet Union would play a real rather than a ceremonial role. (Despite Syria's nominal insistence on Palestinian rights, it was well known that Asad was hostile to Yasir 'Arafat and the Palestine Liberation Organization [PLO], wanted a role for Syria in any Palestinian settlement, and was willing to explore ideas other than an independent Palestinian state.)

When Saudi Arabia presented the Fahd plan in 1981 as an alternative to the Camp David model, Syria played the crucial role in obstructing efforts to pursue it. Less than a year later, however, in a weaker position in the immediate aftermath of the Lebanon War, Syria agreed to the modified version of the Fahd plan presented in Fez. The Fez resolutions demanded a complete Israeli withdrawal from all territories occupied in 1967 and the establishment of an independent Palestinian state. In return, they did not offer a comprehensive peace or an explicit recognition of Israel but proposed that 'the UN's Security Council will provide guarantees for peace among the states of the region including the independent Palestinian state'. Formally, this remains Syria's position. Thus on 27 April 1987, at the conclusion of Asad's visit to the Soviet Union, the joint communique stated that 'the just and comprehensive peace in the Middle East can only be implemented on the basis of Israeli withdrawal from all Arab territories captured in 1967 and the restoration of the legitimate rights of the Palestinian people including its right to return to its country, to self-determination, and to the establishment of its own state'. The Soviet Union and Syria rejected the notion of 'separate and partial solutions', particularly the Camp David Accords, and expressed support for the holding of 'a genuine and effective international conference'.[5]

While this has remained Syria's stated position, its actual position has been modified by several developments during the 1980s. The experience and lessons of the 1982 War and the ensuing two years in Lebanon led Asad to believe that he could confront Israel effectively. This conclusion has been reinforced by a belief that political negotiations as such are futile and that only negotiations conducted from a position of superior strength can yield results. Asad does not believe that the United States will exert sufficient pressure on Israel to produce a settlement to his liking. But scornful as Asad was of the efforts sponsored by the United States in 1982 and 1984–87 to generate an Israeli-Jordanian or Israeli-Jordanian-Palestinian settlement, he still invested effort and exerted pressure to obstruct them.

The intifadah, the Palestinian uprising, which broke out in the occupied territories in December 1987, and the ensuing changes in the PLO's position and political strategy have created a fresh difficulty for Syria. Asad treats 'Arafat with hostility and suspicion. He resents 'Arafat's recent successes, and he suspects that 'Arafat would be willing to come to an agreement with Israel on terms that would be unacceptable, even injurious, to Syria. Despite its formal endorsement of independent Palestinian statehood and praise for the intifadah, therefore, Syria is braced for the prospect of a separate Palestinian-Israeli deal or a new and enhanced role for the PLO in the quest for a comprehensive settlement.

Asad's anxieties have been magnified by the recent changes in Soviet foreign policy. For Syria, the Soviet Union's principal client in the Middle East, the changes of the past three years have had far-reaching ramifications. The Soviet Union has not abandoned its ambitions in the Middle East, but it now seeks to maintain a status quo (in which its own position is recognized) and to avoid a confrontation with the United States. To this end, the Soviet Union has improved its relations with Israel, allowed Soviet Jews to emigrate to Israel, and distanced itself publicly from the offensive implications of Syria's doctrine of 'strategic parity'. Should a breakthrough be achieved in the current efforts to set Israeli-Palestinian negotiations in motion, Asad is worried that one of two undesirable developments may occur: either the Soviet Union will not support his effort to obstruct such negotiations, or the Soviet Union will support an expansion of the negotiations to include Syria and the issue of the Golan Heights but under terms acceptable to Washington and Moscow and not to Damascus.

It is against this background that the various signals sent by Syria at the end of 1989 and in the early months of 1990 should be assessed. In December 1989 the normalization of diplomatic relations between Syria and Egypt was announced. Syria had severed relations with Egypt in 1978 after the signing of the Camp David Accords and had led the all-Arab campaign to punish and isolate Egypt as long as the latter adhered to the peace treaty with Israel. Syria's abandonment of this policy was, therefore, particularly significant. In the ensuing months, the Syrian government indicated to various American officials and dignitaries that it was interested in a settlement with Israel. Among other things, the Syrians told their American interlocutors that they would be willing to demilitarize the Golan Heights once they were restored to Syria and that while Syria still insisted that an international peace conference be convened, bilateral working groups could in fact be formed soon thereafter.[6]

These signals were clearly prompted by the changes in the Soviet Union's Middle Eastern policies. Weakened by a host of other, unrelated developments (the end of the Gulf War, the challenge to its position in Lebanon, the dispute with Turkey over the waters of the Euphrates), Syria is once again indicating an interest in exploring the possibility of settlement with Israel. This new line is designed to facilitate a Syrian dialogue with the United States and to make sure that Syria is not left out, should the Arab Israeli peace process actually be revived – unlikely as this may seem to Asad.

ISRAEL'S POSITION ON A SETTLEMENT

Israel's original position on a political settlement with Syria was formulated by the cabinet in June 1967. The Israeli government made a fundamental distinction between the territory of Mandatory Palestine and that of the Sinai Peninsula and the Golan Heights, which it was willing to return to Egypt and to Syria respectively in return for peace treaties. Its offer to Syria was set out in this way:

> Israel offers the signing of a peace treaty on the basis of the international boundary and Israel's security needs. The peace treaty will require:
> a. Demilitarization of the Syrian heights presently held by Israel.
> b. An absolute guarantee of an uninterrupted flow of water from the sources of the Jordan to Israel.
> Until the signing of the peace treaty with Syria, Israel will continue to hold on to the territories that she is presently holding.[7]

In reality, though, a distinction had already emerged in 1967 between the Israeli attitude towards the question of a potential settlement with Egypt and the less likely prospect of one with Syria. The establishment of Israeli settlements in the Golan and numerous statements by a variety of Israeli spokesmen created the impression that Israel did not really believe that a settlement with Syria was possible. This perception was not translated into a formal stance, however, until the summer of 1977 when Menahem Begin's government clarified its position during its dialogue with the

Carter Administration: 'Israel will remain in the Golan Heights but within the framework of a peace treaty we will be ready to withdraw our forces from their present line to a line that will be determined as a permanent boundary.'[8]

The notion of an Israeli-Syrian settlement is also implicit in the text of the Camp David Accords. Their preamble states that 'to achieve a relationship of peace, in the spirit of Article 2 of the United Nations Charter, future negotiations between Israel and any neighbor prepared to negotiate peace and security with it are necessary for the purpose of carrying out all the provisions and principles of Resolutions 242 and 338'. The text went on to say that the parties recognized that 'for peace to endure, it must involve all those who have been most deeply affected by the conflict. They therefore agree that this framework as appropriate is intended by them to constitute a basis for peace not only between Egypt and Israel, but also between Israel and each of its other neighbors which is prepared to negotiate peace with Israel on this basis'.[9]

The exacerbation of the Israeli-Syrian conflict led the Begin government to decide in December 1981 on the extension of Israeli law to the Golan Heights. Technically, this step fell short of annexation, but the Israeli move reinforced the belief that a Syrian-Israeli agreement was not feasible. This view would be strengthened by developments later in the decade.

In the late 1970s and up until the 1982 War, a school of thought existed in Israel, which argued that Syria's predicament in Lebanon might provide the basis for a Syrian-Israeli 'package deal' involving Israeli concessions in the Golan Heights. Mordechai Gur, Israel's chief of staff in the mid-1970s, was a strong exponent of this view. The idea was never explored seriously, but by 1983 its rationale had been undermined: Syria was doing very well in Lebanon and would have no motivation whatsoever to seek a trade-off. Indeed, Syria's success and Israel's debacle in Lebanon led instead to an acceptance of the view that the dominant theme in Syrian-Israeli relations was not settlement but war. It was during these years that Syria developed its doctrine of strategic parity and undertook a massive military build-up which raised the spectre of continued war.[10]

The signals sent by Syria to the United States in early 1990 indicating a renewed interest in the prospect of a settlement with Israel evoked a very limited response in Israel. The issue was discussed in the media and was raised once in a political context by the Labour party's leader, Shimon Peres, when he argued in the midst of government crisis that the quest for an Arab-Israeli settlement could be expanded to include Syria. This limited Israeli response can be attributed to several reasons. For one thing, many Israelis treated the reports of a change in Syria's position with scepticism.

The harsh speech delivered by Asad on Revolution Day, 8 March, did much to bolster that scepticism. Furthermore, in the winter and early spring of 1990 Israel was immersed in an intense domestic debate that focused on the prospect of negotiations with a Palestinian delegation in Cairo. It was felt by most political analysts that a political system paralysed by a debate over an interim settlement of the Palestinian issue was simply incapable of dealing with yet another contentious issue, particularly when the prospects for success were rather dubious.

ISRAEL AND THE LEBANESE CRISIS, 1975–89

There is, of course, no denying the close inter-relationship between the Lebanese crisis and the Arab-Israeli conflict, but the precise nature of that relationship is a matter of political and academic disagreement. Some believe that the Lebanese system could have survived all the domestic challenges it faced but collapsed under the impact of the Arab-Israeli and, more specifically, the Palestinian problem. Accordingly, a solution to the Lebanese crisis will not be found until the Arab-Israeli conflict is resolved or at least mitigated. Others argue that the Lebanese political system collapsed under its own weight and that the crisis is perpetuated primarily by domestic factors and Syria's quest for hegemony.[11] The truth is far more complex, but my purpose here is not to analyse the nature of the Lebanese crisis but to provide the background for its study as an Israeli policy problem.

Israel's outlook on and policies towards Lebanon have gone through six main phases. Historically, the Jewish community in Palestine and the early Israeli state viewed Christian Lebanon as a kindred entity, another non-Arab and non-Muslim polity in the region and therefore a potential ally. But as the Ben Gurion-Sharett correspondence regarding Lebanon in 1953 shows, most Israeli policy makers and analysts had realized by then that the vision of a Maronite Christian Lebanon allied with Israel was not realistic. From that time until 1975 Israel accepted the pluralistic Lebanon of those years as an optimal neighbour to the north. The far-reaching visions of the past were forgotten, and Israel was content to have a semi-friendly neighbour, which kept a low profile in the Arab-Israeli conflict. This perspective changed again in the 1970s as the Lebanese state grew weaker, Lebanon became the PLO's chief base, and Syrian influence grew.

The civil war of 1975–77 and the collapse of the Lebanese state presented Israel with a policy dilemma: did it want to watch passively as its neighbour to the north was transformed probably in an undesirable fashion, or did it want to intervene actively in an effort to shape Lebanese politics? Prime Minister Yitzhak Rabin and his government finally resolved the dilemma (at least temporarily) by making the 'Red Line' agreement with Syria. Reached in the winter of 1976 through American mediation, it regulated the Syrian-Israeli rivalry in Lebanon. As long as Syria limited its military deployment and activity in Lebanon, Israel was willing to accept the hegemonic position Damascus had acquired in Lebanese politics. At the same time, however, a limited relationship was also developed with the Maronite militias and the cultivation of Major Sa'd Haddad and his militia in southern Lebanon began.

Rabin's policies on Lebanon were essentially maintained by the Begin government during its first two years in power, but by 1979 significant changes could be noticed. A much closer alliance with and a stronger commitment to the Christian militias had been developed. The conflict with the PLO had grown fiercer, in part because the Camp David Accords exacerbated the conflict over the future of the West Bank. Finally, the acceptance of the security challenge involved in Syria's hegemony in Lebanon had given way to a determination to undermine that hegemony. Begin's policy was founded on a belief that existing policy did not provide an adequate response to Israel's security problem in Lebanon, that in the absence of a real state and an effective central government, the territory of Lebanon (and the south in particular) had become the focus of security threats to Israel from both Syria and the Palestinians. The Labour opposition and Begin's other critics did not dispute these underlying assumptions, but they advocated very different responses. In any event the two Begin governments pursued a policy, which culminated in the 1982 War. This was an overly ambitious and ill-calculated attempt to accomplish at one fell swoop not only a resolution of Israel's Lebanese problem but also a desirable solution to the Palestine problem, a victory over Syria, and a restructuring of the existing regional order.

By September 1982, following Bashir Jumayyil's assassination, the Sabra and Shatila massacres, and the outburst of massive opposition in Israel to the government's Lebanese policies, it became clear that the war had failed to achieve its purposes and that, instead, Israel was faced with the problem of extricating itself from Lebanon. Until June 1985 (and under three different governments) the Lebanese problem remained the dominant issue in Israeli politics. The war and its aftermath presented Israel with new problems, particularly that of Shi'i radicalism. Suicide attacks and widespread popular resistance in Lebanon proved to be very effective against Israeli forces and could also inspire the Palestinians and other opponents of Israel. Syria's success in Lebanon during these years reinforced its position and Asad's self-confidence, and Asad came to be seen as Israel's chief Arab adversary. The Syrian-Iranian alliance and the awakening of the

Lebanese Shi'a led to the establishment of an Iranian presence and influence on Israel's northern border.

It was Israel's National Unity government which finally cut the Gordian knot. Having failed during the final months of 1984 to revive and reformulate the tacit Syrian-Israeli understanding with regard to Lebanon, it decided on a unilateral withdrawal reinforced by two other elements: (1) the creation of a full-fledged security belt along the Israeli-Lebanese border monitored by a strengthened militia commanded by the former general, Antoine Lahad; (2) a small Israeli military presence inside the security belt to be augmented when necessary.[12]

Since the unilateral withdrawal was completed in June 1985, Israel's policy towards Lebanon and the Lebanese crisis has rested on different principles. The Israeli outlook on Lebanon is defined in terms of national security interests. These are focused in the southern part of the country. Israel has waived the ambition or will to shape Lebanon's national politics. This policy could, however, change in the event of a change of government in Israel or under the impact of far-reaching changes in Lebanon. This having been said, Israel is still interested in the larger developments in Lebanon. It maintains contact with various groups and communities but is careful not to offer commitments similar to those given in the 1979–82 period.

Israel now takes an ambivalent view of Syria's policies in Lebanon. It recognizes that in the short term, Asad and his regime are weakened by their difficulties in Lebanon, but it realizes that in the long term, in the absence of serious local or external opposition, Asad may accomplish his aims, which would give him considerable advantages in facing Israel. So far, however, Syria and Israel have found ways of avoiding a collision despite the failure to revive their previous tacit understanding. Israel is likewise ambivalent about Iraq's involvement in Lebanon. It appreciates the fact that Iraq seeks to weaken the positions of Syria and Iran but is worried by some of Iraq's actions in Lebanon as well as by the fact that, contrary to most earlier expectations, Iraq has resumed its involvement and high profile in Arab-Israeli affairs. In that case Iraq's influence in Lebanon coupled with its presence in Jordan could offer a serious threat to Israel. Israel was alarmed by Iraq's attempt to supply its Lebanese clients with Frog-7 missiles. In the circumstances obtaining in Lebanon, missiles supplied to General Michel 'Awn's forces might end up in Shi'i or Palestinian hands. (For this reason the Syrian blockade of Christian seaports was not entirely displeasing to Israel.) The fact of the matter is that throughout the crises of 1988–89 in Lebanon – the failure to elect a president and the imposition of two successive Syrian candidates, the fierce fighting between General 'Awn's forces and Syria's proxies, Syria's shelling of the Christian areas in and near Beirut, and Syria's threat to invade the Christian area – Israel did not intervene and did not threaten to do so.

Let us now turn to examine the four questions posed at the outset.

THE PROSPECTS FOR A COMPREHENSIVE SYRIAN-ISRAELI SETTLEMENT

The question of a Syrian-Israeli settlement is not on the Middle Eastern political agenda at present, but a situation could easily develop that would alter that agenda and raise the question in immediate terms. Such a situation might be created by a Syrian-Israeli War, by an aggravation of the Lebanese crisis and the need to resolve it in a larger context, or, in a more benign way, by a breakthrough in the present diplomatic efforts that would raise the question of Syria's future role and attitude.

Despite recent subtle changes in the positions of the parties, the prospects of a comprehensive Israeli-Syrian settlement are clearly dim. The two parties have radically different concepts of such a settlement; in fact they are convinced that a settlement is not feasible and have a demonized view of one another. Domestic issues in both countries tend to aggravate matters. While there is a bitter controversy in Israel over the future of the West Bank and Gaza, about half of the Israeli population is agreeable to territorial concessions as part of a settlement. But there is no such public debate over the Golan Heights, partly because the question seems irrelevant and partly because there is broad support within the Labour party for continued Israeli control of that territory. It is not possible to judge how the Syrian public views the question of a settlement with Israel, but it is clear that Asad's own convictions, the views of his constituency, the image he needs to project, the army's role in his regime, and his minoritarian background all militate against the prospect of a substantial change in the present policy of the regime.

Furthermore, for both Israel and Syria a settlement appears costlier than the maintenance of the status quo. Israel realizes that the costs of a continuation of the conflict with Syria are enormous – the danger of war, an exhausting and escalating arms race and military build-up, Syrian encouragement of resistance and opposition to Israel in the Palestinian and Lebanese arenas – but these costs still do not outweigh the concessions that would be required for a settlement whose value and longevity most Israelis would question.

The Syrian Ba'th regime managed in 1967, despite its radicalism, not to place the question of the Golan at the top of the national agenda. This was very different from the situation in Egypt where under both Nasser and Sadat the question of the Sinai had to be addressed first. It was perhaps easier for an ideological party to argue that the problem of the Golan is part of a larger problem and will be dealt with when a comprehensive solution to the Israeli challenge is devised. This is not to suggest that the Golan issue is not important to Asad – it is – but rather that at most times since 1970 other issues have been more important. This will remain true only so long as others do not make progress in obtaining territory back from Israel, however. Sadat's success over the Sinai presented Asad with a severe challenge, and he would be hard put to contend with Jordanian or Palestinian success over the West Bank. But as long as that does not happen, Asad believes that it is easier to live with the status quo than to make the concessions required by a settlement. One of Asad's gravest complaints against Sadat was that he changed the rules of the game: since 1979 Asad has known that he cannot expect to regain the Golan Heights for less than a comprehensive peace.

Yet to be addressed is the relationship between the quest for a solution to the Palestinian problem and the Syrian-Israeli conflict. At present the issue is ignored, although Syria does make a subtle effort to undermine 'Arafat. But should current efforts at negotiations proceed, the question will force itself onto the situation. From an Israeli perspective, it will probably be couched in the following terms: a failure to extend the process to include Syria could lead to Syrian efforts to sabotage the settlement while Syria's inclusion would be tantamount to a comprehensive settlement in which Israel would be required to make concessions on both its eastern and northern fronts. This all is highly speculative, but it is doubtful that an Israeli government in the foreseeable future could deal with such a task. As has been pointed out, the issue was raised in the awkward American-Syrian dialogue, but so far it has failed to become part of the overall political or diplomatic agenda.

In the past it has been suggested that the egg could be stood on its head, that a useful approach might be to turn Syria into the linchpin and have it deliver the other components of a settlement. However, such a plan is now unworkable for several reasons, not the least of which is that present-day Syria does not have the domestic strength and regional position which are absolutely essential for the performance of such a role. It should be noted in this context that the formation of a right-wing government in Israel in June 1990 could have the apparently paradoxical effect of regenerating talk of an Israeli-Syrian settlement as the next phase of the Arab-Israeli peace process. This would be a consequence of the Israeli right wing's difficulty in making any substantial concessions on the Palestinian issue. To avoid a stalemate and a conflict with the Bush Administration, a demarche vis-à-vis Syria would provide at least a temporary relief.

THE PROSPECTS FOR AN INTERIM SETTLEMENT

In the absence of any reasonable prospects of a comprehensive settlement, the idea of an interim Syrian-Israeli settlement should be explored, either as a transitional phase or as a long-term arrangement. The first model was used successfully in the Egyptian-Israeli case while the second was attempted unsuccessfully in the Jordanian-Israeli case (spring of 1987).

From an Israeli point of view, even an interim settlement with Syria presents great difficulties. The size and terrain of the Sinai Peninsula were well suited to the concept of a series of interim settlements. Had the need arisen, the al-'Arish-Ras Muhammad line in the Sinai could have provided the basis for a mid- or long-term non-belligerency agreement. The same approach cannot be applied in the Golan Heights where the crucial terrain is very close to the present ceasefire line. In 1975 Israel was willing to offer 'cosmetic' concessions in return for tacit acceptance of the Israeli-Egyptian agreement but Syria spurned this proposition. A more significant withdrawal would have involved then and would involve now the loss of strategically crucial territory, the dismantling of settlements, and the return of the Druze population to Syrian control.

But the main obstacle to any interim settlement is inherent in the position of the Asad regime and derives from the longtime propagation of a hard ideological line on the question of a settlement with Israel. In the final analysis, it is power and not principle that counts in Asad's Syria, but the Ba'th Party and its ideology, and Syria's posture as a leader of Arab nationalism, are all important to the regime. Should the question arise, in the context of a full settlement with Israel, of whether Syria would abandon many of its demands and positions in return for a full Israeli withdrawal, a positive reply can be envisaged. But this is not the case when an interim settlement is discussed. Asad would have to abandon his principles for only a part of the Golan Heights, and it is most doubtful that he would agree to that.

ISRAEL, SYRIA AND LEBANON

Having earlier surveyed the evolution of Israel's policies in Lebanon, it is essential to offer a brief overview of Syria's interests and policies before proceeding to assess their relationship in this context.[13]

Syria's massive involvement in the Lebanese crisis dates back to 1976.[14] During the past thirteen years its investment and position in Lebanon have at some times served as a principal source of regional influence and at others have drained the Asad regime's resources to the point of nearly toppling it. Thus the years 1983–85 were ones of great success for Syria in Lebanon, but since 1986 it has encountered increasing difficulties in that arena.

Asad views his position in Lebanon as a most precious investment. Lebanon is the focus of crucial Syrian interests whose loss cannot be contemplated by the regime. Furthermore, the regime faces the classical interventionist dilemma – having invested so much in Lebanon, the loss of that investment has come to be perceived as an unthinkable blow. Asad thinks of Lebanon in terms of hegemony – limited hegemony. By now he knows the domestic limitations of his own system and is familiar (though, not sufficiently so, it would now seem) with the complexities of Lebanese society and politics. Whatever visions of control he may have had in 1976 were subsequently replaced by more modest expectations. For the time being Asad seeks to exercise his limited hegemony in Lebanon by projecting power across a long border, by maintaining a military presence in Lebanon, by relying on local proxies and allies, and by exerting direct influence on the institutions of the state (presidency, government, army), such as they are. In the longer term Asad hopes to grind down the opposition to Syria's sway in Lebanon so as to be able to exercise direct and easy control over a subservient Lebanese state.

Clearly, Syria is encountering increasing difficulties in implementing this policy. Of the various challenges posed to Syria in Lebanon in recent years, General 'Awn's has been the most severe. In Asad's view, 'Awn's defiance not only threatens his position in Lebanon but, if successful and unpunished, could undermine his authority in Syria as well. This accounts for his ruthless response, and he is likely to maintain the same policy whatever the external pressures.

Israel figures prominently in Asad's assessment of Lebanon and the Lebanese arena. His original investment in Lebanon of the early 1970s was conceived, among other things, as part of the effort to 'organize' (in his biographer's language) Syria's Arab environment into a strategic asset vis-à-vis Israel. Lebanon's territory was and is crucial for both defensive, and offensive purposes. Until 1982 the possibility that Israel would move into the Baqa' Valley and menace Damascus was a theoretical threat; in June of 1982 it became a reality. Syria, in turn, if it increases its military commitment and stations additional forces in Lebanon could threaten to engage Israel on two fronts.

Asad regards Israel's interest, influence, and continued involvement in Lebanon as one of the chief constraints on his freedom of action there. This was evident in 1976 and was reinforced by the events of 1979–82. Curiously, despite everything that has happened since 1982, Asad still credits Israel with a great deal of influence on Lebanese national politics. He probably thinks (erroneously) that 'Awn is in league not only with Iraq but also with Israel, as are some of Syria's other foes. This perception is difficult to dispel and, to the extent that it has a restraining influence on Syria's conduct, may have some positive value.

Asad's attitude to Israel's presence and influence in southern Lebanon is somewhat different. Without endorsing Israel's pre-1982 security arrangements, he seems to have made a distinction between them and the post-1982 additions – the creation of a full-blown security zone, and the strengthening of the militia, its conversion into a multi-confessional rather than a Christian body, and the extension of its sway into the important town of Jizzin. Recently Asad has been preoccupied with more urgent concerns in Lebanon, but he has been fighting by proxy against these aspects of the Israeli presence and has also supported and encouraged occasional operations by Lebanese and Palestinian groups against Israel proper.

At the other end of the spectrum from the question of a potential Syrian-Israeli military clash in Lebanon (discussed below) lies the notion of a Syrian-Israeli agreement predicated on Israeli recognition of Syria's supremacy in Lebanon. While such a school of thought existed in Israel in the past, it has, for the time being at least, disappeared from the options under public discussion in Israel. There remains the possibility that a demand that all foreign troops and presence, Israeli as well as Syrian, be removed from Lebanon would be given more teeth as part of an effort to resolve the current crisis. It is not very likely, however, and it is even less likely that Syria would acquiesce in such a demand. As has been suggested, it is determined to preserve and develop its Lebanese domain. Syria would also strongly object to the view that its presence in Lebanon should be put on the same level as Israel's. For Israel the matter is one of practicality not principle. Israel could give up its own limited direct presence in southern Lebanon as part of such a larger settlement but would probably seek to ensure that it is not asked to take the first concrete step in what might prove to be an otherwise futile exercise.

THE DANGER OF A SYRIAN-ISRAELI WAR

In 1982 it was the Israeli government which sought a military confrontation with Syria. It had a dual purpose. First of all, Syria's defeat was correctly perceived as a prerequisite for the establishment of 'a new order' in Lebanon. Second, the Israelis were worried about Syria's military build-up and saw the Lebanese arena as an advantageous one for conducting a sort of 'pre-emptive war'. Asad, in turn, miscalculated and misread the Israelis and his own conduct played into their hands. The present Israeli government is not likely to initiate war against Syria. It is also worried (with more reason) by Syria's military build-up, but its approach to questions of war and peace is different. Should war between Syria and Israel break out in the near future, it is more likely to arise from one of three causes: (1) a deliberate Syrian decision to launch war; (2) as a result of uncontrolled escalation, deterioration, or miscalculation in Lebanon or elsewhere; (3) a Syrian attempt to obstruct a political settlement from which it is excluded.

A Deliberate Decision to Launch War

Syria's policy towards Israel has been conducted since the early 1980s under the doctrine and slogan of strategic parity. The term has been defined in different fashions on different occasions but in essence it denotes Syria's determination to acquire the ability to stand on its own, without other Arab support, against Israel. The Syrians acknowledge that such parity with Israel has yet to be achieved.

Since the mid-1980s Israeli and other experts have debated whether strategic parity is a defensive or an offensive doctrine.
The defensive school argues that Asad wants to ensure that the events of 1982 are not repeated, that an aggressive Israeli government does not seek at some future date to manhandle him in Lebanon or elsewhere. This would also suit Asad's concept of negotiations as an exercise that can only be engaged in successfully from a position of strength. The offensive school argues that the nature of Syria's build-up, deployment, and training program in 1986 and again in 1988–89 was such that it indicated an actual decision to launch war. According to this line of argument, Asad believes that he will not get anything from Israel through negotiation and that military action alone can regain the Golan Heights.

The issue subsided in 1987 when a severe economic crisis forced Syria to slow its military build-up, but the trend was reversed in 1988–89. First, a variety of Israeli spokesmen, alarmed by their reading of military developments, once again sounded the alarm bells. Then the Soviet Union, on different occasions but most notably through its ambassador in Damascus in November 1989, took exception to the doctrine of strategic parity. By dissociating itself from this doctrine and by arguing that what Syria needed was a defensive capability, the Soviet Union did two things. First, it suggested that in its view the doctrine or strategic parity had an offensive edge and that this was not a doctrine, which fitted with the new Soviet foreign policy. Second, its dissociation from this policy seriously weakened Syria's strategic posture. Syria had never had an explicit Soviet commitment to intervene on its behalf in the event of an unsuccessful war, but the prospect of such an intervention, dim as it was, was an important component of

Syria's military posture. Its removal seriously weakened Syria and reduced (though it did not totally eliminate) the prospect of a deliberate Syrian decision to launch war.

Deterioration, Miscalculation and Escalation

As was suggested at the outset, Syria and Israel have a remarkable record of avoiding collisions in difficult circumstances. But the record is not perfect. Begin miscalculated in March–April 1981 and Asad did in 1982. In November 1985 after the shooting down of two Syrian fighter aircraft, a second missile crisis nearly developed. Syrian engagement in anti-Israeli terrorism, culminating in the Hindawi affair, is a striking example of both gross miscalculation and an event that could have had far-reaching consequences.

The potential for a Syrian-Israeli flare-up as a result of miscalculation or deterioration still exists, particularly in the Lebanese arena. In the aftermath of the November 1985 episode, Syria and Israel seemed to have found a modus vivendi in Lebanon's air space but the margin of error is extremely narrow. Furthermore, Lebanon's coastal waters could develop into another Syrian-Israeli zone of conflict. Clear rules do not exist in this arena. While Israel was not entirely unhappy with Syria's interdiction of Iraqi missile supplies to Christian ports in Lebanon, it is unhappy with the notion and fact of a Syrian naval blockade.

Syria's sponsorship or support of Palestinian or Lebanese groups who operate against Israel could also lead to an unanticipated Israeli response and to an unplanned escalation. In 1987 an unusually successful attack by a lone Palestinian in a hand glider was launched from the Baqa' Valley with Syrian support. The attack provoked an outcry, and Syria in fact braced itself for some sort of Israeli retaliation. It failed to come but a similar, or larger, operation could bring it about.

Finally, should the intifadah escalate, the pressure on Syria and its Palestinian supporters to act is likely to increase and with it the danger of a larger Syrian-Israeli conflict.

Syrian Obstruction of an Arab-Israeli Settlement

In November 1981, when it suspected that Jordan was about to join the Egyptian-Israeli peace process, Syria concentrated troops on the Jordanian border thus threatening to intervene militarily, should King Husayn proceed with his plans. In the event the king had no such plans and Syria's troops were withdrawn, but the lesson was not lost on Husayn. During the mid- and late 1980s he was concerned that if his negotiations with Israel succeeded he would have to contend with Syrian threats or possibly military action. This was not the main reason for the failure to reach an agreement, but it was a contributing factor.

A Jordanian-Israeli agreement is not on the agenda at present, but Asad is determined to prevent or obstruct any separate Israeli-Palestinian agreement. If considerable progress is made towards such an agreement, there is no Palestinian border along which to concentrate troops, but Syria could act through Lebanon to raise Arab-Israeli tensions.

CONCLUSION

Thus far, this article has described and analysed the principal components and phases of the Syrian-Israeli relationship. But this relationship has unfolded within a regional and international context that has had a significant, sometimes decisive, impact on its evolution. In the mid-1970s, the October War, the Lebanese Civil War, and the Soviet-American detente provided the context; later in the decade the new policies of the Carter Administration, the Egyptian-Israeli peace process, and the Iranian revolution provided a different backdrop.

Similar changes occurred in the 1980s. Syria did well in the mid-1980s when it successfully undid the consequences of the 1982 War in Lebanon, made the most of its alliance with Iran, and contributed its share to the failure of all efforts to promote Arab-Israeli settlements along lines unacceptable to itself. Later in the decade changes in the Soviet Union's position and policies, the end to the Gulf War, the intifadah, and developments in the Lebanese crisis once again turned Syria's position in Lebanon from an asset into a liability.

In recent months there have been two fresh developments, which are likely to affect the course of Syrian-Israeli relations. One has been the Arab campaign against the prospect of massive Jewish emigration from the Soviet Union to Israel. The language of that campaign alongside the cumulative effect of the Israeli-Palestinian conflict has reversed the trend to normalization in Arab-Israeli relations that had been the primary outcome of the Egyptian-Israeli peace. This development must be pleasing to the regime of President Asad who had consistently advocated that the Arabs must hold to their fundamental position in the conflict with Israel. However, Syria is likely more ambivalent towards Iraq's new role in the conflict with Israel. Iraq's threats to use its non-conventional arsenal against Israel not only if Israel stages another pre-emptive raid against it but also in the event of an Israeli attack on another Arab country has introduced a new element into the Arab-Israeli military equation. While this is probably pleasing to Syria, Iraq's increased power and prominence are not.

This paper was written in the summer of 1990 shortly before the Iraqi invasion of Kuwait, which set in motion a whole new chain of events – the Gulf War, the convening of the Madrid Conference and the inauguration of a decade long Syrian-Israeli peace process. In 1992 I was invited by Prime Minister Rabin to become Israel's Chief Negotiator with Syria.

The peace process of the 1990s is described and analysed further below in this volume.[15] The Gulf War and the disappearance of the Soviet Union were the two principal reasons for a profound change in Hafiz al-Asad's position: he agreed in principle to sign a peace agreement with Israel in return for a full Israeli withdrawal from the Golan. On the Israeli side four Israeli Prime Ministers (Rabin, Peres, Netanyahu and Barak) accepted in principle the same equation. But the decade long effort to translate these changes into an actual peace agreement failed. Yet the failed negotiations left a legacy: an adumbration of a potential settlement, an explicit change in Syria's view of the conflict with Israel from an 'existential' one to a 'territorial' one and a de facto separation of the Israeli-Syrian dispute from the Palestinian issue.

This did not happen in the Syrian-Lebanese-Israeli triangle, the focus of this paper.

During most of the 1990s, when it was hoping to reach an agreement with Syria, Israel was in practice willing to acquiesce in Syria's hegemony in Lebanon. In 1994 Israel and Syria in fact reached an oral understanding, according to which once a Syrian Israeli breakthrough had been achieved, Syria would agree to the signing of a comparable Israeli Lebanese peace and would prevent attacks on Israel from Lebanon's territory. All this time Syria continued to support Hizballah in its conflict with Israel and Israel was willing to accept this Syrian conduct as one of the rules of the game in their complex relationship.

This phase ended in 2000 due to the convergence of several developments: (1) the final collapse of the Israeli-Syrian negotiation; (2) Ehud Barak's decision to withdraw from the 'security zone' in South Lebanon and change the rules of the game within the Israeli-Syrian-Lebanese triangle; (3) Hafiz al-Asad's death and the accession to power of his son, Bashar; (4) Iran's emergence as a regional power with a particular interest in Lebanon's Shi'i community and Hizballah, a political movement cum militia cum terrorist organization and Iran's long arm in Lebanon; (5) the change in Syria's position in Lebanon expedited by her apparent role in the assassination of Rafiq al-Hariri, Lebanon's former Prime Minister, in February 2005. Syria's miscalculation, the hostility of US President George W. Bush and the crystallization of a strong Lebanese opposition forced Syria to withdraw her forces from Lebanon and to rely on other assets in order to preserve a hegemonical position in what used to be a virtual Syrian patrimony.

The Iranian-Syrian strategic partnership with collaboration in Lebanon as an important component dates back to 1979. During the last few years the balance within that partnership changed with Iran clearly becoming a dominant hegemonic power. Iran and Syria collaborated in building Hizballah's arsenal of rockets and missiles both viewing it as a detent against the US and Israel. In July 2006 the explosive potential inherent in this state of affairs was triggered by a Hizballah attack across the Israeli border and an ill-calculated massive Israeli response.

The war ended after five weeks with mixed results. It certainly failed to bring resolution or clarity to the Lebanese arena. The Lebanese political system is divided between two principal coalitions: (1) the one rallied around Fuad Seniora's government supported as a rule by the Maronite, Sunni and Druze communities and by the US and France; (2) the other composed of Hizballah and a variety of pro-Syrian fractions and politicians supported by Syria and Iran.

The risk of another military conflict breaking out in or spilling over into Lebanon remains high. Israel and Syria are in a position reminiscent of the Israeli-Egyptian relationship in 1970–73 – Bashar al-Asad speaks both of renewing the negotiations with Israel and of resorting to military actions. With Iranian and Russian help he is rebuilding Syria's military capabilities. And over the scene hovers the spectre of Iran's build-up as a powerful regional actor ceaselessly seeking to obtain a nuclear arsenal. The role played by Iraq in the 1980s has shifted to the east.

NOTES

1. This article was published in *International Journal*, 45 (Summer 1990), pp.529–52. The author would like to thank the Council on Foreign Relations, which commissioned the original paper on which this article is based.
2. For some illuminating studies, see Y. Evron, *War and Intervention in Lebanon: The Israeli-Syrian Deterrence Dialogue* (London: Croom Helm, 1987) and A. Yaniv, 'Syria and Israel: the politics of escalation', in M. Ma'oz and A. Yaniv (eds), *Syria under Asad* (London: Croom Helm, 1986), pp.78–157.
3. For Asad's outlook, see two biographies: Patrick Seale, *Asad of Syria* (London: I.B. Tauris, 1988) and Moshe Ma'oz, *Asad: The Sphinx of Damascus* (London: Weidenfeld and Nicolson, 1988). Both the strengths and the weaknesses of Seale's biography derive from his closeness to Asad. Ma'oz, an Israeli scholar, had no access to Asad and Syria, and his book is a rare academic study of Asad's regime.
4. For Jimmy Carter's own view in this matter, see his *Keeping Faith* (Toronto, ON: Bantam Books, 1982), p.286. Syria's role throughout that period is discussed by William Quandt in *Camp David* (Washington, DC: Brookings Institution, 1986), passim.
5. Radio Damascus, 27 April 1987.
6. See, for instance, *Ha'aretz* (Tel Aviv), 15 and 20 March 1990.
7. Moshe Dayan, *Milestones* (Jerusalem and Tel Aviv: Idanim, 1976), pp.1–400 [in Hebrew].
8. Moshe Dayan, *Breakthrough* (Jerusalem: Idanim, 1980) [in Hebrew].

9. United States, Department of State, *Bulletin* 78 (October 1978), pp.7–8.

10. See in this volume, I. Rabinovich, 'Syria's Quest for a Regional Role'.

11. See Iliya Harik, 'The Economic and Social Factors in the Lebanese Crisis', *Journal of Arab Affairs*, 1 (April 1982), pp.209–41, and Halim Barakat, 'Social and Political Integration in Lebanon: A Case of Social Mosaic', *Middle East Journal*, 27 (Summer 1973), pp.301–18.

12. For a fuller treatment of these issues, see I. Rabinovich, *The War for Lebanon, 1970–85* (Ithaca, NY: Cornell University Press, 1985).

13. William Harris, 'La Politique Libanaise de Hafez al-Asad', in Basma KodmaniDarwish (ed.), *Liban: Espoirs et Réalités* (Paris, 1987), pp.91–117.

14. For the best account of Syria's original intervention in Lebanon, see N.J. Weinberger, *Syrian Intervention in Lebanon: The 1975–1976 Civil War* (New York, NY: Oxford University Press, 1986).

15. See, in this volume, I. Rabinovich, 'Ehud Barak and the Collapse of the Peace Process'.

17

From Deposit to Commitment: The Evolution of US-Israeli-Syrian Peace Negotiations, 1993–2000[1]

During his two terms in office, US President Bill Clinton invested considerable time and effort in Arab-Israeli peace making. His achievements and failures on the Israeli-Palestinian track – the signing ceremony on the White House lawn in September 1993 and the collapse of the Camp David Conference in July 2000 – drew the greatest deal of attention and comment; but in fact during most of his presidency Clinton and his team assigned priority to the Israeli-Syrian track. Together with three Israeli prime ministers, Yitzhak Rabin, Shimon Peres and Ehud Barak, they sought to achieve an Israeli-Syrian breakthrough and predicate further progress in the peace process on it.

The key development in the trilateral American, Israeli, Syrian negotiations occurred in August 1993, when Prime Minister Rabin deposited with Secretary of State Warren Christopher a hypothetical, conditional willingness to withdraw from the Golan as part of a peace settlement between Israel and Syria on terms acceptable to Israel. Rabin's vision of an acceptable settlement was modelled after the Israeli-Egyptian peace treaty of 1979. He outlined to Secretary Christopher the details of both the substance and procedure that would make a withdrawal from the Golan justifiable and politically feasible. He emphasized that for the time being it was a secret deposit to be kept in the US 'pocket' and not to be laid on the table: He expected the US to act nimbly and discreetly.

This episode is alluded to briefly in Bill Clinton's autobiography My Life published in 2004: 'Before he was killed, Yitzhak Rabin had given me a commitment to withdraw from the Golan to the June 4, 1967 borders as long as Israel's concerns were satisfied.'[2] How was Rabin's 'deposit' transformed into a 'commitment'? The explanation concerns one of the most significant and intriguing turning points of the Israeli-Arab peace process of the 1990s.

Rabin's meeting with Christopher took place on 3 August 1993. The Secretary of State arrived in Jerusalem from Washington, after negotiating an end to Israel's 'Operation Accountability' in South Lebanon. His host was facing a difficult decision. The secret negotiations with the PLO had been practically concluded and a draft agreement was almost ready to sign. The Oslo Accords carried the promise of a historic breakthrough, but were fraught with risks and uncertainties. Was there a Syrian option, an alternative to the Oslo Accords? Rabin would like to know, but all efforts during the previous year, conducted directly and through the United States to divine an answer to this question, were to no avail. Syrian President Hafiz al-Asad would not enter into a substantive negotiation over the nature of a prospective peace agreement unless given a prior Israeli commitment to withdraw from the Golan.

And so Rabin decided to resort at the last moment to the 'hypothetical question' technique. He deposited his positive answer to Asad's fundamental question with the US in order to find out whether Asad would follow Egyptian President Anwar al-Sadat's example in substance and process. Substance meant contractual peace, normalization and adequate security arrangements; process meant a phased withdrawal over several years with a large measure of normalization given to Israel upfront, so as to enable Rabin to build political support for a very controversial prospective withdrawal from the Golan.

Christopher, who knew something but not everything about Israel's negotiations with the PLO, asked about Rabin's intentions with regard to the Palestinians, should the gambit toward Syria prove successful. In that case, Rabin answered, he would limit his deal with the Palestinians to the Gaza Strip.[3] Christopher and his team went to Damascus on 4 August and met again with Rabin the next day. The Secretary of State thought that he brought back a positive answer. Asad said yes in principle but rejected most of the details in Rabin's model: he took exception to the term 'normalization', he insisted that the security arrangements had to be 'equal' and he wanted Israel's withdrawal to be completed in six months. There was a serious discrepancy between Rabin's and Christopher's interpretation of Asad's response. From the lofty heights of a superpower's perspective, Asad's positive-in-principle response provided an adequate basis for further progress. He travelled back to Washington and to California for summer vacation, confident that the Israeli-Syrian track had been opened up and placed on firm footing.

Rabin's perspective was very different. He was disappointed by Asad's response and by Washington's reaction to it. To him, Asad's agreement in principle was less significant than his rejection of the details of Rabin's model. Rabin had created some bargaining space but Asad set the bar at a very low level. He could see how the US team, by conveying Asad's response as it was, positioned itself as an honest broker who would ultimately propose that the parties compromise somewhere in the middle. Israel's withdrawal from the Golan would remain the cornerstone of any future agreement, while Rabin's package would be whittled down in the bargaining process. And so, after Christopher's departure, Rabin authorized his Foreign Minister, Shimon Peres, to conclude and sign the Oslo Accords. In August, Peres flew to California together with Johan Jorgen Holst, the Norwegian Foreign Minister, to brief the Secretary of State on the Oslo Accord and ask him to endorse and help implement them.

The Clinton Administration was initially surprised and furious. It had been briefed in general terms about the negotiations with the PLO, but was not aware of the imminence of a signing. Furthermore, it was persuaded that the breakthrough in the peace process would occur in the Syrian track. From its perspective, that was the correct sequence. It also felt beholden to Asad who, according to its interpretation, had just agreed to go along with Washington.

But in a pragmatic spirit, Clinton's team overcame and concealed its anger and decided promptly to endorse the Oslo Accords and convert them into the Washington signing ceremony. If Israel and the PLO were ready to recognize each other and sign a framework agreement on a resolution of the Israeli-Palestinian conflict, it was up to Washington to seize the moment and make the most of it.

Syria, of course, would be disappointed and angry. It was Washington's task to calm Asad and reassure him that this was not the end of his part in the peace process, just a temporary delay. Once Israel and the Palestinians concluded their agreement, the US would resume its role as a broker between Jerusalem and Damascus and proceed from the premises established in August 1993.

In order to do that, the Clinton Administration asked for Rabin's commitment to resume the give-and-take with Syria on that basis. Rabin did give his commitment to do so and the term 'commitment' was thus explicitly introduced into the vocabulary of the American-Israeli-Syrian negotiations. Rabin's 'commitment' referred specifically to a revival of the negotiations but the US team used it rather loosely and soon extended it to the whole package discussed in early August. The deposit that Rabin defined so precisely and offered in hypothetical and conditional terms was thus converted in Washington's parlance into a 'commitment'.

This process was taken a step further after Rabin's assassination. On the day of Rabin's funeral, President Clinton met in Jerusalem with his designated successor, Shimon Peres. Having made sure that Peres was briefed in advance about the history of Rabin's secret dealings with Washington and

– indirectly – with Damascus, Clinton asked Peres whether he intended to fulfil Rabin's 'commitments' with regard to the Golan and was given a positive answer. The notion of a 'commitment' rather than a 'deposit' was thus further cemented.

At this point, it is important to emphasize that President Clinton's peace team had a different view of the 'hypothetical question' technique and of the terminology used in its implementation.

As recounted by Dennis Ross in his memoirs, Rabin 'proposed to have us convey the following. He would be willing to commit to the US that Israel would withdraw fully from the Golan Heights provided Israel's needs were met and provided Syria's argument was not contingent on any other agreement ... He went on to explain Israel's needs ... '[4] Ross thus begins his account with an Israeli 'commitment' to the US. He later modifies it by writing that 'From this point onward Rabin's conditional offer on full withdrawal became referred to as 'the pocket'.'[5]

But when describing the transition from Rabin to Peres, Ross writes that when he briefed Clinton for his first working meeting with Rabin's successor: 'I began by reminding the president what we had in our pocket from Rabin – a conditional commitment on full Israeli withdrawal from the Golan Heights. After the funeral the President met alone with Peres for 45 minutes and discussed Rabin's commitment on the Golan Heights.'[6]

After the collapse of the Israeli-Syrian negotiations in the spring of 1996, Asad's regime was anxious to salvage from the wreckage a formal legacy. It was particularly anxious to be able to claim that it had obtained from Israel a formal commitment to withdraw to the lines of 4 June 1967. This would enable Syria to argue that in the absence of an actual Israeli withdrawal, there was at least an Israeli commitment to do so as well as an implicit Israeli acknowledgement of Syria's sovereignty over this disputed territory. Should the negotiations be renewed at some point in the future, Syria would be able to insist that this be the starting point of any give and take.

Asad's anxiety was exacerbated by Benjamin Netanyahu's electoral victory over Shimon Peres just a few weeks after the negotiations' collapse. Given Netanyahu's stated positions, the prospect of an agreement with his government on the basis of a full withdrawal from the Golan seemed dim. Syria's president, his aides and spokesmen launched a campaign designed to prove that such a commitment had, indeed, been made.

Unfortunately, from their point of view, Israel's new prime minister was quite effective in his effort to establish the opposite case. Netanyahu presented the Secretary of State with a formal question and received a formal answer – in the State Department's view, nothing of a binding nature had been concluded in the Israeli-Syrian negotiations of the 1993–96 period.[7]

Since September 1996 two efforts were made to achieve an Israeli-Syrian breakthrough – Ronald Lauder's mediation mission on behalf of Benjamin Netanyahu in late 1998 and Ehud Barak's sustained effort in 1999–2000. Lauder, on behalf of Netanyahu, conveyed a willingness to withdraw from the Golan as part of a peace settlement, but his mission collapsed when Asad insisted that he provide a map showing the lines of withdrawal acceptable to Netanyahu.

Barak's negotiation with Asad collapsed during the latter's meeting with President Clinton in Geneva in March 2000, but the moment of truth had occurred earlier, in January, during Barak's negotiation with Syria's Foreign Minister, Faruq al-Shara', in Shepherdstown. Shara' demanded that Barak go beyond an indication of willingness to withdraw from the Golan and make an explicit, formal commitment. Barak declined and explained subsequently that he refused to offer Syria the bottom line before the conclusion of the negotiations. This, he explained, would have left him without any leverage in the final phases of an unfinished negotiation.[8]

From the perspective of the summer of 2004 the issues discussed below seem academic. Hafiz al-Asad died and was succeeded by his son, Bashar, who has yet to consolidate his rule. Israel's Prime Minister, Ariel Sharon, is fully focused on the Palestinian issue and is not interested in resuming negotiations with Syria. President George W. Bush, unlike his predecessor, is critical of Syria and his interest in the Israeli-Arab peace process is limited to the Road Map for resolving the Palestinian issue.

But there is a lesson to be drawn for future Israeli-Arab negotiations from this episode. It concerns the nature of collaboration and coordination between a superpower and a small state in a joint effort on conflict resolution. The superpower is determined to move the process forward. Minor details such as the difference between 'deposit' and 'commitment' seem insignificant, even 'petty'. To the small state they seem significant and crucial. As we saw above, once Rabin indicated to the Clinton Administration that he was in principle willing to withdraw from the Golan, the door was opened for a Syrian-Israeli deal. Terms like 'commitment' or 'conditioned willingness' could be used and indeed were used loosely and interchangeably.

During most of the 1990s the US and Israel cooperated closely in the conduct of the peace process. Much of the time their interests converged. But at some points, interests diverged. At other points the Clinton Administration felt that, as the patron and orchestrator of the peace process, it had to overrule Israeli considerations and protestations in order to move the process forward. In such a division of labor, however, the smaller party has its own interests to protect and its own role to play. And part of that role is to insist on formulating and using a well-thought out and precise terminology.

NOTES

1. This article was published in Elie Podeh and Asher Kaufman (eds), *Arab-Jewish Relations: From Conflict to Resolution?* (Brighton: Sussex Academic Press, 2005), pp.277–82.

2. Bill Clinton, *My Life* (New York: A.A. Knopf, 2004), p.893.

3. For two versions of Rabin's meeting with Christopher and 'the deposit', see I. Rabinovich, *The Brink of Peace: The Israeli-Syrian Negotiations* (Princeton, NJ: Princeton University Press, 1998), pp.104–8; and Dennis Ross, *The Missing Peace: The Inside Story of the Fight for Middle East Peace* (New York: Farrar, Straus and Giroux, 2004), pp.111–13. Ross and I compared our notes in November 1996 in order to present Shimon Peres with an authoritative account after Rabin's assassination, but our published accounts vary slightly.

4. Ross, *The Missing Peace*, p.111.

5. Ibid., p.113.

6. Ibid., p.212.

7. *Ha'aretz*, 16 August 1996; 20 January 1997; 24 October 1997.

8. I. Rabinovich, *Waging Peace* (Princeton, NJ: Princeton University Press, 2004), pp.132–4.

18

Israel and Syria, Rabin and Asad[1]

Of all the conflicts between Israel and her Arab neighbours, the Syrian-Israeli dispute has traditionally been regarded as the most bitter. The Palestinian-Israeli conflict is the core conflict of the Arab-Israeli dispute, and Israelis and Palestinians have for over a century now fought over land, rights, and power – over the most fundamental and the most mundane. But the very close contact and interaction of the two societies, hostile as it has been, has also served to mitigate the mutual abstract demonization that is so characteristic of such conflicts.[2]

For many years Egypt had been Israel's most formidable military and political adversary. When the power of the Egyptian state and the mass of its population were mobilized against Israel, they presented her with the most severe challenges. But the challenge of Egypt had from the beginning been softened by *raison d'état*, the interests of the Egyptian state that set it apart from the Arab collective. And when an Egyptian president, Anwar al-Sadat, decided in the early 1970s that these interests required Egypt's disengagement from the conflict with Israel, it took less than a decade to complete the process of disengagement by signing the first Arab-Israeli peace agreement.[3]

Syria does not possess the weight of Egypt, but it has more than made up for the paucity of resources by zeal and perseverance. Syria's commitment to the issues of Palestine and the Palestinians and its opposition to the state of Israel and its Zionist antecedents have been profound and durable. To Israelis, Syria and the Syrians came to represent Arab enmity and rejection in their most entrenched and significant form.

This Syrian attitude, its evolution over time, and its translation into actual policies have derived from several sources. The weakness of the young Syrian state, its own search for identity, the hold of pan-Arab nationalism on its political classes, and its proximity and closeness to the Palestinian Arabs combined to produce a particularly strong commitment to the Palestinian cause. The ambiguous situation along the Syrian-Israeli armistice lines, the early role played in Syrian politics by army officers and by ideological parties, and Syria's drift into the Soviet orbit and Israel's own reaction and response to these developments turned the foothills of the

Golan Heights into the most active front of the unfolding Arab-Israeli conflict in the 1950s and 1960s.[4]

Syria played a major role in generating the crisis that led to the 1967
War. Having lost the Golan Heights, Syria participated in formulating an
Arab consensus which rejected the notion that in order to regain the land
they lost in 1967 the Arabs should make their peace with the state of Israel
as it had emerged from the 1948 War. Syria joined Egypt in the October
War of 1973, but Hafiz al-Asad's agenda was different from that of Sadat.
Unlike his Egyptian partner, he did not launch war in order to set a peace
process in motion. While Egypt mounted the track that led to the 1979
peace treaty with Israel, the Syrian-Israeli negotiating process dissolved in
the aftermath of the May 1974 Disengagement Agreement. As Sadat's Egypt
became increasingly committed to peace, Asad's Syria led the Arab campaign against Cairo's reconciliation with Israel. Throughout these years, the
intensity of Syria's continued enmity and opposition to Israel was matched
by an Israeli perception of Damascus as an implacable foe, a source of hostility, and definitely not a candidate for a future settlement.

The arena of Syrian-Israeli hostility was expanded by the collapse in
1975 of the Lebanese state, Syria's military intervention, and the establishment of Syrian presence and paramount influence in Lebanon. Initially
Israel and Syria found a *modus vivendi* in Lebanon, but in 1981 they mounted a collision course in that country that led them to a limited war in 1982
and the war by proxy during the following years. Buoyed by her success
against Israel (and the United States) in Lebanon and by her alliance with
revolutionary Iran, Syria championed the doctrine of 'strategic parity' with
Israel and became embroiled in the mid-1980s in a campaign of terrorism
against Israel and America. In 1986 and early 1987 the prospect of a
Syrian-Israeli negotiation, let alone accommodation, seemed very remote.
And yet forces were then at work that in less than five years made the
unthinkable happen and brought Israel and Syria to the negotiating table
as part of a larger effort to arrive at a comprehensive settlement of the
Arab-Israeli conflict. The tale of Hafiz al-Asad's and Yitzhak Shamir's journey to the Madrid peace conference in October 1991 is scintillating. But in
order to appreciate it fully we need to take a closer look at the evolution of
the Syrian-Israeli dispute during the previous forty-odd years.

BETWEEN TWO WARS, 1948–67

When the Arab armies invaded the territory of the young Israeli state in
May 1948, they were implementing the Arab League's resolutions seeking
to support the Palestinian Arabs in their war with the Jewish community

and to prevent the establishment of a Jewish state in their midst. The United Nations General Assembly may have voted on the partition of mandatory Palestine, but for the Arabs this was an illegitimate act, giving birth to an illegitimate state, violating Arab rights, and creating an alien entity in a particularly significant part of the Arab homeland.

Of the five Arab armies taking part in the invasion, the Syrian army came closest to acting in this spirit. King 'Abdallah of Jordan maintained a clandestine relationship with the Jewish leadership, but at the same time pushed hard for an Arab invasion that would provide him with the opportunity to take over the Arab part of Palestine. Egypt's decision to join the war was finally made precisely in order to deny 'Abdallah and his Hashemite cousins in Iraq any such aggrandizement. Lebanon was a reluctant participant in the Arab coalition, yielding to domestic and external pressures to conform to the Arab consensus. Syria had her own share of calculating politicians and generals, but more than in the other Arab states her enthusiastic participation in the war reflected the hold that the ideology of pan-Arab nationalism had both on the political establishment and, in a more radical fashion, on many of its younger challengers. The impact of these ideas and sentiments was magnified by the war and its outcome. To the radical Arab nationalists the defeat sustained by the established Arab regimes was further proof of the corruption of the existing order and its inability to cope with the challenge of the West.

The 1948 War ended with a series of armistice agreements brokered by the UN mediator Ralph Bunche. Egyptian, Jordanian, Lebanese, and Israeli delegations negotiated and signed three armistice agreements on the island of Rhodes in the early part of 1949. Syria avoided the Rhodes talks altogether. Syrian negotiations with Israel began later and proved to be the most protracted and the most difficult. It is ironic from the present perspective that the chief stumbling block in these negotiations was Israel's insistence that Syria withdraw to the international border (between Syria and mandatory Palestine) and Syria's refusal to evacuate the (fairly small) territory she occupied west of that line at the war's end. The negotiation was further compounded by other issues: Syria's vague claim to parts of the Galilee, her refusal to acknowledge Israel's control of land not assigned to her by the UN partition plan, and her attempt to obtain a better hold over two important keys to the region's scarce water resources – the Jordan River and Lake Tiberias. Beyond these concrete impediments lay the reluctance of all Syrian governments and political leaders to defy the Arab nationalist taboo and sign an agreement that would recognize the state of Israel.[5]

The man who broke the taboo was Syria's first military dictator, Husni Za'im. Za'im was an unconventional leader whose person and regime were full of contradictions and incongruities. A former officer in France's colonial levy in the Levant, Za'im was at loggerheads with the Arab nationalist leaders who constituted the backbone of the civilian regime overthrown by his soldiers. In retrospect, it is clear that Za'im was a transitional figure whose regime opened the door to the radical, ideologically bent military that have dominated Syrian politics since the mid-1950s. But during his brief reign (March–August 1949), he did introduce several important changes and did take several bold decisions, one of which was the conclusion of an armistice agreement with Israel. Za'im in fact went further, to the point of proposing a meeting between himself and Israel's prime minister, David Ben-Gurion, and told his American interlocutors that he was willing, in return for significant Israeli territorial concessions, to sign a peace treaty and even to settle Palestinian refugees in Syria. Ben-Gurion refused to meet with Za'im before the conclusion of an armistice agreement, and by the time he was willing to explore the prospects of dealing with him, Za'im was deposed and killed by a fresh group of military conspirators.

This curious episode has yet to be fully explained. Za'im had close links with the CIA, and his initiative may have been part of a larger US effort to resolve the Arab-Israeli conflict in league with a would-be 'reformist army officer'. Ben-Gurion refused to take Za'im seriously, and though his caution may have been well warranted, his initial refusal to deal with Za'im's initiative was quite startling. In Syria and in subsequent Syrian historiography and polemics, this episode left no trace. It was probably seen as too embarrassing and as an inconsequential aberration from the mainstream of Syrian politics and policies.[6]

This failure fitted into a larger pattern. In 1949 and 1950 all efforts to impose a comprehensive settlement of the Arab-Israel conflict or to resolve Israel's disputes with Egypt, Jordan, Lebanon, and the Palestinians were to no avail. To the extent that an Arab party was willing to negotiate or explore the prospect of accommodation with Israel, it insisted on terms that the Israelis found unacceptable. The concept of armistice agreements proved very effective in helping the parties to end the fighting, but not in settling their conflict and in making the transition to a state of peace. Stalemate led to festering, and by the mid-1950s the Arab-Israeli conflict reached its full-blown form: total political boycott by the Arab side, political warfare, border conflicts, and, in October 1956, a second Arab-Israeli war.[7]

Israel's specific conflict with Syria was exacerbated by geography, topography, and the complexities of the armistice agreement. The key to Israel's further development was water and irrigation, and the keys to Israel's water economy were perilously close to the armistice lines, with

Syria: Lake Tiberias and the Jordan River and its tributaries. Syria in this instance was not merely an unfriendly neighbour. It carried an Arab nationalist burden of responsibility to prevent Israel from constructing the overland water carrier from the northern edge of the country to the empty spaces in its southern part, thereby laying the foundation for a larger and more viable Jewish state.

The armistice agreements of 1949 were, as the term suggests, designed to end the hostilities and facilitate the transition to a state of peace. The complex arrangements designed along the Israeli-Syrian line or, for that matter, in Jerusalem, were not meant to linger for nearly twenty years. But they did, and along the Syrian-Israeli armistice lines this prolonged arrangement served to fan an embryonic conflict into active hostility. Perched on the bluff of the Golan Heights, the Syrian army was determined to enforce its own strict interpretation of the agreement and to improve and expand Syria's territorial position. This Syrian pressure and Israel's own assertiveness in claiming and exercising sovereignty accounted for much of the strife along the Syrian-Israeli armistice line in the 1950s. During these years, Syria registered two principal territorial accomplishments: it took over the Hamah enclosure south of Lake Tiberias, and established a de facto presence on and control of the eastern shore of Lake Tiberias.[8]

The Syrian-Israeli conflict of the 1950s underwent a qualitative leap in the early 1960s. A series of developments combined to radicalize Syria's policy toward Israel and to turn it into the principal actor in the chain of events that was set in motion in 1963 and took the region into the May 1967 crisis and the Six Day War.

At the core of these developments was a quest for legitimacy. After they broke away from their union with Egypt, Syria's secessionist rulers (September 1961–March 1963) and their Ba'thist successors were hard-put to stand up to the still formidable 'Abd al-Nasir. In order to embarrass him and to justify Syria's separate existence as the bastion of genuine Arab nationalist opposition to Israel, they adopted a particularly radical position toward Israel and accused Nasir of selling out to the United States and to the Israelis by endorsing the Johnston Plan for Arab-Israeli water sharing. When Israel announced in 1963 that it was about to complete the overland water carrier, Syria threatened to go to war in order to abort the project. This forced Egypt to convene the first Arab Summit conference in Cairo in January 1964.[9] At the conference, a decision to divert the tributaries of the Jordan was made as part of a comprehensive Arab strategy to confront Israel.

Egypt's hope that the formation of a new Arab framework and the formulation of a new Arab strategy would moderate Syria's position failed to materialize. Internecine strife, Soviet support, interaction with the new wave of Palestinian nationalism, and Israel's own miscalculations all served as catalysts of further radicalization. An uninterrupted cycle of violence was unleashed in which a clear distinction no longer existed between cause and effect. When Israeli tanks hit Syrian bulldozers implementing the Arab diversion scheme, Syria retaliated by sending a Palestinian terrorist squad through the territory of Jordan, to which Israel retaliated with an air raid, only to invite the Syrian response of laying a mine in the Israeli patrol road in the valley dominated by the Golan Heights.

Matters came to a head in the spring of 1967. On 7 April six Syrian planes were shot down by Israeli planes in the course of an air battle near Damascus. The Israeli government came to the conclusion that the radical wing of the Ba'th, in power since February 1966, was set on a course of further and escalating friction. It felt that domestic weakness coupled with a sense that the Soviet Union and Egypt were committed to its survival kept propelling the Syrian regime toward further and more dangerous confrontation. The Syrians, Egyptians, and Soviets, in turn, became persuaded that Israel was trying to bring down the Ba'th regime. It was apparently in order to preempt this notion that the Soviets told the Egyptians in May 1967 that Israel had amassed fifteen brigades on its northern borders in order to mount an offensive against Syria.

'Abd al-Nasir decided to deter Israel by breaking the 1957 arrangements and remilitarizing the Sinai. By the time he had established that there was no Israeli military build-up in the north, a process was set in motion that could not be stopped. 'Abd al-Nasir realized that his bold moves had restored his stature in Egypt and the Arab world, and he continued to press forward. He crossed the point of no return on 23 May, when he closed the Straits of Tiran to Israeli shipping.[10]

This turn of events confronted Syria with unexpected problems. Once Egypt took charge, Syria was relegated into a subsidiary role. Furthermore, her leaders realized that, given their contractual obligations vis-à-vis Egypt and their partnership in the Unified Arab Command, a war between Egypt and Israel was bound to involve them as well. Brave rhetoric notwithstanding, this was not what they had in mind. They were willing to go to the brink of war in pursuit of their political ends, but they never planned to cross it. As they later claimed, they thought that Egypt should not have made the decision to close the Straits of Tiran, thereby creating a *casus belli*, and they certainly thought that Egypt was not entitled to make on her own a decision that had such far-reaching ramifications for her partners.

Syria's unhappiness with Egypt's conduct accounted at least in part for the very modest role it chose to play once war broke out on 6 June. While war raged on the Egyptian and Jordanian fronts, Syria was willing to settle on shelling parts of northern Israel and on staging one small land attack. In the early afternoon of the same day the Israeli air force destroyed the Syrian air force and brought the fighting along the Israeli-Syrian front to a virtual end. In the event, this strategy was nearly successful in steering Syria safely through the crisis. Israel's defence minister, Moshe Dayan, was quite willing to let this happen. Having accomplished his original aims, he was reluctant to launch an offensive and capture the Golan Heights. Dayan was anxious that if Israel scaled the Golan Heights, defeated the Syrian army, and seemed to threaten Damascus, the Soviet Union might be provoked into intervening in the war. As he tells it in his autobiography, the defence minister was also worried by the prospect of Egyptian refusal to accept a ceasefire and, therefore, by the risk of a lengthy conflict on two fronts. But there was a more profound dimension to Dayan's hesitation. In his own words, 'Thirdly, the long term consequences of our action: The Syrians would not accept our permanent presence on the Golan Heights and we would be in a state of war with three Arab states. Having crossed the armistice lines on two fronts was quite sufficient. Let us not add a third state to the war against us.'[11]

Dayan's position drew criticism from two quarters. There were those inside the government and among the military who felt and argued that Syria was responsible for the war, and by allowing her to escape its consequences Israel would be sowing the seeds of the next crisis. Another lobby, headed by residents of the valley dominated by the Golan Heights, argued that they must no longer be left to the mercy of Syria's artillery, and exerted pressure on Prime Minister Levi Eshkol and other cabinet members not to end the war without capturing the Golan Heights.

During the night of 8 June Moshe Dayan reconsidered his position, and at dawn he called General David Elazar, General Officer Northern Command, on the telephone and instructed him to launch an offensive against the Golan Heights in the morning. It took Israel about thirty hours to capture the Golan Heights. Given the terrain, fighting was tough and costly. The Syrian army fought well, but the country's leadership took two controversial decisions during the war. The elite units of the Syrian army were not thrown into battle in order to defend the national territory but were kept back in order to protect the regime. And during the final hours of fighting Radio Damascus announced the fall of Kuneitra, the provincial capital of the Golan Heights, several hours before it was actually taken by the Israeli Defense Forces (IDF). The radio bulletin was probably designed to exert pressure on the Soviet Union to expedite the imposition of a ceasefire by the Security Council. In the event it did cause a panicky flight from Kuneitra.

The loss of the Golan and the circumstances under which it happened were to haunt the Ba'th regime in the coming years. The party that claimed to have the formula for liberating Palestine could not protect the integrity of Syria's own territory and lost a piece of it under apparently questionable circumstances. Within the regime's own ranks the warring factions tried to pin responsibility on each other's chests. Hafiz al-Asad was acting defence minister and air force commander during the war. His rivals charged that as such he was formally responsible for the war's conduct and outcome. Asad argued back that instructions were given by others through informal channels and, in any event, he settled the argument by seizing full powers in November 1970.[12]

FROM WAR TO WAR, JUNE 1967–JUNE 1974

On 10 June a ceasefire was arranged between Israel and Syria. The whole of the Golan Heights was captured by Israel; the region's civilian population of about 100,000 fled north. Only the Druze population in several large villages at the foothills of Mt Hermon stayed in place.

War was soon replaced by diplomacy. The United States maintained that the territories captured in war should be exchanged for a solid political settlement. Israel's position diverged at two significant points: it put the West Bank and Gaza in a different category, and it insisted that a political settlement be nothing short of full-fledged formal peace. From that premise the Israeli cabinet (with Menahem Begin in its ranks) decided on 19 June 1967, with regard to Syria that:

> Israel proposes that a peace treaty be signed on the basis of the international border and Israel's security needs.
> The peace treaty will require:
> 1. Demilitarization of the Syrian Heights presently held by the IDF;
> 2. Absolute guarantee of the uninterrupted flow of water from the sources of the Jordan to Israel.
> Until the peace treaty with Syria is signed, Israel will continue to hold the territories it is holding now.[13]

The Arab consensus and the Soviet Union totally rejected this position. To them Israel was an aggressor and the territories captured in the war should be returned to their owners without any conditions. The Arab states consensus was formalized on 1 September 1967, at the Khartoum Arab Summit.

This clash of perspectives and the balance of power between their respective supporters in the international arena produced a diplomatic stalemate. It was formalized by Security Council Resolution 242 in November 1967. The resolution drafters were masters of ambiguity and equilibrium. The Arabs welcomed the preamble that spoke of 'the inadmissibility of the acquisition of territory by war' and the call to 'withdrawal from territories occupied in the recent conflict'. The Israelis, in turn, pointed to the call for 'just and lasting peace in which every state in the area can live in security' and to the assertion of the right of every state in the area 'to live in peace within secure and recognized boundaries', and underlined the fact that the resolution spoke of withdrawal from 'territories' and not from 'the territories'. According to the Israeli interpretation, this meant partial withdrawal. Alongside with the reference to secure boundaries it implied, so the Israelis argued, a territorial compromise over the territories captured in June 1967 in return for genuine peace.

The Syrian Ba'th regime, like the other Arab regimes, was effective and successful in coping with the immediate repercussions of its military defeat. There was no organized opposition to take advantage of the regime's failure and humiliation. In short order, as behooves an ideological regime, a proper explanation for the defeat was produced and a policy line was formulated.[14] For the Syrian Ba'th, dealing with the 'results of 1967' was a subsidiary issue. The fundamental issue was that of 1948, and once this fundamental issue was dealt with, the territorial losses of 1967 would in any case be rectified. Syria took a dubious view of Egypt's willingness to cooperate with the efforts of the United Nations and the superpowers to implement Security Council Resolution 242. But Syria's criticism of Egypt's diplomatic efforts was implicit. If the improbable were to happen and these efforts were to produce an Israeli withdrawal, Syria did not want to legislate herself out of the receiving line.

In a similar vein, Syria was also a partial participant in the 'war of attrition', the limited war launched by Egypt against Israel in 1968. Several serious clashes took place along the Israeli-Syrian ceasefire line during this period, but in comparison to the sustained fighting along the Suez Canal and to the Israeli-Palestinian clashes along the Jordanian border the Golan front was rather quiet.

Syria also encouraged Palestinian attacks against Israel as long as they were carried out through Lebanese or Jordanian territory. Her relations with the PLO and its constituent organizations were compounded by the Syrian claim to be as legitimate a custodian of the Palestinian cause as any Palestinian organization.

Custodianship of the Palestinian cause became excessively demanding in September 1970 – 'Black September' – when King Husayn and his army took on the Palestinian nationalists who had challenged and sapped their power during the previous three years. Intervention on the side of the Palestinians was debated in Syria. Initially the radical faction, arguing that Syria must intervene on the side of the Palestinian nationalists, won, and a Syrian armoured column invaded Jordan. Hafiz al-Asad, defence minister and commander of the air force, argued against intervention. He could not prevent the invasion, but held back the air force. By that time, Israel in league with the United States was deployed to act against the Syrian invasion if necessary. Asad was not willing to have his air force decimated by the Israelis. Without aerial support, the invading Syrian armoured column was easily repelled by the Jordanians and retreated ignominiously.[15] In the ensuing altercation, Asad's Syrian rivals charged him with responsibility for Syria's defeat and humiliation. He finally settled the issue in November by staging 'the corrective movement' and seizing full power in Syria.

Asad's seizure of power was, of course, first and foremost a domestic Syrian affair, but in retrospect it can also be seen as part of a broader development that took the region to the October 1973 war: the Egyptian-Israeli ceasefire that ended the war of attrition, the death of 'Abd al-Nasir, Anwar al-Sadat's rise to power, and Black September.

Syrian politics in the late 1960s were governed by the conflict between Hafiz al-Asad and his rivals. At the core it was a personal and factional struggle for power compounded by genuine disagreements over policy. Asad represented a more pragmatic school that viewed the radical vision of his rivals and their call for a 'popular war of liberation' as hollow posturing. Domestically, he wanted to find a modus vivendi with the middle classes. In foreign policy he wanted Syria to act in concert with the Arab mainstream in order to formulate a joint strategy for dealing with Israel and the territorial losses of 1967.[16]

'Abd al-Nasir's disappearance from the scene and his replacement by the less intimidating Anwar al-Sadat facilitated the formation of an Egyptian-Syrian coalition. That Asad accepted the principle of a diplomatic settlement as an alternative to a military solution was made clear in March 1972. In the course of his Revolution Day speech Asad, for the first time, accepted Security Council Resolution 242, albeit in a conditional and very specific fashion:

> I say this in reply to several inquiries which say we in Syria are against the Security Council's resolution and that Egypt supports the resolution. We support the Security Council Resolution when interpreted as providing for the withdrawal of the enemy from the Arab territory occupied in 1967 and as a confirmation, assertion, and realization

of the rights of the Palestinian people. We are against this resolution when it is interpreted as the realization of new gains for the enemy, consolidation of the aggression, and a stab at the rights of our Arab people in Palestine.[17]

By 1973 Sadat decided to go to war. He was not hoping for a military victory, but reasoned that if the Arabs launched a war and held their own for a couple of days, the international system would be mobilized into forcing on Israel a political settlement acceptable to the Arab side. Syria was a vital military partner to such a war. A simultaneous attack on the Suez and Golan fronts was an essential component of an Egyptian strategy seeking to neutralize Israel's military superiority.

Sadat's invitation to Asad to join him in launching the war presented the Syrian president with a dilemma. The war was to set in motion a diplomatic process that was likely to develop in ways unacceptable to him, and over which he would have very little control. Yet Asad knew very well that he could not afford to reject the invitation. He may also have hoped to secure a territorial gain at the war's outset that would remain his achievement even if the anticipated diplomatic process were to develop in an undesirable direction.

Indeed, neither the war nor its diplomatic sequel unfolded according to plan. The initial Egyptian and Syrian offensive caught Israel by surprise and met with unexpected success. But Syrian Egyptian coordination soon foundered. Syria's troops were pushed back from the Golan Heights, and as Israel regrouped it captured additional Syrian territory, getting ever closer to Damascus. Asad complained later that by stopping his troops in place and by failing to launch additional attacks Sadat was denying Syria support while the latter was being pressed hard by Israel. Sadat, in turn, complained of Syria's attempt to obtain an early ceasefire through the Soviet Union, without consulting Egypt. On 22 October, Syria was surprised both by the ceasefire arranged at Egypt's behest and by its terms (Security Council Resolution 338). During the following weeks and months, Asad had to come to terms with the emergence of direct Egyptian-Israeli negotiations, the formation of a close Egyptian relationship with the United States, and the signing of the Israeli-Egyptian Disengagement Agreement.[18]

Asad's bargaining chips were quite inferior. Syria ended the war with a new loss of territory. Its patron, the Soviet Union, did not prove to be very effective in that role, and it had yet to build a relationship with the United States. It was Asad's ability to maximize his assets and to emerge from this period with a Disengagement Agreement comparable to the one signed earlier by Egypt that first established his international reputation as a masterful negotiator and a formidable adversary. While he negotiated with the American secretary of state, Asad conducted his 'war of attrition' against Israel in the spring of 1974. Both Israel, anxious to put the debacle of the October War behind it, and the United States, worried by the danger of renewed warfare at the height of the energy crisis, were willing to offer Asad better terms than he had expected in the war's immediate aftermath. Henry Kissinger's attempt to use the negotiations to lure Asad away from the Soviet Union failed. Asad wanted to build a new relationship, with the United States, but he was determined to do it on his terms.[19]

The Disengagement Agreement that was finally signed between Syria and Israel in May 1974 has by now governed relations between the two countries for twenty-four years. It has been observed quite scrupulously by both sides, so much so that when they fought in Lebanon in 1982, peace and quiet prevailed along the Golan front. The agreement stipulated an Israeli withdrawal from the territory captured in 1973 as well as from the town of Kuneitra and a small adjacent area. Syria thus regained the best-known site in the Golan Heights while Israel kept the bulk of the territory. This included Mt Hermon (site of a very valuable monitoring station) and the defence line along the hills to the east. A UN force, the United Nations Disengagement Observer Force (UNDOF) was created in order to monitor the agreement, whose mandate was to be renewed every six months.

It is noteworthy that the Disengagement Agreement was not actually signed by Syria. When the time came to sign the agreement in Geneva in June 1974, Syria authorized an Egyptian general to sign on its behalf. The message was clear – Syria was willing to negotiate with Israel indirectly in order to deal with the outcome of the 1973 War and, marginally, with that of the 1967 War, but it was not willing to extend the recognition implied by signing the same agreement. Denying recognition and avoiding or at least minimizing direct contact were traditional tools of Arab nationalist resistance to Israel, and Hafiz al-Asad was determined to demonstrate that he remained the champion of that resistance. Indeed, although the Disengagement Agreement between Egypt and Israel was seen as a first step in an unfolding process, as time went by its Syrian-Israeli counterpart came to be seen more as the final chapter of the October War and less as the initial phase of a potential peace process.[20]

This was not only Syria's choice. Israeli attitudes and policies toward Syria and the Golan had changed considerably soon after 19 June 1967. The positions adopted by the Arab consensus and Syria's own contribution to that consensus persuaded Israeli opinion and the Israeli government that peace with Syria was a remote possibility. Israel dug in for a long stay in the Golan Heights. By the end of 1967 the first Israeli settlements were established. Unlike most of the early settlers in the West Bank, the settlers in the Golan Heights tended to be identified with the Labour party and came to the Golan with the government's encouragement. At the same time, a defence line and monitoring stations were built in the Golan and integrated into Israel's national security doctrine.

The Disengagement Agreements of 1974 were negotiated on the Israeli side by the government of Golda Meir. But she was forced to resign by an Israeli public still smarting under the impact of the October War. Responsibility for the conduct of Israel's relations with the Arab world passed to her successor, Yitzhak Rabin. Together with his friend Henry Kissinger, he chose to proceed with a phased approach, 'step-by-step diplomacy' in the language of that time. Rabin saw Egypt as the key to war and peace with the Arabs. The Sinai, furthermore, afforded the possibility of going through two more interim agreements before coming to a comprehensive agreement for which neither side was yet ready. Rabin was less keen on parallel progress with Syria. If Asad's bargaining style in 1974 was an indicator, the prospect of a further round of negotiations with him was quite alarming. Also, in contradistinction to the Sinai the Golan offered very little manoeuverability. It was difficult to envisage a second interim agreement with Syria that would not affect either some of Israel's settlements or her defensive capability in the Golan. The notion of a full-fledged agreement with Syria was not considered a realistic option.[21]

The actual outcome of this round of diplomacy was the Israeli-Egyptian interim agreement of 1 September 1975. Syria rejected an offer to join the process on the basis of 'cosmetic concessions' by Israel, and mounted instead an all-out campaign against Egypt's 'sellout'. But in short order the altercations over 'Sinai II' were marginalized by three major developments: the Lebanese Civil War, the formulation of a new American policy in the Middle East by the Carter Administration, and Menahem Begin's rise to power in Israel.

THE UNITED STATES, ISRAEL AND LEBANON, 1976–84

By the mid-1970s it became clear that Hafiz al-Asad had transformed Syria's role in the region. The emergence of a comparatively stable and durable regime in Syria after decades of proverbial instability had for the first time enabled a Syrian government to pursue a systematic, ambitious regional policy rather than be buffeted by other forces. The essence of that policy was the quest for hegemony over Syria's weaker Arab neighbours: Jordan, Lebanon and the Palestinians. As the hegemonial Arab power in that part of the Middle East, Asad's Syria planned to stand up to Egypt and to deal with her Soviet patron and with the United States from a hitherto unfamiliar position of strength. From that perspective Israel was not only the traditional enemy of Arab nationalism and the usurper of the Golan Heights but a geopolitical rival in the same part of the Middle East.

The emergence of a powerful Syrian state was an important catalyst to the collapse of the Lebanese state and political system through the civil war of 1975–76. For Syria this presented an opportunity to establish and con-solidate her hegemony over both Lebanon and the PLO, and a danger – a premature collision with Israel, which had its own vital interests in Lebanon. In March 1976 Asad, after much agonizing, decided on a direct military intervention in Lebanon. Through Henry Kissinger, a tacit, indirect understanding was worked out between him and Israel's Prime Minister Yitzhak Rabin. The Red Line agreement, as it came to be known, stipulated that Syria's troops would not cross a line drawn across the southern part of Lebanon. Thereby a Syrian-Israeli conflict was avoided for the time being, and the two countries displayed a surprising ability to tread softly in Lebanon when it came to each other's respective interests.[22]

For Syria the formation of its Lebanese patrimony brought about a pro-found change in perspective. The lines separating between great success and major failure, between lucrative opportunities and severe risks were very fine. As long as Syria's hold over Lebanon was not consolidated, Asad and his regime were preoccupied with their Lebanese investment, often at the expense of other foreign policy issues and considerations.

In November 1976, Jimmy Carter defeated Gerald Ford in the US pres-idential elections. The administration he formed in January 1977 had a view of the Arab-Israeli problem that was dramatically different from the policies identified with the person and era of Henry Kissinger. Several members of the new team were among the authors of the Brookings Report, a policy study sponsored by the Brookings Institution in 1976 in anticipation of the elections. In several respects the new administration seemed to have adopted the report as a blueprint for its Middle Eastern pol-icy. This meant abandoning the phased approach, a quest for a compre-hensive settlement, and a special emphasis on the Palestinian issue as the core of the conflict and the key to its resolution.[23]

The new policies led the Carter Administration to attach a particular importance to Syria. A comprehensive solution required an Arab consen-sus, and Syria's participation was deemed essential. Its pre-eminence in Lebanon also gave Syria a veto power over the PLO, and Syria offered an additional challenge of particular interest to American policy makers – it was the unfriendly actor, a Soviet client, a regime that had to be won over. Asad was invited to a meeting with Carter in Geneva in May 1977. The results were mixed. Carter was profoundly impressed by Asad and left with the impression that he had persuaded him to participate in his efforts. As he wrote in one version of his memoirs:

> I came away from our first meeting convinced that he would be powerful and flexible enough to modify his political tactics to changing times and circumstances. Even in his bitterness toward Israel, he retained a certain wry humor about their conflicting views, and he seemed to derive great patience from his obvious sense of history. He professed to speak for other Arabs, but seemed confident that his influence would be felt in seeking any permanent resolution of differences.[24]

But in the other version of his memoirs, the same US president vented his frustration with the same Syrian leader: 'This was the man who would soon sabotage the Geneva peace talks by refusing to attend under any reasonable circumstances, and would, still later, do everything possible to prevent the Camp David Accords from being fulfilled.'[25]

The policies of the Carter Administration in the Middle East had one unintended consequence: they encouraged Anwar al-Sadat and the newly elected prime minister of Israel, Menahem Begin, to establish a direct channel and to seek a separate Egyptian-Israeli agreement. Washington abandoned its original scheme and moved to play a crucial role in accomplishing the Camp David Accords (September 1978) and the Egyptian-Israeli Peace Treaty (March 1979). Israel agreed to withdraw in phases from the whole of the Sinai and to remove all Israeli presence, military and civilian. In return Egypt agreed to full peace and normalization, with Israel as well as to severe limitations on her own military presence in the Sinai, so as to turn it into an effective buffer zone between the two states. The agreements also provided for Palestinian self-rule in the West Bank and the Gaza Strip for an interim period of five years, and stipulated that 'the principles and provisions described below should apply to peace treaties between Israel and each of its neighbors: Egypt, Jordan, Syria, and Lebanon.'[26]

But Syria was not mollified by this implicit reference to the Golan. Asad had rejected Sadat's invitation to join him in his journey to Jerusalem in November 1977, and he had followed the ensuing chain of events with a mixture of disbelief and rage. As he saw it, Sadat broke ranks with him and the other Arabs, betrayed the most sacred Arab causes, and undermined everybody else's capacity to stand up to Israel or to negotiate with it properly if it ever came to that. The specific terms of the Camp David Accords were seen by him as a bad deal, an outcome to be expected when an Arab leader reverses the obvious sequence in negotiations with Israel and begins by offering the ultimate concession – recognition and acceptance. Yet as the

Egyptian-Israeli peace process progressed into implementation, Asad had to confront a significant body of opinion in Syria that pointed to the fact that Sadat did succeed in regaining the whole of the Sinai while Syria seemed to opt neither for war nor for diplomacy.[27]

Together with Iraq, Syria led the Arab opposition to Sadat's policies, and once Iraq became embroiled in war with Iran Damascus remained the sole leader of the campaign to isolate and punish Egypt and to undermine the peace that had been made with Israel. Like most Arab states, Syria severed diplomatic relations with Egypt and Asad vowed that Syria's flag would not be hoisted in Cairo as long as Israel's flag flew in that city.

The challenge presented by Egypt's peace with Israel was but one of the difficulties that plunged Asad's Ba'th regime into a long and deep crisis in the late 1970s and early 1980s. Domestically the regime contended for several years with the radical Islamic opposition that it finally crushed in the blood bath of Hamah in February 1982. The Israeli government of Menahem Begin sought to take advantage of this weakness in order to change the rules of the game in Lebanon. Begin was of the opinion that Rabin's 'Red Line agreement' with Syria gave the latter undue advantages in Lebanon, that under its terms Syria was consolidating her control over Lebanon, and the PLO was building a virtual ministate in Beirut and south Lebanon. Various members of Begin's government formulated different strategies for dealing with the Israeli Syrian-Lebanese-Palestinian quadrangle: some thought that Asad would be willing to give up the Golan in return for Israeli recognition of Syria's control of Lebanon. Others cultivated an ever-expanding alliance with Bashir Jumayyil's Lebanese forces as a strategic partner against both Syria and the PLO.

In 1981 the Begin government sustained three setbacks: Syria's tactical victory in the 'missile crisis' in Lebanon during the spring, the unsuccessful artillery duel with the PLO that ended with a ceasefire in July, and Sadat's assassination in October. Begin struck back by extending Israeli law over the Golan on 14 December 1981 (by choosing this formula he stopped short of actual annexation). But his more fundamental response to the growing sense that the hopes he had pinned on his peace agreement with Egypt were being frustrated was the green light he gave in November 1981 to the authors of the Lebanon War.[28]

The war was finally launched in June 1982. Its chief architect, Defence Minister Ariel Sharon, set himself ambitious goals: to destroy the PLO's infrastructure in Beirut and south Lebanon, to help Israel's ally Bashir Jumayyil take over the Lebanese state, to destroy Syria's position and military presence in Lebanon and, ultimately, to create a new balance in the region and in Israeli-Arab relations. Asad assumed erroneously at the war's outset that it was directed solely at the PLO, and sought to avoid direct confrontation with the more powerful IDF. When he discovered his mistake his anti-aircraft missile batteries and more than a hundred airplanes had been destroyed. Syria fought well on the ground and its troops' performance played a significant role in slowing down and confounding Israel's original plan.

Yet even Israel's partial success presented Syria with a dangerous challenge. By early September, Bashir Jumayyil was elected Lebanon's president and the country was likely to come under American and Israeli influence. Syria's enormous investment in Lebanon was about to be lost, and the probable repercussions for Asad's regime were alarming. Against this background Asad's ability to regroup, fight back and, ultimately, win was most impressive. He was ruthless in his choice of method (from Bashir Jumayyil's assassination to close collaboration with Iran and Lebanese Shi'ite terrorists), and cunning in manipulating the Lebanese arena, maximizing his assets, and taking full advantage of American and Israeli vulnerabilities. By 1984 the Reagan Administration withdrew the troops it had dispatched to Lebanon, Israel withdrew her forces to the Awali River in the south, and the Lebanese Administration of Amin Jumayyil abrogated the 17 May agreement with Israel that US Secretary of State George Schultz had brokered in 1983.

In September 1984 a national unity government was formed in Israel with Shimon Peres as prime minister and Yitzhak Rabin as defence minister. Peres and Rabin carried the cabinet with them against the opposition of most of the Likud ministers to decide on a withdrawal from Lebanon. Rabin tried to repeat his success of 1976 and to negotiate through the United States a tacit understanding with Asad with regard to south Lebanon. But by that time Asad felt secure in Lebanon and saw no reason to limit his position through an agreement with Israel. Given his attitude, Israel decided on a unilateral withdrawal to the line that has since defined her 'security strip' in south Lebanon.[29]

Asad's impressive string of successes against the United States, Israel, and his Lebanese adversaries endowed him with a fresh sense of confidence and security. Even a serious illness and its domestic political ramifications (November 1983–May 1984) did not cause more than a temporary setback. An emboldened Asad developed a doctrine of 'strategic parity' with Israel. According to the new doctrine Syria could and should build her military forces to the point of being able to face Israel on her own without Egyptian or Iraqi participation in a prospective confrontation.

Another manifestation of Asad's new boldness was his readiness to rely on terrorism as an instrument of foreign policy, and to allow Syria to become directly involved (and implicated) in operations directed at the

United States and Israel in the mid-1980s. But the methods that served Syria well in Lebanon backfired later. Syria was put on the State Department's list of states supporting terrorism and was subjected to British sanctions. Without ever accepting the Western definition of terrorism, Asad modified Syria's policies in 1986. Asad apparently instructed his subordinates to avoid direct Syrian involvement in terrorist activities, but he allowed Palestinian and other groups engaged in terrorism to remain on Syrian and Syrian-controlled soil. This fine distinction has not been shared by successive US Administrations that kept Syria on the terrorism and (separately) drug lists even as relations improved and a dialogue was established.[30]

In any event, Asad's sense of complacency in the mid-1980s was short-lived. By 1987 the Soviet Union was in rapid decline and Asad's universe was being transformed.

THE ROAD TO MADRID

In 1987 Hafiz al-Asad and Yitzhak Shamir, Menahem Begin's successor as leader of the Likud, probably did not envisage that in four years' time they would be taking their countries into an international peace conference seeking a comprehensive solution to the Arab-Israeli conflict and predicated on a set of terms that was as yet unacceptable to both. The remarkable transformation that accounted for this evolution resulted from the combined effect of the decline of the Soviet Union, the Palestinian *intifadah* (uprising), and the Gulf crisis and Gulf War.[31]

The decline and subsequent dissolution of the Soviet Union and the end of the Cold War had a profound impact on Syria and on its Middle Eastern environment. The Soviet-Syrian relationship was rich in tension and ambivalence, but the Soviet Union was a superpower patron, the principal source of weapon systems, Syria's mainstay in the international arena and, ultimately, the guarantor of the regime's security. From mid-1987 it became increasingly and painfully clear that the Soviet Union was improving its own relationship with Israel, avoiding confrontation with the United States in the Arab-Israeli arena, and ceasing to subsidize and fund the supply of armaments to Syria. The Soviets told the Syrians that the doctrine of 'strategic parity' should be replaced by a more realistic doctrine of 'defensive sufficiency'. Other related developments – Soviet-Jewish immigration to Israel, in particular – indicated to Syria, and to other proponents of Arab steadfastness, that after all time might not be on their side.

The first clear sign that Asad had thought through the implications of these developments for his country's foreign policies came in December 1989, when he paid his first visit to Egypt since the breakdown of the late 1970s.

During his visit he accompanied President Mubarak to Sharm al-Shaykh in the Sinai Peninsula and soon thereafter restored diplomatic relations with Egypt. The message and the symbolism could not have been clearer. After twelve years of leading the campaign against Sadat and his policies, Asad was laying down his arms. The Syrian flag was hoisted in Cairo alongside the Israeli flag; and Asad must have realized that by visiting Sharm al-Shaykh he was visiting a particularly significant part of the Sinai – a territory lost in 1967 and recovered through the very peace negotiation that Asad had denounced so vehemently. Beyond the symbolism lay a substantive change of policy and direction. The disappearance of Soviet patronage required that a new relationship be built with the United States. Like Sadat in the early 1970s, Asad understood that for a qualitative change to take place in his relationship with Washington he would have to enter into a peace process with Israel.

During the same years Israel was going through a rude awakening of its own. The outbreak of the Palestinian intifadah in December 1987 and its subsequent unfolding altered a fundamental reality of Israeli-Palestinian relations during the previous twenty years. Israel had coped successfully with all forms of Palestinian resistance and opposition, so that the Israeli body politic did not feel an urgent need to make the painful choices that any solution regarding the West Bank required. The form of opposition developed spontaneously through the intifadah, however, was exacting a price that large segments of Israeli society were not willing to pay.

The Israeli elections of 1988 produced a second national unity government. But given the slight edge it acquired, the Likud was given the prime minister's position for the full period. Yitzhak Rabin remained defence minister, and Shimon Peres became minister of finance. Tensions surfaced soon thereafter. Labour was determined to work together with the Bush Administration in order to start a negotiation process with the Palestinians. Prime Minister Shamir and some of his colleagues rejected the terms put forth by Secretary of State James Baker. In March 1990 the Labour party's leader, Shimon Peres, seized on the Likud's rejection of James Baker's 'five-point plan' to start negotiations with the Palestinians, and brought the government down. His expectation that he would be able to form a new government was ultimately frustrated, and on 11 June 1990, Yitzhak Shamir formed a Likud government in coalition with his customary partners.

These developments and their immediate repercussions were soon overshadowed by the Iraqi invasion of Kuwait and the ensuing Gulf crisis and Gulf War. Syria's particular reaction to Saddam Husayn's move and its conduct during the following months were fashioned by a complex set of considerations. Given the profound hostility between the two regimes and the two leaders, Syria was alarmed by the prospect of an Iraqi success. If

Saddam's gambit were to prove successful, a stronger and bolder Iraq would present an even greater threat to Hafiz al-Asad and his regime. As the United States began to organize an Arab and international coalition against Iraq, the potential advantages of Syrian membership were obvious – obstructing Saddam Husayn, building the dialogue with Washington that Asad had always wanted and was now eager to have and, if Damascus played its cards wisely, additional advantages that could be obtained as inducements for joining. There was also a down side. Joining the United States and Saudi Arabia in a wartime coalition against a Ba'th regime in Iraq might be awkward, and would expose the regime to domestic criticism. Asad was conscious of the fact that while Saddam Husayn was trying to rekindle the ashes of revolutionary pan-Arab nationalism he, Asad, was mounting the post-Cold-War path of dialogue with the United States and with Israel.

Asad's progression along that path was not swift or linear. He did join the coalition and did dispatch a reinforced division to Saudi Arabia, but his troops did not participate in the actual fighting. This did not constitute a real problem for the senior American partner. The United States needed Syria in the coalition not as a fighting force but in order to demonstrate that it was not a Western conservative alliance against radical Arab nationalism. On the domestic front, the regime mounted an effective campaign explaining and defending its choice of allies, and in fact encountered very little overt criticism. As a foreign policy investment Syria's participation in the coalition paid off handsomely. A new relationship was formed with the United States, Saudi Arabia provided Syria with three billion dollars, and the United States and Saudi Arabia, the two principal champions of the Taif Accords, were willing to look the other way when Syria tightened its grip on Lebanon.[32]

The Bush Administration, true to its word, moved soon after the end of the Gulf War to set an Arab-Israeli peace process in motion. President Bush and Secretary Baker felt that the crisis and the war served both to underline the urgency and to improve the prospects of a major effort to resolve or at least ameliorate the Arab-Israeli conflict. During the next seven months they devoted considerable resources to the task of narrowing the differences between the Arab and Israeli views of substance and process. Some of them had to do with the Palestinian issue, but Secretary Baker's greatest effort had to be invested in finding a format and a set of terms that would be acceptable to both Hafiz al-Asad and Yitzhak Shamir.

Asad's original concept was that of an international conference in which the Arab parties, Israel, the United States, and the USSR as well as the United Nations and the European Community would participate. The conference would remain in session and would serve as the principal arena of negotiation, with bilateral negotiations limited to a minimum. According to Asad

the scope of negotiations would be very limited, anyway, since he demanded that the conference be convened on the basis of Security Council Resolutions 242 and 338 and on the principle of 'territories for peace'. Israel's
full withdrawal from the Golan Heights was to be a point of departure and
the negotiations could focus on the implementation of that withdrawal.

Little of this was acceptable to Shamir. He saw the international conference as a festive inaugural event to be followed by direct bilateral Israeli
negotiations with the different Arab delegations. He championed the Israeli
interpretation of Resolution 242 (withdrawal from some of the territories)
and the Likud view that Israel had already met that demand when it withdrew from the Sinai. He was adamantly opposed to the notion of 'territories for peace' and objected to the participation of the United Nations and
the European Community in the conference.

In nine trips to the Middle East, Secretary Baker worked out a compromise. The conference, to be held in Madrid, would be attended by representatives of the United Nations and the European Community (as well as
the Gulf Cooperation Council) but would actually serve as a prelude to
bilateral negotiations. The letter of imitation would rely on Resolutions
242 and 338, but the term 'territories for peace' would be used in letters
of assurance addressed by the United States to the Arab participants but not
to Israel. Multilateral working groups would meet to discuss five regional
issues, but Syria (and Lebanon) would not attend.[33] This accomplished, the
Madrid conference was convened.

There are two ways of looking at the first phase of Syrian negotiations
that emerged from the Madrid conference. One would emphasize, as most
accounts have, the harsh and negative aspects of what seemed more like a
confrontation than a negotiation. After an initial encounter in Madrid,
Israeli and Syrian delegations began to meet in scheduled negotiating
rounds in Washington. Three Israeli delegations met with three Arab delegations — Syrian, Lebanese, and Jordanian-Palestinian. Progress was not
made on any of the four tracks, but while civility was maintained in the
Jordanian and Lebanese tracks the meetings with the Syrians and
Palestinians were tense.

As his negotiator with Israel, Asad appointed Muwaffaq 'Allaf, a retired
Syrian diplomat who had served as an Arab diplomat at the United Nations
and as Syria's ambassador to Vienna before his retirement. Except for one
army officer, General 'Adnan Tayyarah, in charge of foreign liaison, the delegation was composed entirely of diplomats. The Israeli delegation was
headed by Yossi Ben-Aharon, the director general of the prime minister's
office, a member of the inner core of Yitzhak Shamir's government, and
one of the chief architects of its policies. The members of his delegation,

in the best tradition of the Israeli government's pluralistic approach, represented a plethora of government departments and agencies.

Neither Ben-Aharon nor 'Allaf came to Washington to look for the middle ground on which a deal was to be made. Both represented leaders who sent their men to Madrid and Washington with a message defined by reluctance, scepticism, and suspicion. For both delegations the conference room in the State Department building was as much an arena for debate and vindication as a site for potential peacemaking. Since both countries assumed that the negotiations were likely to fail, much of what was said in the conference room and in the media stakeouts was designed for immediate and future public consumption.

The atmosphere in the conference room was tense and unpleasant. The Syrians, in the familiar tradition of denial of recognition, refused to shake hands with their Israeli counterparts. When a coffee break was announced they darted out of the room lest they be perceived to have shared a cup of coffee with the Israelis. In the absence of a chairperson there was often acrimonious squabbling over the right to speak. Much of the speaking was actually closer to haranguing. Yet through the rhetoric the two diametrically opposed positions could be discerned. The Syrians insisted that for peace to happen Israel had first to agree to a full withdrawal from the Golan Heights as decreed by Security Council Resolution 242 and by 'international legitimacy'. The Israeli position was a derivative of the Shamir government's 'peace for peace' policy. Security Council Resolution 242 demanded that the Arabs give Israel peace within 'secure and recognized' boundaries in return for withdrawal from some of the territory captured in June 1967. By withdrawing from the bulk of the territory (the Sinai) Israel had met her obligations and was now entitled to peace with her other Arab neighbours without offering any additional territorial concessions.

The two positions were, needless to say, irreconcilable. The gap was compounded by sharp disagreements over the past and by mutual demonization. In Syria's version Israel was an expansionist aggressor who had been violating the armistice agreement between 1949 and 1967 and then had launched an aggressive war through which it added the Golan Heights to its unlawful possessions. Israel's narrative was that of an aggressive Syria that for nineteen years had been shelling and shooting at Israeli civilians from the Golan Heights and in the 1960s plunged the region into the 1967 War. Israel took the Golan Heights in self-defence and was holding on to them lawfully. And if the Syrians condemned the Israelis as expansionist oppressive usurpers and occupiers, the Israelis retorted by denouncing the Syrians as the oppressive occupiers of Lebanon and merchants of regional and international terrorism.

It is easy to make light of this chapter in the history of the Israeli- Syrian negotiations and to register their negative impact in reinforcing the negative views and stereotypes that Israelis and Syrians had of each other. But when I was entrusted in July 1992 with the conduct of Israel's end of the negotiations, and took a closer and better informed look at the first five rounds of negotiations, I could also see their valuable side. Israeli and Syrian representatives had not met and talked for forty years. A pre-negotiating phase was required before a real negotiation could begin. The contradictory versions of the past had to be confronted and the legacy of grievances unburdened before a rational negotiation and quest for settlement began. Even when we met under different and more pleasant circumstances in August 1992 a new page could not simply be turned, but a great deal of aggravation could be and in fact was saved.

I subsequently found out that there was more to the Shamir government's policies and to Syrian-Israeli contacts than in the formal accounts of the first five rounds. Alongside the mainstream Likud position that opposed any, let alone major, territorial concessions in the Golan as part of a settlement with Syria, there had for years been voices in the Likud that argued the merits of repeating with Syria what Begin had done with Egypt, as long as the principal task of preserving Israel's control of the land of Israel was accomplished. Early in 1992, a secret, parallel, channel to Syria was opened. I later came to know the person who had carried the messages between Jerusalem and Damascus. He continued to carry messages between some Israelis and some Syrians in later years, as well. Official negotiators are probably never enamoured of emissaries whose *raison d'être* is to bypass official channels, but I had additional reasons for doubting the value of this particular go-between. In any event, he was authorized in 1992 to convey to his Syrian contacts that, contrary to the line projected by Yossi Ben-Aharon in the Washington talks, the Shamir government did not rule out the possibility of some territorial concessions in the Golan as part of an Israeli-Syrian settlement. But in the spring of 1992 the Syrians lost whatever interest they may have had in the Shamir government's gambit, as the June elections in Israel drew closer.

ISRAEL AND SYRIA, RABIN AND ASAD

The Israeli-Syrian negotiations of the years 1992–95 were shaped by numerous forces, but they were dominated by the personalities of Yitzhak Rabin and Hafiz al-Asad. In the summer of 1992 both men were at the apex of long and impressive military and political careers that had unfolded during the previous five decades in very different environments. Both leaders had interacted in the past and had developed a grudging respect for each other. Asad, of course, was the one unquestioned leader of a person-alized one-party regime whereas Rabin headed a coalition government resting on a small parliamentary majority, and was also constrained by sig-nificant limitations within his own party, cabinet, and government. Yet, in their different styles both men shaped their countries' approach to negoti-ations and conducted them directly or through their emissaries.

When the Labour party won the Israeli elections on 23 June 1992, Yitzhak Rabin became prime minister for the second time, fifteen years after he resigned that post in March 1977. This unusual return to power reflected Rabin's perception by the Israeli public as 'Mr National Security', the authoritative figure who could lead their country through a peace process without eroding its security. Rabin's stature was the product of his career and personality. He had volunteered for the Palmach, the elite unit of the Haganah, the IDF's precursor, in May 1941, was a young and promi-nent brigade commander in Israel's War of Independence, and in 1964 became the IDF's chief of staff. In that capacity he prepared and led the IDF through the brilliant military victory of 1967. Rabin had to share the glory with another major figure – Moshe Dayan, who became defence minister on the eve of the war. But to Israelis and Arabs, in the Jewish world and in the international arena, he was to remain the great chief of staff of the Six Day War.[34]

In 1968, when he retired from the IDF, he chose to become Israel's ambassador to the United States. His tenure as ambassador, the relationships he built with Richard Nixon, Henry Kissinger, and the congressional lead-ership, and the role he played in the high international drama of the war of attrition and the Jordanian crisis of September 1970 added significant new dimensions to his persona and public image. Rabin was designated by Golda Meir and the Labour party to a leadership role upon his return to Israel in 1973. His election to the Knesset and his appointment as minister of labour in Golda Meir's last cabinet were the standard fare for a senior Israeli gen-eral entering the political fray. It. was the fall of Golda Meir's government in the aftermath of the October War debacle that catapulted Rabin to the cen-ter of Israeli politics. As a venerable military commander with international stature and diplomatic experience, his reputation untarnished by the October debacle, he was chosen by the parry elders as Golda Meir's succes-sor in May 1974. The choice was challenged by Shimon Peres, and the issue was decided by a vote in the party centre; which Rabin won by a 60:40 ratio. A deal was made whereby Peres was given the Ministry of Defence in Rabin's government, and the mixed pattern of the two men's rivalry and partnership was set for the next twenty-two years.

A comparison of Rabin's two terms as prime minister reveals his capacity to learn, grow, and develop. Yitzhak Rabin of the years 1974–77 was not the mature, confident, and authoritative statesman of the 1990s. He had been, at 52, his country's youngest and first Israeli-born prime minister. The young prime minister was not comfortable with politics and politicians. He was cerebral, direct and blunt. His government rested on a narrow parliamentary basis and within the government he felt challenged and undermined by the defence minister. Domestically, the country and the government were buffeted by the forces that were about to end some fifty years of Labor hegemony in pre-state and independent Israel. In Israel's relations with the Arab world crucial choices had to be made. Rabin preferred a careful, gradual approach. An important interim agreement was concluded with Egypt and a crisis was averted in Lebanon, but painful decisions concerning the Palestinian issue and the future of the West Bank were avoided.

In March 1977 Rabin resigned over a personal embarrassment – a bank account maintained by his wife in Washington. It was the right thing to do, and it also kept him at some distance from the Labour party's first electoral defeat in May of that year. The next seven years were an awkward, difficult period for Yitzhak Rabin, involving the continuing rivalry with Shimon Peres inside the Labor party and the need to form responses to the policies of Menahem Begin, who took Israel to the heights of peace with Egypt and to the depth of the Lebanon War. Rabin emerged from this period with his stature rebuilt as the authority on national security, a leader who was somewhat removed from partisan politics. Within the Labour party a truce was achieved whereby Shimon Peres remained the party's leader and its candidate for prime minister, and Rabin was second in command and candidate for the post of defence minister.

These roles and images were reinforced by two versions of national unity governments between 1984 and 1990. While Peres and Menahem Begin's successor, Yitzhak Shamir, alternated as prime minister, Rabin served through the period as a powerful and quite autonomous defence minister. After March 1990, when the Labour party brought down the second national unity government, Rabin launched yet another challenge to Shimon Peres's leadership. The next parliamentary elections were scheduled for June 1992, and the thrust of Rabin's campaign within the Labour party was that he alone could return the party to power, that the particular image he projected and the more centrist policy he presented would provide the victory that had eluded Shimon Peres in 1981, 1984 and 1988.

Rabin at seventy won the Labour party's primaries in February 1992, and moved on to the general elections campaign. It was a very personalized campaign ('Labour headed by Rabin') that criticized the Likud government on two inter-related principal issues: its inability to manage both the Madrid peace process and the American-Israeli relationship. Rabin and Labour won and on 13 July 1992, he presented his new government to the Knesset.

The new prime minister was determined to effect real changes. He had a clear sense that he was not given a rare opportunity – a second term fifteen years after his first one – just in order to spend time in office. He was determined to change the national agenda set by the previous government by reigniting the Madrid peace process. This was important in itself and key to improving relations with the United States. That accomplished, the loan guarantees would be released and the necessary investments could be made to absorb the new wave of immigrants and to build the infrastructure for the next phase in Israel's development.

Rabin saw no problem in removing the two difficulties that had obstructed Israel's relationship with the United States and their co-operation in moving the peace process forward. He was willing to suspend the construction of new settlements and to accept the principle of peace based on territorial compromise (as distinct from the previous government's formula of 'peace for peace'). As defence minister he had been willing to resort to harsh measures in order to defeat the Palestinian *intifadah*, because in his view it was a new round in conflict between Israel and Palestinian nationalism that Israel could not afford to lose. But the lesson of the *intifadah* was not lost on him – after twenty years of futile resistance the Palestinians had stumbled upon an effective form of resistance that made the price of continued control of Gaza and the West Bank prohibitive. Rabin's approach to the issue was pragmatic not ideological or moral. Israel in his eyes had as good a claim to the West Bank as the Palestinians, but the bulk of the West Bank was inhabited by Palestinians and that was an unchangeable fact. That being the case, he saw no point in constructing new settlements in the midst of Palestinian areas, in expending a significant portion of Israel's resources in the West Bank, in keeping the IDF busy policing the area, or in spoiling Israel's relationship with the United States over these issues. Nor did he believe in packing and leaving. He believed – and so stated in his election campaign that a genuine autonomy could be agreed upon between Israel and the Palestinians, and that this could be accomplished within nine months.

Rabin was less sanguine with regard to an Israeli-Syrian settlement. The former general commanding officer of the Northern Command and the former chief of staff had vivid memories of the fierce conflicts with Syria in the 1950s and 1960s. He was impressed by his ability to reach a tacit agreement with Asad over Lebanon in 1976 and by Syria's strict enforcement of the

Disengagement Agreement since 1974, but he was doubtful that Syria's concept of peace and Israel's stake in the Golan Heights could be reconciled. This view informed his election campaign, which laid the emphasis on reaching an agreement with the Palestinians and made virtually no mention of a serious prospect of negotiations with Syria.

Rabin's own perspective changed soon after his election. Secretary of State Baker came for his last visit in that capacity to the Middle East. He travelled first to Damascus and then to Jerusalem, where he told Rabin that Asad was seriously interested in making peace with Israel and that the Bush Administration was ready to make a significant investment in obtaining and securing an Israeli-Syrian agreement. Rabin was impressed but not persuaded, and he was certainly ready to explore Syria's position and its repercussions for the peace process that he was about to galvanize.

In the mid-1940s, when Yitzhak Rabin was an officer in the Palmach, Hafiz al-Asad, born in 1930, was a high-school student in Latakiyya, a provincial port in north-western Syria. Asad came from the large village of Kardaha in the hills just east of the coast. This was the land of the 'Alawis, a heterodox Islamic sect that makes up about 12 per cent of Syria's population. The 'Alawis were rural, tribal, and downtrodden. For centuries they had been persecuted, exploited, and despised by Muslim-Sunni central governments and by Muslim-Sunni landlords living in cities like Hama and Latakiyya. When France took control of Syria, it cultivated the 'Alawis, encouraged their separatism, and recruited many of them into the colonial levy. But by the mid-1940s France was on her way out, and the 'Alawis were being integrated into the state of Syria by the Arab nationalist government in Damascus. Young men of Asad's generation were undergoing political socialization in a very politicized high school in the provincial capital. Of the variety of ideological movements that competed for the allegiance of his generation, Asad, like so many other young 'Alawis, chose the Ba'th. The Ba'th offered a radical secular version of Arab nationalism that proved to be particularly attractive to members of the minority communities.

The pattern continued. Like so many other young 'Alawis (and members of other minority communities), Asad proceeded from high school to the military academy in Homs. A military career was a major channel of upward mobility in Syria in the 1940s and 1950s. In the military academy and later as an air force pilot, Asad continued his membership and activities in the ranks of the Ba'th. These were exciting years. Army officers and their civilian allies toppled the old order in Syria, plunged the country into a series of *coups d'état*, and turned it into the focal point of regional and international conflicts. The Ba'th party allied itself with Gamal 'Abd al-Nasir, the messianic leader of pan-Arab nationalism, and in February 1958 led Syria into an unsuccessful union with Egypt. The union broke up in September 1961, but successive Syrian governments were hard put to consolidate Syria's existence as an independent state.

Hafiz al-Asad, now a retired air force major, was a member of a small secretive group that masterminded the coup which on 8 March 1963, brought the Ba'th to power in Syria. Their experience during the previous five years had set them against 'Abd al-Nasir and against the founding fathers of the Ba'th party. But as a small cell operating behind the scenes and through the military and political powers of others, they had to dissimulate and to act cautiously, It was only after the intra-Ba'th coup of 23 February 1966, that they rid themselves of their partners and took full power into their hands. Asad became acting minister of defense but retained his personal power base as commander of the air force, Asad's title 'Acting Minister of Defense' was an early and curious manifestation of Asad's fondness for the formalistic and legalistic side of things. The Ba'th party's rules stipulated that a member could hold either a military command or a ministerial post. Asad was determined to hold both, but also to observe the letter if not the spirit of the party's constitution.

A much more significant aspect of Syrian politics in the mid-1960s and of Asad's rise to power was the emergence of sectarian loyalties and rivalries as a governing factor and a major issue. As we saw earlier, members of the 'Alawi and other minority communities (primarily Druze and Isma'ili) tended to join both the military and the Ba'th party. Consequently, when a group of Ba'thi army officers seized power in Syria it included a disproportionate number of minorities. In the factional and personal conflicts of the 1960s primordial group solidarity became an important factor. And once the sectarian genie was out of the bottle, there was no containing it. At some point an invisible line was crossed and an innocuous sense of familiarity and solidarity turned into deliberate coordination. And once Asad and a group of 'Alawi military and civilians found themselves in control of the regime (having eliminated the Druze and Isma'ili factions) they felt threatened by the resentful Sunni majority. The tension between a regime dominated by a sectarian minority and a resentful majority remained acute for nearly twenty years.

It was hardly surprising that when members of the core group of the Ba'th regime had eliminated all their partners they turned upon each other. The unexpected development was Hafiz al-Asad's victory. During the Ba'th's first years in power Asad was considered a grey, slow, somewhat awkward politician, while his chief rival Salah Jadid was regarded as a political mastermind, a cunning manipulator. But when matters came to a head in 1969–70, it transpired that behind the stodgy facade lay a brilliant tactician. Asad was deliberate, patient, and cool-headed. He had gradually built a power base in both the army and the party. And when he decided to act in November 1970, he did not stage a coup but took full power into his hands and was soon ready to present a complete governing apparatus as well as a set of integrated policies.

The intra-Ba'th conflict of the late 1960s was first and foremost a personal and factional struggle for power. But there were also genuine differences of policy and substance. Asad represented a pragmatic approach. Within Syria he was not interested in deepening the social and economic revolution but in finding a *modus vivendi* with the Sunni urban groups, as long as they accepted the regime and did not meddle in politics. Regionally he sought accommodation and cooperation with Egypt and the Arab mainstream. And internationally, although he continued to rely on the Soviet Union as Syria's superpower patron, he was anxious to open a dialogue with the United States.

Asad's first years in power were on the whole a remarkable success. After twenty-five years of proverbial instability he formed a comparatively stable and durable government. On the basis of that stability he conducted an effective foreign policy that turned Syria into a regional power. His conduct of the post-October War negotiations, his role in the Lebanese crisis, and the anti-Egyptian campaign he mounted in the aftermath of the second Sinai agreement all bore testimony to Syria's new status in Middle Eastern and international politics.

Asad's personality was an important component of Syria's newly acquired stature. By the early 1980s Asad had built a reputation as a cunning and effective negotiator, an excellent strategist and tactician, and a leader whose personal charm and sense of humour served to conceal the brutal power that he and his regime would use when challenged. In the international arena it was Henry Kissinger's memoirs that did more than any other publication to build Asad's complex image. In the Middle East context it was Karim Pakradouni, a Lebanese politician, the principal liaison between Syria and the Phalanges (the essentially Maronite-Christian party), who drew Asad's fullest and most flattering profile. Despite the occasional over-statement, Pakradouni's account is very useful in offering both a description of Asad's *modus operandi* in the 1970s and early 1980s and a sense of the image Asad himself sought to project.

> In carrying out his designs, Asad is implacable, cautious and unyielding. He has built his authority stone by stone; he is never in haste, he never gets excited and rarely raises his tone. He prefers to get what he wants by stealth and he employs persuasive before dissuasive methods.

He chooses his moment perfectly, waiting for the right opportunity, letting his own strength build up while his opponents get weaker. He will not negotiate from a position of weakness, lest his adversary be tempted to wring something out of him; when he is in a position of strength he regards any concession as an unnecessary gift. He believes that everything has its price, but that it is up to him to decide what the price shall be. He will not let himself be constrained by limits or conditions laid down by others.

When entering negotiations he adopts an impassive face. The stage setting is always the same. He usually knows his subject in depth; be has an elephantine memory and a prodigious ability to concentrate.

Sometimes, the meeting itself will be the subject of negotiation. He is an unpredictable, wily negotiator who is as capable of treating a serious problem in cavalier fashion as he is of declining to give an exact reply to a simple question. If be promises something it is as good as done, but when he wants to refuse he will say 'I shall talk this over with X or Y' or 'I shall examine this question'.[35]

Asad's initial achievements were marred in the latter half of the 1970s by a host of domestic and external problems: the lingering animosity of the urban Sunni population, the Muslim fundamentalist offensive, dissension and corruption within the regime's ranks, the rivalry with Saddam's Iraq and Husayn's Jordan, the challenge of Israeli-Egyptian peace, and the mounting cost of maintaining Syria's new fiefdom in Lebanon. The difficulties reached their zenith in 1982. In February of that year Asad's soldiers quashed yet another Muslim rebellion in the city of Hama with unprecedented brutality, killing some 15,000 of the city's residents. In June Israel launched its war in Lebanon and in early September seemed to have destroyed Syria's enormous investment there. But Asad fought back, and did so with great success and brought his and his country's prestige to a new height.

The same pattern – oscillation between periods of success and achievements and points of crisis – continued in the latter half of the 1980s. Its persistence was a reflection of Asad's personal and political strengths, and of his unwillingness and inability to deal with his regime's structural flaws. Thus in the late 1980s, in response to the collapse of the Soviet Union and of close allies like Romania's Nicolae Ceausescu, Asad moved to build new relations with the United States and Egypt, but he failed to introduce meaningful political reforms in Syria. Having faced no serious domestic opposition in recent years, Asad may very well feel that he did the right thing.

During the four decades of his political career Hafiz al-Asad went through several radical changes of direction. A member of the Ba'th party, a paragon of Arab union in the 1940s and 1950s, he played a crucial role in the consolidation of Syria's independent existence in the 1960s. The leader of the Syrian Ba'th party and regime that had at one time been closely identified with notions of revolution, radicalism, and anti-imperialism, he took his country in 1990–91 into the American-led war coalition against the other Ba'th regime in Iraq. In some respects Asad's gradual acceptance of the notion of a political settlement with Israel in the late 1980s and early 1990s represented a similar departure from a seminal dimension of his personal and political history and make-up. And yet it was a different development. In Asad's own mind the transition from the role of Arab nationalism's standard bearer in the struggle against Israel to that of a peacemaker was more difficult than the decision to join the coalition against Iraq. Nor was Asad's soul-searching alleviated by the need to make sharp choices. It had been difficult to join the United States and Saudi Arabia in a wartime coalition against a radical Arab regime, but Asad's decision was eased by the obvious threat that the prospect of Saddam's victory represented. When it came to reconciliation with Israel, an equally dramatic threat or attraction was absent. The Bush Administration's invitation to Madrid required a significant decision by Asad. Yet Asad could tell himself that, important as his positive answer was, it fell short of a final, irreversible choice and commitment. Whatever his concept of settlement, the Shamir government's reluctance combined with his own reservations to produce meaningless negotiation requiring no painful choices. It was the arrival of Rabin's government that forced Asad to grapple fully with the most fundamental issues that the prospect of a genuine settlement with Israel raised for him and for Syria.

CONCLUSION

This account of nearly four years of serious negotiations between Israel and Syria raises several questions: why did the negotiations fail to produce an agreement? Was there a deal on the cards that was not turned from potential to reality? If so, why was a deal not made and what roles were played in this regard by the three participants in the negotiations, Israel, Syria, and the United States? Given the failure to reach an agreement, did the parties actually seek an agreement, or were they negotiating with other purposes in mind? What was the significance of the Israeli-Syrian negotiation within the larger scheme of the Israeli-Arab peace process and the regional politics of the Middle East? And finally, what has happened between Israel and Syria since the suspension of their negotiations, and what are the prospects of resuming a serious negotiation between the two countries in the foreseeable future?

At no time during this period (August 1992–March 1996) were Israel and Syria on the verge of a breakthrough. A breakthrough occurs when both sides realize that the main elements of the deal have been agreed upon; various details, some of them important, have yet to be finalized, a crisis may yet develop, but an invisible line has been crossed and both sides know that they have an agreement in hand.

The potential of getting to that point existed twice – in August 1993 and during the first few weeks of Shimon Peres's tenure as prime minister in November–December 1995. In early August 1993, Rabin sought to establish whether he had a viable option for a settlement with Syria as the cornerstone in his peacemaking strategy. Having failed in his persistent efforts to form a direct channel to Asad, he relied on the US secretary of state and authorized him to use the 'hypothetical question' technique in order to find out whether Asad was ready for the very specific package that Rabin regarded as acceptable to him and, ultimately, to the Israeli public. An element of flexibility was built into the package to be used in the inevitable process of bargaining, but a trained eye could easily identify the hard core of Rabin's position.

Asad's response was positive in principle, in that he told the secretary of state for the first time that, in return for the withdrawal he was asking for, he was willing to offer a full contractual peace. But his response to Rabin's specific peace package was disappointing. Two core elements were unacceptable to Asad: normalization and interface – Rabin's insistence on applying the Israeli-Egyptian model whereby a limited withdrawal would be matched by a comparatively long period of normalization so as to 'test' the new relationship before a large-scale withdrawal was undertaken. Asad also rejected Rabin's demands in two procedural matters (which for the Israeli prime minister were most important) – engaging in public diplomacy and establishing a discreet, bilateral channel. On other issues – the security arrangements and the time frame – his response indicated that a long and arduous bargaining process lay ahead. Asad, in other words, had his own specific peace package and he was willing to come to an agreement only on the basis of that package or a close approximation of it.

Rabin's package reflected his principal considerations: peace with Syria was important in itself and as an indispensable component of an eventual comprehensive settlement. But Asad would not make peace unless offered a full withdrawal. This was a price Rabin was most reluctant to pay. Furthermore, even if he personally overcame his own feelings he would find it difficult to rally a majority of Israelis to endorse it unless Asad was willing to make an investment in converting the Israeli public. Rabin's package and his procedural concomitants were designed to guarantee that

Israel ended up with a genuine peace, that the political and security risks were minimized, and that a political base of support for it could be built in Israel.

Rabin's reluctance was matched by Asad's ambiguity. He had made 'a strategic decision for peace' in the sense that he was now willing to make a contractual peace with Israel. He wanted to regain the Golan and to build a new relationship with the United States, and he had come to the conclusion that the two could not be obtained unless he were willing to sign a peace treaty with Israel. Asad believed that he could cope with this radical emotional and ideological departure from his past record, and that his regime could absorb the shock waves and the impact of the changes entailed in this decision. But this could only be done within a very particular definition of peace and of the procedure that led to it. Dignity was an important consideration, as were the sense of lingering geopolitical rivalry with Israel and of Syrian society's and political system's vulnerability to the impact of opening up in general, and to Israel specifically. Hence the insistence on a modest set of political and security arrangements to be offered in return for a withdrawal that Asad regarded as his due. Here, too, was a curious symmetry between the Israeli and Syrian positions. Asad believed that Israel was bound to withdraw; in his terminology it was 'an obligation' decreed by 'international legitimacy'. Israel did not deserve to be rewarded for fulfilling its obligation, and therefore everything that Syria might agree to that was not specified in Resolution 242 would be a concession. For Rabin, Israel's and his personal agreement to a massive withdrawal in the Golan would be a major concession, a radical departure from an entrenched policy, and a risky and costly step. For him what Syria was asked to give were not concessions but prerequisites for making his decisions justified and viable.

The gap between these two outlooks could conceivably be closed by the United States as the facilitator of the peace process and of the Israeli-Syrian track in particular. In Rabin's eyes this should have been done by pressuring Asad to accept the basic premises of his position. If the United States were to play the classic role of a mediator and come out with a compromise formula of sorts, his package would be eroded to the point of making the deal unacceptable. It is moot to speculate on the potential course of events had Asad accepted a greater part of Rabin's package or had the Clinton Administration decided to tell Asad that it viewed Rabin's package as an integrated whole and expected him to accept it if he wanted to move on in the peace process. Given the history of Washington's relations with Asad this could hardly be expected and, indeed, did not happen. During the previous two decades only one administration, Reagan's, was willing to be tough with Asad to the point of colliding with him in Lebanon, and it ended by withdrawing ignominiously. The Nixon, Ford, Carter, and Bush Administrations all tried with varying degrees of success to engage Asad. The Clinton Administration adopted the same approach. Nor did the administration expect Rabin to conclude the agreement with the PLO in Oslo within such a short time span. But under the combined impact of Asad's response and the administration's attitude, Rabin chose to make his move on the Palestinian track.

Given this turn of events, the prospect of an agreement with Syria before the end of Rabin's first term diminished progressively. True, some very significant negotiations took place (the 'ambassadors' channel' and the chiefs of staff's meetings in 1994 and 1995) and progress was made in the negotiations and in Asad's give-and-take with President Clinton and Secretary Christopher, but the passage of time had a negative effect on the Israeli-Syrian track. The events of August 1993 predicated the peace process on the Israeli-Palestinian track. The accent then shifted to the Israeli-Jordanian track. As time went by, Asad's ability to obtain an agreement with Israel that would be implemented within Rabin's term was lost. The passage of time also meant that opposition in Israel to Rabin's policy in the peace process and specifically to a settlement with Syria was building up. Asad in turn felt more relaxed in 1995 than he had in 1991–92, when the impact of the Soviet Union's collapse and the Gulf crisis was fresh.

Asad and Rabin became increasingly sceptical of each other. Rabin suspected that Asad was less interested in making peace than in obtaining Israeli and American commitments for withdrawal, that he was not interested in a genuine negotiation but in an American mediation that would meet him half-way without addressing the fundamental elements of Rabin's package. Asad suspected that Rabin had decided not to conclude an agreement with him during his first term and that he was keeping him last in line, expecting to consolidate the peace process, negotiating with Asad from a position of strength, and seeking to force him to come to an agreement on Israel's terms.

Asad's suspicions were not totally unfounded, in that Rabin had indeed believed since August 1993 that an agreement with Syria during his first term was unlikely. The events of August 1993, Clinton's summit with Asad in January 1994, Asad's stiffer position in April of that year, and the two crises that followed the chiefs of staff's meetings in 1994–95 all indicated to him that even if Asad had made a 'strategic choice for peace' it was encumbered by so many conditions, reservations, and inhibitions as to make it impractical. Rabin did not expect the Clinton Administration to deal with Asad more forcefully, and despite occasional references to the greater effectiveness of exerting geopolitical pressures on Asad he did not pursue this approach seriously.

Rabin knew that in the long term an agreement with Syria would have to be made for Israel's reconciliation with her Arab neighbours to be viable. But he was not in a hurry, and was certainly not willing to pay the price exacted in negotiations for being or appearing to be in a hurry. The Oslo agreements, peace with Jordan, and a degree of normalization with the Arab world were not a bad record for one term. If reelected, then from a stronger domestic base and with the achievements of the peace process under his belt he could continue the negotiations with Asad and seek closure with a surer hand. In the meantime he would respect his commitments to the American president and secretary of state, and keep Asad engaged in the negotiations even if that required occasional verbal concessions. Asad could, of course, upset this complex calculus by accepting the bulk of Rabin's package or by agreeing to a meeting, but this was not likely to happen.

Rabin was not alone in casting doubt on Asad's determination actually to conclude an agreement with Israel. Israeli politicians from both ends of the spectrum, policy analysts, and media commentators shared his scepticism. The fullest presentation of this interpretation was made by the American analyst Daniel Pipes. Writing in January 1996 at the high point of the Wye Plantation negotiations, Pipes argued that 'the Syrian and Israeli governments – despite their tense relations – have established the general contours of a peace agreement. In the four principal areas of negotiations, the two sides have no profound differences'. And yet, Pipes continued, an agreement had not been made and was not likely to be made because of President Asad's domestic political constraints and considerations. As a member of the 'Alawi minority community, he wrote, Asad was primarily concerned with his regime's survival and in a smooth succession, and he felt that by making peace he would be undermining the position and loyalty of the defence and security establishment, generating expectations for greater freedom and democracy, and opening Syria to Israeli tourists and influence. Asad was, therefore, not interested in making peace but rather in participating in a peace process so as to improve his standing in Washington and to distinguish himself from countries like Iran and Libya. With more than a touch of irony, Pipes added that this policy 'worked best when Likud was in power, for Asad could rely on Yitzhak Shamir's government to maintain a hard line as well'. But the advent of the Labour government, ready to make concessions for peace with Syria, undermined the policy that Asad had pursued so successfully since the Madrid conference.[36]

I do not share this interpretation. I believe that when he agonized over George Bush's invitation to the Madrid conference, Asad did think through the full ramifications of a positive answer and made a decision to join a process that could very well lead him to sign a peace treaty with Israel. I am also certain that there is a Syrian narrative of this four-year saga that is very different from the Israeli and American views of the same period and chain of events. But when all is said and done it is difficult to understand why Asad, despite his suspicions, reservations, and inhibitions, failed to take the steps that would have produced an agreement on terms that should have been quite acceptable to him.

These questions arise with greater poignancy with regard to the second point in time at which a breakthrough was feasible, November 1995 to January 1996. The Syrian negotiator, Walid Mu'allim, by way of expounding his government's line, argued that given the unprecedented pace of progress at Wye, 'Uri Savir, Dennis Ross and I ... decided that we would hold continuous talks to finalize the structure of an agreement on all issues ... We set a deadline for ourselves agreeing to close the remaining gaps and finalize all the elements of an agreement by June of 1996 ... The expectation was that by September 1996 the final document would be ready ... So we were very surprised when soon afterward Mr Peres called early elections.'[37] The Israeli negotiator Uri Savir has not complained of missed opportunities and has not allocated blame or responsibility, but he has argued in a television interview that much had been accomplished at the Wye negotiations and that Israel and Syria were on the verge of coming to an agreement.

But in December 1997 the Israeli newspaper *Ma'ariv* published a story under the headline 'This Is How We Missed the Peace with Syria'. Savir was not quoted directly in the story, which revolved mostly around him, but what the Israeli press likes to call 'sources close to him' argued, in line with Mu'allim's claim, that Savir, Mu'allim, and Ross brought the negotiations to the verge of agreement − 'all disputes between the two states could be bridged with relative ease. All that had to be done was to make a decision, but Peres could not make that difficult decision, not he, not in the position he was in'. And in case this was not clear enough, and as if the unwarranted insinuation concerning Shimon Peres did not suffice, the correspondent summed up: 'The bottom line is that at the end of the first round at the Wye Plantation Uri Savir presented Shimon Peres with the general contours of the peace agreement he could bring to Jerusalem before November 1996 ... Peres equivocated ... he knew that he would have to make difficult decisions; to moderate the army's demands, to give up the Golan Heights. He knew that Rabin could have done it; he was not certain that he could. Peres decided to move up the elections ... This is how the opportunity was missed for a peace agreement between Israel, Syria, and the rest of the Arab world.'[38]

Secretary of State Christopher, during an interview granted to the diplomatic correspondent of *Ha'aretz* in late October 1997 when he came to

Israel to take part in the inauguration of the Peres Peace Center, spoke at some length and quite freely about these issues. When asked whether Asad miscalculated and missed an opportunity, or whether he saw peace as a long-term threat to his regime, the former secretary argued:

> My own view is that he missed an opportunity, an historic opportunity to achieve the return of the Golan, or return of territory. I account for it not by his fear, but his mistrust and suspicion of what was being offered. He examined it so extensively and exhaustively that he missed the opportunity. If he had been responsive and done the public things that we urged and also responded substantively I think much more progress would have been done. Rabin had the strength and the conviction that Syria was and is a threat and it would be a great service to Israel if that threat were removed. One of Asad's miscalculations was that time is and was on his side.

From a perspective of nearly two years Secretary Christopher argued that, in fact, there was no real possibility of concluding an agreement during Peres's brief tenure:

> I really respected that when Prime Minister Peres felt that he needed a mandate for himself ... and I think that pushed him to the early election decision. The time was very late then, even if the elections had been held in November [October 1996]. They were supposed to conclude a deal in the midst of an election campaign when there had been kind of a historic event like an assassination and then a change of government. That would have been very, very short, very tight.'[39]

Asad's biographer, Patrick Seale, in addressing the same issues took an entirely different line. Under the subtitle of 'Missed Opportunities', he begins by referring to the argument 'that Asad missed the chance of peace with Israel – and of a return of the Golan – when Rabin was alive and then, when Peres inherited the prime minister's mantle ... Peace was there for the taking, it is said, if only Asad had made some gesture such as agreeing to meet Peres, or allowing Israeli journalists to visit Syria'. Seale opens his response to this argument by admitting that 'Asad had always been extremely cautious in negotiation, insisting on proceeding step by careful step, seeing a trap in Israel's repeated probing for 'back channels ... Asad seems unable to set aside his deep conviction that Israel is not ready for an honorable peace, not ready to be simply one player among others in the Middle East system ... but conspires instead to hold sway over the whole region ... with the aim of reducing the Arabs to a subject people'. Seale quotes in this context Asad's interview to *al-Ahram* in October 1995 and his scathing attack on Peres's vision of a 'New Middle East'.[40]

With regard to the Wye Plantation negotiations, Seale maintains that 'while Syria offered total peace for total withdrawal' Israel never responded in a clear-cut fashion. The withdrawal:

> was always hedged around by numerous preconditions. First it was to be subject to an Israeli national referendum then it was to be accompanied by such draconian conditions as the thinning out and restructuring of the Syrian armed forces, the placement inside Syrian territory of an Israeli warning station, only token Israeli withdrawal pending proof of Syrian good behaviour and full normalization: in the sense not just of diplomatic relations but of the free movement of goods and people, joint projects, integration of utilities and the like.

Seale then complains that at one of the last sessions at Wye Plantation the Israelis apparently submitted more than a score of projects for integrating the two economies. 'Most Syrians,' he says, 'would have seen any such settlement as exposing their society, nascent industries, cultural traditions and national security to hostile Israeli penetration. For Asad it would have made a mockery of his entire career.'[41]

Seale ends with two very different conclusions. One is that an agreement between Israel and Syria during these years was not in fact feasible. For one thing, on the key issues – withdrawal, security, the timetable, and normalization – 'no agreement was reached'. But beyond this lay the more fundamental incompatibility between two very different visions of peace. For Asad, he says, the essence of any settlement is not the recovery of this or that piece of occupied territory but the 'containment' of Israel, just as his notion of a 'comprehensive peace is not about normalization but ... about holding the line against Israel ... to shrink its influence to more modest and less aggressive proportions, which the Arab players in the Middle East could accept and live with'. This vision could not coexist with Israel's view, which sees peace as a means to extend its influence to every corner of the Arab world. But while Seale writes that 'it was these conflicting visions of peace which very probably doomed the talks to failure', the blame for missing the opportunity to make peace was Israel's rather than Syria's. 'Israel wanted too much and overreached. It could have peace but she wanted peace and hegemony, and that was not and is not realistic.'[42]

Seale is not a Syrian spokesman, but he is Asad's semi-official biographer, and he has access to and he understands Asad and his policies. When Ambassador Mu'allim argues that peace at the Wye talks was within reach, he has an axe to grind. His government's line is that much was accomplished at the Wye Plantation, that it was formalized, that it is binding, and that the negotiations should be resumed at the point at which they were interrupted. Seale's version, while not free from partisan baggage, is less self-serving and offers a valuable insight into Asad's view of the negotiations with Israel and of the contours of an acceptable settlement.

Asad was probably genuine when he spoke of concluding a settlement in 1996, but his definition of an acceptable settlement was far apart from that of Shimon Peres. It might have been possible to bridge that gap, but certainly not within the time frame dictated by the Israeli prime minister's domestic political calculus. This was an issue that Asad failed or refused to understand. He did not want to make the investment that Peres viewed as indispensable if he were to commit himself right away, and he responded angrily when Peres decided a few weeks later to move up the elections. By venting his anger in Lebanon, where he gave Hizballah a free hand and possibly a green light to ignore the 'understanding', he drew Peres into launching Operation Grapes of Wrath, which contributed to his electoral defeat and to the rise of an Israeli government that he found far more difficult to comprehend and contend with.

Asad's failure to empathize with his Israeli counterpart's domestic political constraints and calculus reflected the deliberate and limited fashion in which he and his subordinates came to accept the complexities of and rules of the game in the Israeli political system. It was a slow, manifold process. It began with a stereotypical view of Israeli society and politics, coloured by hostility and lack of interest, a tendency to view all Zionist parties as being essentially the same, and a suspicion that what we viewed and presented as complexities and difficulties were in fact finely orchestrated negotiating tactics. Over time a more credulous and nuanced view was adopted in Damascus, but the extent and pace of this development were too limited to have a real impact at the crucial moment. The election results of 29 May 1996, and their subsequent impact on the Syrian-Israeli track provided a rude awakening and led Asad in the summer of 1997 to start addressing the Israeli political system as such, but for the 1995–96 window of opportunity it was too late.

Asad's Israeli counterparts had an easier task in dealing with a centralized, stable system dominated by one person. They realized, of course, that authoritarian leaders are not free from opposition, that they have to contend with their brand of public opinion and prepare it for changes of line and policy, but they believed all along that they had to focus their efforts on one person, who had the power to make the decisions and carry his country with him. The Israelis assumed that the Syrian public was ahead of its government in being willing to settle with Israel, that opposition to a decision by Asad within the regime could transpire but would remain marginal, and that the real impediments were to be found within Asad's own mind. Asad had been a significant figure in Syrian politics since the mid-1960s, and Rabin and Peres in the course of their public and political careers had each formed a view of the Syrian ruler. These personal views were supplemented by the contribution of Israel's national security bureaucracy, whose analysts had scrutinized Asad's actions and statements over the years. The missing element was personal acquaintance. It is difficult to envisage the Egyptian-Israeli Peace Treaty of 1979 without the meetings between Sadat and Begin (not to speak of the personal relationships between several other Egyptians and Israelis), or Oslo II without the personal give-and-take that Rabin and Peres had with 'Arafat and his group during the previous two years. Except for two formal meetings with General Shihabi, personal contact with Asad and his team was denied to the two Israeli prime ministers who dealt with him. For them he remained an abstract enigma, his aims and motives undeciphered.

It is this view of the discrepancy between the influence of the domestic dimension on the respective positions and conducts of Israel and Syria in their negotiation which accounts for the meager space devoted in this book to the political and socioeconomic aspects of Asad's policies.[43] During the past three decades Syria has undergone profound demographic and socioeconomic changes that will probably be translated to political changes at some future points. But thus far Syria is governed by a stable, powerful, and monolithic regime that is totally dominated by one person. This person has undoubtedly thought through the potential repercussions of a prospective settlement with Israel on the nature and stability of his regime, and he has defined his concept of an acceptable peace arrangement in this context, as well. A close scrutiny could possibly identify nuances regarding the issue of a settlement with Israel within the Asad regime's political spectrum, but Asad's unquestioned dominance has denied such nuances any practical significance. From Henry Kissinger's memoirs we know that during the negotiations he conducted in 1974 before signing a Disengagement Agreement, Asad invested a visible effort to insure the support of the senior military echelon for his policies and arranged for frequent meetings between these officers and the secretary of state. The year 1974 was Asad's fourth in power, and he had yet to consolidate his position fully. Twenty years later Asad was firmly entrenched, and if he had to invest efforts in keeping the defence establishment's support, he certainly did not have to involve the secretary of state in them.

An entirely different set of domestic issues came to the surface in late 1995 and early 1996, due to the special emphasis on the economic dimension of peace and the issue of Israeli-Syrian economic cooperation in

Shimon Peres's concept of peace. The Israeli prime minister's approach was unacceptable to Asad for a number of reasons: he opposed any component in the peace settlement that could be perceived as an Israeli *diktat* and therefore humiliating; he was opposed to any expansion of the notions of peace and normalization; and he rejected anything that he perceived as an attempt to interfere in his regime's internal affairs, be they political or economic. Seale's description of Asad's response to Peres's new ideas seems authentic.

In the absence of an agreement, what did the Israeli-Syrian negotiations produce? In fact, quite a lot. Both sides became thoroughly familiar with each other's positions. The general contours of a prospective settlement were sketched and several important barriers were crossed. Two Israeli prime ministers have indicated to the Israeli public their willingness to make massive concessions in order to achieve peace with Syria, and Hafiz al-Asad has publicly agreed to make full peace and to offer normalization with Israel. But the negotiation has created a negative legacy, as well. A powerful opposition was built in Israel to the notion of a settlement based on withdrawal from the Golan. Asad, on the other hand, by claiming publicly to have obtained an American and Israeli commitment to such withdrawal will be hard put to settle for less, and so will his successors. The present Israeli government was elected on a platform rejecting the model of an Israeli-Syrian agreement that was adumbrated in its predecessors' negotiations with Syria. It is now trying to construct an alternative model, one that Asad is vowing to reject. It will be difficult, though perhaps not impossible, to obtain an agreement under these circumstances.

The Syrian-Israeli negotiation of the years 1992–96 had a significance that exceeded the bilateral relationship between the two countries. Hafiz al-Asad and Syria had a special role and a special status in the Madrid process. President Bush and Secretary Baker invested a special effort in bringing Asad to Madrid. They wanted his prestige and his resources harnessed to the peace process rather than mobilized against it. His resources included Syria's innate power, its influence over the Palestinians, and its position in Lebanon. Asad's prestige rested on his record and on his claim to pan-Arabism's residual mantle. President Clinton and Secretary Christopher inherited this view of the peace process, and viewed a Syrian-Israeli agreement as the key to a durable comprehensive settlement.

This view was shared some of the time by Rabin and Peres. But Rabin also drew on his experience as a peace negotiator in 1949 and as the prime minister who cooperated closely with Henry Kissinger in making the interim agreement of 1975. If Syria was not a genuine partner to a comprehensive settlement that Israel could live with, he would rather proceed gradually and incrementally, and deal with individual Arab partners and not with the Arab collective. Ironically Asad found himself hemmed in by his participation in the peace process and by the prospects opened to him in the negotiations with Israel, and was unable to put up serious opposition to Israel's agreements with the PLO and Jordan and the normalization process with the larger Arab world.

The chapters of this book are rich in raw material that would interest students of the arts of negotiation and bargaining. No attempt will be made here to fit this raw material into a general theory of negotiations. But it is important to make some comments with regard to academic literature on negotiations, as well as draw some lessons in the specific context of Israeli-Arab peacemaking.

The failure to come to an Israeli-Syrian agreement should naturally be measured against the three achievements of the peace process – the much earlier Egyptian-Israeli peace, and the contemporaneous negotiations and agreements with the PLO and Jordan.

The Camp David Accords of September 1978 and the Israeli-Egyptian peace treaty of March 1979 were the culmination of a diplomatic process that began in the immediate aftermath of the October 1973 War. The October War ended the stalemate that followed the 1967 Six Day War, and enabled two of the parties to the conflict to end their bilateral dispute by trading the Egyptian territory that Israel captured in 1967 for peace and acceptance. There was much more to Israeli-Egyptian peacemaking than this simple formula, of course. Egypt made peace with Israel as part of a comprehensive reorientation of her domestic and foreign policies. Egypt was led by a bold visionary leader who made big decisions and refused to be bogged down by details. In his different style, his Israeli counterpart, Menahem Begin, was capable of breaking the mould and taking a decision that ran against the grain of his public image. Sadat did not act in a vacuum. He spoke and acted with the confidence of a leader who came from the heartland of a country with a long tradition of *raison d'état*. Begin had the advantage of being a right-wing leader who could afford to antagonize some of his own supporters, knowing that he could count on the centre and left-wing's support when making peace. Sadat and Begin had the support – and prodding – of an American president who, having overcome his initial reluctance, devoted himself to seeing the negotiation through. And they had the Sinai Peninsula as a natural buffer zone between the two countries. Both leaders understood the value of an early secret 'walk in the woods', and both allowed their military establishment to build channels of communication and a relationship of trust that facilitated the agreement.

The dramatic impact of Israel's agreement with the PLO was at least equal to that of Sadat's journey to Jerusalem. It is easier to explain the PLO's or Yasir

'Arafat's decision to make the agreement. They were at a low ebb and they could see the value of making the concessions that were required on their part in order to reach a compromise that brought 'Arafat from Tunis to Gaza. These were decisions he could have made in the past, probably on better terms, but in 1993 he finally chose to act rather than let another opportunity slip by. The Israeli government's calculus was more complex. Israel was clearly the stronger party in the conflict, and the temptation to hold on to Israel's traditional position vis-à-vis the PLO or to try to dictate terms to a weakened PLO was there. But Rabin and Peres decided as a lesson of the *intifadah* that Israel had to seek a political settlement with the Palestinians, and were persuaded by the course of the Washington talks that the PLO was indeed the *interlocuteur valable*. Constructing the agreement as a phased agreement with the more painful final-status issues left to the end made the pill easier to swallow, at least at the outset. The availability of the Oslo channel was of immense value in making these decisions. For several months authorized representatives could meet and negotiate secretly, away from public scrutiny and political interference. An effective private channel and the direct contact between authorized representatives were indispensable for effecting the Israeli-Palestinian breakthrough.

When it came to peacemaking between Israel and Jordan, the difficult decision was King Husayn's. Compared to the concessions it had to make in other tracks, Israel's concessions to Jordan were not particularly painful. It was the king who had to overcome his reluctance to antagonize Asad and a significant segment of his own constituency by making full peace with Israel. His decision was facilitated by the resolution of disputed land and water issues, by the Clinton Administration's encouragement, and by the new realities of Palestinian politics in the aftermath of the Oslo Accords. Between Jordan and Israel there existed a long tradition of contact and cooperation that was one of the best-advertised secrets of Middle Eastern politics. This enabled the two governments to negotiate at the highest level. It was at that level that the special personal relationship between King Husayn and Prime Minister Rabin was formed.

Against the backdrop of these three breakthroughs, both the missing elements and the principal impediments in the Israeli-Syrian negotiation become more clearly apparent. Hafiz al-Asad is not Anwar Sadat. He is not a bold and visionary decision maker but a meticulous tactician. Yitzhak Rabin was ready to make a bold decision, but he ended up making it in the Palestinian and not in the Syrian context. Bill Clinton is a different president from Jimmy Carter and George Bush, and during his first term he found out that even if his priorities lay in the Israeli-Syrian track he could with less pain and cost push the Israeli-Arab peace process on other tracks. Moreover, the Golan Heights are different from the Sinai. It is a comparatively small area, bordered by four states, close to Damascus as well as to Israeli-populated areas, militarily crucial, and commanding Israel's water resources. Another factor was that Yitzhak Rabin and Shimon Peres realized, as they had suspected, that it was indeed more difficult for leaders relying on a center-left coalition to make peace than it would have been for a right-wing leader. Their efforts to come to terms with Syria generated opposition from the right as well as from segments of the centre. In the absence of Syrian cooperation in addressing Israel's public opinion, the domestic political price seemed prohibitive.

Asad's refusal to meet personally with his Israeli counterparts and the restrictions he imposed on his negotiators were another major obstacle. At any given point during the four-year negotiation a decision by Asad to come to a meeting with President Clinton and the prime minister of Israel would have produced an agreement based on a compromise. But Asad was hoping to do better than the projected compromise, and was not willing to take the small risk that the meeting would not produce an agreement.

For adversaries like Israel and Syria to make the difficult decisions that produce an agreement, a combination of pain and hope is required. The pain makes the status quo unbearable, the hope and vision of a better future facilitate the decision. That combination was glaringly absent during four years of negotiation.

The academic literature dealing with conflict resolution refers to such a combination of actual pain and anticipated gain as 'ripeness' (and more recently 'readiness'). Those writers who advocate the usefulness of this concept have argued that as long as a conflict has not reached a point of ripeness, be it 'positive' (when expectations of relief or gain provide the momentum that is indispensable for overcoming the forces acting to perpetuate the conflict) or negative (when the pain or cost exacted by the status quo become the primary motive for accepting a compromise), all efforts to resolve it are bound to fail. Conversely, they maintain that the availability of such ripeness will account for the success of negotiations or other efforts at reconciliation and settlement.[44] The concept of ripeness can be a very useful analytical tool in understanding the course of a successful or abortive negotiation; but it is less valuable as an operational tool to serve policy makers in making the decision to launch an effort to resolve a particular conflict or in formulating their strategy.

The same academic literature that has provided us with the concept of ripeness has also offered us important distinctions between a very basic and broad term – negotiations – and the more specific terminology of pre-negotiations, bargaining, and mediation. The distinctions are not merely semantic.

The term 'bargaining' refers to the give-and-take between two parties, each seeking to make the best deal from its point of view. The process of bargaining is obviously a very significant part of the larger negotiations in the context of which it is being conducted. Without a successful conduct and conclusion of the bargaining process a negotiation will not be brought to a successful end. But this does not quite sum up the complex interplay between the bargaining dimension and the broader negotiation.

In a successful negotiation, the process of mutual discovery and confidence building should facilitate the bargaining, while the emerging shape of a mutually acceptable deal would reinforce an unfolding reconciliation. Together they create a new and shared calculus that replaces the erstwhile zero-sum game, a distinctive component of conflict situations. Thus on the way to the Oslo Accords the Israeli side chose to moderate its bargaining position, having recognized its greater power and having decided that by dictating terms to the weaker Palestinian party Israel might end up undermining her future partner in the implementation of the agreement. No such dynamics developed in the Israeli-Syrian dialogue, when the deal defined by Asad as the essential minimum was well above the line drawn by Israel. The tough bargaining combined with Syria's reluctance to accept reconciliation and normalization as legitimate elements of the negotiation to produce a negative dynamic much of the time.

The mediation between Israel and Syria was, as we know, conducted by the United States. Other actors, governments, and individuals tried their hand at mediating but ended up adding curious episodes to the saga of the negotiations rather than affecting their course. Of the two protagonists it was Syria that was more interested in Washington's mediation. For both Washington and Damascus this was also a mechanism for building an American-Syrian dialogue, so much so that in short order the negotiation turned into a three-way negotiation. Within this triangle it was often clear that Damascus was more interested in its dialogue with Washington than in its bargaining with Jerusalem.

In fact, Israel also wanted the United States to play a role, but from her perspective a successful negotiation with an Arab party should rest on the right mixture of direct negotiations and American involvement (as was the case between Israel, Egypt, Jordan, and the Palestinians). The Clinton Administration was willing, indeed eager, to play the roles of sponsor, mediator, and arbitrator in a negotiation it regarded as the cutting edge of the peace process. But at the end of the day Washington lacked the will and the power to force on the parties a formula and was unable to bridge the gap that separated them.[45]

An important recent trend in academic writing on conflict resolution and negotiations emphasizes the distinction between the actual negotiation and an earlier phase – 'pre-negotiations'. The earlier phase is defined as the time span during which the parties make the transition from a unilateral search for conflicting solutions to a shared problem, to a joint search for a common solution. The passage from one phase to the next is marked by the inauguration of a formal negotiation. In operational terms the pre-negotiating phase is to be used in order to maximize the prospects of success once a full-fledged negotiation is launched. The underlying assumptions are that the opportunity for a formal negotiation must not be squandered – it would be dangerous and wasteful – and that a correct construction of the pre-negotiating phase by narrowing differences and reducing scepticism and hostility is essential for a subsequent success.[46] Unfortunately, in reality it is quite difficult to construct the process of reconciliation according to the optimal model proposed by the experts. At the end of the war, in the shadow of a crisis, given the fear that the window may close, the parties will begin to talk or be summoned to the table according to the circumstances of the moment.

In the history of Israel's peacemaking with Egypt, the years 1973 to 1977 can be seen as a phase of pre-negotiations, which effectively set the stage for a successful negotiation that was concluded less than a year after its formal inauguration. But this course of events was not foreseen when both a direct dialogue and an American mediation between the two countries began in the murky aftermath of the October War. By the same token, the architects of the Madrid process did not know at the time that from the perspective of August 1993 the formal talks between Israeli and Palestinian delegations would appear as part of a preparatory phase for the informal and semi-formal give-and-take that led to the Oslo breakthrough.

The course and outcome of Israel's negotiation with Syria contain many lessons for those interested in conflict resolution and negotiations either in general or in their Middle Eastern context, but the principal lessons concern the Israeli-Syrian relationship itself. The conflict between the two countries is open and it needs to be managed, settled, and resolved. Some would argue that given the failure of the major effort invested in the early and mid-1990s one should wait for a profound change in the Israeli-Syrian equation – a geopolitical change in the region, a political change in Syria, the introduction of novel and hitherto unfamiliar elements into the proposed formula – that would provide for an entirely different negotiation. But such changes may never happen or may happen at such a late point as to make them irrelevant.

Discussion of the prospect of renewing the negotiations should focus on Israel and Syria as we know them. Hafiz al-Asad has no intention of lowering his demands. He has also managed to tie the hands of his successors by publicly claiming that he had obtained an Israeli commitment to and an American endorsement of an agreement predicated on full withdrawal. But if Asad wants to reach an agreement with Israel, he will have to offer more for what he demands. The United States will remain a crucial intermediary between Israel and Syria, but without a direct, discreet dialogue between the two countries it will be very difficult to reach an agreement. The hard core of bargaining and deal-making will have to be wrapped with a thick and effective crust of public diplomacy, without which the Israeli public will not endorse an agreement with Syria predicated on a territorial concession. Only if Israel, Syria, and the United States draw the lessons offered by three and a half years of negotiation and a year and a half of breakdown in communication will Israel and Syria be able to cross at the decade's end the brink they failed to cross in the early and mid-1990s.

NOTES

1. This article was published in I. Rabinovich, *The Brink of Peace* (Princeton, NJ: Princeton University Press, 1998).
2. The best and most comprehensive book on Israel's conflict and relations with Syria in those years is Moshe Ma'oz, *Syria and Israel: From War to Peacemaking* (Oxford: Clarendon Press, 1995). For illuminating insights into the Syrian point of view and Asad's perspective on the conflict and on the early peace process with Israel, see Patrick Seale, *Asad of Syria* (London: I.B.Tauris, 1988).
3. For Egypt's position see Itamar Rabinovich, 'Egypt and the Palestine Question before and after the Revolution', in Shimon Shamir (ed.), *Egypt from Monarchy to Republic* (Boulder. CO: Westview Press, 1995), pp.325–39.
4. For a thorough study of the armistice regime between Syria and Israel, see Nisim Bar Ya'acov, *The Israel-Syrian Armistice* (Jerusalem: Magnes Press, Hebrew University, 1967) [in Hebrew]. Among the several general studies of the first two decades of the Arab-Israeli conflict, see especially Nadav Safran, *From War to War: The Arab-Israeli Confrontation, 1948–1967* (New York, NY: Pegasus, 1969).
5. These differences are described in Itamar Rabinovich, *The Road Not Taken – Early Arab-Israeli Negotiations* (New York, NY: Oxford University Press, 1991), pp.65–82.
6. Ibid., pp.99–110.
7. This process is analysed by Safran, *From War to War*, who describes it as 'the festering of the conflict'. A different version, more sympathetic to the Arab view of the process, is Fred Khouri, *The Arab-Israeli Dilemma* (New York, NY: Syracuse University Press, 1968).
8. Bar Ya'acov, *Israeli-Syrian Armistice*, pp.77–9.
9. For an analysis of the interplay between Syria's domestic politics and its conduct on the issue of the Israeli overland water carrier, see Itamar Rabinovich, *Syria under the Ba'th* (Jerusalem and New York, NY: Israel Universities Press, 1972), pp.94–5.
10. A particularly useful analysis of the process of deterioration leading to the Six Day War is Shimon Shamir 'The Middle East Crisis: On the Brink of War', in Daniel Dishon (ed.), *Middle East Record, 1967* (Tel Aviv: Israel Universities Press, 1971), pp.183–204.
11. Moshe Dayan, *Moshe Dayan: The Story of My Life* (New York: Warner Books, 1976), p.475.
12. Itamar Rabinovich, 'Continuity and Change in the Ba'th Regime in Syria 1967–1973', in Itamar Rabinovich and Haim Shaked (eds), *From June to October* (New Brunswick, NJ: Transaction Books, 1978), pp.219–28.
13. Dayan, *Story of My Life*, p.491.
14. The best account of the Arab regime's success in coping with the impact of the 1967 defeat is Fuad 'Ajami, *The Arab Predicament: Arab Political Thought and Practice Since 1967* (Cambridge: Cambridge University Press, 1982).
15. See the complementary versions by Henry Kissinger, *White House Years* (Boston, MA: Little, Brown, 1979), pp.597–617, and Yitzhak Rabin, *The Rabin Memoirs* (Berkley, CA: University of California

Press, 1996), pp.178–9.

16. The best account of the internal conflict within the Ba'th regime in the late 1960s is Nikolaos van Dam, *The Struggle for Power in Syria* (London: Croom Helm, 1981).

17. 'Al-Asad Notes Progress on Revolution Anniversary', FBIS, 9 March 1972, pp.1–15.

18. Itamar Rabinovich 'The October War's Impact on Syrian Position and Policy in the Conflict with Israel', in Adir Cohen and Efrat Karmon (eds), *In the Shadow of the October War* (Haifa: University of Haifa, 1976), pp.211–22 [in Hebrew].

19. See Kissinger's classic account of his negotiations with Asad in Henry Kissinger, *Years of Upheaval* (Boston, MA: Little, Brown, 1982), pp.777–87.

20. Ma'oz, *From War to Peacemaking*, pp.144–52.

21. Rabin, *The Rabin Memoirs*, pp.242–5.

22. Itamar Rabinovich, *The War for Lebanon 1970–1983* (Ithaca , NY: Cornell University Press, 1985).

23. Steven L. Spiegel 'The Carter Approach to the Arab-Israeli Dispute', in Itamar Rabinovich and Haim Shaked (eds), *The Middle East and the United States* (New Brunswick, NJ: Transaction Books, 1980), pp.93–117.

24. Jimmy Carter, *The Blood of Abraham* (Boston, MA: Houghton Mifflin, 1985), p.73.

25. Jimmy Carter, *Keeping Faith*, pp. 285–6.

26. See the text of the Camp David Accords in Appendix E to William B. Quandt, *The Peace Process: American Diplomacy and the Arab-Israeli Conflict since 1967* (Washington, DC: Brookings Institution, 1993), pp.445–56. The book itself contains the most complete study and analysis of the Accords.

27. Asad's response to the Camp David accord is vividly described by Seale, *Asad of Syria*, pp.304–10.

28. For the origins of the 1982 war in Lebanon, see Ze'ev Schiff and Ehud Ya'ari, *Israel's Lebanon War* (New York, NY: Simon and Schuster, 1984).

29. David Kimche, *The Last Option* (London: Weidenfeld and Nicolson, 1991), passim.

30. See, in this volume, Itamar Rabinovich, 'Syria's Quest for a Regional Role'.

31. For three Israeli versions of Shamir's path to Madrid, see Yitzhak Shamir, *Sikumo shel Davar* (In Conclusion) (Tel Aviv: Idanim, 1994) [in Hebrew], pp.263–91; Moshe Arens, *Broken Covenant* (New York, NY: Simon and Schuster, 1995); and Eitan Bentzur, *The Road to Peace Goes through Madrid* (Tel Aviv: Yediot Aharonot, 1997) [in Hebrew].

32. Eyal Zisser, 'Syria', in Ami Ayalon (ed.), *Middle East Contemporary Survey*, 14 (1990) and 15 (1991), pp.649–68 and 664–89, respectively. The Taif Accords were signed in Taif in Saudi Arabia in 1989 with a view to normalizing the political conditions in Lebanon. They also provided rather vaguely for the future departure of Syria's troops.

33. The efforts invested in and negotiations conducted before the Madrid conference are described in detail by the architect of the conference James A. Baker, *The Politics of Diplomacy: Revolution, War, and Peace, 1989–1992* (New York, NY: G.P. Putnam's Sons,1995), pp.417–20, 425–8, 447–9, 454-7, 459–63, 468–9, 487–9, 500–7.

34. Lea Rabin, *Our Life – His Legacy* (New York, NY: G.P. Putnam's Sons, 1997).

35. Karim Pakradouni, *Stillborn Peace* (Beirut: FMA, 1985), pp.71–4.

36. Daniel Pipes, 'Just Kidding', *New Republic* (8 and 15 January 1996), pp.18–19.

37. See Mu'allim's interview in *Journal of Palestine Studies*, 26, 2 (Winter 1997), p.40l.

38. 'Kakh Fisfasnu et hashalom im Surya' ('This is how we missed the peace with Syria), section 2, *Ma'ariv*, 12 December 1997, pp.1–3.

39. 'A Believer in the Road already Traveled', section 2, *Ha'aretz* (English edition), 24 October 1997, p.5.

40. Patrick Seale, 'Asad's Regional Strategy and the Challenge from Netanyahu', *Journal of Palestine Studies*, 26, 101 (Fall 1996), p.36.

41. Ibid., p.36.

42. Ibid., pp.36–7.

43. For a detailed account of these issues see Volker Perthes, *The Political Economy of Syria under Asad* (London: I.B. Tauris, 1997). For a comprehensive and updated review of the relationship between political and economic issues in Asad's Syria and their relationship to his policies in the peace process, see Glenn E. Robinson, 'Elite Cohesion, Regime, Succession and Political Instability in Syria', *Middle East Policy*, 4, 4 (January 1998), pp.159–79.

44. The concept of ripeness is treated by a rich body of literature. Some of the important original contributions to that literature were made by Richard Haass, who left Harvard University to serve in the Bush Administration's National Security Council. In the Middle Eastern context, William Zartman of Johns Hopkins University's School of Advanced International Studies has devoted a particular effort to the development and application of this term; see William Zartman, 'Explaining Oslo', *International Negotiation*, 2, 2 (1997), pp.195–215; and also Dean Pruitt, 'Ripeness Theory and

the Oslo Talks', *International Negotiation*, 2, 2 (1997), pp.237–50.

45. For intervening mediation by a superpower, see Sa'adia Touval, 'The Superpowers as Mediators', in J. Bercovitch and J. Rubin (eds), *Mediation in International Relations* (New York, NY: St Martin's Press, 1992), pp.232–48.

46. On pre-negotiation, see William Zartman, 'Prenegotiation: Phases and Functions', in J. Gross-Stein (ed.), *Getting to the Table: the Processes of International Prenegotiation* (Baltimore, MD: Johns Hopkins University Press, 1989), pp.1–17. Alongside the academic literature in this field, mention should be made of the book written by the American diplomat Harold Saunders, published under the title *The Other Walls* in the mid-1980s and in revised form in the early 1990s. Saunders, who played a senior role in the formation of Middle Eastern policy under Nixon, Ford, and Carter, devoted the core of this book to a discussion of the construction of the correct process of dialogue between Israel and the Palestinians. See Harold Saunders, *The Other Walls: The Arab-Israeli Peace Process in a Global Perspective* (Princeton, NJ: Princeton University Press, 1991). Saunders draws a clear distinction between the early phase of pre-negotiation and the negotiation itself. For another study by a former diplomat in collaboration with an academic student, see Samuel Lewis and Kenneth Stein, *Making Peace among Arabs and Israelis: Lessons from Fifty Years of Negotiating Experience* (Washington, DC: United States Institution of Peace, 1991).

19

On Public Diplomacy and the Israeli-Syrian
Negotiations During the Waning
of Hafiz al-Asad's Rule

In December 1999 and in February 2000 Faruq al-Shara', Syria's Foreign Minister, spoke in public regarding the negotiations that were being conducted by his country and Israel. In both cases Shara' deviated from the official Syrian line and shared with his audience novel ideas and formulations. But the sense and some of the formulations of Shara''s two statements were contradictory. When he spoke in Washington in December 1999 Shara' sought to persuade Israeli and international opinion that the 'existential conflict' between Syria and Israel had ended. But in Damascus in February 2000, speaking to the Arab Writers Union, Shara'went back to the 'Phased Approach' held by Syria in the 1970s and intimated that a peace treaty with Israel may very well be a temporary expediency.[1] The discrepancy between the two statements was not merely a failed effort to speak differently to different audiences. It rather reflected the Syrian-Israeli disagreement over the issue of 'public diplomacy' as well as the growing importance of public opinion as a political factor in Syria during the waning of Hafiz al-Asad's regime.

'Public Diplomacy' is a crucial component in conflict resolution in the contemporary international arena. The term refers to the actions, rhetoric and symbolic acts – addressed at public opinion by governments engaged in negotiations or conflict resolution in order to facilitate the process of reconciliation, acceptance and concession indispensable to agreement. In a world open to the media the differences between actions directed at the domestic arena and those focused on the other side are minimal: both constituencies will monitor every word and action. Furthermore, as part of the mutual inspection built into contemporary negotiations both parties will seek to ascertain that their counterpart is preparing public opinion for concessions and acceptance and refrains from double talk.

In the context of the Israeli-Arab peace process public diplomacy played a prominent and crucial role in the successful resolution of the Israeli-Egyptian conflict. Egypt's president, Anwar al-Sadat, instinctively understood the need to transform Israeli public opinion both with regard to the prospect of real peace with the Arab world and to the conviction that holding onto the Sinai Peninsula was vital to Israeli's national security.

Sadat understood that without such a change, his partner, Menahem Begin, would not be able to sign a peace treaty predicated on full withdrawal from the Sinai Peninsula – a *sine qua non* for himself. Sadat understood also the importance of two other foundations of the Israeli psyche – the sense of security (or insecurity) and the urge to obtain acceptance and legitimacy from the Arab parties to the conflict.[2] Consequently Sadat was willing to reverse the conventional sequence. Having been reassured by the messages transmitted through an authoritative Israeli representative, Foreign Minister Moshe Dayan, in a secret pre-negotiation, Sadat decided to grant to Israel a sizeable portion of the elements of recognition and legitimacy associated with a peace agreement at an early phase, prior to the start of the formal negotiation and to continue in the same vein during the negotiations' early stages. Hence the visit to Jerusalem in November 1977, the speech in the Knesset, Begin's invitation to Isma'iliyya, the invitations extended to other Israelis and the willingness to host an Israeli military delegation in Cairo.

Sadat did accomplish his aims with regard to Israeli opinion and the Israeli political system. His impact on Egyptian and Arab opinion was more complex. Whether he meant it or not, Sadat administered 'shock therapy' to these two constituencies. He met with fierce opposition from Nasserist and Islamic groups, but he was able to carry Egypt with him. In the rest of the Arab world he was ostracized by both governments and popular opinion.

The first, Egyptian, phase of the Israeli-Arab peace process withered in 1981. It was revived a decade later by the Bush-Baker Administration through the construction of the Madrid Process. The Madrid conference was convened in October 1991 and was followed by several rounds of talks in Washington, but the negotiating tracks with Syria, Jordan and the Palestinians were only energized after the formation of Yitzhak Rabin's government in the summer of 1992. A balance sheet of the Madrid process, which run its course by 2001 points to a mixed outcome:

1) The signing of a framework agreement for a resolution of the Israeli-Palestinian conflict, mutual recognition between Israel and the Palestinian national movement, the formation of a Palestinian Authority holding sway over most of the population of the West Bank and the Gaza Strip, continuation of the Israeli-Palestinian conflict, collapse of the effort to reach a final status agreement, and the resumption of armed conflict in September 2000.

2) The signing of a Jordanian-Israeli peace treaty.
3) Failure to reach a Syrian-Israeli agreement despite the significant progress made in the negotiations.
4) The establishment of a considerable degree of normalization in Israel's relationship with the larger Arab world and the suspension of a large part of that progress after the collapse of the peace process.[3]

Public diplomacy had a different role in each of these different tracks. The measure of normalization achieved in Israel's relationship with the Arab collective – a softening of the Arab economic boycott, the establishment of semi-diplomatic relations with several countries in the Gulf and North Africa and Israel's participation in the regional economic conferences in Casablanca, Amman and Cairo – were to a large extent acts of 'public diplomacy' designed, with Washington's active encouragement, to demonstrate to the Israeli public that the Arab world was reciprocating for the gestures and concessions of the years 1993–94.

The signing of the Jordanian-Israeli peace treaty in October 1994 was yet another dividend accruing to Israel as a by-product of the Oslo Accords. The new open peaceful relationship with Jordan was very valuable in its own right but it was also supplemented by a series of goodwill gestures offered by King Husayn to his friend Yitzhak Rabin. The gestures were made in the larger context of Arab-Israeli relations rather than in the framework of Israeli-Jordanian diplomacy. For Israeli public opinion there was nothing controversial about a peace treaty with a second Arab country that involved only minor concessions.

This certainly was not the case with regard to Israel's negotiation with the PLO. Rabin anticipated a harsh reaction in Israel to the very signing of the Oslo Accords, to the essence of the agreement and to the recognition extended to the PLO. He chose a tactic reminiscent of Sadat's conduct in 1977 – the negotiation was kept under a tight lid until the last moment and the signing of the agreement was announced to the Israeli public in a manner bound to have a shocking effect. The signing ceremony in Washington was prepared as a mega act of public diplomacy directed at several constituencies – Israeli, Palestinian, Arab and international opinion.

It was designed to send the message that a historic compromise had been reached between Israel and Palestinian nationalism and to prepare the ground to compromises and concessions likely to be required further down the road. Rabin himself through his demeanour during the signing ceremony and through the text of his speech projected a degree of ambivalence given the agonizing choices confronting himself and the Israeli public.

In theory both Israel and the emerging Palestinian Authority were to continue to invest considerable efforts in public diplomacy in the aftermath of the signing ceremony. After all, a simple act, impressive as it was, did not suffice in order to bring about real changes in the attitudes of two communities after decades of a bitter national conflict. But such efforts were not invested primarily due to difficulties inherent in the very nature of the Oslo Accords. These Accords did not resolve the Israeli-Palestinian conflict but rather created a framework for reaching a final agreement. Consequently the parties became engaged in both the next phases of their negotiations and in efforts to pre-determine the shape of the final settlement in line with their divergent, often contradictory, concepts of that settlement. Both leaderships invested a greater effort in their domestic arenas than in trying to affect public opinion on the other side. In the Israeli-Palestinian relationship more that public diplomacy was required. Nothing short of massive investment in peace-building would suffice. The failure to make such an investment was an important contributor to the outbreak of the Israeli-Palestinian crisis in the summer and fall of 2000.

As for the Syrian track, the decade of Israeli-Syrian negotiations can be clearly divided into five phases determined primarily by the tenures of five Israeli Prime Ministers: Yitzhak Shamir (October 1991–Spring of 1992), Yitzhak Rabin (July 1992–November 1995), Shimon Peres (November 1995–March 1996), the secret negotiations during Benjamin Netanyahu's tenure (1998–99) and Ehud Barak (May–June 1999–March 2001).[4] During each of these phases public diplomacy was assigned a different role.

During its first phase the Syrian-Israeli negotiations were to a large extent an exercise in negative public diplomacy. The meetings between the two delegations were held in a very formal setting in a conference room at the State Department building. The Syrian delegation adhered to the Syrian-Arab policy of boycott – separate entry and departure and refusal to shake hands and to accept any other form of informal or personal interaction. Both parties openly recorded the negotiating sessions and both were clearly speaking to the microphone, creating their own record of the history of the Syrian-Israeli dispute and documenting their version of the talks' anticipated failure. When entering and exiting the State Department's building the delegations held separate press briefings consisting mostly of mutual recriminations. A Syrian-Israeli dialogue failed to develop first and foremost due to the absence of a mutually acceptable basis for a negotiation but the negative atmosphere surrounding the meetings became part of the problem.

This state of affairs was transformed by the formation of Yitzhak Rabin's government in July 1992. Rabin decided to move the peace process

forward and was willing to offer significant concessions to either Syria or
the Palestinians in order to effect a breakthrough. During his first year in
office Rabin realized that the concessions required on either track – willingness to withdraw from the Golan Heights or recognition of the PLO and
an Oslo-like agreement – was grater than he had originally assumed. In
early August 1993 Rabin faced the need to choose between the two tracks
with the drafts of the Oslo Accords ready on the Palestinian track and the
'deposit' – Rabin's conditional readiness to withdraw from the Golan in
return for a particular peace settlement – having been conveyed by
Secretary of State, Warren Christopher, to Hafiz al-Asad.

Rabin's choice of the Palestinian track derived largely from Asad's disappointing response to his gambit. The Israeli Prime Minister saw a
prospective agreement with Syria as a late by-product of the Israeli-
Egyptian peace settlement put together in 1977–79. Important differences
notwithstanding Israel's conflict with Egypt and Syria were essentially territorial disputes between two sovereign states. Once Menahem Begin's government had signed with Egypt a peace treaty predicated on full withdraw
from the Sinai, it was inconceivable that Asad would agree to less than a
full withdrawal from the Golan. But Rabin insisted that the Egyptian precedent also apply to Asad's part of the deal and demanded a package of concessions and gestures comparable to the one granted by Sadat to Begin: full
peace, a heavy dose of normalization upfront matched by phased withdrawal over three years, massive security arrangements as compensation
for withdrawal from the high ground and willingness to engage in public
diplomacy in order to persuade the Israeli public that a change had indeed
taken place in Syria's attitude that would justify Rabin's willingness to
break a taboo and agree to get off the Golan. Asad conveyed his willingness
to sign a full peace agreement with Israel in return for withdrawal from the
Golan, but he rejected the rest of Rabin's package.

One important difficulty built into that negotiation was the discrepancy between Rabin's insistence on a replicating the Egyptian model and
Asad's determination to do better than Sadat. How else could he justify a
fifteen-year delay in signing an agreement identical to the one he had
scorned and vilified in the late 1970s.

In the give and take of August 1993 issues of public diplomacy were
hardly discussed but the Israeli negotiator had already come to realize that
much could not be expected from Asad in this area. During the previous
year, once the negotiation had mounted a more fruitful course, the Israeli
delegation made several efforts to raise the issue and met a brick wall.
While Rabin and other Israeli leaders spoke at length about the new
prospect for peace with Syria, Asad made just one oblique reference to 'the

peace of the knights, the peace of the brave'. On 16 January 1994 Presidents Clinton and Asad met in Geneva. In the course of the subsequent press conference Clinton had to invest considerable efforts in order to extract from Asad a brief statement concerning his readiness for peace and normal relations with Israel. This episode led to a minor US Israeli diplomatic incident – the US peace team saw Asad's statement as a breakthrough while Rabin bluntly dismissed the whole press conference as a failure.

Asad's negotiators were quite clear in explaining his position in this matter. Public diplomacy as such had no value. Substance alone had value, and the one substantive issue was Israel's withdrawal from the Golan. Israel should begin by committing to Syria to withdraw from the Golan. On this basis peace could be made. When the Syrian public finds out that Israel is withdrawing from the Golan it will support the motion of peace.

Each party was responsible for mobilizing support for peace-making in its own constituency and if the Israeli government is hard put to build support for withdrawal from the Golan, it should deal with this problem by itself. It must not try to shift it in Syria's direction.

The gap between Israelis and Syrians respective outlooks in this matter was not narrowed during the next two years despite the upgrading of their channels of communication through the 'ambassadors' channel in Washington and through two meetings of the Chiefs of Staff of the Syrian and Israeli armies. Under US pressure Asad agreed to a potentially major gesture – an interview by Foreign Minister, Faruq al-Shara' to Israeli television.[5] But the exercise backfired – Shara''s sour tone and demeanour and the negative slant of his statements served to reinforce Syria's negative image in Israel. This futile effort coupled with President Clinton's two failed efforts to extract a gesture or a statement from his Syrian counterpart in their joint press conferences (January and October 1994) clearly indicated that Asad, beyond his distaste for public diplomacy in sharp contrast to Sadat, did not quite grasp the interplay between media and politics in countries like the US and Israel.

During the final months of Rabin's life and tenure the negotiation with Syria had been suspended. It was renewed with fresh vigour by Shimon Peres upon assuming the country's leadership. Early in his tenure Peres made the decision to hold the next parliamentary elections on schedule (October 1996) and to seek victory not as Rabin's avenger but on his own track record. He also decided to reinforce that record by completing the negotiations with Syria within a few months rather than proceed with the full implementation of the Oslo Accords with which he was so closely identified. But Peres encountered a disappointing Syrian response. Peres was ready to move forward with break-neck speed and was willing to announce his willingness to withdraw from the Golan, but he insisted that this be matched by Asad's agreement to a public meeting of the two leaders. Like Rabin, Peres saw such a dramatic act of public diplomacy as a *sine qua non* for a successful negotiation with Syria.

Asad declined altogether; his response to Peres' enthusiastic overtures was disappointing. Thus, he refused to raise the level of the negotiations and kept his ambassador in Washington as the chief negotiator. Walid Mu'allim was in fact an authoritative and effective negotiator but Peres, for obvious reasons, wanted to raise the negotiations to the political level. Asad, in turn, would only agree to send a delegation composed of diplomats and army officers to a conference site near Washington to negotiate with a comparable Israeli delegation. Asad carefully monitored all aspects of the negotiation with Peres. His delegates to the Wye Plantation were allowed a new level of 'personal normalization' with their Israeli counterparts, but no change was allowed with regard to public diplomacy.

In substantive terms quite a bit of progress was made at the Wye Plantation, but Asad dictated a slow pace that failed to match Peres' political calendar. When Peres decided, as a result, to move up the elections from the fall to the spring of 1996 Asad responded angrily. The negotiations stumbled on until early march 1996 when Peres, frustrated by Syria's refusal to publicly condemn the wave of Palestinian terrorism launched at the time, decided to suspend the talks with Syria.[6]

During Benjamin Netanyahu's three-year tenure the saga of the Israeli-Syrian negotiations was enriched by an intriguing episode, that has yet to be fully studied. Netanyahu authorized his friend and supporter, the American business magnate, Ronald Lauder, to negotiate with Asad. Asad met several times with Lauder who shuttled between Jerusalem and Damascus. Some light was shed on Lauders mission at the end of Netanyahu's term in the late spring of 1999. Lauder apparently conveyed Netanyahu's willingness in principle to withdraw from the Golan to the lines of 4 June 1967 while Asad was surprisingly forthcoming on the issue of the Israeli monitoring station on Mt Hermon and agreed that it would continue to be operated by American (and according to some reports some Israeli) personnel. Lauder's mission came to an end when Netanyahu declined to provide the map with a demarcation of Israel's line of withdrawal.[7]

Naturally this episode had no public dimension during Netanyahu's period, but it had a negative impact in Ehud Barak's quest for a swift resumption and conclusion of the negotiations with Syria. Barak acted for several months in the (wrong) assumption (created by Lauder's initial report) that Asad would settle on withdrawal to the international border (rather than to the lines of 4 June 1967). Still more important was his conclusion that in a direct negotiation with Asad rather than with his emissaries a greater degree of flexibility could be expected. These assumptions played an important role in Barak's decision to focus on Syria as the first and primary target of his peace policy and to devote ten crucial months to this futile effort. The summer and fall of 1999 were consumed by an American-Israeli effort to overcome a familiar dilemma – Asad insisted on an explicit commitment to withdrawal to the lines of 4 June as a pre-condition to renewing the negotiations. Barak, who, like his three predecessors, was ready in principle to withdraw from the Golan refused to offer a commitment that would deny him leverage and manoeuverability once the actual negotiation begun.

In early December 1999 Asad surprised everybody by agreeing to renew the negotiations and, to boot, by appointing his Foreign Minister, Faruq al-Shara', to lead the Syrian delegation. Bark in turn decided to ignore the difference in rank and to come in person to the first round of negotiations in Washington on 15 December 1999. The gesture made by Asad in raising the negotiation to the political level was offset to a degree by lowering the level of authorized normalization – Shara' would not shake Barak's hand in public. But Shara''s public statement reflected an effort to set a positive tone. He drew an equation whereby 'For Syria the significance of peace lies in regaining all occupied lands' while 'for Israel the significance of peace lies in the end of psychological fear … the end of occupation will for the first time be balanced by destroying the barrier of fear and anxiety and replacing them with a candid and mutual sense of peace and security'. In a similar vein Shara' spoke about the 'establishment of dignified peace for the sake of the two parties that will preserve rights, honor and sovereignty because only a dignified and just peace will be accepted by future generations; it is the only peace that will open new horizons for entirely different relationships between the peoples of the region'.

Shara''s statement included two novel motifs. They were formulated with a degree of prudence reflecting ambivalence. Those in Israel, he said, who are opposed to returning occupied lands to their original owners 'are sending a message to the Arabs that the conflict is existential … rather than a conflict over borders that could be concluded as soon as the parties regain their rights'. He then added: 'A peace agreement between Syria and Israel and Lebanon and Israel would signify for our region an end to a history of war and conflicts and will also ensure a dialogue between cultures and a dignified competition in various fields such as politics, culture, science and economy.'[8]

The Syrian-Israeli round of talks in Washington laid the foundation for the effort to effect a breakthrough in a meeting convened by the US in Shepherdstown, West Virginia between 3–10 January 2000. The meeting ended in failure and the negotiation was frozen for several weeks when yet another effort was made to break the ice through a meeting held between Presidents Clinton and Asad in Geneva on 26 March.

In the coming years several of the American and Israeli participants in these events criticized Ehud Barak, citing his refusal to give Faruq al-Shara' a clear commitment to withdraw to the 4 June lines as the chief reason for the collapse of the negotiation. In their view a real opportunity to reach an Israeli-Syrian agreement was missed, when Barak was discouraged by his pollsters, who alerted him to the massive opposition to a withdrawal from the Golan.[9]

Barak rejects this criticism and argues that he was ready to complete the negotiation but, like his predecessors, refused to give away his negotiating assets by succumbing to the persistent Syrian demand to receive a commitment to withdrawal as a pre-condition.[10] Even if we accept Barak's version it is clear that the Israeli public's negative view of Hafiz al-Asad's Syria and opposition to withdrawal from the Golan was a significant element in Barak's calculus. That Israeli attitude was informed by the cumulative effect of a decade of negative public diplomacy. In any event, Barak did not abandon the Syrian track and deposited with President Clinton a new compromise formula and his 'bottom line' in anticipation of Clinton's third and final summit with Hafiz al-Asad in Geneva on 26 March. The meeting ended quite abruptly with yet another failure thus marking the end of a decade-long effort to resolve the Israeli-Syrian conflict. Hafiz al Asad died on 10 June and was succeeded by his son Bashar.

Hafiz al-Asad's health had been the subject of rumours and speculations for nearly two decades but in the late 1990s the impact of his declining health was evident and it clearly affected the conduct of the Syrian-Israeli negotiation of 1999–2000. Asad was losing physical strength and political power. Members of his government such as Faruq al-Shara' took liberties that had been inconceivable previously while others became openly critical of the ailing President. Their criticism focused on two issues: the idea of appointing his son as successor and the motion of a peaceful settlement with Israel. A linkage was created between the two issues and Asad was required to pay a political price for introducing the dynastic principle into Syrian politics. Asad and his immediate circle felt vulnerable and their response to the criticism was apologetic. The harshest criticism was launched by a Ba'th Party member, 'Aqleh 'Ursan, Chairman of the Damascus based Arab Writers Union:

we reject and will keep rejecting any prospect of recognizing the Zionist enemy, and we will go on fighting against all manifestation of normalization with that enemy because we view the struggle against him as an 'existential conflict' rather than a 'conflict over borders' ... The question is whether this [our] position will come to an end when this Israeli-Syrian and this Israeli-Lebanese negotiation will yield peace agreements? ... Will an era in our history come to end to be replaced by a new era? Are we going to be left with just a sense of despair and possibly also with the bitter memories of our defeat? Will we be left with just the prospect of eating at the table of those who defeated us in negotiations and feel as if we have accomplished 'miracles' ... will the ghosts of millions of Palestinians expelled from their homes vanish?[11]

'Ursan and others, whose criticism did not get published, were explicitly critical of Shara''s statement in Washington and challenged the Ba'th regime's willingness to recognize Israel and sign with her a peace treaty, albeit a formal one. Shara' replied to this criticism in the speech mentioned above. He chose to address the Arab Writers Union and delivered to them an unprecedented apologetic speech. He began by explaining that Asad's way was sort of 'a third way' in the Arab world: not a surrender (like Sadat's, Husayn's and 'Arafat's) and not a refusal to make peace that the rest of the world would not understand. It was Syria's middle of the road way – willingness to make peace but in a dignified fashion, insisting on her principles – which kept the Arab nationalist cause on the right track. According to Shara' Syria was left with no choice but to enter into a peace process with Israel because it had been betrayed at every stage: first by Egypt, then by Iraq (who went to war first against Iran and then against Kuwait) and during the Madrid process by Jordan and the PLO. Moreover, what was Syria to do given Israel's power? Israel is stronger than all the Arab states put together. She enjoys the unprecedented support of the United States and is successful in misleading international public opinion into believing in her peaceful intentions.

Speaking to the Arab Writers Union Shara' took two of the main motifs of his Washington statements and turned them around. If he implied in Washington that in return for regaining the Golan Syria was willing to resolve a conflict with Israel that had once been existential and was now territorial, he now explained that he had something far more complex in mind. In his own words:

I am repeating what I said in Washington; and there were those who understood the opposite of what I had in mind, possibly due to a bad translation, and there were those who took it from the press without looking at the [original] text ... I encumbered Israel with responsibility vis-à-vis the international community when I said 'if Israel wants to continue the occupation of Arab lands and to hold on to them she is sending a message to the Arabs that they have no choice but to continue in an existential conflict, namely we or they'.

Shara' also endowed his statement on the transition from military conflict to political competition with a meaning different from the one it seemed to have when made in Washington. As he put it now, it was not in the Arabs' interest to continue the military confrontation because in the absence of military balance between Israel and the Arabs such a confrontation could play into Israel's hands and help her in implementing her expansionist plans, Zionism's vision, with greater speed. 'But if we convert the military confrontation into a political, economic, commercial and cultural competition with all its aspects and isolate her military arsenal and neutralize it ... the results could be better and the disasters less numerous, because we would be forcing Israel to resort to the other non military measures.'

Later on in this address Shara' repeated the Syrian demand for withdrawal to the lines of 4 June, denied the news reports (concerning the Lauder mission) that Syria had agreed to Israeli presence in the monitoring station and denied also fresher news reports that Syria had taken a more flexible position with regard to the security arrangements. Shara' emphasized once again the importance of winning international public opinion and presented a Syrian version of Ehud Barak's 'mask tearing' thesis: 'Even if we fail, we do not lose, because we will gain the support of Arab and international opinion. The Arabs will take our side willy-nilly because we will tell them that we did our best.'

Shara' then proceeded to take questions from audience and his answers to some of them went further than his original text. Thus he explained that in certain contexts peace could be 'an empty word devoid of content, having no significance from Israel's perspective – Israel made peace with Egypt but I don't see peace between Israel and Egypt'. According to Shara', Israel carried the blame for this state of affairs, because it was only interested in the external paraphernalia of peace: handshakes, embassies and the like. But real peace can only come when Israel respects Arab culture and civilization, and experiences soul-searching over her past sins and denounces them. In other words, only a process comparable to the South African Truth and Reconciliation would enable Israel to be accepted in the region. Shara' was swept by his own rhetoric to the period of reendowing the 'phased doctrine' favoured by the Syrian Ba'th regime in the 1970s:

> I am a member of the Ba'th Party and I have the honor of being a
> member in a party aware of the fact that regaining the whole of
> Palestine is a long-term strategic goal, that cannot be achieved in one
> phase. I am talking of the Ba'th Party and not about the negotiations
> or about other ideologies. Even the ideology of the Ba'th Party sets a
> number of phases for the liberation and these statements have been
> made for more than thirty years. In the phase of liberation the first
> stage is regaining the captured Arab lands and securing the solid
> national rights of the Palestinian Arab people.

Shara''s statement was clearly addressed to a particular segment of Syrian
public opinion. But which segment? The answer to this question can be
found in a most interesting essay published by a Syrian intellectual, Sadiq
al-'Azm in *The New York Review of Books* on 15 June 2000 under the title 'The
View from Damascus'. 'Azm is a son of a great Damascus family that in the
eighteenth century created a dynasty of local governors in the Othman
Province of Damascus. Several family members played important roles in
the politics of the Syrian state into the middle of the twentieth century.
'Azm received his PhD in philosophy at Yale and served as professor at the
American University of Beirut and at the University of Damascus and built
a reputation as a radical critic of Arab and Islamic society through such
books as *Self-Criticism in the Wake of the Defeat* and *A Critique of Religious Thought*.
After years of a self-imposed exile 'Azm came back to the University of
Damascus and found an unarticulated *modus vivendi* with the Ba'th regime
predicated on an understanding of the boundaries that must not be crossed
by a critical public intellectual in a country like Syria.

'Azm opened his essay with a question: 'Is Syria as Syria, not just as a
regime and a government, ready at this time for peace with Israel?' His
answer was 'a qualified, limited yes'. He drew a distinction between two
components of Syrian opinion: one consists of 'the men of profound rejection – those who refuse to accept Israel's existence'. 'According to my best
judgment' he wrote:

> these are now in the minority, but they certainly do exist. Their
> position has an entrenched emotional attraction and under the right
> circumstances they could regain their strength, reach an understand-
> ing with the main stream of public opinion and become the decisive
> force in Syria's culture and politics. Prominent in this group are
> members of the civil society's Islamic currents who are presently
> rallying around an Islamic version of the doctrine that views Palestine
> as the promised land. The doctrine regards Palestine as a *Waqf*, a reli-
> gious endowment ... The other type of adherents to the profound

rejection are the radical nationalists who rally around a watered down and secularized version of the *Waqf* doctrine.

Shara''s apologetic speech was clearly addressed at this group. But 'Azm is more interested in Syria's civil society. For him, even after nearly forty years of Ba'th rule, Syria's real public discourse is conducted within Damascene civil society. Since the Madrid Conference (October 1991), he argued, intense debates have taken place in Syrian society with regard to Israel, 'with regard to the peace process, with regard to our future relations with the neighbor as well as with regard to the fears, anxieties, disappointments, failures and expectations emanating from the imminent deal, like it or not, with the old enemy'. 'Azm made it clear that at issue was not a debate conducted in the media but 'charged exchanges, comprehensive, penetrating, conducted in the age old tradition of an informal dialogue among people'. 'It is at one and the same time the Damascus rumor mill and people's free press.' The cumulative effect of these informal talks and debates is 'a public opinion that the power centers take into account without admitting as much. This public opinion has questions and queries regarding peace with Israel, but at the end of the day it has accepted it'. For 'Azm this is the decisive fact.

'Azm's essay dealt explicitly with the issue of public diplomacy and fully endorsed the Ba'th regime's position. He attributed great importance to Asad's cryptic support for peace with Israel and the tacit measures of normalization with Israel facilitated also through the Syrian media. If the Syrian media refers to Israel's Prime Minister by using his name and title rather than speak of 'he who calls himself prime minister of the Zionist entity', that is good enough. And as for Israel's demand that Asad's regime should invest a far more dramatic effort vis-à-vis Israeli public opinion, he endorsed the complaint made by Walid Mu'allim, Syria's former ambassador to Washington (and presently Foreign Minister): 'We have always felt that the Israelis wanted us to do their own work. They wanted us to persuade their public that peace was in their own interest. We prepared our public for peace with Israel. Many things changed in our media, but they wanted us to speak in the Israeli media in order to prepare Israeli opinion … we saw this insistence as a negative symptom.'

Ironically 'Azm's essay appeared in print five days after Hafiz al-Asad's death. Asad's death, his son's accession and several other changes terminated a decade of Israeli-Syrian negotiations and militated against their resumption.

NOTES

1. Radio Damascus, 15 December 1999. Al-Safir, Beirut, 13 February 2000. The Syrian 'phased approach' consisted of two stages: a political one, to which Hafiz al-Asad's regime assigned priority and which aimed at liberating the Syrian and the Palestinian territories occupied by Israel in June 1967, and an ideological long-term one designated to fully liberating Palestine. The means for the achievement of the first stage were both military and diplomatic while the means for implementing the second stage were left vague by Asad. See, Moshe Ma'oz's works *Asad: The Sphinx of Damascus – A Political Biography* (London: Weidenfeld and Nicolson, 1988); and *Syria and Israel: From War to Peacemaking* (Oxford: Clarendon Press, 1995).

2. B. William Quandt, *Camp David: Peacemaking and Politics* (Washington, DC: Brookings Institution, 1986).

3. For the Madrid Process, see Eitan Bentzur, *The Road to Peace Goes Through Madrid* (Tel-Aviv: Yediot Aharonot, 1997); Uri Savir, *The Process* (Tel-Aviv: Yediot Aharonot, 1998); Itamar Rabinovich, *Waging Peace: Israel and the Arabs, 1948–2003* (Princeton, NJ: Princeton University Press, 2004).

4. For a detailed description of the Israeli-Syrian negotiation, see Itamar Rabinovich, *The Brink of Peace: The Israeli-Syrian Negotiations* (Princeton, NJ: Princeton University Press, 1998).

5. Ibid., pp.159–60.

6. Savir's assessment of this issue is different of mine, see Savir, *The Process*, pp.298–326; and Rabinovich, *The Brink of Peace*, pp.196–247. See as well Dennis Ross, *The Missing Peace: The Inside Story of the Fight for Middle East Peace* (New York, NY: Farrar, Straus and Giroux, 2004), pp.238–45.

7. See an article by the Israeli journalist, Ben Aluf, in *Ha'aretz*, 24 June 1999.

8. Radio Damascus, 15 December 1999.

9. Raviv Druker, *Hara-kiri* (Tel-Aviv: Yediot Aharonot, 2002), pp.70–111; see as well an interview given by Ambassador Martin Indyk to *Yediot Aharonot*, 16 March 2001. For Ehud Barak's version see an interview given to *Ha'aretz*, 19 May 2000; 'The Myths Spread About Camp David are Baseless', in Shimon Shamir and Bruce Maddy-Weitzman (eds), *The Camp David Summit – What Went Wrong?* (Brighton: Sussex Academic Press, 2005), pp.117–47. See also Dennis Ross, *The Missing Peace*, pp.549–90. About the meetings in Shepherdstown and Geneva see Madeleine Albright, *Madam Secretary* (New York, NY: Miramax Books, 2003), pp.474–9 and Bill Clinton, *My Life* (New York, NY: A.A. Knopf, 2004), pp.882–7; 903–4. For an overall view of the negotiation between Barak and Asad, see Eyal Zisser, 'The Israel-Syria Negotiations: What Went Wrong?', *Orient*, 42, 2 (June 2001), pp.225–51.

10. *Ha'aretz*, 19 May 2000. See also in this volume, I. Rabinovich, 'Ehud Barak and the Collapse of the Peace Process'.

11. 'Ursan's article was published on 18 December 1999 on the website of al-usbu' al-adabi. An earlier article of the same vein was published by 'Ursan on 12 December 1999.

20

Ehud Barak and the Collapse of the Peace Process[1]

Ehud Barak was elected as Israel's prime minister on 17 May 1999; on 6 July he presented his coalition government to the Knesset. He had conducted his election campaign as Yitzhak Rabin's heir – a high-ranking military man and a former chief of staff of the IDF – who went into politics in order to provide Israel with peace embedded in a solid new security regime.[2] But as prime minister, Barak adopted a style radically different from Rabin's. Rabin moderated his bold decisions through his preference for gradualism; Barak sought to cut the Arab-Israeli Gordian knot with one bold stroke. He concluded that the phased approach to Israeli-Arab peacemaking had run its course, and acted out of a deeply held conviction that the failure to reach a swift comprehensive Arab-Israeli settlement would inevitably lead to a large-scale collision.

Barak set a formidable challenge for himself by formulating ambitious goals and a brief timetable in his public statements. During his first visit to the United States as prime minister, Barak's spokesmen told Israeli reporters that he had presented President Clinton with a programme for a final peace agreement that would resolve all outstanding issues among Israel, the Palestinians, Syria, and Lebanon. These issues would include the most intractable problems, such as Jerusalem and the resettlement of the Palestinian refugees. The Israeli reporters were told that 'Barak wants to remove the phased approach once and for all off the agenda and proposes that Arab leaders come to discuss the whole gamut of issues ... The Barak plan sets a timetable of fifteen months, until October 2000, to reach a breakthrough on all tracks: a final-status Israeli-Palestinian agreement, peace agreements with Syria and Lebanon, and regional arrangements for the refugee and water problems.'[3]

On other occasions, Barak emphasized that he was setting a fifteen-month deadline in order to find out whether Israel had a 'real partner' on the Arab side. Barak and his spokesmen did not elaborate in public on the essential components of his plan, but they let it be understood that he estimated an agreement could be reached on terms that were quite acceptable to both Palestinians and Israelis. This agreement would include an independent Palestinian state, contiguous in the West Bank and connected to the Gaza Strip through an elevated bridge; a unified Jerusalem under Israeli sovereignty; the Jordan River serving as a security border; and refugees rehabilitated in their countries of residence without 'right of return' to Israel. Barak was said to be willing to predicate the peace settlement with Syria on Israel's withdrawal from the Golan Heights, while insisting that the border be pushed back from the shoreline of Lake Tiberias.[4]

Barak's domestic political moves reflected his decision to devote his first two years in office to completing – or at least significantly advancing – the peace process. The elections of May 1999 were conducted by the 'two ballots' method, which meant that the voter cast one ballot for the direct election of the prime minister and another for a party list. Barak won an impressive personal majority (56.08 per cent) but emerged with a weak parliamentary basis. His own list won only 26 out of 120 seats, and the larger center-left bloc, the natural supporter of his peace policy, failed to obtain the requisite number of seats for building a coalition.

Against this backdrop the prime minister-elect had two choices. One option was to form a coalition government with the Likud, with a parliamentary caucus decimated to nineteen; to settle on modest progress in the peace process; and to seek to turn the Likud into a partner for an ambitious program of sociopolitical reform. The second option was to add the Orthodox Sephardi Shas (the third largest party, now holding seventeen seats) to the coalition alongside the left-wing Meretz Party, in the hope that in return for the accommodation of its agenda on funding a separate school system and 'church and state' issues, the Shas leadership would overcome the nationalistic proclivities of its voters and support Barak's bold vision for ending the Arab-Israeli conflict.

Barak chose the second option, working on the assumption that under the leadership of Rabbi Ovadya Yossef, Shas would become an effective partner to his peace policies. On 4 July 1999, he introduced a government resting on a coalition composed of seventy-three members of the Knesset. He also assumed that a government conducting an energetic peace policy could rely on the votes of the Arab Knesset members without adding them to the coalition.

This strategic choice was supplemented by a second major decision: to focus the initial and main effort of the government's peace policy on the Syrian, rather than Palestinian, track. Barak did not advertise this choice. According to his own statements, Barak remained committed to the idea of reaching final-status agreements with both Syria and the Palestinians

within a reasonable time frame, but he clearly preferred a 'Syria first' policy, seeking to obtain an early agreement with Syria and then proceed to
negotiate with the Palestinians from a better bargaining position.

This premise – as well as the whole tenor of Barak's policy – was ques-
tioned by a significant portion on Israel's foreign policy and national
security establishment. Questions were raised as to whether a government
resting on a fragile coalition would be able to complete agreements entail-
ing significant concessions on both the Syrian and Palestinian tracks.
There were also more specific questions regarding Barak's ability to
achieve an agreement with Syria, based on withdrawal from the Golan
and approved by a referendum, with the Palestinian issue hovering in the
background.

Barak's preference for the Syrian track was shaped by the same considerations that had guided his three predecessors – Rabin, Peres, and
Netanyahu – to choose a 'Syria first' policy. The Syrian-Israeli conflict was
perceived as less complex than the Israeli- Palestinian dispute, as an essentially territorial conflict between two sovereign states rather than a nationalist and communal conflict over land and rights. Asad was also seen as a
better partner than Yasir 'Arafat for a swift negotiation. Barak, in a typically
determined fashion, pushed from this vantage point to an early resumption and conclusion of the Israeli-Syrian negotiations.

Given the comparatively cordial welcome offered to Israel's new leader
by both the Syrian government and media, it began to seem that the
prospects of an Israeli-Syrian agreement were better in the latter half of
1999 than they had been in the previous decade. And yet the efforts to
resume the negotiations met with a series of unanticipated difficulties. It
took a full six months – until December 1999 – to restart the negotiation.[5]
Two of the difficulties were of an apparently technical nature. For one,
Hafiz al-Asad continued to insist (as he had done vis-à-vis Netanyahu) that
the negotiations be resumed only 'at the point at which they had been
interrupted', and that 'point' included an Israeli agreement to withdraw to
the lines of 4 June 1967. Barak was familiar with the history of the Israel-
Syrian negotiations and well knew that Asad would not sign a peace treaty
with Jerusalem without a full Israeli withdrawal from the Golan. Even if he
accepted this as part of the negotiation's bottom line, Barak was not willing to accept it as the point of departure. By effectively surrendering his
trump card before the start of the negotiations, he would be left without
any leverage or bargaining chips once the negotiations began to unfold.
Barak also wanted to establish the degree of flexibility in the Syrian insistence on Israel's withdrawal to 'the lines of 4 June 1967'. Such lines had
never been drawn on a map. Barak wanted to ascertain Asad's willingness

to settle on a formal Israeli acceptance of his demand, in return for Syrian flexibility regarding the actual location of the lines. When this issue was first put on the agenda in the mid-1990s, the Israeli negotiators and their colleagues on the US 'peace team' assumed that what mattered to Asad was the principle of obtaining an Israeli withdrawal beyond the (1923) inter-national boundary, that he was primarily interested in the al-Hammah salient (south of Lake Tiberias), and that he would be willing to accom-modate Israel's needs regarding the shoreline of Lake Tiberias and north-ern Jordan. It was made amply clear to Asad that this was a 'Red Line' for a country preoccupied with its water supply.[6]

A second difficulty arose from the loose ends left in the aftermath of the negotiation conducted with Asad in the fall of 1998 by the American business magnate Ronald Lauder on behalf of Benjamin Netanyahu. Lauder, a Republican who had served as ambassador in Vienna on behalf of the Reagan Administration, was supposed to conduct the negotiation unbeknownst to the Clinton Administration. Yet Lauder was accompanied on his trips to Damascus by a Lebanese-American middleman who was connected to several parties, including the Clinton Administration. Later, Lauder gave the US government a report, and a version was leaked to the Israeli media. According to Lauder's early report to the Clinton Admin-istration (subsequently modified), his negotiation with Asad was conduct-ed on the basis of an Israeli agreement to withdraw to the international boundary (rather than the lines of 4 June). This led Barak to believe that he could restart negotiations on terms that were more comfortable from an Israeli point of view. It took several weeks to discover that the report – and the set of assumptions it produced – were erroneous. (The Syrians contin-ue to deny this version of events and have sought to belittle the significance of the whole Lauder episode.)

Beyond these particular issues lies the more fundamental question of Asad's intention ever to consummate negotiations with Israel. There was, in the 1990s, a school of thought that had argued all along that Asad never intended to reach an agreement with Israel, and that his participation in the peace process was motivated purely by the political dividends he expected to reap in Washington. But even those who did not share this view had to contend with the question of the extent to which – and the conditions under which – Asad was interested in resuming and complet-ing negotiations with Israel in 1999–2000.

The principal change during this period was the decline of Asad's health, and the subsequent urgency that was now vested in the issue of succession. Asad died in June 2000. During the preceding months his physical and mental decline was all too evident. This decline was matched by a loss of authority and political power. The process of promoting his son, Bashar, and building him up as heir apparent, was accelerated. Some of Hafiz al Asad's closest friends and associates were removed by younger men who were closer to Bashar and viewed as better partners for the new ruler. Asad's gradual decline gave Syria's foreign minister, Faruq al-Shara', a degree of authority and freedom of action that he had not known in the past.

Hafiz al-Asad's power remained unchallenged, but the removal of several former partners and associates, the widespread unhappiness with the adoption of the dynastic principle, and the discontent with Bashar's persona created significant pockets of criticism and opposition for the first time in many years. Part of the criticism was directed at the very idea of settlement with Israel and the compromises and concessions it entailed; these were easier targets than Asad's nepotism. Asad, aware of his decline, chose to focus on his chief priority: ensuring the succession to his son.

But this was not the only set of forces brought to bear on Syria's negotiations with Ehud Barak. Asad's desire to regain the Golan before stepping offstage, the need to secure Washington's goodwill and cooperation at this sensitive juncture, and the potential for conflict in Lebanon (given Barak's pledge to the Israeli public to get the IDF out of Lebanon within his first year in power) all modified and affected the Syrian-Israeli negotiations.

Barak first made that pledge during the election campaign, and it was, indeed, dismissed by many as a mere campaign promise. But he did repeat it after his election and thereby changed the dynamic shaping the Israeli-Lebanese-Syrian triangle throughout the 1990s. Israel's policy had been predicated on the assumption that its problems in South Lebanon could be resolved only through an agreement with Syria. The hegemonic power in Lebanon, Syria in fact encouraged Hizballah's attacks in order to extract greater concessions from Israel. Barak's promise (or threat) to take Israel out of South Lebanon by July 2000 altered this equation. How would Hizballah conduct itself if Israel were to withdraw unilaterally from South Lebanon? How should Syria act on its own and with regard to Hizballah and its Iranian sponsors? Could Damascus risk escalation along the Israeli-Lebanese border, given the complex state of affairs in Syria's domestic politics?

Against this backdrop, the quiet diplomacy of the summer and fall of 1999 yielded a positive outcome. In December 1999 the resumption of the Israeli-Syrian negotiations was announced. Moreover, Asad agreed to upgrade the negotiation from the bureaucratic to the political level and nominated Foreign Minister Faruq al-Shara' as the Syrian negotiator. Barak, in turn, decided to overlook the difference in rank and status and put himself at the head of the Israeli delegation. Negotiations began in Washington on

15 December. Barak was accompanied by his foreign minister, David Levy; the minister of tourism (and former chief of staff of the IDF), Amnon Shahak; and a team of negotiators headed by Reserve General Uri Sagie (who, like Barak and Shahak, had participated in earlier phases of the Israeli-Syrian peace process).

In December 1999 and January 2000 two rounds of negotiations were held under President Clinton's aegis, in Washington and in Shepherdstown, West Virginia. The Washington talks were overshadowed by Faruq al-Shara's sulking conduct, notably his refusal to shake Barak's hand and his strident speech.[7] Such details may seem trifling within the larger context of two enemies making an effort to move from a state of hostility and belligerency to a state of peace, but symbols and rituals are significant both in conflict and during a transition to peace. This was particularly true for the Israeli-Syrian relationship. It was widely assumed that in the event of an agreement with Syria, Barak would have to hold a referendum. It was also assumed that in order to win this referendum, he would have to persuade Asad to engage in 'public diplomacy' – a series of gestures designed to persuade the Israeli public that Syria had had a change of heart and was now ready for genuine peace with yesterday's enemy. But during the Washington talks and throughout this period, Syria held on to its familiar position: refusal to engage in any public diplomacy, and continued pressure exerted on Israel in the Lebanese and Palestinian arenas as long as an agreement had not been reached.

However, in the closed sessions held in Washington, Shara' was more forthcoming than his public conduct suggested. Furthermore, strident tone notwithstanding, he incorporated two intriguing phrases in his public statement: that the conflict with Israel was no longer existential but territorial, and that peacemaking with Israel constituted a transition from struggle to competition.[8] This motif was essential to Syria's concept of a prospective settlement with Israel – Israel would no longer be an enemy but would remain an adversary and a competitor. By signing a peace treaty with Israel, Syria could end active conflict with the Jewish state but not reconcile itself to its legitimacy. The struggle would therefore continue in other (that is, non-military) ways. This concept of peacemaking with Israel is, in fact, not so different from the policies pursued by Egypt, although the latter's leaders stopped short of an explicit adoption of the notion of 'an ongoing struggle', preferring to use sifted terms such as 'cold peace' and opposition to 'normalization'.

The Shepherdstown talks took longer than the brief meeting in Washington but ended in failure. The chief obstacle was familiar: Syria's insistence on an explicit Israeli commitment to withdraw to the lines of 4

June 1967, as a pre-condition to any progress. Barak alluded to his willingness to withdraw, and to start preparing Israeli public opinion for withdrawal to the lines of 4 June 1967, as an abstract concept, but he refused to make an explicit commitment prior to assessing Asad's flexibility regarding the actual demarcation of the 4 June lines and in particular the shoreline of Lake Tiberias. According to American diplomats who participated in the talks, Syria's Foreign Minister Shara' indicated that Syria could be flexible in this matter. But he refused to elaborate, and, as it turned out during the Clinton-Asad meeting in Geneva in March 2000, his statement had no real value.

The failure of the Shepherdstown talks subsequently became a bone of contention between Barak and his critics. Participants such as Ambassador Martin Indyk and Barak's own chief negotiator, Uri Sagie, have argued that Barak developed 'cold feet'. They felt that his failure to make an explicit commitment prevented a breakthrough with a Syrian partner otherwise ready to make a deal. Raviv Druker's critical book on Barak's tenure claims that pollsters warned Barak that Israeli public opinion was opposed to the concessions demanded by Syria.[9] Robert Malley, a former official of the National Security Council, argued that Clinton was resentful of Barak's conduct at Shepherdstown – so much so that, angered by a change in Barak's position during the Camp David Summit in July 2000, he told him: 'I can't go to 'Arafat with a retrenchment! You can sell it ... This is not real. This is not serious. I went to Shepherdstown ... and was told nothing by you for four days. I went to Geneva and felt like an Indian doll doing your bidding ...'[10]

Barak still insists that it would have been a grave mistake to offer Asad an explicit commitment to withdraw, and that it was Asad's insistence on this pre-condition that obstructed the talks. Barak also attributes great importance to the fact that an American draft of a proposed text for an Israeli-Syrian peace treaty was leaked to the Israeli press. The US peace team prepared the draft in an effort to demonstrate how close the parties were to agreement. The Syrians leaked a doctored version of the text, to show that it was in fact closer to a 'non-belligerency' agreement than to a peace treaty. Later, (in order to counter this attempt or perhaps owing to another consideration by an American or Israeli participant) a different, more attractive version of the text was leaked to an Israeli journalist. Indeed, in the post-mortem of the Shepherdstown talks, the Syrians complained that the leak embarrassed Asad and made it difficult for Syria to resume the negotiations.[11]

As had been the case in earlier instances, the very fact that a high-level Israeli-Syrian meeting took place agitated the Israeli political system. The prospect of an agreement with Syria predicated on a full Israeli withdrawal from the Golan seemed close and realistic. The Golan Lobby had become powerful during the past decade, and its campaign against Barak's Syrian gambit was facilitated by two crucial forces: Hafiz al-Asad's refusal to invest any effort to win over Israeli public opinion, and the inherent difficulty of persuading the public to endorse an agreement that had yet to be made.

In hopeful anticipation, Barak's government began a campaign to build support in the United States for a massive aid package, to be received when an agreement with Syria was signed. It suggested that the Clinton Administration should ask Congress for a special aid package of up to $17 billion, allowing Israel to build up and modernize the IDF to compensate for the loss of the Golan.[12] This was a staggering amount that would be difficult to get endorsed by any Congress, let alone a Republican one explicitly hostile to Syria and reluctant to assist the Clinton Administration in attaining its foreign policy objectives. Moreover, during the brief period of high expectations of an Israeli-Syrian breakthrough, the Golan Lobby in Israel and its allies in the American-Jewish community launched a campaign against US support of a would-be Israeli-Syrian agreement. The campaign was reminiscent of the one conducted in the mid-1990s. As it turned out, the campaign was superfluous – cut short by the collapse of the negotiations in March 2000.

In contradistinction to the familiar arguments of Israeli and American opponents of a Syrian-Israeli settlement were the novel voices of a domestic Syrian opposition to accommodation with Israel. There were some indications of such opposition in the early and mid-1990s, but at that time they seemed marginal and muted. The domestic criticism of Asad's policies that surfaced in late 1999 and early 2000, however, was systematic and sustained. He and his regime were taken to task for their very willingness to accept the state of Israel, as well as for their apparent readiness to withdraw from some of Syria's original positions in negotiations. An article published by 'Aqleh 'Ursan, a Ba'th Party member and chairman of the Arab Writers Union headquartered in Damascus, was a particularly harsh example of such criticism. 'Ursan stated, 'We reject and will continue to reject any recognition of Zionism.'[13] Echoing the bitter tone of Syria's greatest poet, Nizar Qabbani, 'Ursan asked rhetorically, 'Are we to remain with nothing but a sense of despair and possibly the bitter memories of our defeat? Will the ghosts of millions of Palestinians who were expelled from their homes disappear?' He asserted that he and his colleagues saw the struggle against the 'Zionist enemy' as an 'existential' conflict – and not as a conflict over borders – in a clear, sardonic reference to Faruq al-Shara's statement.

On 13 February, Shara' appeared before the members of the Arab

Writers Union and delivered a speech explaining and defending Syria's policy toward Israel. It was an uncharacteristic speech for a foreign minister to make. In ordinary circumstances, it would have been Asad's responsibility to offer an authoritative exposition of his regime's policy. But Asad's health had deteriorated to the point that he was incapable of exercising his customary leadership role.

Shara's speech was not a coherent, focused text but rather a patchwork of ideas and arguments that constituted an effort to address different constituencies – and was therefore full of contradictions. In defence of the regime's policies, he explained that the Arabs had been defeated by Israel, and Syria had been abandoned by its Arab partners. Therefore there was no choice but to make peace with Israel. In a similar apologetic vein, Shara' repeated in a modified version the statement he had made in Washington in December 1999 that the conflict with Israel had been transformed from an existential to a territorial dispute and was accordingly ripe for resolution. The foreign minister also repeated another motif from his Washington speech in stating that peace, in fact, meant a transformation of the military conflict to a political, economic, and cultural competition – one in which the Arabs stood a better chance.

However, in other segments of the 13 February speech Shara' denounced Israel and Zionism, pledging his allegiance to the original vision and long-term goals of the Ba'th. In response to a question from the audience, Shara' went so far as to revive the 'phased approach' of the 1970s: 'The Ba'th Party believes that regaining the whole of Palestine is a long-term strategic goal that could not be implemented in one phase ... the Ba'th Party's doctrine draws a distinction between the different phases of the struggle for the liberation of Palestine.'[14]

The failure of the Shepherdstown talks resulted in a stalemate that lasted for about two months. Both the Clinton Administration and the Barak government were worried by this passage of time. The date of Israel's withdrawal from Lebanon was getting closer and Asad's health continued to deteriorate, exacerbating the Israeli debate on a prospective agreement with Syria. Proponents argued that it was preferable to conclude the agreement with a leader who commanded the stature and authority necessary to both make and implement the agreement. They also believed that the majority of Syria's political system and public had come to accept the notion of peace with Israel, so an agreement made by Asad would be kept by his successors even if he died shortly after signing. They further argued that if an agreement failed to be signed during Asad's lifetime, it would take his successor a long time to establish enough sway to complete the peace process with Israel. On the other side of the debate, opponents of a settlement with Syria reinforced their original criticism by arguing that handing over the Golan to a dying autocratic ruler would be an egregiously reckless act.

In any event, the United States and Israel reached the conclusion that a face-to-face meeting between Presidents Clinton and Asad was the only possible way to break the deadlock and reach a swift agreement. Washington and Jerusalem therefore acted on the assumption that Asad alone possessed the authority to make crucial decisions for breakthrough and accommodation, and that absent the prospect of a meeting between Barak and Asad, the closest approximation to an Israeli-Syrian Summit was an American-Syrian one. Clinton was familiar with Barak's position and could be trusted to present and represent it well. And furthermore, Asad was believed to be more interested in a dialogue with Washington than in making peace with Israel.

This technique constituted a new version of Rabin's position with Warren Christopher in August 1993. Like that original deposit of Israel's willingness to withdraw from the Golan, Barak's reliance on Clinton reflected his exasperation by his repeated failure to reach Asad directly. He learned from the Lauder episode that it was easier to persuade Asad to make concessions when negotiating with him in person. But Christopher's meeting with Asad in August 1993 was a first step calculated to set a process in motion. The Clinton-Asad meeting in March 2000 was rather a final measure, a last-ditch effort to prevent total collapse of the Israeli-Syrian negotiation.

The 26 March meeting in Geneva ended in swift, resonant failure. We have yet to find out the extent of the efforts invested to secure the success of the meeting and to save Clinton from another embarrassment. Clearly, the US president acted on the assumption (derived from statements made by Faruq al-Shara' in earlier discussions) that Asad would be willing to show flexibility in drawing the lines of 4 June 1967, and to allow a strip of land along Lake Tiberias and the Upper Jordan to remain under Israeli sovereignty. The strip would be wider than the ten metres stipulated by the 1923 agreement, which established the boundary between the British Mandate in Syria and the French Mandate in Syria.

In Geneva, Asad rejected these ideas out of hand. He made it amply clear that if Shara' had spoken to that effect, he had exceeded his authority. And so the ten-month effort launched in May 1999 collapsed – under Asad's insistence on obtaining part of the Lake Tiberias shore, and under Barak's insistence that even if Israel agreed to withdraw from the Golan Heights and to give up the al-Hammah enclave, it could not and would not give up full sovereignty over the lake. Barak viewed full control of Lake Tiberias as key to Israel's water regime; he also sensed that this represented a political red line that the Israeli electorate would not cross in a referendum or a fresh election.[15]

The collapse of the fourth effort of Israeli-Syrian resolution in the final decade of the twentieth century had several causes. Asad's uncompromising position and Washington's and Jerusalem's tactical errors were two of them. But the prime reason seems to have been Asad's physical and mental decline. During the last months of his life, Asad focused his residual powers on securing the succession to his son. He felt weak, and vulnerable, and was sensitive to criticism that he was willing to sacrifice his principles for a compromise with Israel. This criticism may well have reflected a minority view and was probably also an expression of opposition to the introduction of the dynastic principle into the political system of a formerly revolutionary republic. Nonetheless, on the eve of a problematic transition, Asad and his loyalist core were defensive. Had Israel succumbed to all his demands and provided him with 'the peace of the victors', he might have signed an agreement – but for Ehud Barak this was not a viable option.

The failure of the Geneva Summit provided fresh ammunition to those who had argued since the early and mid-1990s that Asad never intended to consummate the negotiations with Israel, and that he was merely interested in the political dividends accruing to participants in the peace process. For advocates of this interpretation, the Geneva meeting in March 2000 was a moment of truth that illuminated Asad's conduct throughout the previous decade. An entirely different interpretation argues that the failure of the 1999–2000 negotiation could have been avoided altogether. My own view is that the spring of 2000 cannot necessarily explain the previous decade owing to the profound change in Asad's outlook once he realized that his death was imminent.

Several attempts were made to revive negotiations in the aftermath of the failed summit in Geneva, but they were nipped in the bud by two developments: Israel's withdrawal from Lebanon in May and Asad's death in June.

Israel's withdrawal from South Lebanon ended a nine-year link between the Israeli-Syrian negotiations and the security issues along the Israeli-Lebanese border. Israel no longer expected an agreement with Syria to also provide a fundamental solution to its Lebanese dilemma. It also reached, independently, the conclusion that large-scale military operations in Lebanon, attacks on Hizballah, and exercising indirect pressure on Beirut were all ineffective strategies. Syria was the hegemonic power in Lebanon, and Israel's quest for security along its northern border would now rest on a classic deterrence equation. Attacks on Israel across an internationally recognized border would lead – it was suggested – to a full-fledged Israeli-Syrian collision.[16]

From Barak's point of view, the unilateral withdrawal from Lebanon was a gamble. There was no guarantee that either Syria or Hizballah would act cautiously. However, in reality it proved to be at least a short-term success. Hafiz al-Asad died on 10 June. Bashar's succession proceeded smoothly, and the new president was clearly interested in consolidating his position rather than in risky adventures. Nor were Teheran and Hizballah interested in a wave of violence in South Lebanon at that time. For them, Israel's withdrawal was a great victory – a vindication – and they were determined to exploit it politically by bolstering Hizballah's standing in Lebanon.

For nearly five months, Hizballah's leadership did indeed refrain from initiating dramatic attacks against Israel. Instead, it settled on digging in along the border and encouraging Lebanese civilians to come to the fence in an effort to defy and provoke IDF guards. While Israel claimed that its withdrawal from Lebanon was final and definitive, Hizballah argued that the issue remained open as long as Israel continued to hold Lebanese prisoners and failed to withdraw from the Shaba Farms. According to Israel (and the UN), the Shaba Farms were Syrian territory and should be dealt with by Israel and Syria. Hizballah (and eventually other Lebanese actors), however, saw fit to argue that this was Lebanese territory and that Israel's refusal to withdraw from it constituted an act of occupation and aggression. The organization was thus laying the groundwork for new attacks on Israel at some future date.

That future date came in early October 2000. After the outbreak of Palestinian-Israeli violence in late September, Hizballah was confronted with both opportunity and pressure to join the fray. From Iran's and Hizballah's perspective, the Palestinians were inspired by their exploits in Lebanon and applied the lesson that there was no need to make concessions to Israel. If one stood one's ground and fought for one's rights, the Israelis would pack up and leave. How could Hizballah's leadership remain an idle spectator under these circumstances? Hizballah's radical proclivities were reinforced by two developments: its poor performance in Lebanese elections and Bashar al-Asad's weakness. Bashar not only failed to restrain the organization but seemed to be under its leadership's spell. For Hafiz al-Asad, Hizballah had been an actor on the Lebanese scene, an arm of the Iranian government, and an occasional ally of Syria's policy. But while he had sought to use and manipulate the organization, his son seemed to admire it.

With this backdrop of events spurring them on, Hizballah launched an offensive against Israel by abducting three Israeli soldiers who were patrolling the border on 7 October. A week later it abducted an Israeli businessman in Europe. Other attempts did not materialize. Israel, reluctant to open a second front, decided to refrain from a military response.

Israel's policy changed after the formation of Sharon's government in February 2001. Hizballah attacked twice, and on both occasions Israel retaliated by attacking Syrian positions. Sharon thus implemented the deterrence equation established by Barak and underscored the view that Syria was the effective address for Israel's deterrence. In both cases Syria refrained from responding despite pressures that were reportedly exerted on Bashar al-Asad by his more radical associates.

The calming effect of Israel's actions evaporated after a few months. The Palestinian-Israeli war of attrition intensified, as did Iran's determination to destabilize the region. Hizballah's attacks grew in scope and boldness.

The tension and violence along Israel's northern border in 2001 and 2002 provided yet another manifestation of the 'shifting horizon' phenomenon in Arab-Israeli relations. Even when Israel withdrew to the international border – and did so in cooperation with the United States – Hizballah (and subsequently Lebanon's government) have argued that Israel's withdrawal was less than complete. Furthermore, the Arab Summit conference in Beirut in March 2002, meeting to adopt the Saudi 'peace initiative', endorsed this position as well.

It was only in the early summer of 2000, after the final collapse of the Syrian negotiations and his unilateral withdrawal from Lebanon, that Barak devoted his full attention to negotiations with the Palestinians – protestations notwithstanding. It had been to the detriment of Israel's dealings with the Palestinians that Barak had focused primarily on the Syrian track during his first year in office.

These new dealings consisted of several meetings with 'Arafat, of give-and-take with him through a discreet channel, and of a formal negotiation on the implementation of the Wye Agreement signed by Netanyahu's government in October 1998. Barak confronted a double dilemma: how to preserve 'Arafat's and the Palestinians' goodwill while assigning a clear priority to the Syrian track, and how to proceed with the implementation of the Wye Agreement without spending territorial assets that he would rather use in the final-status negotiations. Barak viewed himself as a leader possessed of capabilities and style different from those of Netanyahu and believed in his ability to accomplish final-status agreements with both Syria and the Palestinians. The agreement with the Palestinians would perhaps be reached and implemented in phases, but Barak was reluctant to offer massive concessions during the interim phases. (As a member in Rabin's cabinet in the Summit of 1995 he abstained during the vote on the Oslo II Accord in disagreement with the phased withdrawals that were built into it.)

In any event, on 4 September 1999, Barak signed the Sharm al-Sheikh agreement for the implementation of the Wye Agreement that had been signed by Netanyahu in October 1998. The withdrawal that had originally been envisaged in two phases was now to be implemented in three, but the Palestinians were compensated by a verbal promise that they would be given contiguous 'quality' territory. Agreement was also reached regarding a familiar set of issues including the port in Gaza, safe passage between the West Bank and the Gaza Strip, and prisoner release. The parties agreed on a continuous accelerated negotiation with a view to reaching agreement in two phases: a framework agreement within 2000 and a final status agreement within a year.

The final-status negotiations were conducted in a secret channel. The Palestinian delegation was headed by Abu 'Ala', chairman of the Legislative Council and 'Arafat's chief negotiator in Oslo. Barak was represented by Shlomo Ben-Ami, minister of domestic security, and Gilead Sher, an attorney who negotiated the Sharm al-Sheikh agreement on Israel's behalf. In May 2000, details of the secret Israeli-Palestinian negotiation began to leak. Natan Sharanski, minister of the interior in Barak's government and a prominent member of the right wing of the coalition, publicized these details and began to build up opposition to what he saw as excessive concessions on Israel's part.[17]

The formulas which underlay the understandings that coalesced in Stockholm were reminiscent of the core of the Beilin-Abu Mazen draft agreement put together in the fall of 1995: Israeli readiness to withdraw from the bulk of the West Bank and the Gaza Strip, and Palestinian acceptance of Israeli annexation of the large settlement blocs in return for an asymmetrical exchange of territories. Barak felt that a swift final-status agreement with 'Arafat was within reach on the basis of this formula, and he began to urge President Clinton to summon the parties to a summit modelled on the 1978 Camp David Conference, in order to reach such an agreement.

Barak was acting under the pressure of two ticking political clocks. In the United States, President Clinton's second term was drawing to a close. The presidential election was scheduled for early November, and Clinton's own assessment was that he could be effective only through September in helping the parties reach agreement and mobilizing support in Congress for the financial aid packages indispensable for its implementation. In Israel, Barak was acutely aware that his coalition was shrinking with the passage of time and a hostile majority was coalescing in the Knesset. These calculations were reinforced by the prime minister's sense that tensions were building up and that, barring an agreement, Israel and the Palestinians were on a collision course. The eruption of violence on 'Nakba Day' (the term used by the

Palestinians to designate Israel's independence and their defeat) in May 2000 lit a significant red light. The level and intensity of the violence were an indication of the potential for greater conflict, as well as of the fact that 'Arafat did not fully control the Palestinian 'street', and that the popular rage was directed in part at him and at the Palestinian Authority.

In the summer of 2000, an intricate and intriguing link developed between the dynamics of Israeli domestic politics and Israel's conduct in its negotiation with the Palestinians.

As mentioned above, the elections of May 1999 produced a discrepancy between Barak's impressive personal achievement and the further fragmentation of the Knesset and weakening of the two large parties. In the two ballot election, Barak won 56 per cent of the vote; the list composed of the Labour Party and its partners won twenty-six seats in the Knesset (as compared to thirty-four in the 1996 elections). The Likud list was decimated to a mere nineteen (as compared to thirty-two). The ultra-Orthodox Sephardi Shas rose from ten to seventeen, the left-wing Meretz from nine to ten, and the new Shinuy (defined by an assertive secularist platform) won six seats. Several Arab members were elected, most of them through anti-Zionist lists.

From this fragmented picture, three major conclusions could be drawn. First, the Israeli public gave Barak an impressive personal victory but denied him the possibility of forming a stable coalition government. Second, Netanyahu was personally defeated, but 'Netanyahu's coalition' suffered only a minor loss and commanded fifty-eight seats in the new Knesset. And last, with regard to the principal issue on the national agenda – Israel's relationship with the Arab world – the Israeli body politic remained more or less evenly divided.

With these conclusions setting the stage, it is quite possible that Barak's choice of Shas as a principal partner to his 'peace coalition' was doomed to fail. This inherent difficulty was then compounded by Barak's failure to learn from Rabin's mistake in 1992. At the time, Rabin had formed a coalition government with Shas and Meretz, and assigned the education portfolio to the latter's leader, Shulamit Aloni. Friction soon erupted over the budgeting of Shas's independent educational system (one of the party's principal mainstays). This was one of the main reasons for Shas's decision to withdraw from the coalition in 1993. In 1999, it was Meretz's new leader, Yossi Sarid, who became the minister of education. A tug-of-war soon started between Sarid and Shas, exacerbating the party's relationship with Barak and keeping their relationship on the edge of a permanent crisis. In June 2000, Meretz withdrew from the coalition, promising to support the government 'from the outside'. By this point Barak's relationship with Shas was beyond all repair.

Nor did Barak fare well in his relations with the other coalition partners. The ultra-Orthodox Yahadut Hatorah left the coalition as early as 1999; Natan Sharanski, the former anti-Soviet activist, was openly critical of Barak's style of governance and his willingness to offer far-reaching concessions in order to reach agreements with Syria and the Palestinians. The effect of these tensions in the coalition's ranks was magnified by endemic criticism and challenges to Barak's leadership in his own party.[18]

The disintegration of Barak's coalition was accelerated by the decision to go the Camp David Conference. Shas, the National Religious Party, and Sharanski and his faction were all opposed to the anticipated concessions and left the coalition. Foreign Minister David Levy was offended by the fact that the minister of domestic security, Shlomo Ben-Ami, was put in charge of the negotiations and was accompanied by his brother Maxim. Barak was left with a coalition of thirty. He managed to keep his government afloat for several more months, through parliamentary manoeuvers and owing to the reluctance of several Knesset members to end their term and face a new election. But by late November, Barak had reached the end of his rope and called for a new election. On 9 December, he formally resigned and became the prime minister of a transitional government.

One important outcome of this chain of events was that Barak conducted both the negotiations at Camp David and the crisis that broke out at the end of September 2000 without parliamentary majority and through a diminished cabinet. It was an extraordinary set of affairs. A prime minister preoccupied with his own political survival and devoid of parliamentary support could hardly be expected to manage a profound and sustained national security crisis.

When Barak lost his coalition on the eve of his departure for Camp David, he established an unhealthy connection between his own political future and the success of the negotiations. The conventional wisdom at the time stated that a majority of Israelis supported an agreement with the Palestinians but opposed the concessions that such an agreement entailed. It was widely assumed that the Knesset would approve neither an agreement based on massive concessions nor a referendum that would endorse such an agreement. To facilitate one of these scenarios, Barak would have had to dissolve the Knesset and bring about a fresh election. Barak's supporters and opponents alike estimated that in that situation, he would be reelected. However, as the Camp David Conference failed, the issue remained moot.

The expectations generated by the very term 'Camp David', as well as the changes in Israel's position in the negotiations, turned the second Camp David Conference in July 2000 into the high (and eventually low) point of Ehud Barak's effort to reach an accord with the Palestinians. Despite its saliency, the

July Summit should be seen as a phase in a negotiation that lasted for almost a year – from the spring of 2000 to the eve of the February 2001 elections.

As time goes by and accounts of that negotiation accumulate, it increasingly appears to have been a journey by Barak and his government from the centre-right of the Israeli political spectrum to its left wing. This journey did not produce a comparable shift on the Palestinian side and did not obtain an agreement. Furthermore, since the end of September, the effort had been overshadowed by 'Arafat's attempt to exploit the outbreak of violence as another means of pressure on Israel. The Barak government's journey unfolded through five main phases. (The rest of the chapter, dealing with the Israeli-Palestinian negotiation is not reproduced here.)

NOTES

1. This article was published in Itamar Rabinovich, *Waging Peace – Israel and the Arabs*, 1948–2003 (Princeton, NJ: Princeton University Press, 2004).
2. The first book written on the Barak period was by the journalist Raviv Druker, *Hara-kiri* [in Hebrew] (Tel Aviv: Yediot Aharonot, 2002). It is a critical book, relying mainly on interviews with disappointed assistants and partners and internal material from the Prime Ministry Office that was handed to the author. Later on another book was published, Ran Eddelist, *Ehud Barak: His War against the Demons* (Or-Yehuda: Kineret, 2003) [in Hebrew]. This book attempts to form a reaction to Druker's book, and it is based, although this is not explicitly stated, on long hours of conversations with Barak himself as well as with other participants in the events of the period.
3. Ibid., and Aluf Benn in *Ha'aretz*, 19 July 1999.
4. Ibid.
5. For an overview of the Israeli-Syrian negotiations during Barak's period, see Eyal Zisser, 'The Israel-Syria Negotiations: What Went Wrong?', *Orient*, 42, 2 (June 2001), pp.225–51.
6. See Uri Savir, *The Process* (Tel-Aviv: Yediot Aharonot, 1998) [in Hebrew], pp.298–326, and Itamar Rabinovich, *The Brink of Peace* (Princeton, NJ: Princeton University Press, 1998), pp.248–93, 305–19.
7. For the public diplomacy in the Israeli-Syrian negotiations, see in this volume the chapter: 'On Public Diplomacy and the Israeli-Syrian Negotiations During the Waning of Hafiz al-Asad's Rule'.
8. Ibid.
9. See Druker, *Hara-kiri*, pp.70–110; American ambassador in Israel Martin Indyk in *Yediot Ahronot*, 16 March 2001. Ehud Barak's version was published in an interview for *Ha'aretz*, 19 May 2000; Uri Sagie (during a conversation with the author, May 2003). Another American version is that of Robert Malley, a member of the National Security Council during the Clinton Administration; see Robert Malley 'Middle East Endgame III: Israel, Syria and Lebanon – How Comprehensive Peace Settlements Would Look', *International Crisis Group Middle East Report*, 4 (16 July 2002), p.4.
10. See Robert Malley and Hussein Agha, 'Camp David: The Tragedy of Errors', *The New York Review of Books*, 48, 13, 9 August 2001.
11. Zisser, 'The Israel-Syria Negotiations', p.237.
12. Aluf Benn in *Ha'aretz*, 4 January 2000.
13. See note 6.
14. Ibid.
15. See Zisser, 'The Israel-Syria Negotiations'; Malley, 'Middle East Endgame III'. Additional details of the negotiations can be found in Madeleine Albright, *Madam Secretary* (New York, NY: Miramax Books, 2003), pp.476–82.
16. For an analysis of the new power equation created in South Lebanon, see Robert Malley, 'Old Games in Search of New Rules', *International Crisis Group Middle East Report*, 7 (29 October 2002).
17. Druker, *Hara-kiri*, pp.189–208.
18. Ibid., pp.167-78.

21

The Bush Administration, Israel and Syria,[1] 2001–2008

The nature and landscape of the trilateral relationship between the US, Israel and Syria were transformed during the final months of 2000 and the early months of 2001. To begin with, all three countries underwent significant domestic political changes that had major repercussions for the conduct of their foreign policies.

As has already been mentioned, Hafiz al-Asad died in June 2000 and was succeeded by his son, Bashar. His original heir apparent, Basil, was killed in a car accident in 1994 and Bashar, an ophthalmologist, who studied and worked in England, was drafted into the role.

During the next six years Hafiz al-Asad had to deal with two principal questions in this context:

1. Could the dynastic principle be introduced in a regime that used to be defined as socialist and revolutionary?
2. How suitable was Bashar to the task of leading a difficult and complex country like Syria?

Asad Père had to invest considerable political capital in order to secure the succession to his son. His efforts were facilitated by the apparent decision by the other potential contenders to avoid a power struggle and to hold on, instead, to their respective power bases.

Bashar's assumption of power was smooth, but it did not take long for the world to find out that Syria's new ruler had yet to consolidate and assert his own power vis-à-vis his father's associates and that, more ominously, despite six years of preparation he seemed ill-equipped to navigate the web of domestic and regional forces and issues confronting Syria's ruler.

From a Middle Eastern perspective the US presidential transition of 2000–01 was dramatically different from that of 1992–93. The incoming Bush Administration was determined to distance itself from its predecessor's policies in the Middle East and to replace them with its own distinctive set of policies. The Clinton Administration, it was argued, spent too much time and effort on an Arab-Israeli peace process, that had conveniently collapsed during the latter half of 2000. One of the first measures taken by the new Administration was to dismantle the State Department's peace process team. The office of the Special Middle East Coordinator was abolished and the conduct of Middle Eastern policy was restored to the Bureau of Near Eastern Affairs. As the new National Security Adviser put it: 'We shouldn't think of American involvement for the sake of American involvement ... Washington should consider it a slap at the United States or a disengaged American policy if the parties can progress on their own'.[2]

More significant was the reversal of the logic and essence of the policy. The Clinton Administration's policy departed, as we saw, from a geopolitical premise and sought to pacify and stabilize the Arab-Israeli part of the Middle East so that in addition to the intrinsic value of the resolution of an old conflict, it would provide a solid base for dealing with the severe security challenges presented in the Eastern part of the region by Iran and Iraq.

The dominant strand in the Bush Administration's policy toward the Middle East reversed this line and replaced it with a mixture of ideology and *real politic*. The primary goal was to topple the radical, dictatorial regimes of Iran and Iraq and replace them with more democratic and more moderate regimes. Once implemented, this strategy would dramatically enhance the prospects for peace and democracy in the core area of the Middle East and a different, more successful, peace process could be pursued.

In immediate terms this meant loss of interest in both tracks of the peace process. Secretary of State Colin Powell did travel to the region early in his tenure and he did visit Damascus but the emphasis of that visit was on Syria's role in helping Iraq circumvent the sanctions regime and sell more oil than it was allowed to through the pipeline that led through Syria's territory to the Mediterranean.

Ehud Barak's government and coalition had been waning since the early summer of 2000 and whatever power and prestige he was left with were decimated by the failure of the Camp David Summit, the outbreak of the 'second *intifadah*' and the failure to contain it either by force or through a revival of the 'peace process'. Barak's defeat in the February 2001 elections for the post of Prime Minister (a procedure introduced in the mid 1990s as an attempt at electoral reform, since rescinded) was hardly a surprise. More surprising was the fact that the contender was Ariel Sharon and not Benjamin Netanyahu, the Likud's leader, who insisted that he would only run in a general election that would provide him with a comfortable parliamentary majority.

As Prime Minister, Sharon had clear priorities: defeat the 'second intifadah' and then find a viable formula for dealing with the Palestinian issue. He was not interested in the Syrian track and remained firmly opposed to the notion of withdrawal from the Golan Heights. During his tenure two attempts were made to start an informal (or initially informal) Israeli-Syrian track. The first was an initiative taken by Mahir, Bashar al-Asad's brother, through a Jordanian contact and through a former Director General of the Israeli Foreign Ministry, Eytan Bentzur, to resume the negotiations. The second attempt was conducted by another Director General of the Israeli Foreign Ministry, Alon Liel and a Syrian-American named Ibrahim Sulayman, who had a long record of trying to insert himself into Syrian-Israeli peacemaking. This was a longer effort that was initially facilitated by the Turkish government and subsequently by the Swiss Foreign Ministry. In both cases the top echelons of the Syrian regime were clearly supportive of the attempt, probably as part of a larger effort to mend relations with the US and emerge out of diplomatic isolation. Syria's official line was that it wanted to resume the negotiations with Israel 'at the point at which they had been interrupted' (this was the standard Syrian formula of seeking to preserve 'the deposit') but that in the absence of a diplomatic option Syria would resort to force to liberate its land. With characteristic incongruity Syria's new president also made some virulent anti-Israeli and even anti-Semitic remarks. Sharon, in any event, dismissed the initiatives to start an informal dialogue.

In a similar vein, Sharon refused to become seriously reengaged in Lebanon even in the aftermath of serious provocations by Hizballah. He took limited action against Hizballah and Syrian targets but avoided massive retaliation and refused to deal with the build up of Hizballah's arsenal of rockets. Whether as a product of his 1982 misadventure in Lebanon or because he wanted to focus on the Palestinian issue Sharon would not be drawn to deal thoroughly with Hizballah or its patrons.

This initial configuration did not bode well for either the bilateral American-Syrian relationship or for the trilateral American-Syrian-Israeli relationship. The inauspicious outlook was further compounded by a series of subsequent developments:

1. THE IRAQI ISSUE AND THE WAR IN IRAQ

Syria was not included in the original schedule of Colin Powell's first trip to the Middle East as Secretary of State in 2001, but a visit to Damascus was added later. The purpose, as we saw, was to deal with Syria's aid to Iraq in selling more oil than allowed by the 'oil for food program'. In their meeting

Bashar al-Asad promised Powell that Syria would comply with the sanctions regime. What followed became a pattern. For one thing, the promise was not kept. Bashar tried also to follow in his father's steps by straddling the line and by trying to compartmentalize his relations with the US. He did accommodate the US after 9/11 by offering some intelligence sharing and cooperation against al-Qaeda but acted against the Bush Administration's policies in Iraq, by actively opposing the diplomatic efforts to prepare the ground for the war and by procuring military equipment for Saddam's army (allegations of other forms of collaboration with Saddam's regime have not been proven). But while Hafiz al-Asad had mastered the art of straddling the line his son was far less skilful and as far as the Bush Administration was concerned his efforts were counterproductive.

In the period leading to the war, during the war and in its immediate aftermath the Iraqi issue could be described as an irritant in Syria's relations with the US, but as that initial apparent success of the war turned into a lingering crisis, American anger at Syria's conduct grew dramatically. Syria clearly did not want to see the US or a pro-American government installed safely in Iraq. The Ba'th regime has its own version of a siege mentality and from its perspective American military presence and political hegemony in Iraq were grave threats. In order to remove the threat Syria allowed Damascus Airport and the Syrian-Iraqi border to become the main gateway for the 'Sunni insurrection'. Until well into 2007 all US efforts to persuade Damascus to seal off its border with Iraq met with outright rebuffs or evasive responses.

2. 9/11 AND THE WAR ON TERROR

Syria had no role in 9/11 and, as we saw, was willing to offer the US at least a measure of cooperation against al-Qaeda in its aftermath. But 9/11 changed the prism through which Middle Eastern issues were seen in Washington and from the new perspective Syria could not and did not do well. As Iran's ally, patron of Hizballah, patron and host of Hamas and Islamic Jihad, Syria was bound to be seen by the Bush Administration as being on the wrong side of the essential divide. In time Syria's support for the 'Sunni insurrection' in Iraq in which al-Qaeda played a leading role erased whatever good will which emanated from the initial intelligence sharing with Washington.

3. EFFORTS TO REVIVE THE ARAB-ISRAELI PEACE PROCESS

The Bush Administration's initial dismissive attitude toward and reluctance to engage in Arab-Israeli peacemaking were modified by the lingering and exacerbation of the Palestinian-Israeli fighting. The administration found itself increasingly engaged in efforts to end the fighting and restart the negotiations. These efforts were accelerated by the optimism which prevailed in the immediate aftermath of the war in Iraq, when it was still considered a success. The US used its prestige to force Yasir 'Arafat to appoint Abu Mazen (Mahmud 'Abbas) to the post of Prime Minister thereby providing Israel, at least in theory, with a more attractive negotiating partner.

There were several reasons for the failure of this bid and not least of them was Syria's support for Hamas, Islamic Jihad and other radical groups determined to perpetuate the cycle of violence. Syria was interested under certain conditions to resume its own negotiations and it voted for a watered down version of the Saudi plan to seek an Arab-Israeli comprehensive settlement in 2002, but as long as Washington and Jerusalem were exclusively focused on the Palestinian track Damascus could be relied upon to undermine their efforts. This role was less evident during the heyday of the intifadah when the limelight was on the Palestinian establishment. But with the waning of the intifadah and particularly after Yasir 'Arafat's death Syria's role in league with Iran in stoking the fire of Palestinian-Israeli violence and obstructing Mahmud 'Abbas's policies became all the more prominent and visible.

4. THE ALLIANCE WITH IRAN

The Syrian-Iranian alliance dates back to 1979, but as in so many other respects, the transition from Hafiz to Bashar al-Asad marked a significant change in the nature of that relationship. Hafiz al-Asad knew how to maintain his relationship with Iran on an equal footing. Under his less dexterous son the premise of the relationship shifted over time and by the middle of the present decade it began to resemble a patron-client relationship.

As Iran's power and influence grew and served as the basis for a manifest quest for regional hegemony and with the exacerbation of Sunni-Shi'i tensions in the region, Syria increasingly came to be seen by the US and its Arab friends as an Iranian outpost in the core area of the Middle East. This was clearly illustrated during Israel's war with Hizballah in the summer of 2006, which in regional and international terms was played out as a war by proxy between the US and its allies on one side and Iran and Syria on the other.

In this context it is important to mention Israel's raid in North-Eastern Syria on 6 September 2007. The whole issue has yet to be fully clarified, but it seems fairly safe to accept the press reports and expert analyses stating that Israel destroyed a nuclear reactor supplied by North Korea and being constructed by North Korean technicians. Intriguing and significant questions remain unanswered: was it a bilateral Syrian-North Korean venture, or was Iran involved as well? Did the project begin under Hafez al-Asad or was it launched by Bashar? The Bush Administration decided in September 2007 to join Israel and Syria in playing the event down. It probably sought to minimize the repercussions of this episode on its own impending deal with North Korea to dismantle the latter's nuclear programme. But it could not have overlooked the far-reaching implications of Syria's decision to acquire a nuclear option in league with at least one member of the President's original 'axis of evil'. Indeed in April 2008 in anticipation of and during a congressional hearing of this issue the Bush Administration released a deluge of information on the Israeli raid. The Administration argued forcefully that Israel had destroyed a nuclear reactor built by North Korea and in order to prove its point went to the unusual length of releasing footage of North Korean technicians inside the reactor provided to it by Israeli Intelligence. This was all done in a North Korean context but as a by-product Syria was exposed to a new dose of negative attention and press stories.

In contradistinction to the demonizing effect that Syria's close relationship with Iran had on the Bush Administration's perception of Damascus an alternative perspective would see a positive challenge in either seeking a dialogue with both Iran and Syria or, failing that, to woo Damascus away from Teheran. This was the perspective adopted by the bi-partisan Baker-Hamilton Commission dealt with below.

5. LEBANON

Alongside the war in Iraq and its aftermath, developments in Lebanon since 2004 have had the greatest impact on the Bush Administration's relationship with Syria. For quite some time the US had been resigned to Syria's hegemony in Lebanon. The first Bush Administration complied with a tightening of Syrian control as part of the arrangements that brought Syria into the war coalition against Saddam in 1990. Throughout the 1990s the Clinton Administration was willing to accept the status quo in Lebanon as part of a larger package that would include an Israeli-Syrian peace agreement and a significant upgrading of Syria's relationship with the US. This approach faded away with the transition to the Bush Administration but the chain of events which led to the championing of Lebanese independence and democracy as a major cause of US policy in the Middle East began in 2004.

Syria overplayed its hand twice in an effort to preserve its supremacy in Lebanon. It forced an extension of the term of the pliable president, Emile

Lahoud, and then was probably involved, at a high level, in the assassination in February 2005 of Rfiq al-Hariri, the former Prime Minister. Hariri, a wealthy businessmen and a close ally of Saudi Arabia, was not in office, but was seen by Syria as the most serious threat to its sway in Lebanon. The assassination backfired in that it energized and motivated the domestic and external foes of Syria's ambitions in Lebanon to rally and demand a full withdrawal of Syria's forces from Lebanon. The pressure was such that on 5 March Bashar al-Asad announced that Syria would withdraw its forces from Lebanon. The Lebanese public and political system were divided into two major camps and the next phase in the drama consisted of massive demonstrations staged by the two of them. Hizballah and Syria's and Iran's other supporters organized on 8 March a mass demonstration calling on Syria to keep its troops in Lebanon. A much larger counter-demonstration was held on 14 March relying on the Sunni, Druze and the bulk of the Maronite communities. In May–June 2005 fresh parliamentary elections were held in Lebanon and the 14 March coalition won a majority that led to the formation of Fouad Seniora's government. On another front an international investigation into Hariri's assassination was launched and conducted quite aggressively by a German magistrate, Detlev Mehlis. The spectre of a member or members of the Syrian regime's inner circle being summoned to an international tribunal as suspects became a real prospect.

This chain of events fired the imagination of George W. Bush. Here was a shining example of a successful American effort to bring democracy to a Middle Eastern country and to contend with radical forces resorting to violence and terror in an effort to bring down a fragile, democratically elected government. Lebanon now came to occupy a larger, much more prominent, place on the Administration's Middle Eastern agenda and in its view of and relationship with Syria. An American-Syrian rapprochement or a trilateral American-Israeli-Syrian deal became less likely if Syria were to insist on a restoration of its position in Lebanon as part of the package. On a different level, the issue of the international tribunal and the investigation of Rfiq al-Hariri's assassination became an instrument available to American policy makers. They could push the issue and precipitate a crisis in Syria and around it, or they could tread more gently.

Fashioning a Syria policy that would deal effectively with this complex web of issues has been a challenging issue for the Bush Administration during the past seven years. The administration has consistently avoided the two edges of the spectrum of choices available to it: it would not use force to punish Syria or try to topple the regime nor would it try to engage it in a dialogue. It did threaten and cajole Syria, it has sought to isolate it diplomatically, it has sought to obstruct its policies, it has imposed sanctions on Syria and has tinkered with the Syrian opposition. The two most notable instances of pressure exerted by the Bush Administration occurred in 2003 and 2005.

In the immediate aftermath of the war in Iraq and under the impact of America's military success and Saddam's downfall several senior US policy makers made thinly veiled threats to use force against Syria if it did not change its behaviour. Then, in early May Secretary of State Colin Powell travelled to Damascus and met with President Bashar al-Asad. Less bluntly than some of his colleagues but quite plainly Powell went through the litany of US grievances (Syria's conduct in Iran and Lebanon, support for Palestinian and Lebanese terrorist groups, the arsenal of weapons of mass destruction) and demanded a change in Syria's policies.

In line with the familiar pattern Asad promised to accommodate Washington's concerns, but genuine implementation did not follow. Thus, while the Syrian authorities instructed Hamas and Islamic Jihad to close their offices in Damascus they were also told with a wink and a nod that they 'should work from home'. Washington must have realized shortly thereafter that the pressure it had exerted proved to be ineffective and, worse, that it was put in the awkward position of having made empty threats.

A similar episode took place in 2005 in the Lebanese context. At the height of the crisis that followed Rfiq al-Hariri's assassination and Syria's withdrawal Bashar al-Asad clearly felt that the Bush Administration was seeking to topple him, using the investigation and the prospect of an international tribunal as the chief instruments of that policy. However, if the Bush Administration (or part of it) did entertain such plans, it abandoned them in short order. By that time it was deeply into the Iraqi quagmire and another active front in the Middle East did not fit into the agenda. Furthermore, it was argued that the real alternative to Bashar al-Asad were not the opposition leaders cultivated by the Administration but the Syrian branch of the Muslim Brotherhood. It took some time for Bashar al-Asad and his associates to realize that the acute pressure was off, but once they did, political assassinations targeting Syria's opponents in Lebanon followed suit.

It is important to note that the Bush Administration did not always speak and act with one voice with regard to Syria. As a rule the White House and the NSC adopted a harsher line as compared to that of the State Department.

There was an interesting Israeli dimension to the US Syrian tension. According to a senior Israeli official one of his US counterparts tried to encourage Israel to take action against Syria. According to the same official at the height of the crisis in 2005 the Syrians were prepared to launch missiles against Israel and against US targets in Iraq.

An alternative approach, seeking to engage Syria in dialogue, was suggested, as we saw, by the Baker Hamilton Commission. In the report it published in December 2006 the Commission recommended that:

> Given the ability of Iran and Syria to influence events within Iraq and their interest in avoiding chaos in Iraq, the United States should try to engage them constructively. In seeking to influence the behaviour of both countries, the United States has disincentives and incentives available. Iran should stem the flow of arms and training to Iraq, respect Iraq's sovereignty and territorial integrity, and use its influence over Iraqi Shia groups to encourage national reconciliation. The issue of Iran's nuclear programs should continue to be dealt with by the five permanent members of the United Nations Security Council plus Germany. Syria should control its border with Iraq to stem the flow of funding, insurgents, and terrorists in and out of Iraq. The United States cannot achieve its goals in the Middle East unless it deals directly with the Arab-Israeli conflict and regional instability. There must be a renewed and sustained commitment by the United States to a comprehensive Arab-Israeli peace on all fronts: Lebanon, Syria, and President Bush's June 2002 commitment to a two-state solution for Israel and Palestine. This commitment must include direct talks with, by, and between Israel, Lebanon, Palestinians (those who accept Israel's right to exist), and Syria.

The commission's recommendations were rejected by the Bush Administration, but limited contact in the forum dealing with Iraqi issues was established.

Another discordant American voice was that of Nancy Pelosy, the new speaker of the House of Representatives, elected after the Democrats' electoral success in November 2006. As part of her April 2007 trip to the Middle East the speaker chose to visit Damascus and meet with Bashar al-Asad in stark opposition to the Administration's line. The speaker's main motive may have been the desire to demonstrate that the Administration had no monopoly over the conduct of US foreign policy. In any event if she wanted to find a resonant issue in which the President had strong feelings she chose well. President Bush responded by criticizing what he saw as a 'useless exercise that would lead the Asad government to believe that they are part of the mainstream of the international community when in fact they are a state sponsor of terror, when in fact they are helping expedite the movement of foreign fighters into Iraq, when they have done little to nothing to rein in militant Hamas and Hizballah and when in fact they destabilize the Lebanese democracy.'[3]

The Pelosy episode caused a brief strain in the relationship between the Bush Administration and the Olmert government. When she visited Israel prior to her trip to Damascus, the speaker discussed her plans with the two principal hosts, Prime Minister Olmert and Speaker of the Knesset, Dalia Itzik, who seemed to endorse her trip and sent with her a message of sort to Bashar Al-Asad. This must have incensed the White House and must have led to a phone call or another message prompting Olmert to back away publicly from the original endorsement.

Syria and the US conducted another limited dialogue on the eve of the Annapolis Conference. The US wanted Syria to participate primarily in order to ensure that Damascus did not sabotage a diplomatic initiative cherished by the Secretary of State. The comparative thaw that was part of this effort was manifested by American acknowledgement of a greater Syrian effort to seal the border with Iraq. The language used on the eve of and during the conference suggested that while the initial thrust was on the Palestinian track, Syria's turn would come. Syria participated in the conference but chose to send a relatively junior official. In the event, the whole 'Annapolis initiative' failed to take off and there was no sequel to the modest start of an improvement in US-Syrian relations or a return to Syrian-Israeli diplomacy.

In fact, the whole episode represented a temporary diversion in the Bush Administration's policy which began with an initial lack of interest and shifted to actual opposition to the prospect of reviving the Syrian-Israeli track when Prime Minister Olmert in 2007 changed Sharon's and his own policy.

When Ehud Olmert succeeded Ariel Sharon as (acting) Prime Minister, Head of the Kadima Party and eventually as an elected Prime Minister, he also adopted his negative attitude toward the notion of an Israeli-Syrian settlement and/or renewed negotiation.

Olmert ran in the 2007 elections on a platform of extending Sharon's policy in Gaza to the West Bank. In other words, the focus of the policy remained on the Palestinian issue and the prospect of a deal with Syria and the price tag of such a deal were kept off the agenda by Olmert. While Bashar Al-Asad and other Syrian spokesmen continued to speak of their will to renew the negotiation (coupled with a threat that the alternative to negotiation was war), Olmert rebuffed any such overture. Unofficially he intimated that this line was at least in part the product of the Bush Administration's opposition to a revival of a negotiation that would obstruct its own efforts to isolate and de-legitimize Asad's regime.

Later on, Olmert must have realized that an outright rejection of an Arab foe's apparent peace overture was not a wise policy, and rather than reject the idea out of hand, he presented, whenever asked, a list of conditions that Syria would have to meet before negotiations could be restarted.

In time, George W. Bush changed his own line as well. He ceased to express opposition to the notion of Israeli-Syrian negotiations and said instead, that this was the business of the parties themselves, but that the US would not be a party to such a negotiation. Given the fact that for Syria peace with Israel was seen as a part of a larger settlement with the US, Bush's new position remained a major obstacle to the conclusion if not to the opening of a new Israeli-Syrian negotiation, but it did provide Olmert with additional diplomatic space.

In February 2007 Olmert inaugurated a new phase by authorizing the Prime Minister of Turkey to start mediation between Israel and Syria. The Turkish mediation or the indirect talks between Israel and Syria did not remain secret for very long. This is hardly surprising given the fact that both parties had an interest in publicizing them. Syria was interested in the diplomatic dividends accruing to a country ostracized by the Bush Administration while Olmert wanted to send a message of some hope to an Israeli public worried by a series of negative developments in the Syrian arena. In a series of press interviews he gave in mid-April 2008, on the eve of the Passover holiday, Olmert emphasized that this was a serious dialogue and that he realized the full repercussions of a potential agreement: 'I only say one thing and am saying it with full seriousness and intent: There is room to conduct a process that will produce an Israeli-Syrian agreement. The Syrians know that I want it. They know my expectations and I think I know theirs.'[4]

Olmert's interviewers identified an important element in Olmert's revelations and explained to their readers that: 'Olmert's positive message is Syria.' There was more to the PM's policy than a quest for some good news. He had the full support of the Israeli National Security Establishment for an opening to Syria. Even if the negotiation did not lead to an agreement, it would open a channel of communication with a significant adversary and would reinforce Israel's hand in the direct negotiation with Abu-Mazen and the indirect give or take with Hamas.

The simultaneous announcement by Israel and Syria on 21 May 2008 that they were holding indirect talks that could develop to a full-fledged negotiation was a startling development. Its timing (as distinct from the decision to open the dialogue) may well have been a product of Olmert's political and personal problems.

The Israeli-Syrian announcement generated a wave of speculations as to what may have been accomplished in the indirect talks and as to the prospect of the negotiation given the exacerbation of Olmert's problems and the prospect of imminent political changes in Israel. Most observers share the view that a Syrian-Israeli peace deal is not a likely prospect at the present and that this will remain the case at least until the spring of 2009 with a new US Administration, and the Israeli government at that time being in a position to reconsider their policies in the region.

This chain of events was a source of embarrassment to President Bush and his Administration. Clearly he was briefed by Olmert about the public announcement of the Syrian talks and gave a reluctant green light but he was quite openly unhappy with the seal of approval given to his *bête noire*.

In an interview given to four Israeli journalists prior to the public announcement, President Bush practically let the cat out of the bag by coming close to revealing the impending announcement. He denied that he ever pressured Olmert not to talk to Syria but was fiercely critical of Bashar Al-Asad and his regime. When he spoke at the Knesset on 15 May 2008, during his visit to Israel to celebrate its sixtieth anniversary, Bush denigrated negotiation with 'terrorists and radicals as comparable to an appeasement of the eve of World War Two'.[5]

This statement came back to haunt the President once the Israeli-Syrian talks were announced. *The New York Times* quoted an administration official who described Olmert's actions as 'a slap in the face'.[6] Furthermore, if Bush's statement in the Knesset was aimed at Barack Obama's willingness to talk to Iran and Syria, it became part of the domestic American debate and the President was taken to task for the inconsistency of his own policy. Why would Bush denounce talks with Syria one day and endorse a Lebanese settlement with Hizballah a week later?

During the weeks that followed the May 21 announcement its initial dramatic effect faded as the focal point of Israeli politics shifted to the various parties' calculations and preparations for anticipated major changes: the formation of a new government based on the current coalition or a new election. But the Bush Administration anxiety that the very inauguration of a Syrian-Israeli negotiation would yield diplomatic dividends to Damascus was vindicated. France, Washington's former partner in protecting Lebanon and the March 14 coalition from Syria's ambitions, wasted no time in reaching out to Bashar al-Asad and his regime.

By June 2008 it became clear that the Israeli-Syrian indirect negotiation was not about to produce an agreement, but that both parties were clearly interested in keeping the process they had created going. The Olmert Government, realizing full well that it had a very limited run, was still keen to demonstrate that is was a valid, functioning government. The Asad regime was keen to build a record designated to reinforce its legal and diplomatic case and to reap the diplomatic dividends accruing to it from the very opening of this diplomatic channel. In fact, it did not take long for the Bush Administration's argument, that by negotiating with Asad's Syria, Israel would be legitimizing his regime, to be vindicated. Under the stewardship of President Nicolas Sarkozy and Foreign Minister Bernard Kouchner, Washington's recent partners in protecting Lebanon from Syria's ambitions, rushed to embrace Bashar al-Asad and his regime.

Nicolas Sarkozy went so far as to invite Bashar al-Asad to the meeting of a new forum he initiated – ' The Union of Mediterranean States' on 13 July in Paris. Olmert has been invited to the same forum and the prospect of a meeting or at least a handshake between the Israeli Prime Minister and the Syrian President became the subject of press and diplomatic speculation.

When George W. Bush visited Paris earlier in June the difference of opinion regarding Syria came up in the talks between him and his host. The pattern that first appeared between Bush and Olmert repeated itself. Bush was critical and sceptical regarding the contacts with Syria and the legitimization thus given to the Asad regime but he agreed not to turn it into a subject of open disagreement.

Criticism of Israel's decision to open a negotiation with Syria and of the fashion in which it was made came from an unexpected source. A senior UN official, the Norwegian diplomat Terje Larsen, who handled Lebanon on behalf of the UN, in a meeting with Israeli diplomats criticized their Government's policy. In his words: 'Israel has given Syria a huge gift without getting anything in return'.[7] According to Larsen, Israel has opened the door to all those European countries that are all too eager to renew their contacts with Syria.

Larsen's criticism was reported to the Foreign Office in Jerusalem and, like so many other Israeli diplomatic dispatches, found its way to the Israeli media.

It can be assumed quite safely that the parameters of the trilateral American-Israeli-Syrian relationship will not change prior to the late winter of 2009, when a new US Administration and the Israeli Government of the day are likely to take a fresh look at Middle-Eastern diplomacy.

The Israeli Government that will emerge from the current crisis will have to decide whether it wants to proceed with the negotiation begun by the current government, in what fashion and to what end. It will have to integrate such decisions into a larger strategy that will address the other core issues of Israel's national security policies – its relations with a new US Administration, the Palestinian issue and Iran's quest for regional hegemony and nuclear arsenal.

NOTES

1. This chapter is taken from the text of a monograph written for the Saban Center at the Brookings Institution when the author served as Bronfman Distinguished Fellow in 2007/2008.
2. *The New York Times*, 9 February 2001.
3. President Bush in a news conference, 3 April 2007 (http://www.whiehouse.gov/news/releases/2007/04/20070403.html).
4. Tel-Aviv: *Yediot Aharonot*, 18 April 2008.
5. *Jerusalem Post*, 23 May 2008.
6. *The New York Times*, 22 May 2008.
7. *Haaretz*, 17 June 2008.

Bibliography

Archives
Britain: Public Record Office (PRO), London.
Britain: Tagert Papers, St Antony's College, Oxford.
Britain: Spears Papers, St Antony's College, Oxford.
France: Archives Départementales de la Corrèze.
France: French Military Archives, Chateau Vincennes.
France: Ministère des Affaires Etrangères (M.A.E.).
Israel: Central Zionist Archives (CZA), Jerusalem.
Israel: Ben-Gurion Heritage Center, Sde-Boker.
Israel: Israel State Archive, Jerusalem.
United States: National Archives (NA), Washington, DC, and Maryland.

Published Documents
Documents of the Foreign Policy of Israel (DFPI). Part 3: *Armistice Talks with the Arab Countries*. Edited by Yemima Rosenthal. Jerusalem: Israel State Archive, 1983.
US Government. Foreign Relations of the United States (FRUS).

Books
Abu Maneh, Butrus. *Studies on Islam and the Ottoman Empire in the 19th Century, 1826–1876* (Istanbul: Isis Press, 2001).
'Aflaq, Michel. Fi sabil al-B'ath (Beirut: Dar al-Tali'ah, 1959).
'Ajami, Fuad. *The Arab Predicament: Arab Political Thought and Practice Since 1967* (Cambridge: Cambridge University Press, 1982).
—— *The Vanished Imam: Musa al-Sadr and the Shi'a of Lebanon* (London: I.B. Tauris, 1986).
—— *The Dream Palace of the Arabs: a Generation's Odyssey* (New York: Pantheon Books, 1998).
Albright, Madeleine. *Madam Secretary* (New York: Miramax Books, 2003).
Andrew, C.M. and Kanya-Forstner, A.S. *France Overseas: The Great War and the Climax of French Imperial Expansion* (London: Themes and Hudson, 1981).

Arens, Moshe. Broken Covenant (New York: Simon and Schuster, 1995).

Aron, Raymond. Peace and War (Garden City, NY: Doubleday/Anchor, 1973).

Arslan, 'Adel. The Memoirs of Amir 'Adel Arslan, vol. 2, 1946–1950 (Beirut: Dar al-Taqadumiyya Lil-Nashir, 1983) [in Arabic].

Al-'Azm, Khalid. Mudhakkirat (The Memoirs) (Beirut: al-Dar al-Taqadumiyya lil-Nashr, 1973).

Al-'Azm, Sadiq. Self-Criticism in the Wake of the Defeat (Beirut: Dar al-Tali'ah, 1968) [in Arabic].

—— A Critique of Religious Thought (Beirut: Dar al-Tali'ah, 1969) [in Arabic].

Baer, Gabriel. Population and Society in the Arab East (New York: F.A. Praeger, 1964).

Baker, A. James. The Politics of Diplomacy: Revolution, War, and Peace, 1989–1992 (New York: G.P. Putnam's Sons, 1995).

Bar-Ya'acov, Nisim. The Israeli-Syrian Armistice: Problems of Implementation, 1949–1966 (Jerusalem: Magnes Press, Hebrew University, 1967) [in Hebrew].

Baru, Tawfiq; Ahmad Ibrahim 'Ibad and Mahmud 'Abduh. Ta'rikh al-'arab al-hadith al-mu'asir (al-jiz' ath-than, ath-thalith, ath-thanawi, al-adabi) (Damascus, 1971/2).

Batatu, Hanna. The Old Social Classes and the Revolutionary Movements of Iraq (Princeton, NJ: Princeton University Press, 1979).

Ben-Gurion, David. The War Diary: The War of Independence, 1948–1949. 3 Vols (Tel-Aviv: Ministry of Defence, 1982) [in Hebrew].

Bentzur, Eitan. The Road to Peace Goes Through Madrid (Tel-Aviv: Yediot Aharonot, 1997) [in Hebrew].

British Admiralty. A Handbook of Syria (including Palestine) (London: HM Stationery Office, 1913).

Bulloch, John. Death of a Country: The Civil War in Lebanon (London: Weidenfeld and Nicolson, 1977).

Carter, Jimmy. Keeping Faith: Memoirs of a President (Toronto, ON: Bantam Books, 1982).

—— The Blood of Abraham (Boston, MA: Houghton Mifflin, 1985).

Claude, Inis. Swords into Plowshares (New York: Random House, 1971).

Clinton, Bill. My Life (New York: A.A. Knopf, 2004).

Cohen, G. The British Cabinet and the Palestine Question (Tel Aviv: Tel Aviv University; 1976) [in Hebrew].

—— Churchill and Palestine 1939–1942 (Jerusalem: Yad Izhaq Ben-Zvi, 1976) [in Hebrew].

Commins, D. David. Islamic Reform: Politics and Social Change in Late Ottoman Syria (New York: Oxford University Press, 1990).

Copeland, Miles. The Game of Nations (London: Weidenfeld and Nicholson, 1969).

—— The Game Players (London: Aurum Press, 1989).

Darwaza, M. 'Izzat. *Al-Wahda al-'Arabiyya* (Cairo: al-Maktab al-Tijari lil-Tiba'ah wal-Tawzi'i wal-Nashr, 1957) [in Arabic].

Dayan, Moshe. *Milestones* (Jerusalem and Tel-Aviv: Idanim, 1976) [in Hebrew].

—— *The Story of My Life* (New York: Warner Books, 1976).

—— *Breakthrough* (Jerusalem: Idanim, 1980) [in Hebrew].

Dishon, Daniel (ed.). *Middle East Record, 1967* (Tel-Aviv: Israel Universities Press, 1971).

Druker, Aviv. *Hara-kiri* (Tel-Aviv: Yediot Aharonot, 2002) [in Hebrew].

Drysdale, Alasdair and Raymond, Hinnebusch. *Syria and the Middle East Peace Process* (New York: Council on Foreign Relations, 1991).

Eddelist, Ran. *Ehud Barak: His War Against the Demons* (Or-Yehuda: Kineret, 2003) [in Hebrew].

Entelis, John. *Pluralism and Party Transformation in Lebanon: al-Kataib, 1936–1970* (Leiden: E.J. Brill, 1974).

Esman, J. Milton and Itamar Rabinovich (eds). *Ethnicity, Pluralism and the State in the Middle East* (Ithaca, NY: Cornell University Press, 1988).

Evron, Y. *War and Intervention in Lebanon: The Israeli-Syrian Deterrence Dialogue* (London: Croom Helm, 1987).

Eylath, Eliyahu. *Zionism and the Arabs* (Tel Aviv: Devir, 1974) [in Hebrew].

Fansa, Nadhir. *Days of Husni al-Za'im: 137 Days that Shook Up Syria* (Beirut: Manshurat Dar al-Afaq al-Jadida, 1982) [in Arabic].

Gershoni, I. and James, P. Jankowski. *Islam and the Arabs: The Search for Egyptian Nationhood, 1900–1930* (New York: Oxford University Press, 1986).

Gomaa, A.M. *The Foundation of the League of Arab States: Wartime Diplomacy and Inter-Arab Politics, 1941–1945* (London: Longman, 1977).

Haddad, M. Robert. *Syrian Christians in Muslim Society: An Interpretation* (Princeton, NJ: Princeton University Press, 1970).

Haig, Alexander. *Caveat: Realism, Reagan and Foreign Policy* (New York: Macmillan, 1984).

Haley, P. Edward and Lewis W. Snider. *Lebanon in Crisis: Participants and Issues* (Syracuse, NY: Syracuse University Press, 1979).

Homet, Marcel. *L'Histoire Secrète du Traité Franco-Syrien: Ou Va le Proche Orient?* (Paris: J. Peyronnet, 1938) [in French].

Hoskins, A. *British Routes to India* (New York: Longmans, Green and Company, 1928).

Hourani, Albert. *Syria and Lebanon: A Political Essay* (London: Oxford University Press, 1946).

—— *Minorities in the Arab World* (London: Oxford University Press, 1947).

—— *Arabic Thought in the Liberal Age* (London: Oxford University Press, 1962).

Imam, Samih, Suleiman al-Khuri and Ahmad Bitar. *Ta'rikh al-'arab al hadith* (al-saff al-sadis al-ibtida'i) (Damascus 1971/2, first printed in 1968/9) [in Arabic].

Kedourie, E. In the Anglo-Arab Labyrinth: the McMahon-Husayn Correspondence and its Interpretations, 191 –1939 (Cambridge: Cambridge University Press 1976).

Kerr, Malcolm. The Arab Cold War, 1958–1964: A Study of Ideology in Politics (London: Oxford University Press, 1965).

Khouri, Fred. The Arab-Israeli Dilemma (New York: Syracuse University Press, 1968).

Khoury, Philip. Urban Notables and Arab Nationalism: The Politics of Damascus 1860–1930 (Cambridge: Cambridge University Press, 1983).

Kienle, Eberhard (ed.). Contemporary Syria – Liberalization between Cold War and Cold Peace (London: British Academic Press, 1994).

Kimche, David, The Last Option (London: Weidenfeld and Nicolson, 1991).

Kissinger, Henry. White House Years (Boston, MA: Little, Brown, 1979).

—— Years of Upheaval (Boston, MA: Little Brown, 1982).

Klieman, A.S. Foundation of British Policy in the Arab World: The Cairo Conference, 1921 (Baltimore, MD: Johns Hopkins Press, 1970).

Lammens, Henri. La Syrie: Precis Historique (Beyrouth: Imprimerie Catholique, 1921).

Laqueur, W.Z. Communism and Nationalism in the Middle East (New York: Praeger, 1956).

Lawson, H. Fred. Why Syria Goes to War: Thirty Years of Confrontation (Ithaca, NY: Cornell University Press, 1996).

Lewis, Bernard. Islam in History: Ideas, Men and Events in the Middle East (London: Alcove Press, 1972).

Lewis, Samuel and Kenneth Stein. Making Peace Among Arabs and Israelis: Lessons from Fifty Years of Negotiating Experience (Washington, DC: United States Institution of Peace, 1991).

Longrigg, Stephen Hemsley. Syria and Lebanon Under French Mandate (London: Oxford University Press, 1958).

McGhee, George. Envoy to the Middle World: Adventures and Diplomacy (New York: Harper and Row, 1983).

Ma'oz, Moshe. Ottoman Reform in Syria and Palestine, 1840–1861: The Impact of Tanzimat on Politics and Society (Oxford: Clarendon Press, 1968).

—— Asad: The Sphinx of Damascus – A Political Biography (London: Weidenfeld and Nicolson, 1988).

—— Syria and Israel: From War to Peacemaking (Oxford: Clarendon Press, 1995).

Ma'oz, Moshe and Avner Yaniv (eds). Syria under Asad: Domestic Constraints and Regional Risks (London: Croom Helm, 1986).

Marqus, E. History of the Communist Parties in the Arab Homeland (Beirut, 1964) [in Arabic].

Oren, Michael. *Six Days of War: June 1967 and the Making of the Modern Middle East* (Oxford: Oxford University Press, 2002).

Pakradouni, Karim. *La Paix Manquée: Le Mandat d'Elias Sarkis, 1976–1982* (Beirut: Ed. FMA, 1984) [Pakradouni's book was translated to English under the title *Stillborn Peace: The Mandate of Elias Sarkis, 1976–1982* (Beirut: FMA, 1985)].

Parker, Richard. *The Politics of Miscalculation in the Middle East* (Blooming, IN: Indiana University Press, 1993).

Perthes, Volker. *The Political Economy of Syria under Asad* (London: I.B. Tauris, 1997).

Petran, Tabitha. *Syria* (London: Ernest Benn, 1978).

Philipp, Thomas (ed.). *The Syrian Land in the 18th and 19th Century*, Berliner Islamstudien, Bd. 5 (Stuttgart: Frantz Steiner Verlag, 1992).

Pichon, Jean. *Le Partage du Proche Orient* (Paris: J. Peyronnet, 1938) [in French].

Pipes, Daniel. *Greater Syria: The History of an Ambition* (New York: Oxford University Press, 1990).

Porath, Yehoshua. *The Growth of the Palestine Arab Nationalist Movement 1918–1929* (Jerusalem: Hebrew University Press, 1971) [in Hebrew].

Pryce-Jones, David. *Betrayal: France, The Arabs, and The Jews* (New York: Encounter Books, 2006).

Al-Qasimiyya, Khayriyya. *Al-Hukuma al-'Arabiyya fi Dimashq 1918–1920* (Cairo: Dar al-Ma'arif, 1971) [in Arabic].

Quandt, B. William, Fuad Jabber and Ann Mosley Lesch. *The Politics of Palestinian Nationalism* (Berkeley, CA: University of California Press, 1973).

—— *Decade of Decisions: American Policy Toward the Arab-Israeli Conflict, 1967–1976* (Berkeley, CA: University of California Press, 1977).

—— *Camp David: Peacemaking and Politics* (Washington, DC: Brookings Institution, 1986).

—— *The Peace Process: American Diplomacy and the Arab-Israeli Conflict since 1967* (Washington, DC: Brookings Institution, 1993).

Rabbath, Edmond. *Unité Syrienne et Devenir Arabe* (Paris: Marcel Riviere, 1937) [in French].

Rabin, Lea. *Our Life – His Legacy* (New York: G.P. Putnam's Sons, 1997).

Rabin, Yitzhak. *The Rabin Memoirs* (Berkley, CA: University of California Press, 1996).

Rabinovich, Itamar. *Syria under the Ba'th, 1963–1966: The Army-Party Symbiosis* (Jerusalem and New York: Israel Universities Press, 1972).

—— *The War for Lebanon, 1970–1985* (Ithaca, NY: Cornell University Press, 1985).

—— *The Road Not Taken – Early Arab-Israeli Negotiations* (New York: Oxford University Press, 1991).

—— The Brink of Peace: The Israeli-Syrian Negotiations (Princeton, NJ: Princeton University Press, 1998).

—— Waging Peace: Israel and the Arabs, 1948–2003 (Princeton, NJ: Princeton University Press, 2004).

Ramazani, Rouhullah. Revolutionary Iran: Challenge and Response in the Middle East (Baltimore, MD: Johns Hopkins University Press, 1986).

Al-Razaz, Munif. Al-Tajriba al-Murra (Beirut: Dar Ghandur, 1967) [in Arabic].

Rejwan, N. Nasserist Ideology: Its Exponents and Critics (New York: J. Wiley, 1974).

Ross, Dennis. The Missing Peace: The Inside Story of the Fight for Middle East Peace (New York: Farrar, Straus and Giroux, 2004).

Sa'adeh, Antun. The Leader Through the Phases of the Palestine Question. A party publication (Beirut, 1949) [in Arabic].

Safran, Nadav. Egypt in Search of Political Community: An Analysis of the Intellectual and Political Evolution of Egypt, 1804–1952 (Cambridge, MA: Harvard University Press, 1961).

—— From War to War: The Arab-Israeli Confrontation, 1948–1967 (New York: Pegasus, 1969).

Samné, George. La Syrie (Paris: Bossard, 1922) [in French].

Sasson, Eliyahu. On the Road to Peace (Tel- Aviv: Am Oved, 1978).

Saunders, Harold. The Other Walls: The Arab-Israeli Peace Process in a Global Perspective (Princeton, NJ: Princeton University Press, 1991).

Savir, Uri. The Process (Tel-Aviv: Yediot Aharonot, 1998) [in Hebrew].

Schiff, Ze'ev and Ehud Ya'ari. Israel's Lebanon War (New York: Simon and Schuster, 1984).

Seale, Patrick. The Struggle for Syria: A Study of Post-War Arab Politics, 1945–1958 (London: Oxford University Press, 1965).

—— Asad of Syria: The Struggle for the Middle East (London: I.B.Tauris, 1988).

Shalev, Aryeh. Cooperation in the Shadow of Conflict (Tel-Aviv: Ma'arachot, 1987) [in Hebrew].

Shamir, Yitzhak. Sikumo shel Davar (In Conclusion) (Tel-Aviv: Idanim, 1994) [in Hebrew].

Sharabi, Hisham. Al-Jamr wal-Ramad (Embers and Ashes) (Beirut, 1978) [in Arabic].

Sharif Munir. Al-'Alawiyyun man hum wa-ayna hum (Damascus: Al-maktabah al-kubra liltalif wal-nashr, 1946) [in Arabic].

Shemesh, Moshe. The Palestinian Entity 1959–1974, Arab Politics and the PLO (London: Frank Cass, 1988).

Shibli al-'Aysami, Dawd Nimr and Mahmud al-Shufi. Muhafazat al-Suwayda (Damascus, 1963) [in Arabic].

Sivan, Emmanuel. *Radical Islam, Medieval Theology and Modern Politics* (New Haven, CT: Yale University Press, 1985).

'Ubaid, Salamah. *Al-thawrah al-suriyya al-kubra* (Beirut: matabi' dar al-ghad, 1971) [in Arabic].

'Umar, F. 'Abdallah. *The Islamic Struggle in Syria* (Berkeley, CA: Mizan Press, 1983).

Van Dam, Nikolaos. *The Struggle for Power in Syria: Sectarianism, Regionalism and Tribalism in Politics, 1961–1980* (London: Croom Helm, 1981).

Weinberger, Naomi Joy. *Syrian Intervention in Lebanon: The 1975–1976 Civil War* (New York: Oxford University Press, 1986).

Weulersse, Jacques. *Le Pays des Alaouites* (Tours: Arrault, 1940) [in French].

—— *Paysans de Syrie et du Proche Orient* (Paris: Gallimard, 1946) [in French].

Wilson, Mary. *King 'Abdallah, Britain and the Making of Jordan* (New York: Cambridge University Press, 1987).

Yamak, Z. Labib. *The Syrian Social Nationalist Party: an Ideological Analysis* (Cambridge, MA: Harvard University Press, 1966).

Zak, Moshe. *Israel and the Soviet Union – A Forty-Year Dialogue* (Tel Aviv: Ma'ariv, 1988) [in Hebrew].

Zamir, Meir. *The Formation of Modern Lebanon* (London: Croom Helm, 1985).

—— *Lebanon's Quest: The Road to Statehood, 1926–1939* (London: I.B.Tauris, 1997).

Articles

Abu Manneh, Butrus. 'The Christians between Ottomanism and Syrian Nationalism: The Ideas of Butrus Bustani', *International Journal of Middle East Studies*, 11, 3 (1980), pp.287–304.

Al-'Azm, Sadiq. 'The View from Damascus', *The New York Review of Books* (15 June 2000).

Barak, Ehud. 'The Myths Spread About Camp David are Baseless', in Shimon Shamir and Bruce Maddy-Weitzman (eds), *The Camp David Summit – What Went Wrong?* (Brighton: Sussex Academic Press, 2005), pp.117–47.

Barakat, Halim. 'Social and Political Integration in Lebanon: A Case of Social Mosaic', *Middle East Journal*, 27 (Summer 1973), pp.301–18.

Batatu, Hanna. 'Some Observations on the Social Roots of Syria's Ruling Military Group and the Causes for Its Dominance', *The Middle East Journal*, 35, 3 (1981), pp.331–44.

Bilovich, Yossef. 'The Quest for Oil in Bahrain 1923–1930: A Study in British and American Policy', in Uriel Dann (ed.), *The Great Powers in the Middle East 1919–1939* (New York: Holmes and Meier, 1988), pp.252–68.

Burke III, Edmund. 'A Comparative View of French Native Policy in Morocco and Syria', *Middle Eastern Studies*, 9, 2 (1973), pp.175–86.

Dann, Uriel. 'Regime and Opposition in Jordan since 1949', in Menahem Milson (ed.), *Society and Political Structure in the Arab World* (New York: Humanities Press, 1973), pp.146–81.

—— 'The Jordanian Entity in Changing Circumstances', in Itamar Rabinovich and Haim Shaked (eds), *From June to October* (New Brunswick, NJ: Transaction Books, 1978), pp.231–44.

Dawn, C. Ernest. 'The Rise of Arabism in Syria', *Middle East Journal*, 16, 2 (1962), pp.145–68.

—— 'The Egyptian Remilitarization of Sinai, May 1967', *Journal of Contemporary History*, 3, 3 (July 1968), pp.201–24.

Devlin, F. John. 'The Setting', in F. John Devlin, *The Ba'th Party: A History from its Origins to 1966* (Stanford, CA: Hoover Institution Press, 1976), pp.1–22.

Drysdale, Alasdair. 'The Succession Question in Syria', *The Middle East Journal*, 39, 2 (Spring 1985), pp.246–57.

Evans-Pritchard, E., 'Genesis of a Social Anthropologist – an Autobiographical Note', *The New Diffusionist*, 3, 10 (January 1973), pp.17–23.

Eylath, Eliyahu. 'Antun Sa'adeh – Portrait of an Arab Revolutionary', in *Zionism and the Arabs* (Tel Aviv: Devir, 1974) [in Hebrew], pp.372–86.

Flores, A. 'The Early History of Lebanese Communism Reconsidered', *Khamsin*, 7, 12 (1981–2), pp.7–19

Gelb. H. Leslie. 'Israelis Say Syria Might Seek a War', *The New York Times* (14 July 1986).

Gellner, Ernest. 'The Stakes in Anthropology', *The American Scholar*, 57 (Winter 1988), pp.17–30.

Geertz, Clifford. 'Slide Show, Evans-Pritchard's African Transparencies', *Raritan Quarterly*, 3 (Fall 1983), pp.62–80.

Gershoni, I. 'The Arab Nation, The House of Hashem and Greater Syria in 'Abdallah's Writings', *Hamizrah Hehadash*, 25, 1 and 2 (1975), pp.165–70.

Golan, Galia and Itamar Rabinovich. 'The Soviet Union and Syria: The Limits of Cooperation', in Ro'i Ya'akov (ed.), *The Limits of Power: Soviet Policy in the Middle East* (London: Croom Helm, 1979), pp.213–31.

Gordon, D. 'History and Identity in Arab Text-books: Four Cases', *Princeton Near Eastern Paper*, 13 (1971).

Harik, Ilia. 'The Economic and Social Factors in the Lebanse Crisis', *Journal of Arab Affairs*, 1 (April 1982), pp.209–41.

Harris, William. 'Beirut: The Battle to Come', *The Middle East*, 140 (June 1986), pp.10–11.

—— 'Syria Rides the Tiger', *The Middle East*, 144 (October 1986), pp.8–9.

—— 'La Politique Lebanese de Hafez al-Asad', in Basma Kodmani-Darwish (ed.), *Leban: Espoirs et Realites* (Paris, 1987) [in French].

Hinnebusch, A. Raymond. 'Revisionist Dreams, Realist Strategies: The Foreign Policy of Syria', in Bahjat Korany and Ali E. Hillal Dessouki (eds), *The Foreign Policy of Arab States* (Boulder, CO: Westview Press, 1984), pp.283–322.

—— 'Does Syria Want Peace?', *Journal of Palestine Studies*, 26, 1 (October 1996), pp.42–57.

Hourani, Albert. 'Ottoman Reform and the Politics of Notables', in W.R. Polk and R.L. Chambers, *Beginnings of Modernization in the Middle East* (Chicago, IL: University of Chicago Press, 1968), pp.51–68.

—— 'Ideologies of the Mountain and the City', in R. Owen (ed.), *Essays on the Crisis in Lebanon* (London: Ithaca, 1976), pp.33–41.

—— 'Lebanon, Syria, Jordan and Iraq', in A.L. Udovitch (ed.), *The Middle East: Oil, Conflict and Hope* (Lexington, MA: D.C. Heath, 1976), pp.269–90.

Husry, K.S. 'King Faysal I and Arab Unity 1930–1933', JCH, 10, 2, pp.323–40.

Jabber, F. 'The Palestinian Resistance and Inter-Arab Politics' in W.B. Quandt, F. Jabber and A. Mosley Lesch, *The Politics of Palestinian Nationalism* (Berkeley, CA: University of California Press, 1973), pp.166–7.

Kedourie, Elie. 'Pan-Arabism and British Policy', in *The Chatham House Version and Other Middle Eastern Studies* (London: Weidenfeld and Nicolson, 1970), pp.213–35.

—— 'The Kingdom of Iraq: a Retrospect', in *The Chatham House Version and Other Middle Eastern Studies* (London: Weidenfeld and Nicolson, 1970), pp.236–82.

—— 'Political Parties in the Arab World', in *Arabic Political Memoirs and Other Studies* (London: Frank Cass, 1974), pp.28–58.

—— 'The Sorcerer's Apprentice', in *Arabic Political Memoirs and Other Studies* (London: Frank Cass, 1974), pp.170–6.

Kelidar, A. 'Religion and State in Syria', *Asian Affairs*, 61, 5 (February 1974), pp.16–22.

Khoury, Philip. 'Factionalism among Syrian Nationalists during the French Mandate', *International Journal of Middle Eastern Studies*, 13, 4 (1981), pp.441–69.

—— 'Divided Loyalties: Syria and the Question of Palestine, 1919–1939', *Middle Eastern Studies*, 21, 3 (July 1985), pp.324–48.

Kramer, Martin. 'Azouri: A Further Episode', *Middle Eastern Studies*, 18, 4, (1982), pp.351–8.

—— 'Syria's 'Alawis and Shi'ism', in M. Kramer (ed.), *Shi'ism, Resistance and Revolution* (Boulder, CO: Westview Press, 1987), pp.237–54.

Little, Douglas. 'Cold War and Covert Action: The United States and Syria, 1945–1958', *Middle East Journal*, 44, 1 (Winter 1990), pp.51–75.

Malley, Robert. 'Middle East Endgame III: Israel, Syria and Lebanon – How

Comprehensive Peace Settlements Would Look', *International Crisis Group Middle East Report*, 4 (16 July 2002), p.4.

—— 'Old Games in Search of New Rules', *International Crisis Group Middle East Report*, 7 (29 October 2002).

Malley, Robert and Hussein Agha, 'Camp David: The Tragedy of Errors', *The New York Review of Books*, 48, 13 (9 August 2001).

Mayer, T. 'The Islamic Opposition in Syria, 1961–1982', *Orient*, 24, 4 (December 1983), pp.589–609.

Oron, Y. 'The Attempted NSP Coup', in Y. Oron (ed.), *Middle East Record*, 1961 (Jerusalem: Israel Program for Scientific Translations, 1966), pp.398–404.

Perlman, M. 'Arab-Jewish Diplomacy, 1918–1922', *Jewish Social Studies*, 6, 2, pp.123–54, CZA S/25-3282.

Pipes, Daniel. 'Just Kidding', *New Republic* (8 and 15 January 1996), pp.18–19.

Pruitt, Dean. 'Ripeness Theory and the Oslo Talks', *International Negotiation*, 2, 2 (1997), pp.237–50.

Rabinovich, Itamar. 'Germany and the Syrian political Scene in the Late 1930's', in Y. Wallach (ed.). *Germany and the Middle East, 1835–1939* (Tel Aviv: Tel Aviv University, 1975), pp.191–8.

—— 'The October War's impact on Syrian Position and Policy in the Conflict with Israel', in A. Cohen and E. Karmon (eds), *In the Shadow of the October War* (Haifa: University of Haifa, 1976) [in Hebrew].

—— 'Continuity and Change in the Ba'th Regime in Syria, 1967–1973', in Itamar Rabinovich and Haim Shaked (eds), *From June to October* (New Brunswick, NJ: Transaction Books, 1978), pp.219–28.

—— 'Syria', in Colin Legume and Haim Shaked (eds), *Middle East Contemporary Survey, Vol.* I, *1976–1977* (New York: Holmes and Meier Publishers, 1978), pp.604–18.

—— 'Egypt and the Palestine Question before and after the Revolution', in Shimon Shamir (ed.), *Egypt: from Monarchy to Republic* (Boulder, CO: Westview Press, 1995), pp.325–39.

Ramet, Pedro. 'The Soviet Syrian Relationship', *Problems of Communism*, 35 (September–October 1986), pp.35–46.

Raymond, Andre. 'La Syrie du Royaume Arabe a l'independence 1914–1916', in A. Raymond (ed.), *La Syrie d'aujourd'hui* (Paris: Editions du Centre National de la Recherche Scientifique, 1980), pp.55–85 [in French].

Reed, F. Stanley. 'Dateline Syria: Fin de Regime?', *Foreign Policy*, 39 (Summer 1980), pp.176–90.

Rekhes, Elie. 'Jews and Arabs in the Israeli Communist Party', in Esman, J. Milton and Itamar Rabinovich (eds), *Ethnicity, Pluralism and the State in the Middle East* (Ithaca, NY: Cornell University Press, 1988), pp.121–39.

Robinson, E. Glenn. 'Elite Cohesion, Regime, Succession and Political Instability in Syria', Middle East Policy, 4, 4 (January 1998), pp.159–79.

Rondot, Pierre. 'L'Expérience du Mandate Français en Syrie et au Liban 1918–1945', Revue Générale de Droit International Public (1948), pp.1–23.

Roswald. A. 'The Spears Mission in the Levant: 1941–1944', The Historical Journal, 29, 4 (1986), pp.897–919.

Sadowski, Yahya. 'Ba'thist Ethics and the Spirit of State Capitalism: Patronage and the Party in Contemporary Syria', in Peter J. Chelkowski and Robert J. Pranger (eds), Ideology and Power in the Middle East (Durham, NC: Duke University Press, 1988), pp.160–84.

Salibi, Kamal. 'Islam and Syria in the Writings of Henri Lammens', in Bernard Lewis and P.M. Holt (eds), Historians of the Middle East (London: Oxford University Press, 1962), pp. 330–42.

—— 'The Lebanese Identity', Journal of Contemporary History, 6, 1 (1971), pp.76–86.

Seale, Patrick. 'Asad's Regional Strategy and the Challenge from Netanyahu', Journal of Palestine Studies, 26, 101 (Fall 1996), p.36.

Sela, Abraham. 'Syria and the Palestinian Question from the Establishment of the Arab League to the Armistice Agreement, 1945–1949', Dapei Elazar, 6, 10 (Tel Aviv University 1987), pp.24–42 [in Hebrew].

Seymour, Martin. 'The Dynamics of Power in Syria since the Break with Egypt', Middle Eastern Studies, 6, 1 (1970), pp.35–47.

Shamir, Shimon. 'The Middle East Crisis: On the Brink of War', in Daniel Dishon (ed.), Middle East Record, 1967 (Tel Aviv: Israel Universities Press, 1971), pp.183–204.

—— 'Midhat Pasha and the Anti-Turkish Agitation in Syria', Middle Eastern Studies, 10, 2 (1974), pp.115–41.

—— 'The Arab-Israeli Conflict', in A.L. Udovitch (ed.), The Middle East: Oil, Conflict and Hope (Lexington, MA: D.C. Heath, 1976), pp.195–230.

Shimoni, Ya'acov. 'Syria Between the Coups', Hamizrah Hehadash, 1 (October 1949–50), pp.7–21 [in Hebrew].

Snider, W. Lewis. 'The Lebanese Forces: Their Origins and Role in Lebanon's Politics', Middle East Journal, 38, 1 (Winter 1984), pp.1–33.

Al-Solh, Raghid. 'The Attitude of the Arab Nationalists towards Greater Lebanon during the 1930s', in Nadim Shehadi and Dana Haffar Mills (eds), Lebanon: A History of Conflict and Consensus (London: Center for Lebanese Studies with I. B. Tauris, 1988), pp.149–65.

Spiegel, L. Steven. 'The Carter Approach to the Arab-Israeli Dispute', in Itamar Rabinovich and Haim Shaked (eds), The Middle East and the United States (New Brunswick, NJ: Transaction Books, 1980), pp.93–117.

Steppat, Fritz. 'Eine Bewegung unter den Notabeln Syriens 1877–1878, Neues Licht auf die Enstehung des Arabischen Nationalismus', *Deutscher Orientalistentag*, 17 (1968), Teil 2, ZDMG, Supplementia 1 (1969), pp.631–49.

Stoakes. F. 'The Supervigilantes: The Lebanese Kataeb Party as Builder Surrogate and Defender of the State', *Middle Eastern Studies*, 11, 3 (October 1975), pp.215–36.

Touval, Saadia. 'The Superpowers as Mediators', in J. Bercovitch and J. Rubin (eds), *Mediation in International Relations* (New York: St Martin's Press, 1992), pp.232–48.

Van Dam, Nikolaos. 'Middle Eastern Political Clichés: 'Takriti' and 'Sunni Rule' in Iraq; "Alawi Rule' in Syria, A Critical Appraisal', *Orient*, 21 (January 1980), pp.42–57.

Van Dusen, M. 'Political Integration and Regionalism in Syria', *Middle East Journal*, 26, 2 (1972), pp.123–36.

Vatikiotis, P.J. 'Inter-Arab Relations', in A.L. Udovitch (ed.), *The Middle East: Oil, Conflict and Hope* (Lexington, MA: D.C. Heath, 1976), pp.145–79.

Verte, M. 'Arab-Zionist Negotiations in the Spring of 1919 and British Policy', *Zion*, 1–2, 5277/1967.

Winder, B. 'Islam as the State Religion, A Muslim Brotherhood View in Syria', *The Muslim World*, 49 (1954), pp.215–26.

Zamir, Meir. 'Smaller and Greater Lebanon: The Squaring of a Circle', *Jerusalem Quarterly*, 23 (Spring 1982), pp.215–36.

Zartman, William. 'Prenegotiation: Phases and Functions', in Janice Gross-Stein (ed.), *Getting to the Table: the Processes of International Prenegotiation* (Baltimore, MD: Johns Hopkins University Press, 1989), pp.1–17.

—— 'Explaining Oslo', *International Negotiation*, 2, 2 (1997), pp.195–215.

Zisser, Eyal. 'Syria', in Ami Ayalon (ed.), *Middle East Contemporary Survey*, 14 (1990) and 15 (1991), pp.649–68 and 664–89, respectively.

—— 'The Israel-Syria Negotiations: What Went Wrong?', *Orient*, 42, 2 (June 2001), pp.225–51.

Dissertations

Dawn, C. Ernest. 'The Project of Greater Syria' (Unpublished PhD Dissertation, Princeton University, 1968).

Eldar, D. 'France's Policy in the Levant and French Attitudes to Arab Nationalism and Zionism, 1914–1920' (Unpublished PhD Dissertation, Tel Aviv University, 1978) [in Hebrew].

McDowall, D. 'The Druze Revolt 1925–1927 and its Background in the Late Ottoman Period' (B. Litt Thesis, St John's College, Oxford, 1972).

Susser, A. 'Western Power Rivalry and Its Interaction with Local Politics in the Levant, 1941–1946' (Unpublished PhD Dissertation, Tel Aviv University, 1986).

Van Dam, Nikolaos. 'De Rol Van Sektarisme, Regionalisme en Tribalisme bjj de Strijd on de Politike Macht in Syrie, 1961–1976' (Unpublished PhD Dissertation, University of Amsterdam, 1977) [in Dutch].

Van Dusen, M. 'Intra and Inter Generational Conflict in the Syrian Army' (Unpublished PhD Dissertation, Johns Hopkins University, 1971).

Index

Vallentine Mitchell is a long established international publisher of books of Jewish interest and Middle Eastern Studies, both for the scholar and the general reader. Subjects covered include Jewish history, culture and heritage, religion, modern Jewish thought, biography, reference and the Holocaust. We hope that among our past and present titles you will find much of interest. Vallentine Mitchell also publishes the journals *Jewish Culture and History* and *Holocaust Studies: A Journal of Culture and History*.

Our new and forthcoming publications include several important and eagerly awaited titles.

Visit our website

www.vmbooks.com

to read blurbs, see jackets and journals and more.

Vallentine Mitchell

The Spread of Islamikaze Terrorism in Europe

The Third Islamic Invasion

Raphael Israeli, Harry Truman Institute,
Hebrew University, Jerusalem

Here the outspoken academic Raphael Israeli deals with radical Islam's attempt to gain a solid foothold on the European continent through immigration (legal and illegal) and political refugee status, all calculated to expand the influence of Islam by taking advantage of the Western liberal and democratic governments accommodating them as guests – and then as citizens. The democratic freedom in which they now live allows them to say and do things which the far stricter regimes of Islamic countries do not tolerate.

The three major countries of Europe most affected by Muslim immigration and demographic presence are France, Britain and Germany, who host about half of the total of 30 million Muslims in Europe today. This book examines the increasing presence of radical Islam within this Muslim diaspora in Europe, and the confusions and divisions within Western governments about how to engage with radical Islam and police its criminal elements. It examines the escalating impact of radical Islam in Europe, showing the larger picture.

2008   512 pages
978 0 85303 733 0   cloth   £49.50/$79.95
978 0 85303 734 7   paper   £19.95/$34.95

Palestinians between Nationalism and Islam

Raphael Israeli, Harry Truman Institute,
Hebrew University, Jerusalem

This book is a thematic collection of articles by this author, a recognized authority on contemporary Israeli–Palestinian relations, providing a retrospective on the development of the tension between nascent Palestinian nationalism as articulated by the PLO and Islam as incorporated by Hamas. It illuminates the dynamics of a rapidly changing situation, plotting the development of this volatile region.

The death of Arafat and the rise of the comparatively moderate Abu Mazen provided the final impetus for the dramatic rise of Hamas in Palestinian politics. Hamas strengthened permanently in the grassroots by dispensing welfare to the poor, criticizing the corrupt Palestinian Authority, and providing religious solace for the misery of life. Its stunning victory over the veteran PLO in the 2006 elections has made the matter all the more pertinent. Difficult days lie ahead for those behind international attempts to bring peace to Palestine.

2008   336 pages
978 0 85303 731 6   cloth   £49.50/$79.95
978 0 85303 732 3   paper   £19.95/$34.95

The Palestinian Press as a Shaper of Public Opinion

Writing Up A Storm

Mustafa Kabha, Open University of Israel

With a Foreword by **Israel Gershoni**

This book deals with the development of the Palestinian Arabic press during the years 1929–1939, years in which the national identity of the Palestinian Arab public was formalized and shaped and characterized by the development of the Palestinian National Movement. During this period the Palestinian National Movement, in addition to its struggle with the Zionist Movement, was also involved in a struggle with the British Mandatory government. The primary professed goal of this struggle was to prevent realization of the program for a Jewish National Home, and to lead Britain to a situation in which it would be compelled to grant independence or a certain degree of autonomy to the Palestinian Arabs, as had been granted to other Arab countries, such as Iraq and Egypt.

The press became integrated as a central factor in shaping the development of the Palestinian National Movement in a gradual process: it began emerging in the mid-1920's, its weight increased significantly during the events of 1929, and it peaked in the Great Strike of April–October 1936. The few studies conducted to date on the functioning of the Palestinian press during the Mandatory period dealt with the political aspects of the newspapers and with their articulation of the various political groups and powers in the Palestinian National Movement. In this book Mustafa Kabha emphasize social, cultural, and institutional aspects, in addition to the national-political aspect.

2007 320 pages
978 0 85303 671 5 cloth £60.00/$95.00
978 0 85303 672 2 paper £22.00/$35.00